RAT QUEENS™

VOLUME THREE: DEMONS

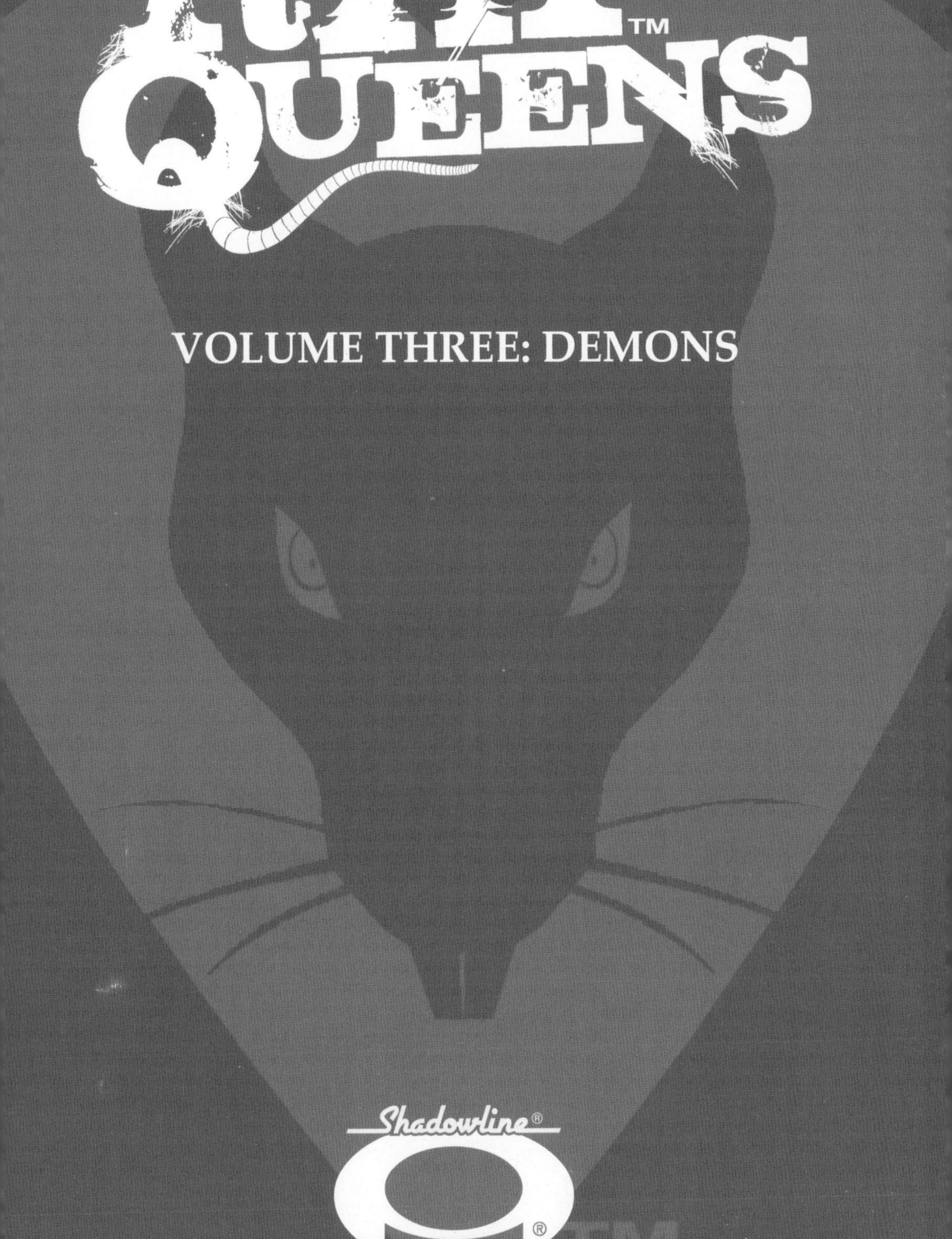

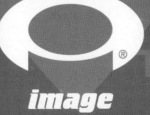

Shadowline®

image

FIRST PRINTING: APRIL, 2016

ISBN: 978-1-63215-735-5

RAT QUEENS, VOL 3: DEMONS. Published by Image Comics, Inc. Office of publication: 2001 Center St. Sixth Floor, Berkeley, CA 94704.

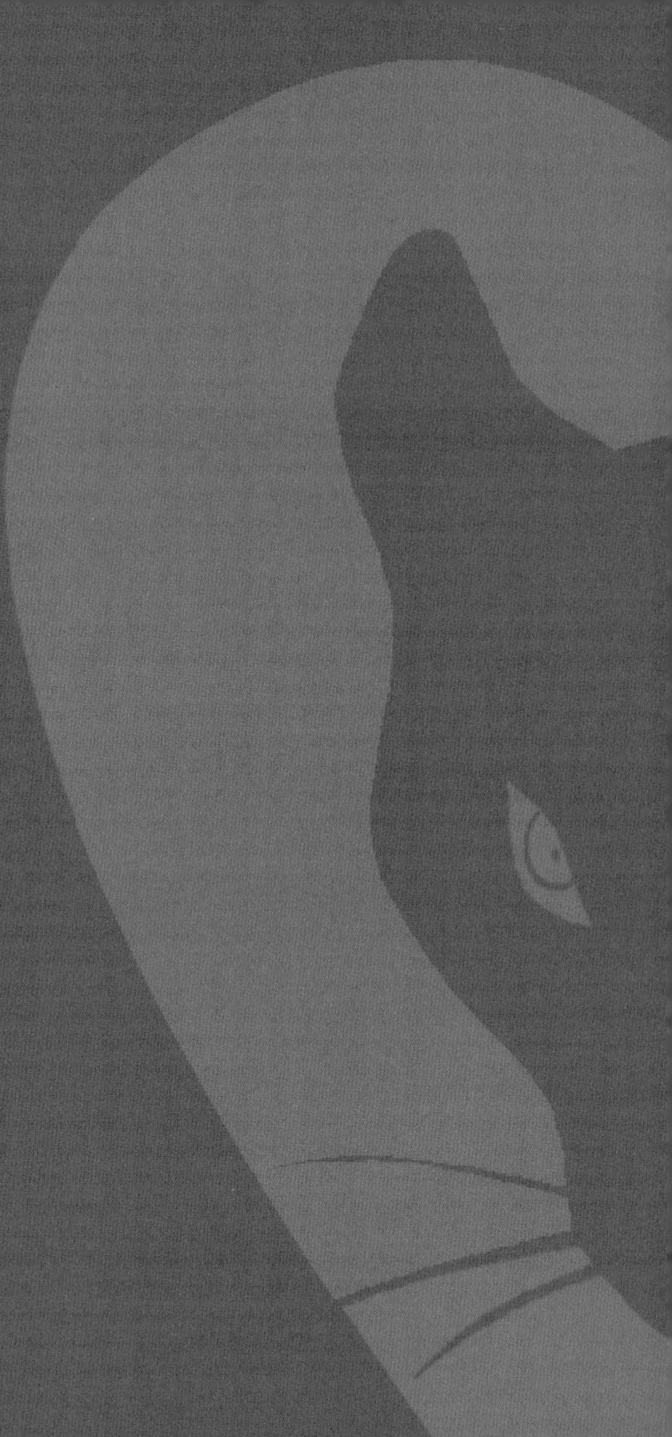

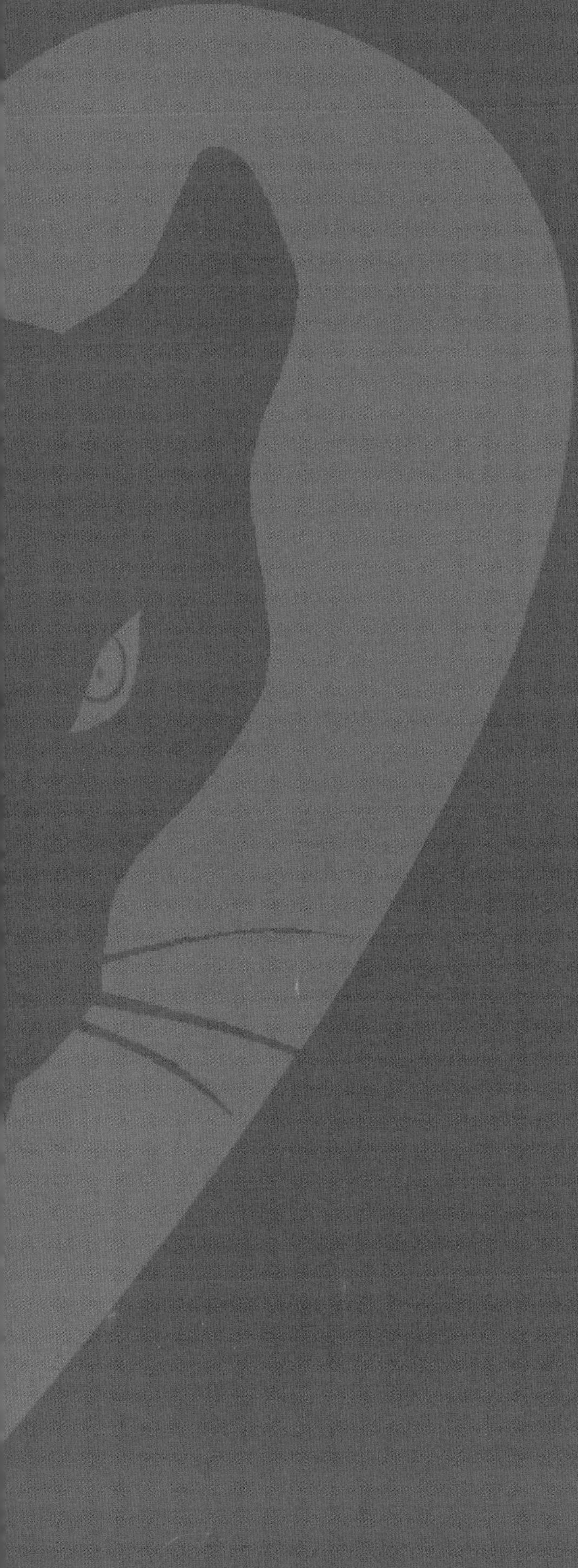

KURTIS J. WIEBE
story

TESS FOWLER
art

TAMRA BONVILLAIN
colors

ED BRISSON
letters

STJEPAN SEJIC
original covers

LAURA TAVISHATI
edits

MARC LOMBARDI
communications

JIM VALENTINO
publisher/book design

IMAGE COMICS, INC.
Robert Kirkman – Chief Operating Officer
Erik Larsen – Chief Financial Officer
Todd McFarlane – President
Marc Silvestri – Chief Executive Officer
Jim Valentino – Vice-President

Eric Stephenson – Publisher
Corey Murphy – Director of Sales
Jeff Boison – Director of Publishing Planning & Book Trade Sales
Jeremy Sullivan – Director of Digital Sales
Kat Salazar – Director of PR & Marketing
Emily Miller – Director of Operations
Branwyn Bigglestone – Senior Accounts Manager
Sarah Mello – Accounts Manager
Drew Gill – Art Director
Jonathan Chan – Production Manager
Meredith Wallace – Print Manager
Briah Skelly – Publicity Assistant
Sasha Head – Sales & Marketing Production Designer
Randy Okamura – Digital Production Designer
David Brothers – Branding Manager
Ally Power – Content Manager
Addison Duke – Production Artist
Vincent Kukua – Production Artist
Tricia Ramos – Production Artist
Jeff Stang – Direct Market Sales Representative
Emilio Bautista – Digital Sales Associate
Leanna Caunter – Accounting Assistant
Chloe Ramos-Peterson – Administrative Assistant
IMAGECOMICS.COM

CHAPTER ELEVEN

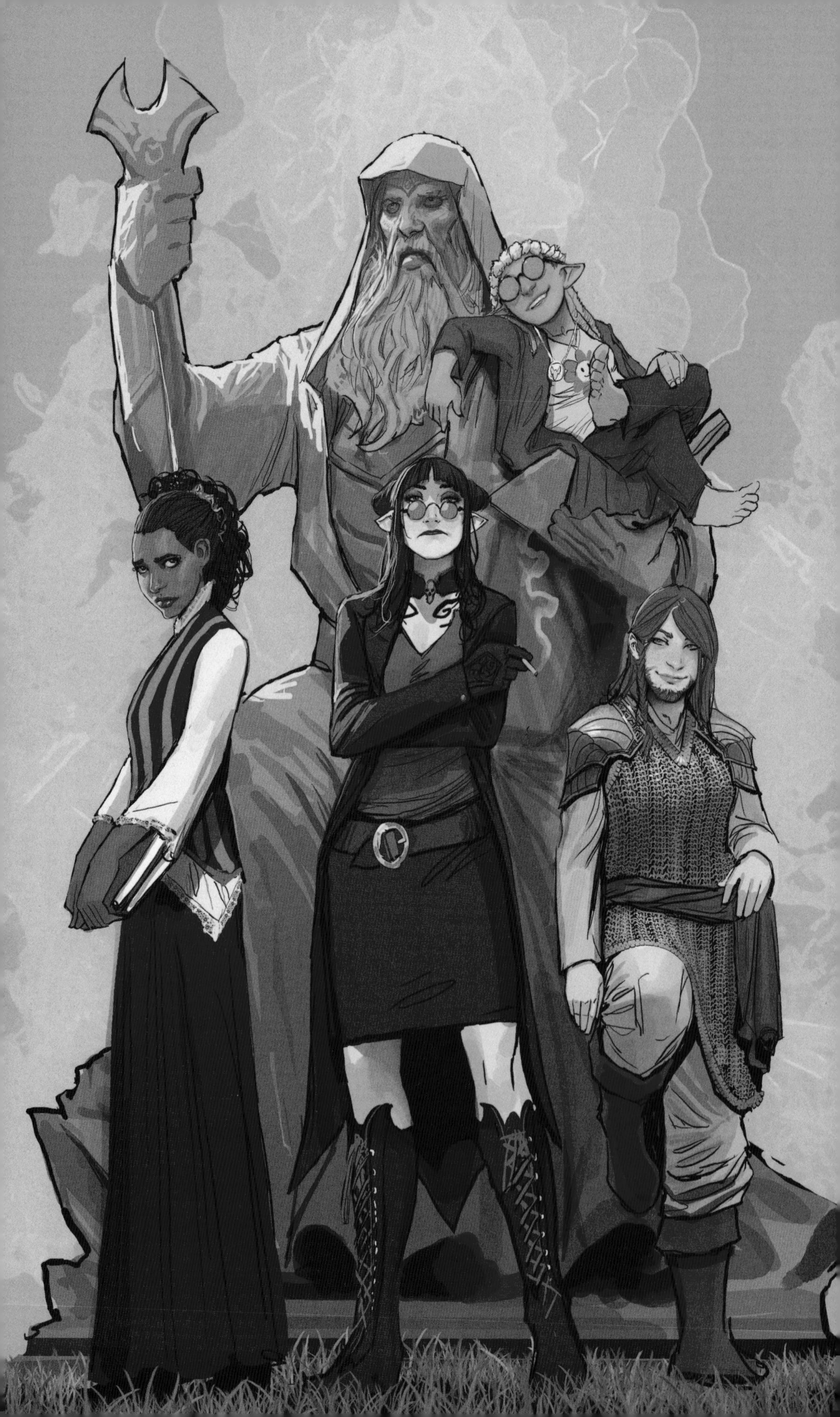

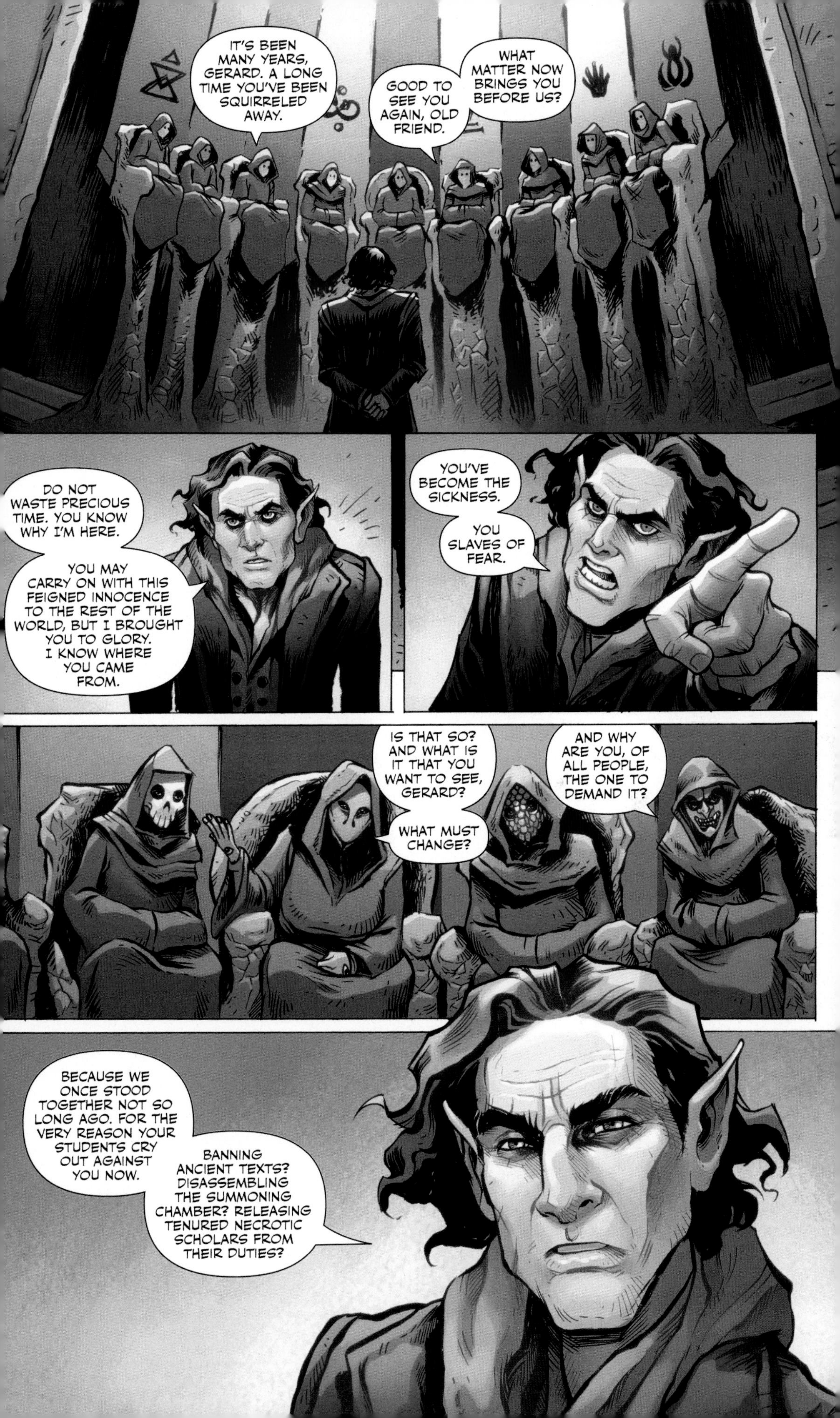
IT'S BEEN MANY YEARS, GERARD. A LONG TIME YOU'VE BEEN SQUIRRELED AWAY.
GOOD TO SEE YOU AGAIN, OLD FRIEND.
WHAT MATTER NOW BRINGS YOU BEFORE US?
DO NOT WASTE PRECIOUS TIME. YOU KNOW WHY I'M HERE.
YOU MAY CARRY ON WITH THIS FEIGNED INNOCENCE TO THE REST OF THE WORLD, BUT I BROUGHT YOU TO GLORY. I KNOW WHERE YOU CAME FROM.
YOU'VE BECOME THE SICKNESS.
YOU SLAVES OF FEAR.
IS THAT SO? AND WHAT IS IT THAT YOU WANT TO SEE, GERARD?
WHAT MUST CHANGE?
AND WHY ARE YOU, OF ALL PEOPLE, THE ONE TO DEMAND IT?
BECAUSE WE ONCE STOOD TOGETHER NOT SO LONG AGO. FOR THE VERY REASON YOUR STUDENTS CRY OUT AGAINST YOU NOW.
BANNING ANCIENT TEXTS? DISASSEMBLING THE SUMMONING CHAMBER? RELEASING TENURED NECROTIC SCHOLARS FROM THEIR DUTIES?

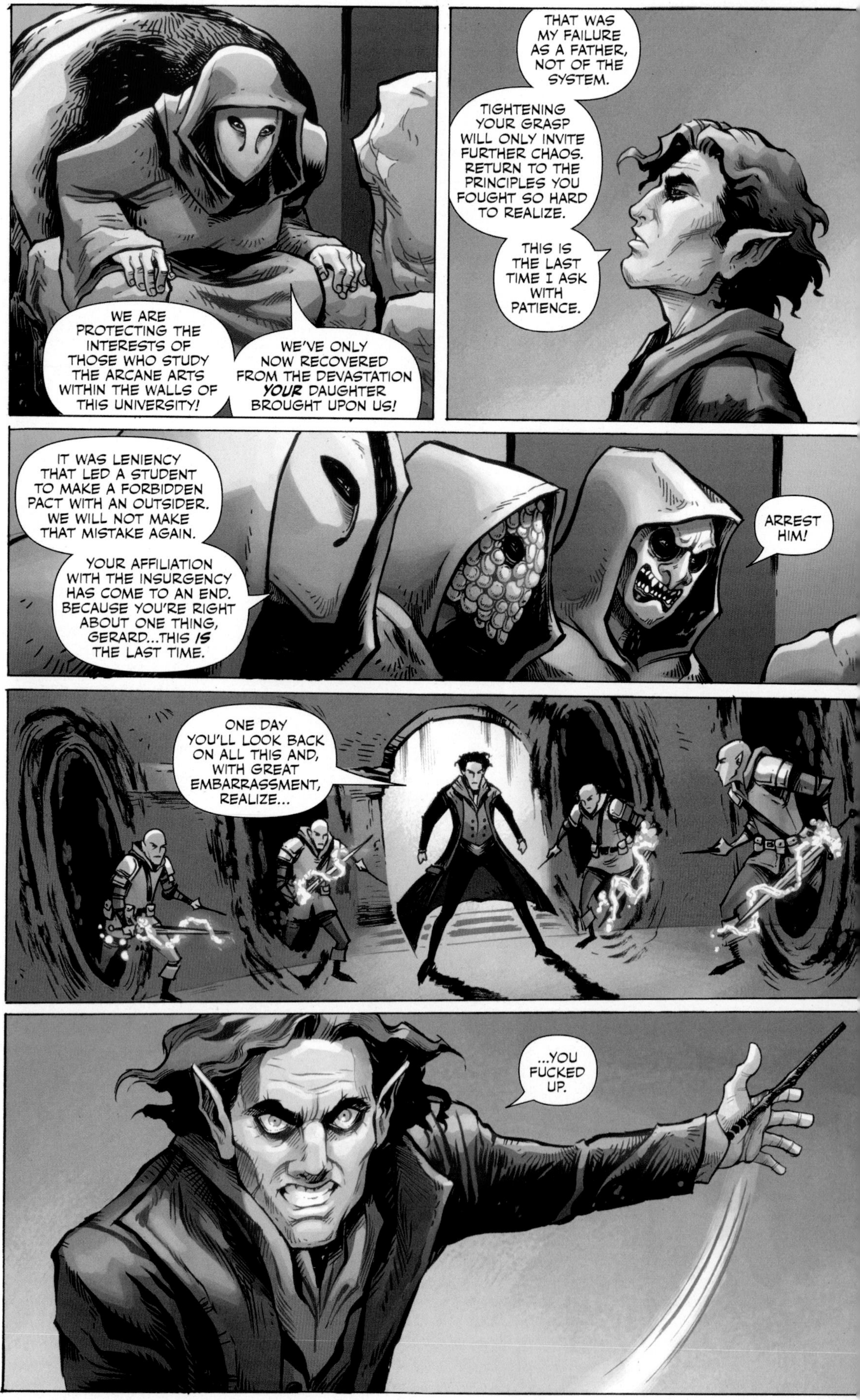
WE ARE PROTECTING THE INTERESTS OF THOSE WHO STUDY THE ARCANE ARTS WITHIN THE WALLS OF THIS UNIVERSITY!
WE'VE ONLY NOW RECOVERED FROM THE DEVASTATION *YOUR* DAUGHTER BROUGHT UPON US!
THAT WAS MY FAILURE AS A FATHER, NOT OF THE SYSTEM.
TIGHTENING YOUR GRASP WILL ONLY INVITE FURTHER CHAOS. RETURN TO THE PRINCIPLES YOU FOUGHT SO HARD TO REALIZE.
THIS IS THE LAST TIME I ASK WITH PATIENCE.
IT WAS LENIENCY THAT LED A STUDENT TO MAKE A FORBIDDEN PACT WITH AN OUTSIDER. WE WILL NOT MAKE THAT MISTAKE AGAIN.
YOUR AFFILIATION WITH THE INSURGENCY HAS COME TO AN END. BECAUSE YOU'RE RIGHT ABOUT ONE THING, GERARD...THIS *IS* THE LAST TIME.
ARREST HIM!
ONE DAY YOU'LL LOOK BACK ON ALL THIS AND, WITH GREAT EMBARRASSMENT, REALIZE...
...YOU FUCKED UP.

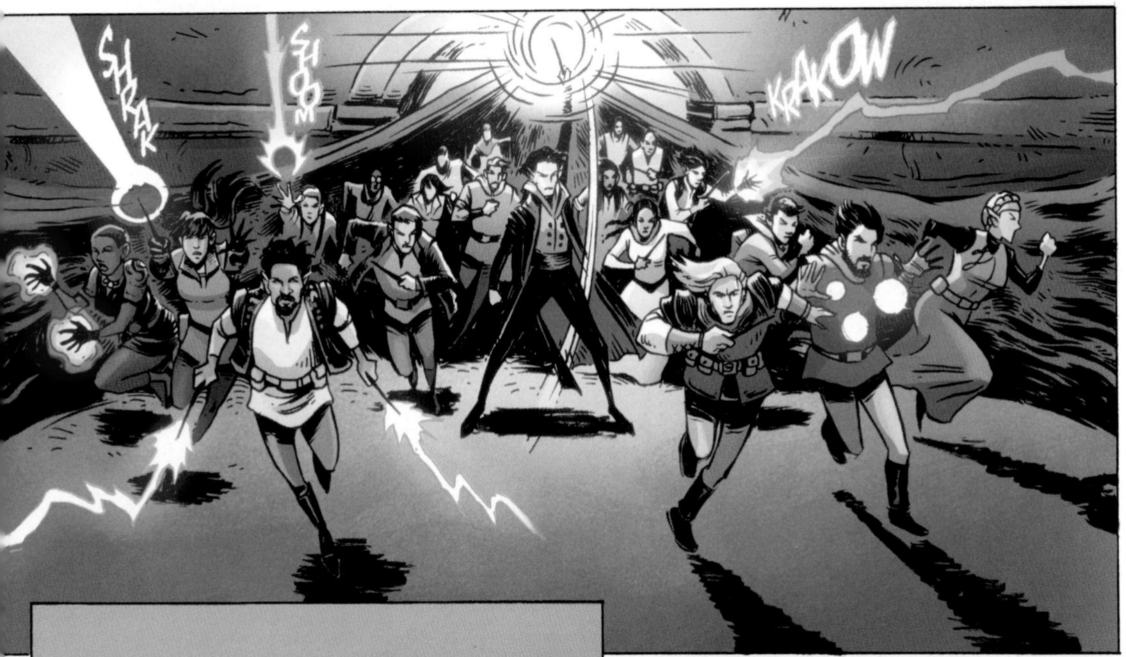
SHRAK
SHOM
KRAKOW

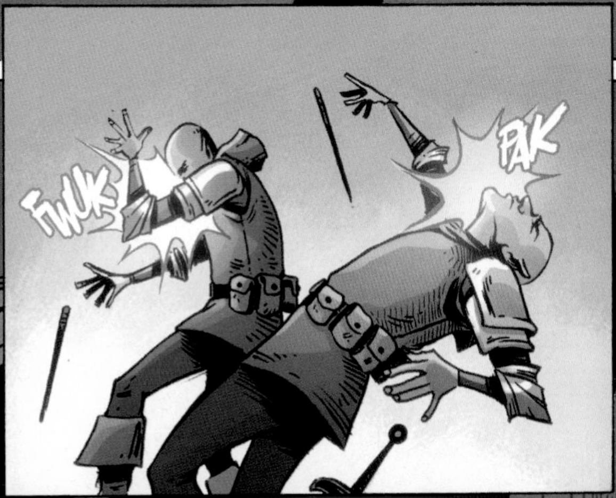
FWUK
PAK

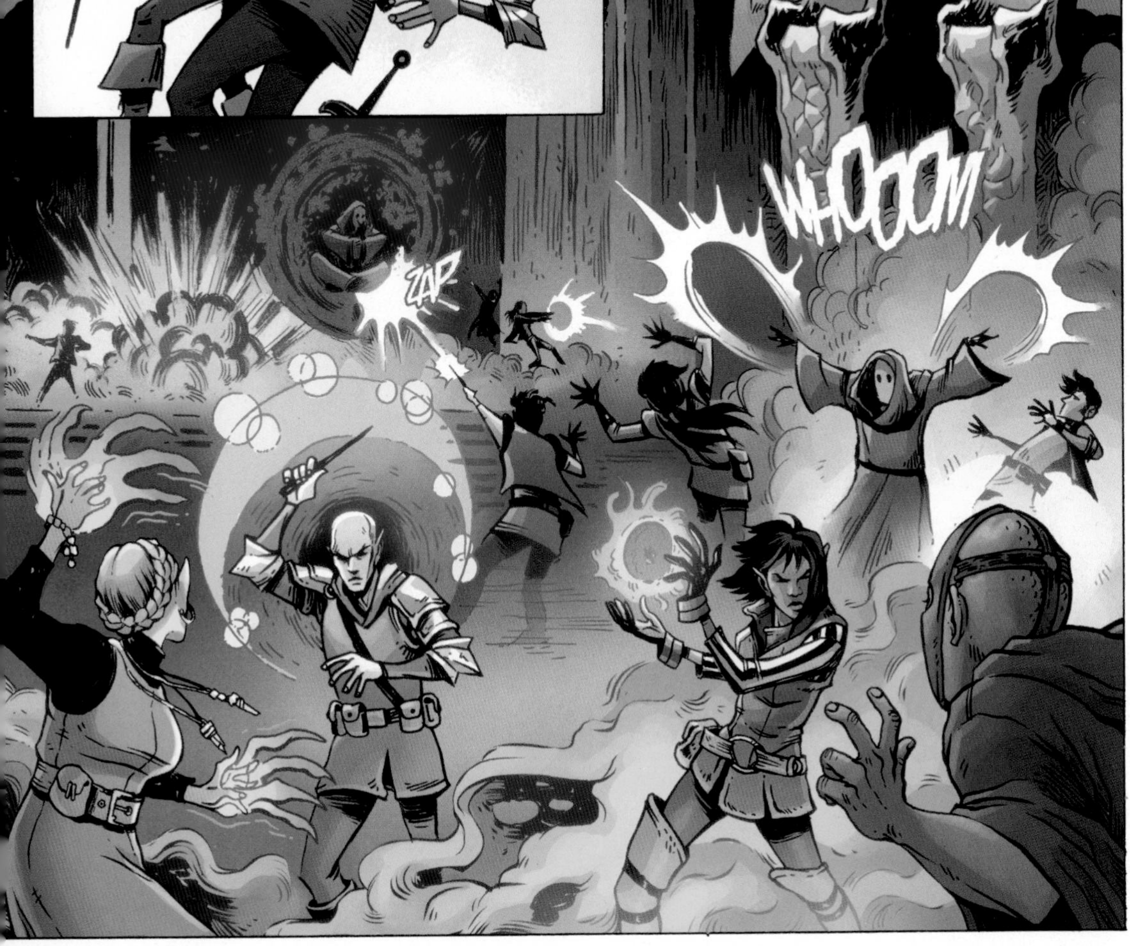
WHOOOM
ZAP

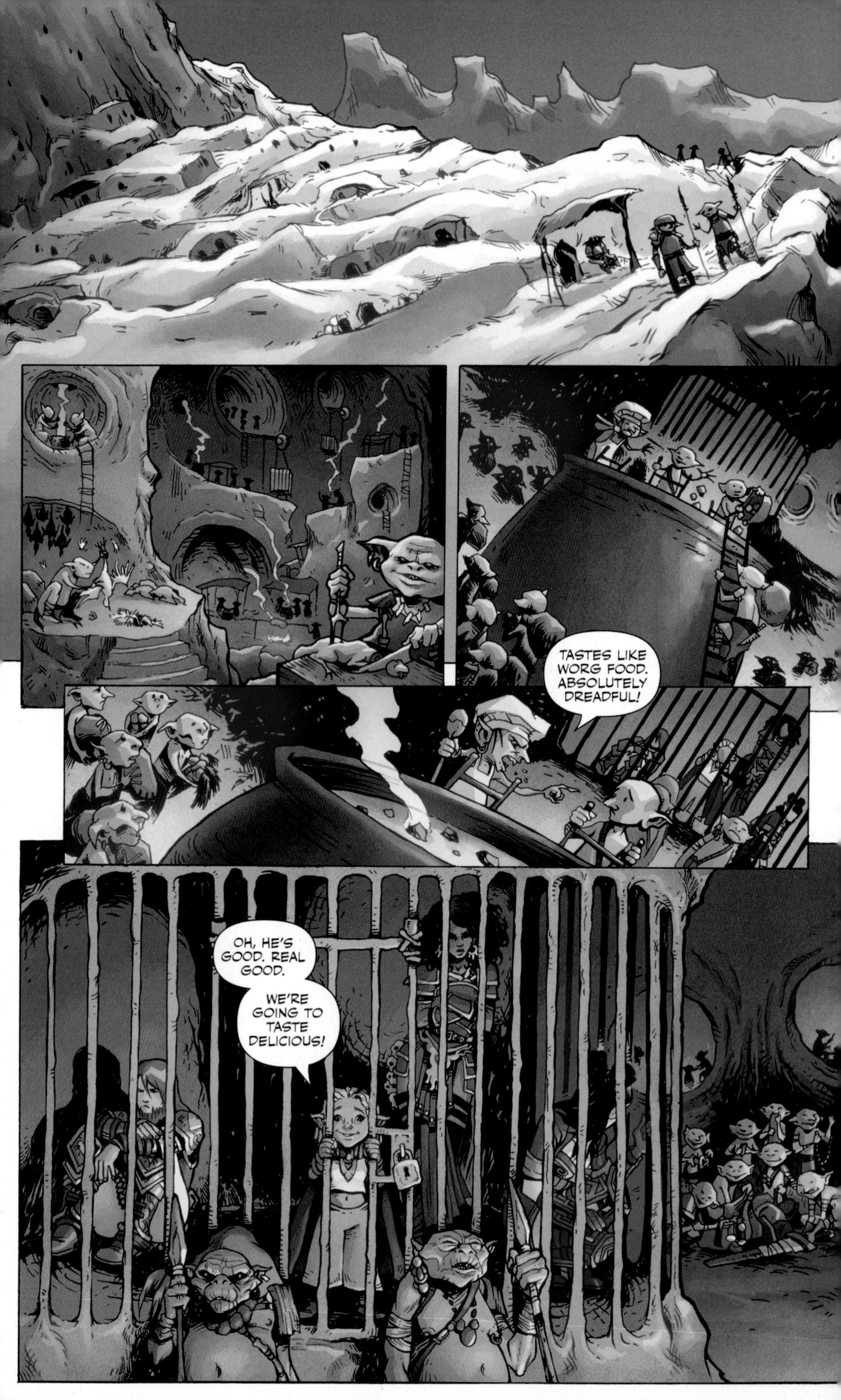
TASTES LIKE WORG FOOD. ABSOLUTELY DREADFUL!
OH, HE'S GOOD. REAL GOOD.
WE'RE GOING TO TASTE DELICIOUS!

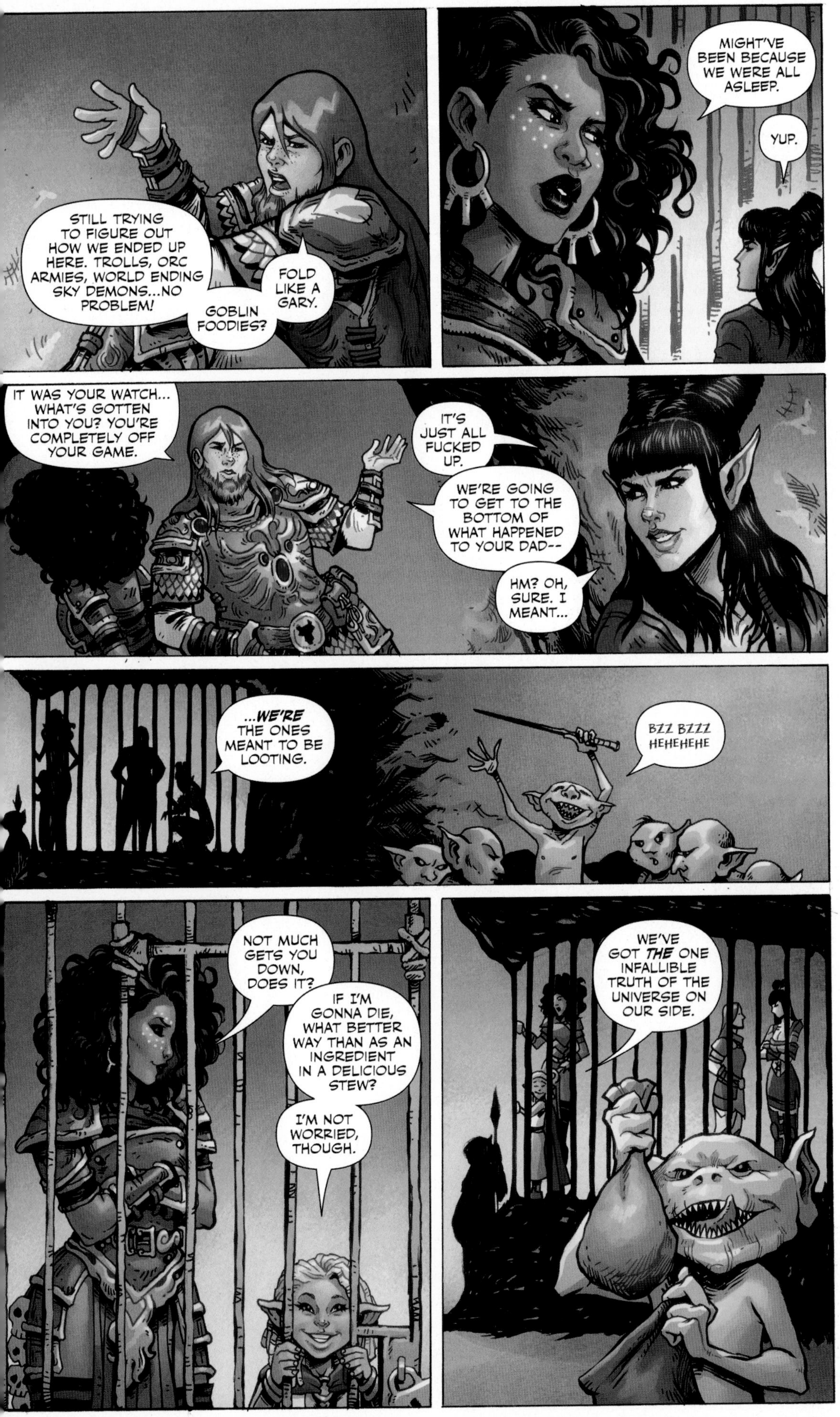
STILL TRYING TO FIGURE OUT HOW WE ENDED UP HERE. TROLLS, ORC ARMIES, WORLD ENDING SKY DEMONS...NO PROBLEM!
GOBLIN FOODIES?
FOLD LIKE A GARY.
MIGHT'VE BEEN BECAUSE WE WERE ALL ASLEEP.
YUP.
IT WAS YOUR WATCH... WHAT'S GOTTEN INTO YOU? YOU'RE COMPLETELY OFF YOUR GAME.
IT'S JUST ALL FUCKED UP.
WE'RE GOING TO GET TO THE BOTTOM OF WHAT HAPPENED TO YOUR DAD--
HM? OH, SURE. I MEANT...
...WE'RE THE ONES MEANT TO BE LOOTING.
BZZ BZZZ HEHEHEHE
NOT MUCH GETS YOU DOWN, DOES IT?
IF I'M GONNA DIE, WHAT BETTER WAY THAN AS AN INGREDIENT IN A DELICIOUS STEW?
I'M NOT WORRIED, THOUGH.
WE'VE GOT THE ONE INFALLIBLE TRUTH OF THE UNIVERSE ON OUR SIDE.

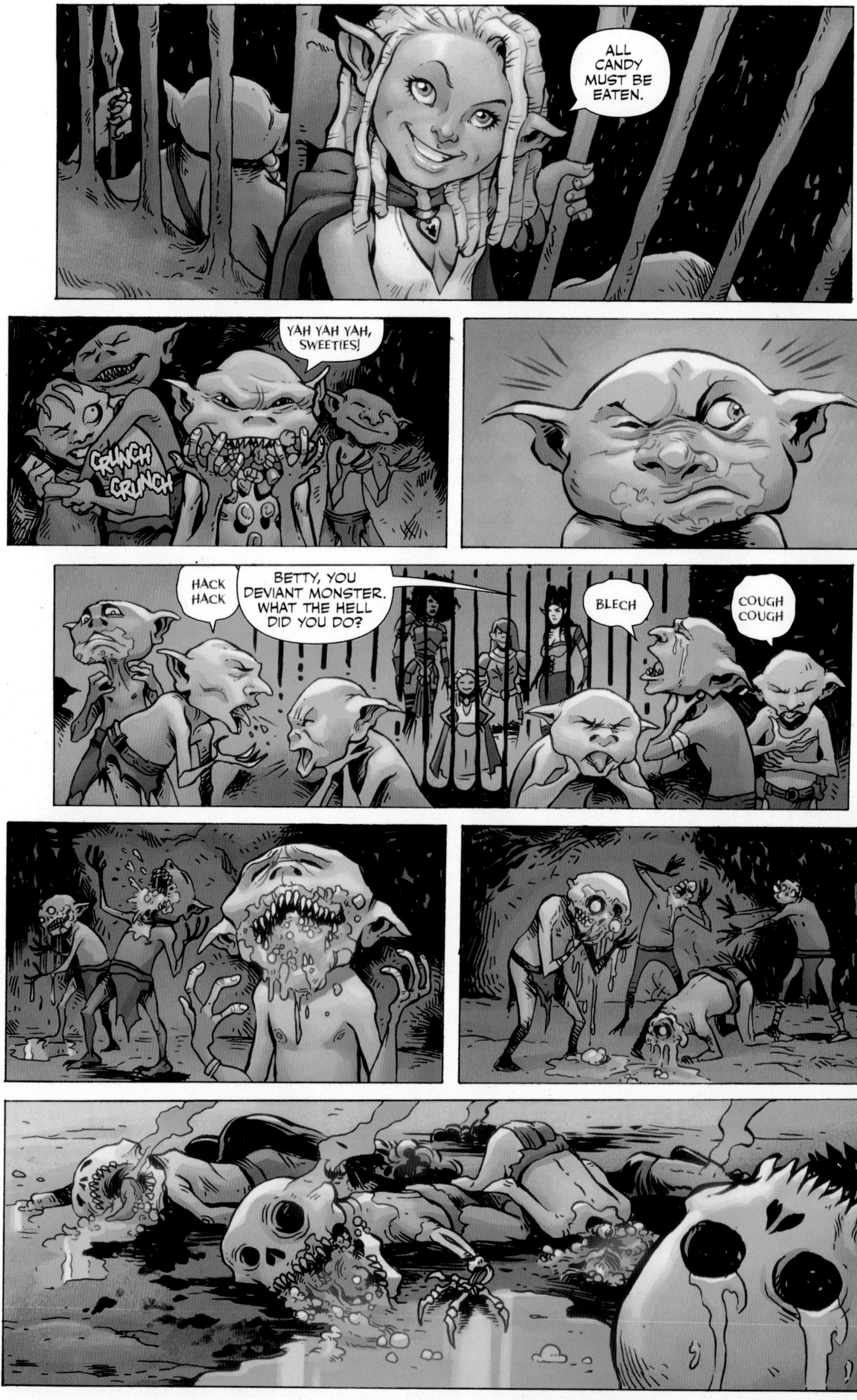
ALL CANDY MUST BE EATEN.
YAH YAH YAH, SWEETIES!
CRUNCH
CRUNCH
HACK HACK
BETTY, YOU DEVIANT MONSTER. WHAT THE HELL DID YOU DO?
BLECH
COUGH COUGH

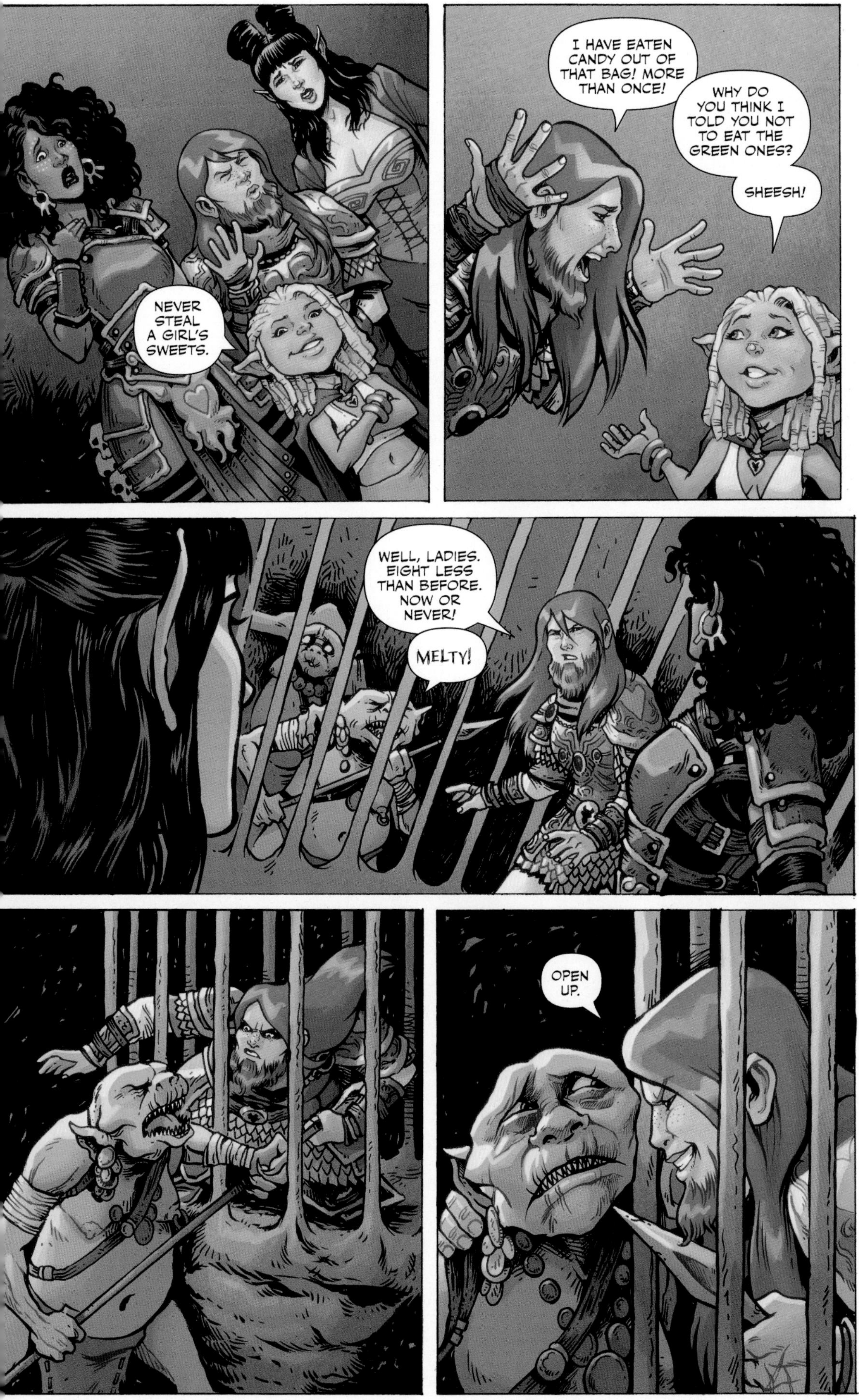
NEVER STEAL A GIRL'S SWEETS.
I HAVE EATEN CANDY OUT OF THAT BAG! MORE THAN ONCE!
WHY DO YOU THINK I TOLD YOU NOT TO EAT THE GREEN ONES?
SHEESH!
WELL, LADIES. EIGHT LESS THAN BEFORE. NOW OR NEVER!
MELTY!
OPEN UP.

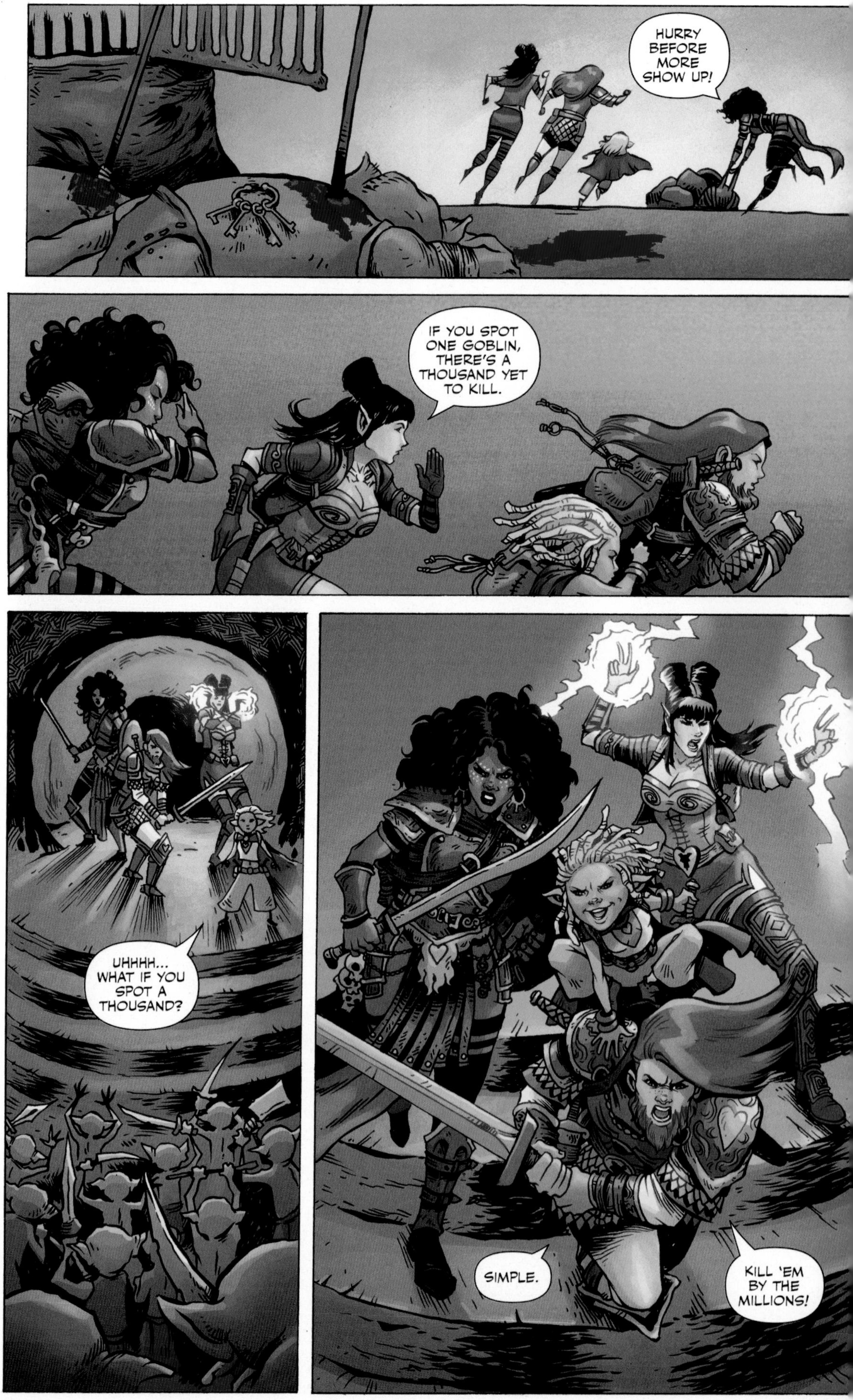
HURRY BEFORE MORE SHOW UP!
IF YOU SPOT ONE GOBLIN, THERE'S A THOUSAND YET TO KILL.
UHHHH... WHAT IF YOU SPOT A THOUSAND?
SIMPLE.
KILL 'EM BY THE MILLIONS!

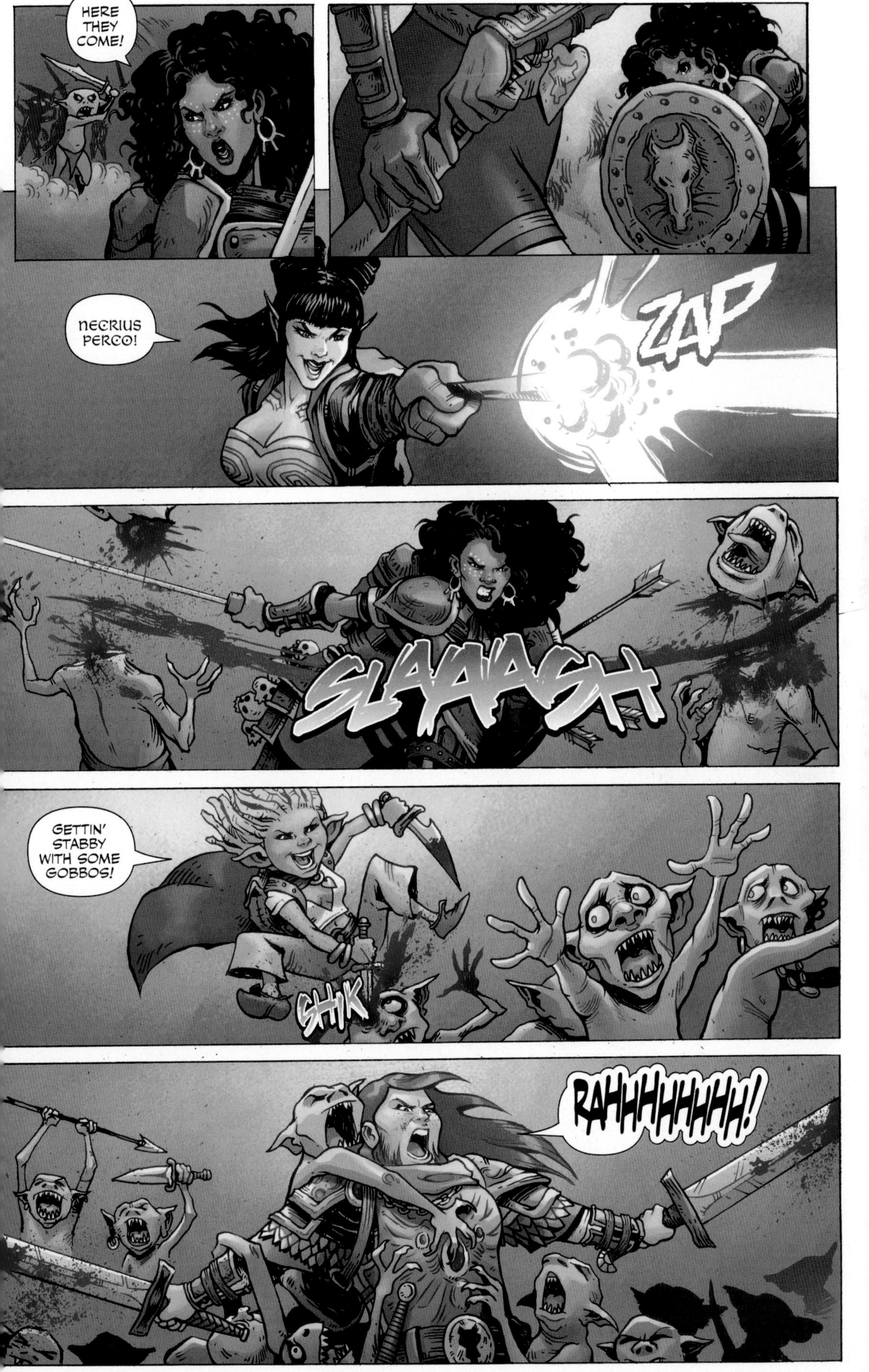
HERE THEY COME!
NECRIUS PERCO!
ZAP
SLAAASH
GETTIN' STABBY WITH SOME GOBBOS!
SHIK
RAHHHHHHH!

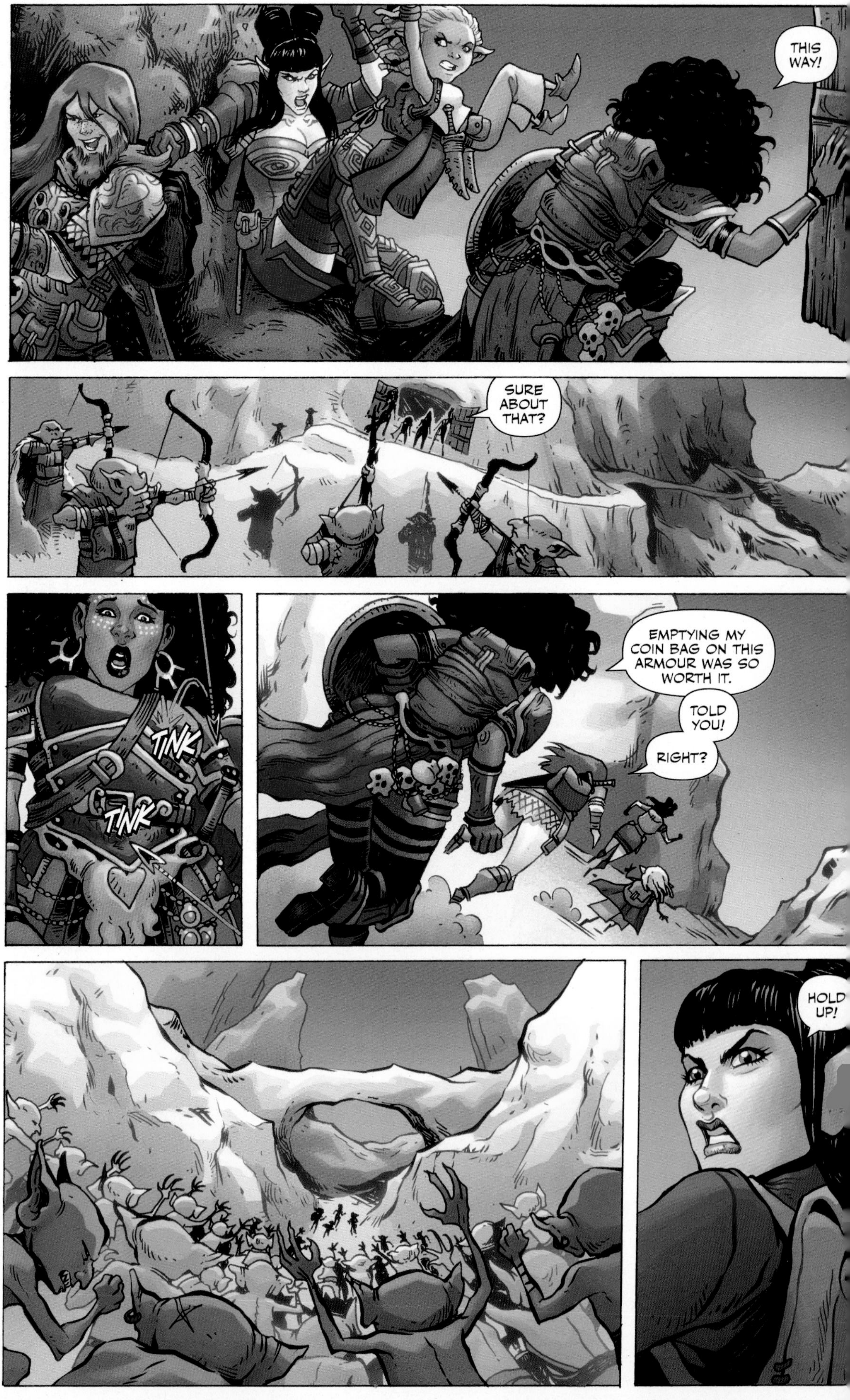
THIS WAY!
SURE ABOUT THAT?
TINK
TINK
EMPTYING MY COIN BAG ON THIS ARMOUR WAS SO WORTH IT.
TOLD YOU!
RIGHT?
HOLD UP!

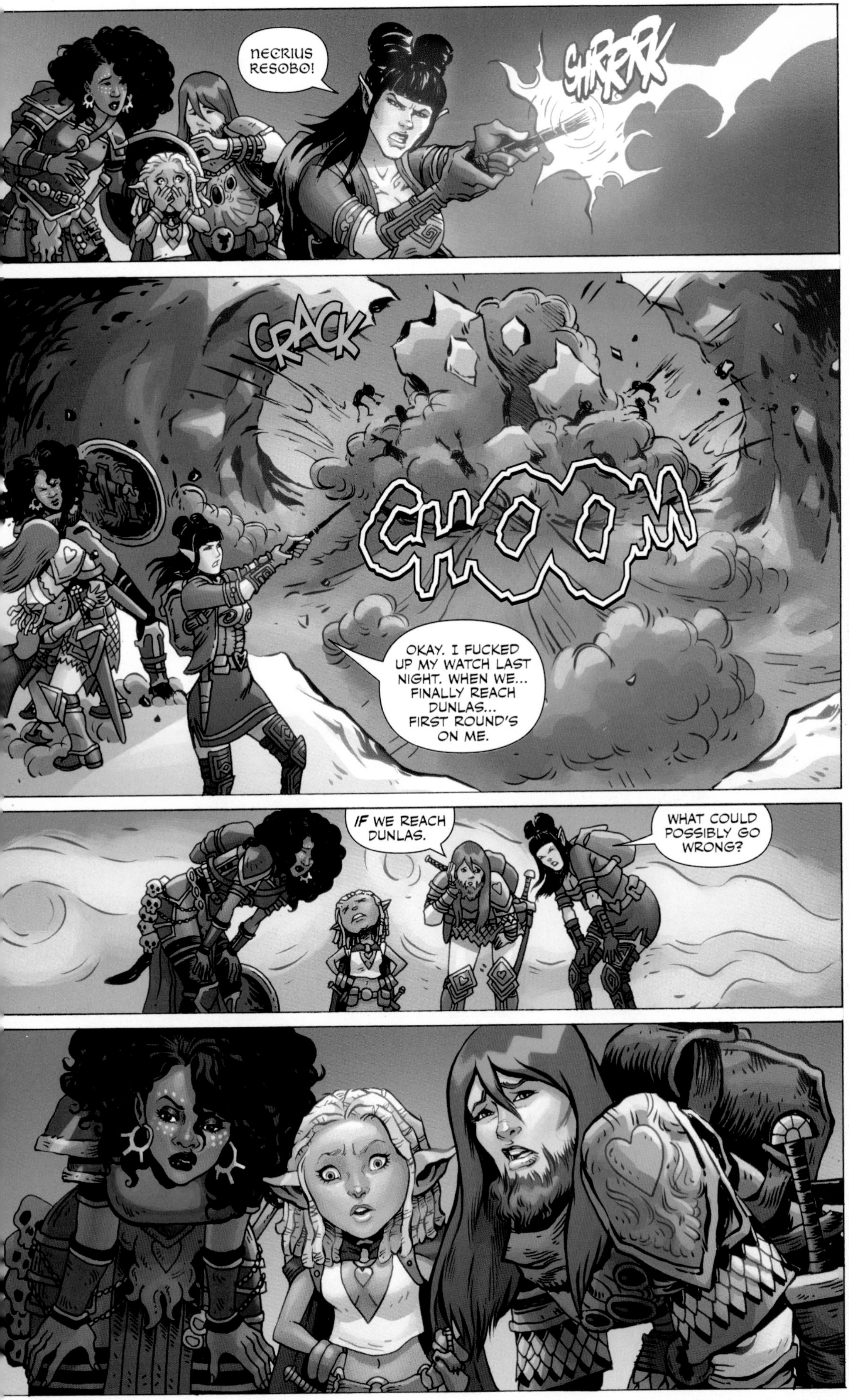
NECRIUS RESOBO!
SHRRRK
CRACK
CHOOM
OKAY. I FUCKED UP MY WATCH LAST NIGHT. WHEN WE... FINALLY REACH DUNLAS... FIRST ROUND'S ON ME.
IF WE REACH DUNLAS.
WHAT COULD POSSIBLY GO WRONG?

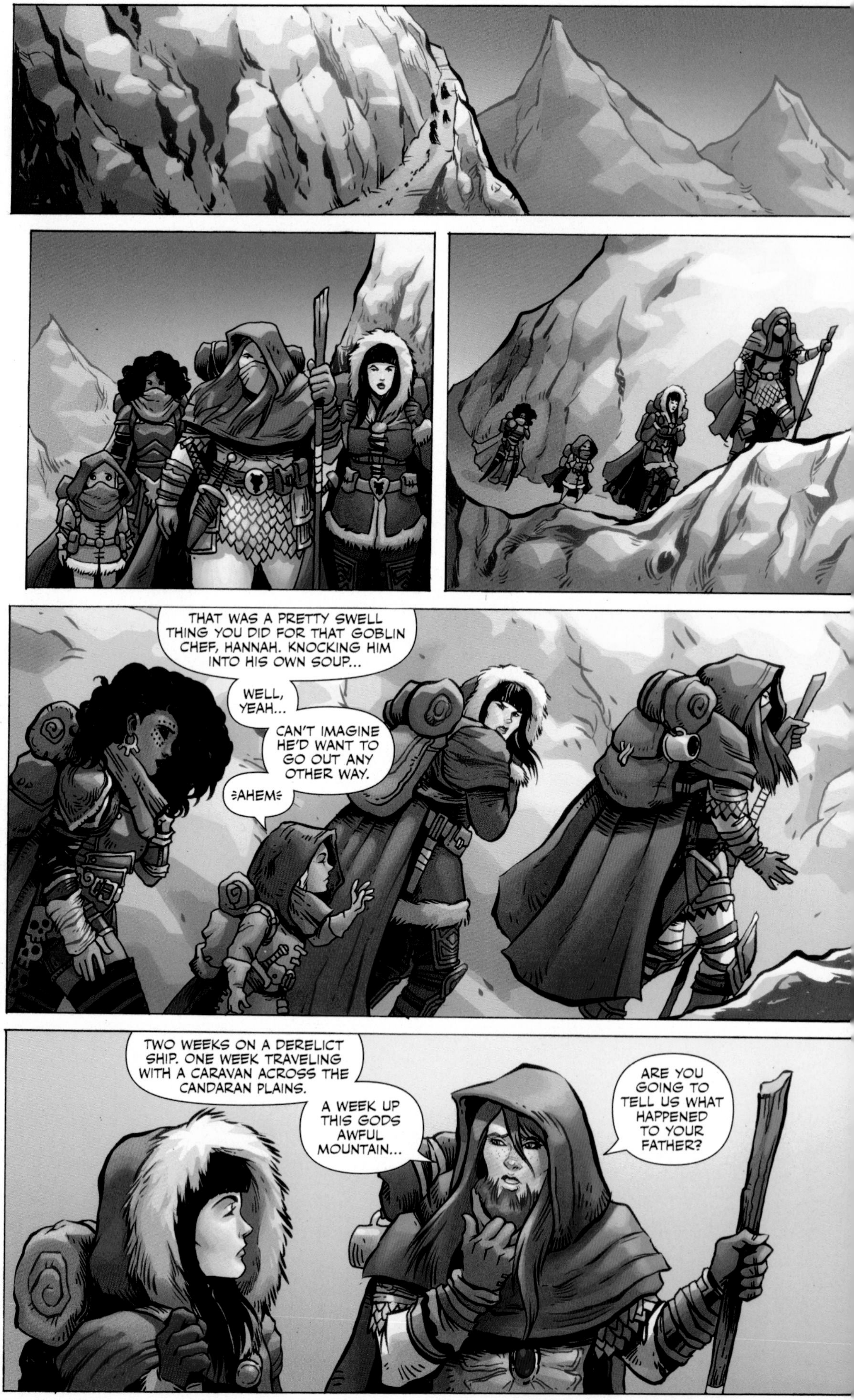

THAT WAS A PRETTY SWELL THING YOU DID FOR THAT GOBLIN CHEF, HANNAH. KNOCKING HIM INTO HIS OWN SOUP...
WELL, YEAH...
CAN'T IMAGINE HE'D WANT TO GO OUT ANY OTHER WAY.
AHEM
TWO WEEKS ON A DERELICT SHIP. ONE WEEK TRAVELING WITH A CARAVAN ACROSS THE CANDARAN PLAINS.
A WEEK UP THIS GODS AWFUL MOUNTAIN...
ARE YOU GOING TO TELL US WHAT HAPPENED TO YOUR FATHER?

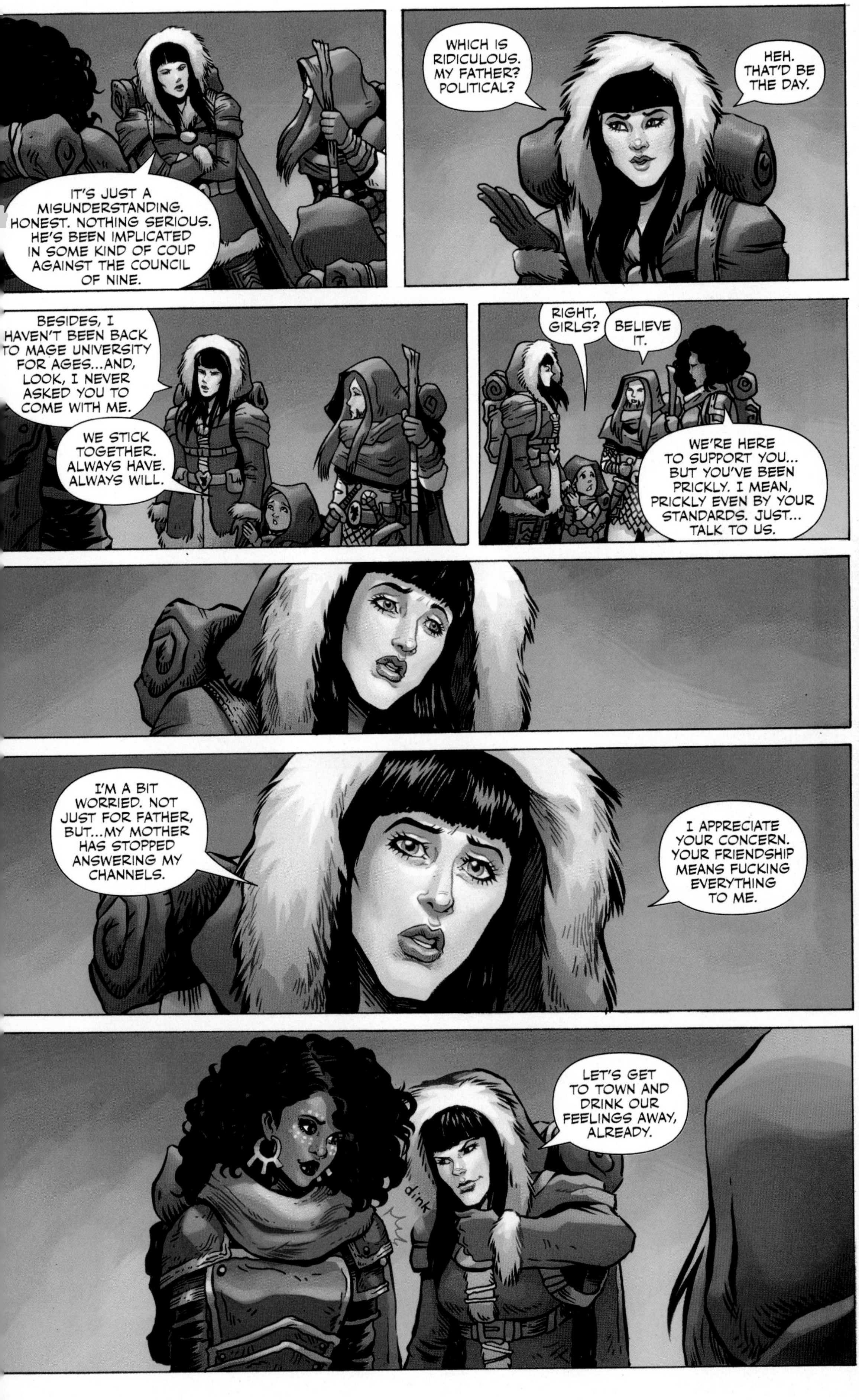
IT'S JUST A MISUNDERSTANDING. HONEST. NOTHING SERIOUS. HE'S BEEN IMPLICATED IN SOME KIND OF COUP AGAINST THE COUNCIL OF NINE.
WHICH IS RIDICULOUS. MY FATHER? POLITICAL?
HEH. THAT'D BE THE DAY.
BESIDES, I HAVEN'T BEEN BACK TO MAGE UNIVERSITY FOR AGES...AND, LOOK, I NEVER ASKED YOU TO COME WITH ME.
WE STICK TOGETHER. ALWAYS HAVE. ALWAYS WILL.
RIGHT, GIRLS?
BELIEVE IT.
WE'RE HERE TO SUPPORT YOU... BUT YOU'VE BEEN PRICKLY. I MEAN, PRICKLY EVEN BY YOUR STANDARDS. JUST... TALK TO US.
I'M A BIT WORRIED. NOT JUST FOR FATHER, BUT...MY MOTHER HAS STOPPED ANSWERING MY CHANNELS.
I APPRECIATE YOUR CONCERN. YOUR FRIENDSHIP MEANS FUCKING EVERYTHING TO ME.
LET'S GET TO TOWN AND DRINK OUR FEELINGS AWAY, ALREADY.
dink

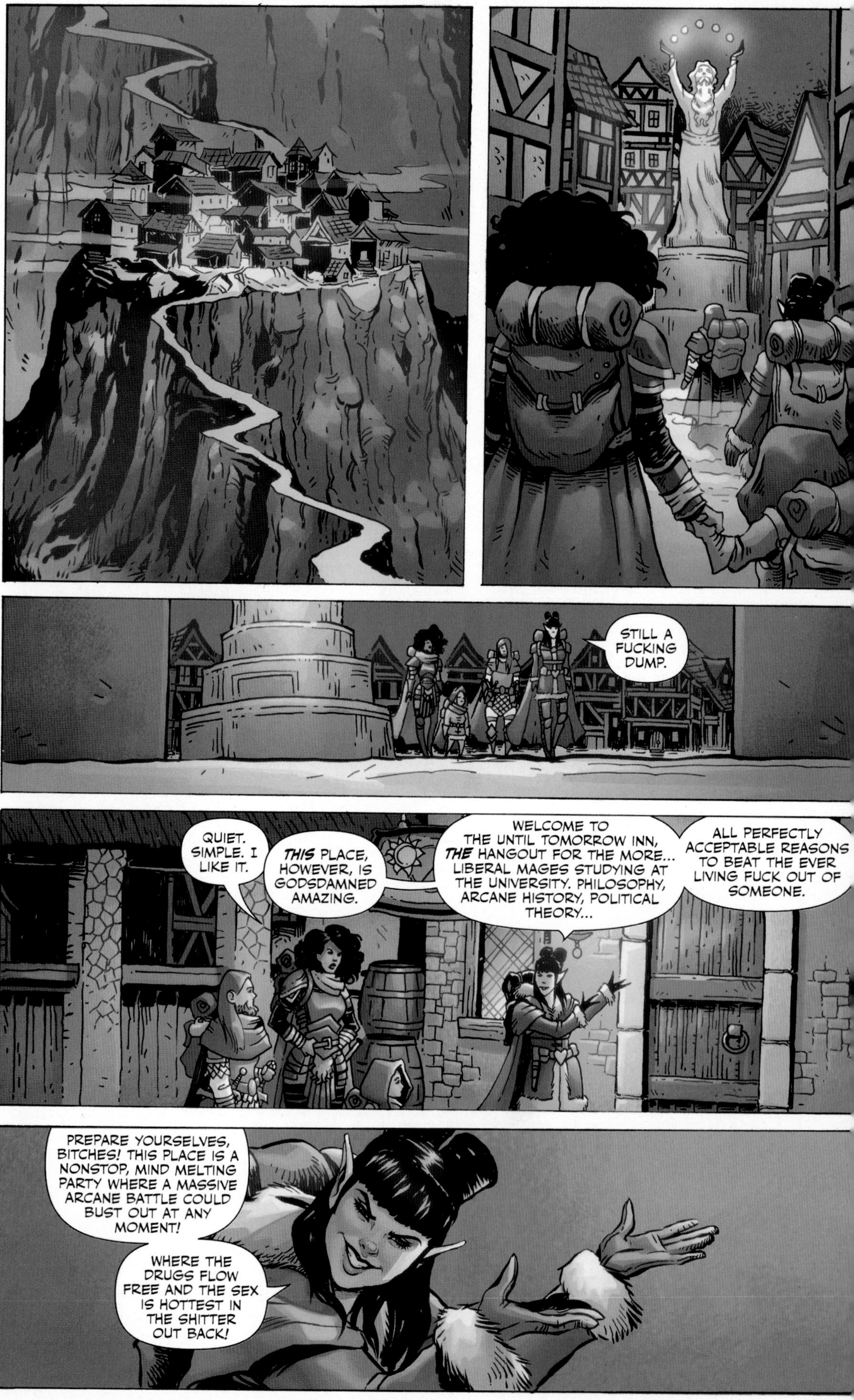
STILL A FUCKING DUMP.
QUIET. SIMPLE. I LIKE IT.
THIS PLACE, HOWEVER, IS GODSDAMNED AMAZING.
WELCOME TO THE UNTIL TOMORROW INN, THE HANGOUT FOR THE MORE... LIBERAL MAGES STUDYING AT THE UNIVERSITY. PHILOSOPHY, ARCANE HISTORY, POLITICAL THEORY...
ALL PERFECTLY ACCEPTABLE REASONS TO BEAT THE EVER LIVING FUCK OUT OF SOMEONE.
PREPARE YOURSELVES, BITCHES! THIS PLACE IS A NONSTOP, MIND MELTING PARTY WHERE A MASSIVE ARCANE BATTLE COULD BUST OUT AT ANY MOMENT!
WHERE THE DRUGS FLOW FREE AND THE SEX IS HOTTEST IN THE SHITTER OUT BACK!

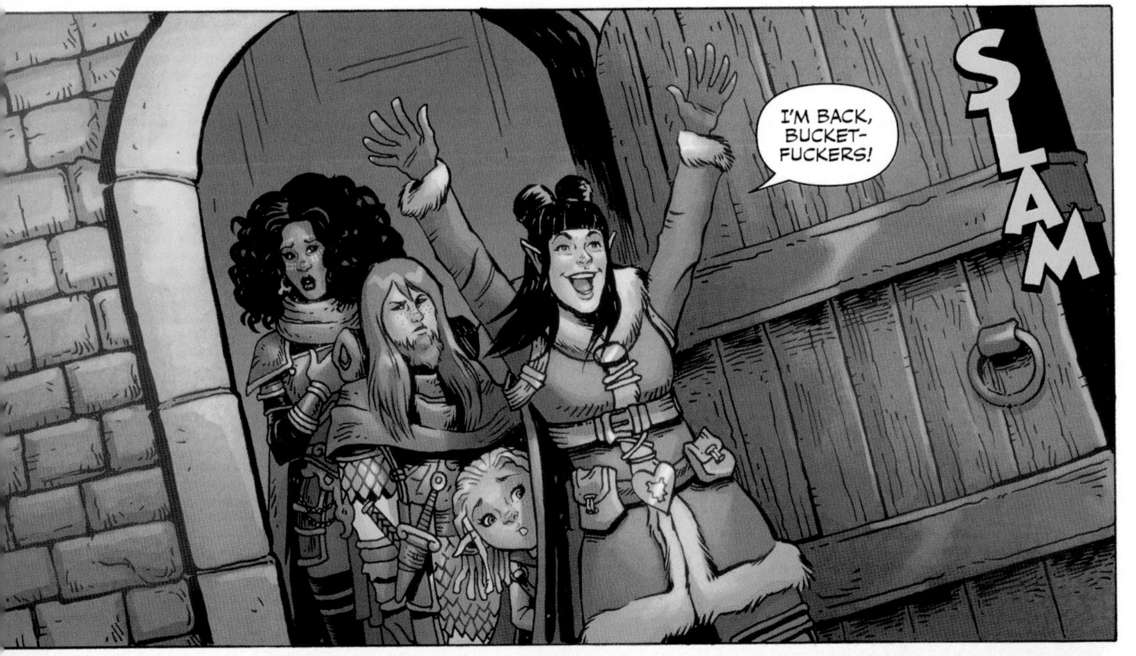
I'M BACK,
BUCKET-
FUCKERS!
SLAM

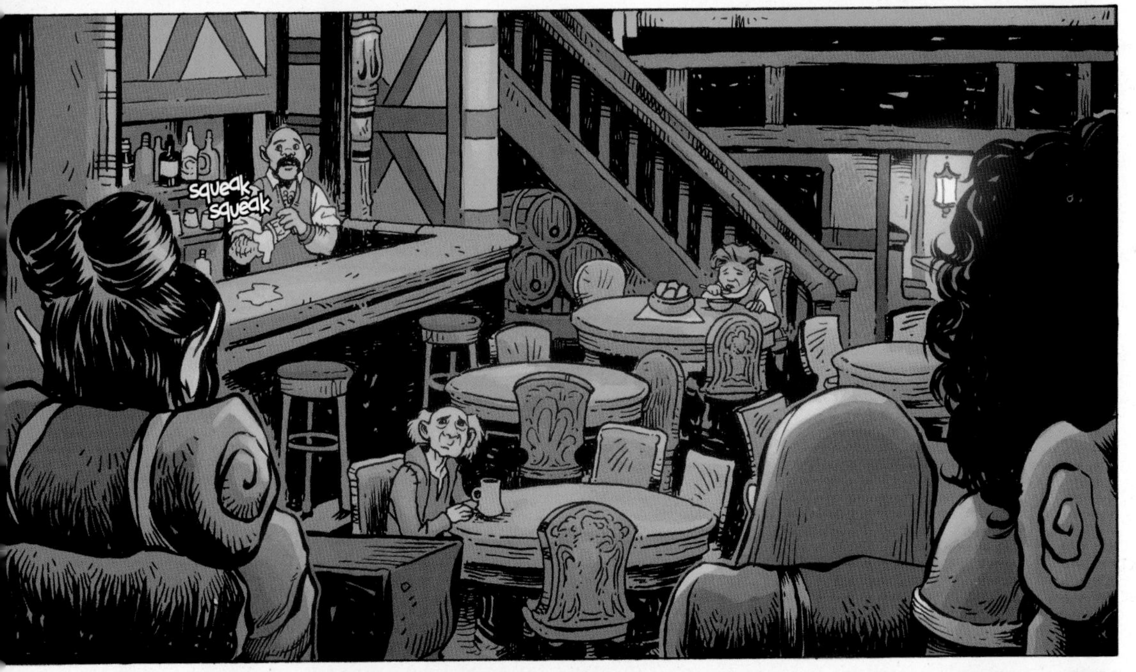
squeak,
squeak

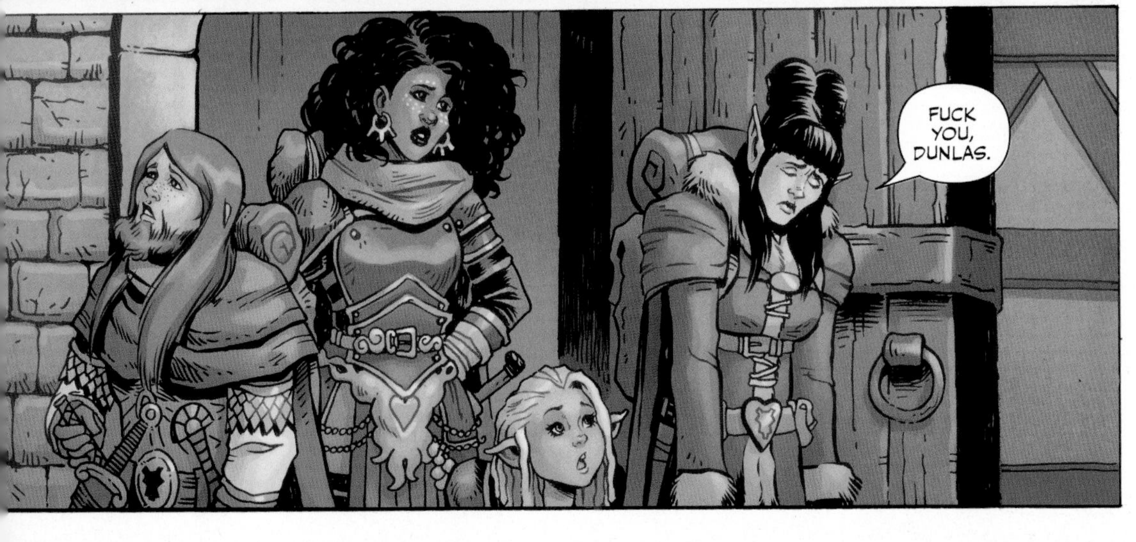
FUCK
YOU,
DUNLAS.

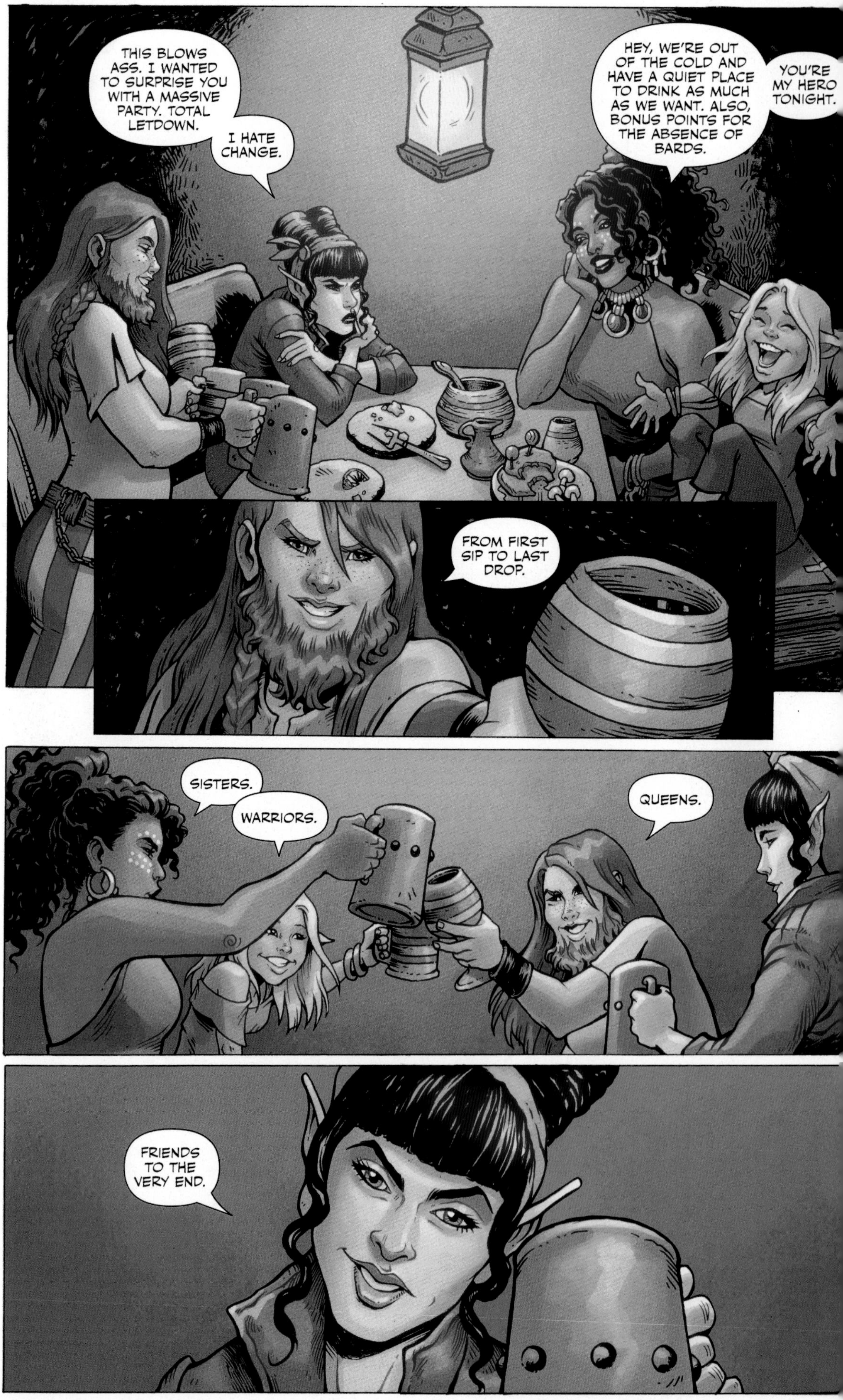
THIS BLOWS ASS. I WANTED TO SURPRISE YOU WITH A MASSIVE PARTY. TOTAL LETDOWN.
I HATE CHANGE.
HEY, WE'RE OUT OF THE COLD AND HAVE A QUIET PLACE TO DRINK AS MUCH AS WE WANT. ALSO, BONUS POINTS FOR THE ABSENCE OF BARDS.
YOU'RE MY HERO TONIGHT.
FROM FIRST SIP TO LAST DROP.
SISTERS.
WARRIORS.
QUEENS.
FRIENDS TO THE VERY END.

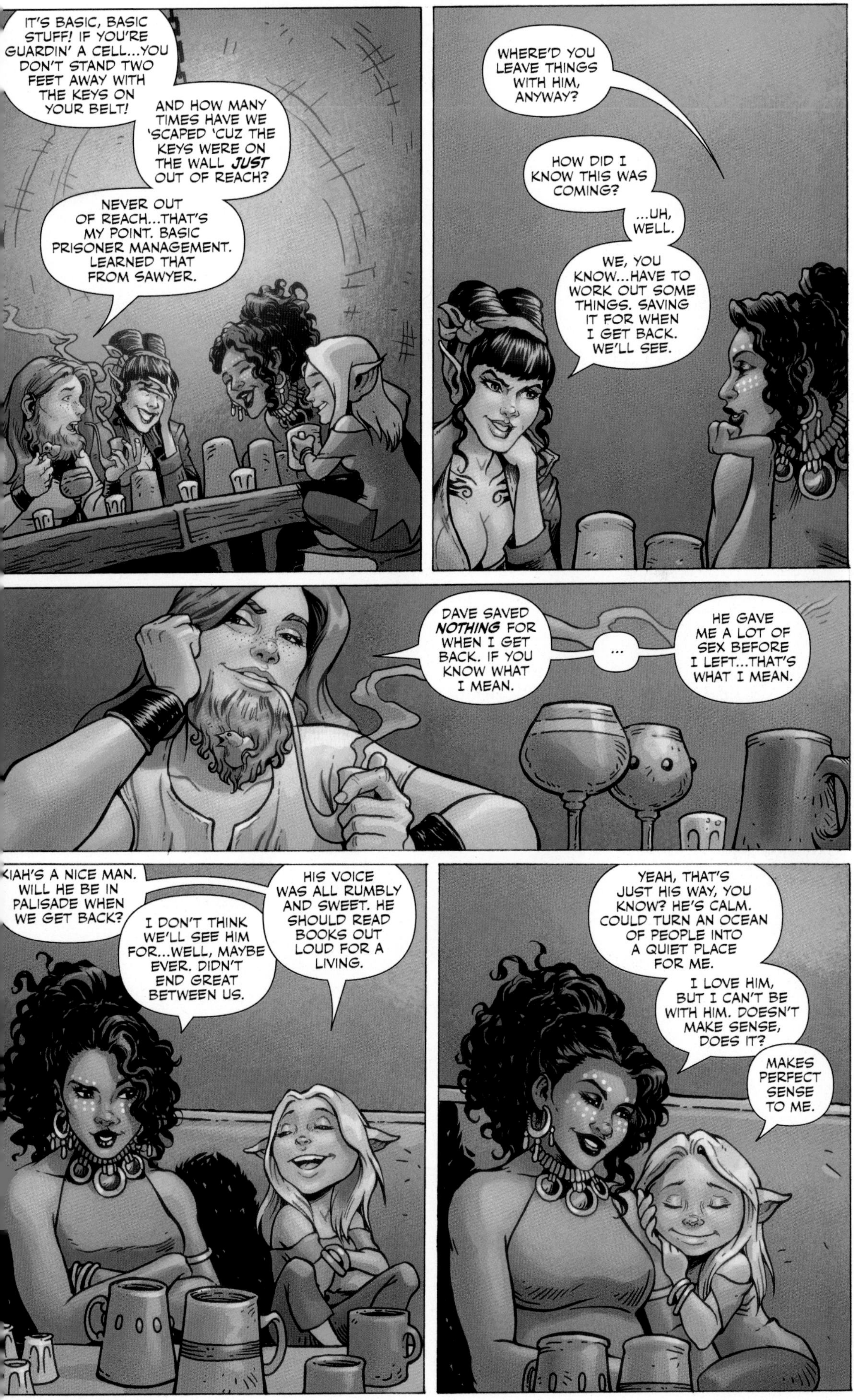
IT'S BASIC, BASIC STUFF! IF YOU'RE GUARDIN' A CELL...YOU DON'T STAND TWO FEET AWAY WITH THE KEYS ON YOUR BELT!
AND HOW MANY TIMES HAVE WE 'SCAPED 'CUZ THE KEYS WERE ON THE WALL JUST OUT OF REACH?
NEVER OUT OF REACH...THAT'S MY POINT. BASIC PRISONER MANAGEMENT. LEARNED THAT FROM SAWYER.
WHERE'D YOU LEAVE THINGS WITH HIM, ANYWAY?
HOW DID I KNOW THIS WAS COMING?
...UH, WELL.
WE, YOU KNOW...HAVE TO WORK OUT SOME THINGS. SAVING IT FOR WHEN I GET BACK. WE'LL SEE.
DAVE SAVED NOTHING FOR WHEN I GET BACK. IF YOU KNOW WHAT I MEAN.
...
HE GAVE ME A LOT OF SEX BEFORE I LEFT...THAT'S WHAT I MEAN.
KIAH'S A NICE MAN. WILL HE BE IN PALISADE WHEN WE GET BACK?
I DON'T THINK WE'LL SEE HIM FOR...WELL, MAYBE EVER. DIDN'T END GREAT BETWEEN US.
HIS VOICE WAS ALL RUMBLY AND SWEET. HE SHOULD READ BOOKS OUT LOUD FOR A LIVING.
YEAH, THAT'S JUST HIS WAY, YOU KNOW? HE'S CALM. COULD TURN AN OCEAN OF PEOPLE INTO A QUIET PLACE FOR ME.
I LOVE HIM, BUT I CAN'T BE WITH HIM. DOESN'T MAKE SENSE, DOES IT?
MAKES PERFECT SENSE TO ME.

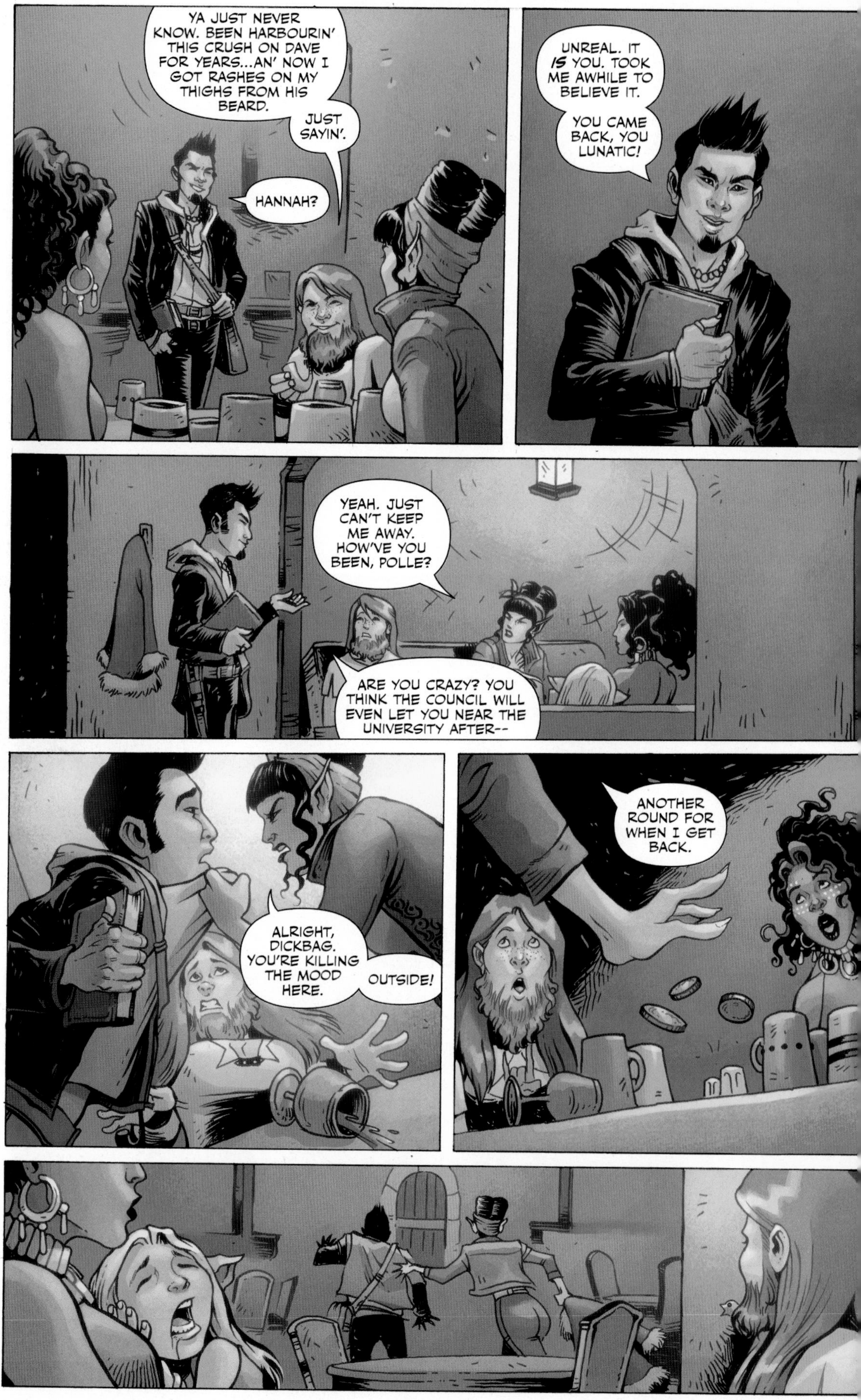
YA JUST NEVER KNOW. BEEN HARBOURIN' THIS CRUSH ON DAVE FOR YEARS...AN' NOW I GOT RASHES ON MY THIGHS FROM HIS BEARD.
JUST SAYIN'.
HANNAH?
UNREAL. IT *IS* YOU. TOOK ME AWHILE TO BELIEVE IT.
YOU CAME BACK, YOU LUNATIC!
YEAH. JUST CAN'T KEEP ME AWAY. HOW'VE YOU BEEN, POLLE?
ARE YOU CRAZY? YOU THINK THE COUNCIL WILL EVEN LET YOU NEAR THE UNIVERSITY AFTER--
ALRIGHT, DICKBAG. YOU'RE KILLING THE MOOD HERE.
OUTSIDE!
ANOTHER ROUND FOR WHEN I GET BACK.

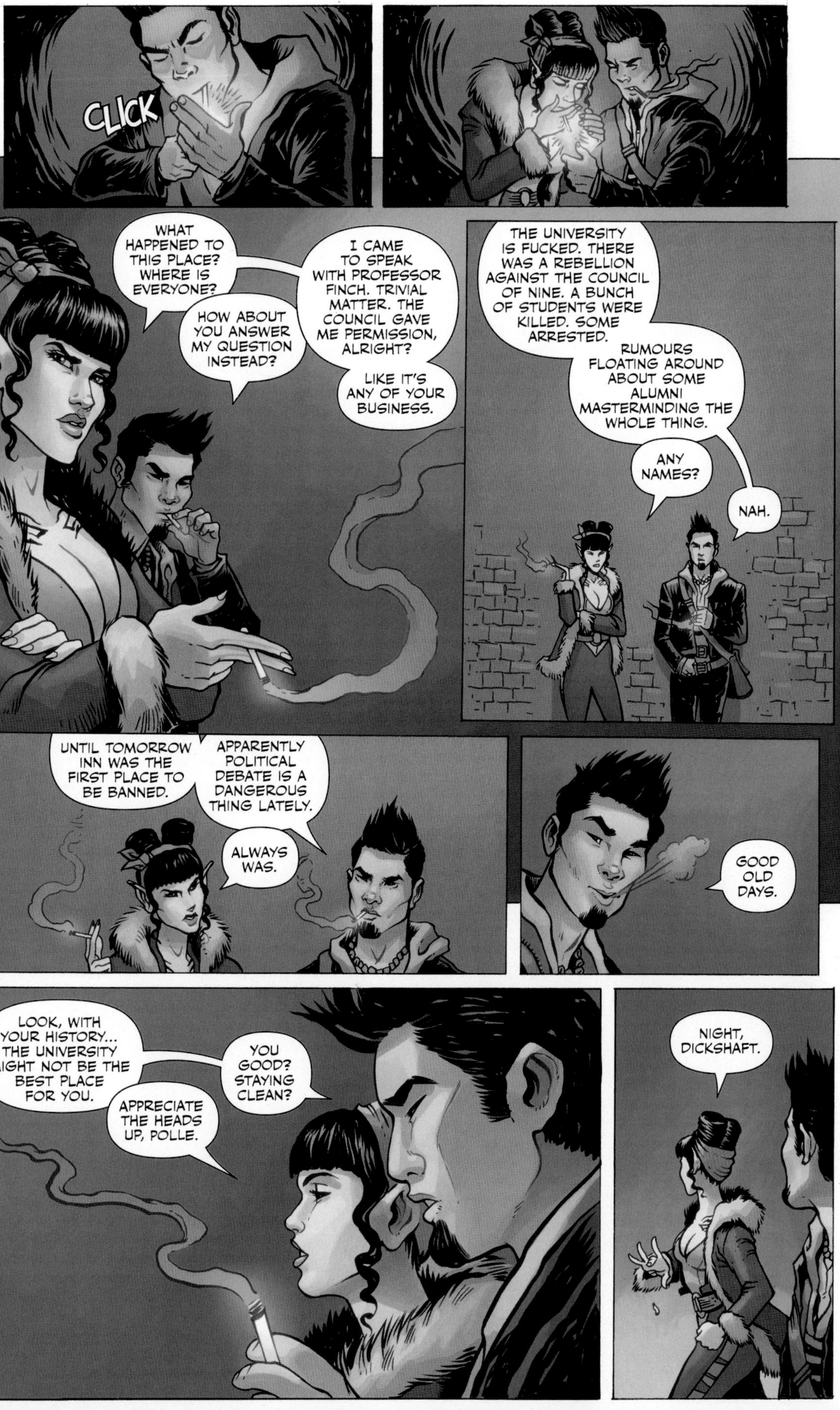
CLICK
WHAT HAPPENED TO THIS PLACE? WHERE IS EVERYONE?
I CAME TO SPEAK WITH PROFESSOR FINCH. TRIVIAL MATTER. THE COUNCIL GAVE ME PERMISSION, ALRIGHT?
HOW ABOUT YOU ANSWER MY QUESTION INSTEAD?
LIKE IT'S ANY OF YOUR BUSINESS.
THE UNIVERSITY IS FUCKED. THERE WAS A REBELLION AGAINST THE COUNCIL OF NINE. A BUNCH OF STUDENTS WERE KILLED. SOME ARRESTED.
RUMOURS FLOATING AROUND ABOUT SOME ALUMNI MASTERMINDING THE WHOLE THING.
ANY NAMES?
NAH.
UNTIL TOMORROW INN WAS THE FIRST PLACE TO BE BANNED.
APPARENTLY POLITICAL DEBATE IS A DANGEROUS THING LATELY.
ALWAYS WAS.
GOOD OLD DAYS.
LOOK, WITH YOUR HISTORY... THE UNIVERSITY MIGHT NOT BE THE BEST PLACE FOR YOU.
YOU GOOD? STAYING CLEAN?
APPRECIATE THE HEADS UP, POLLE.
NIGHT, DICKSHAFT.

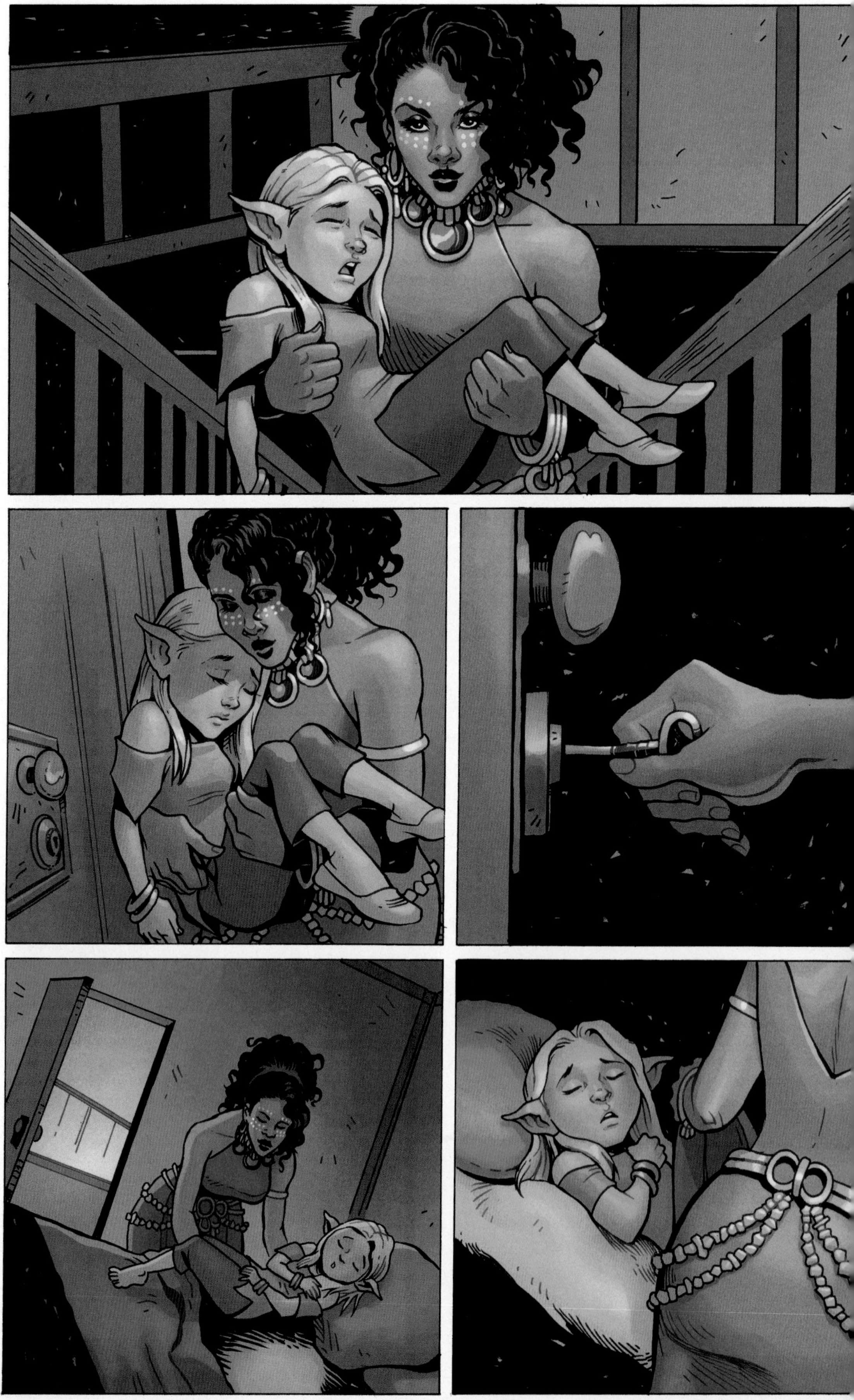

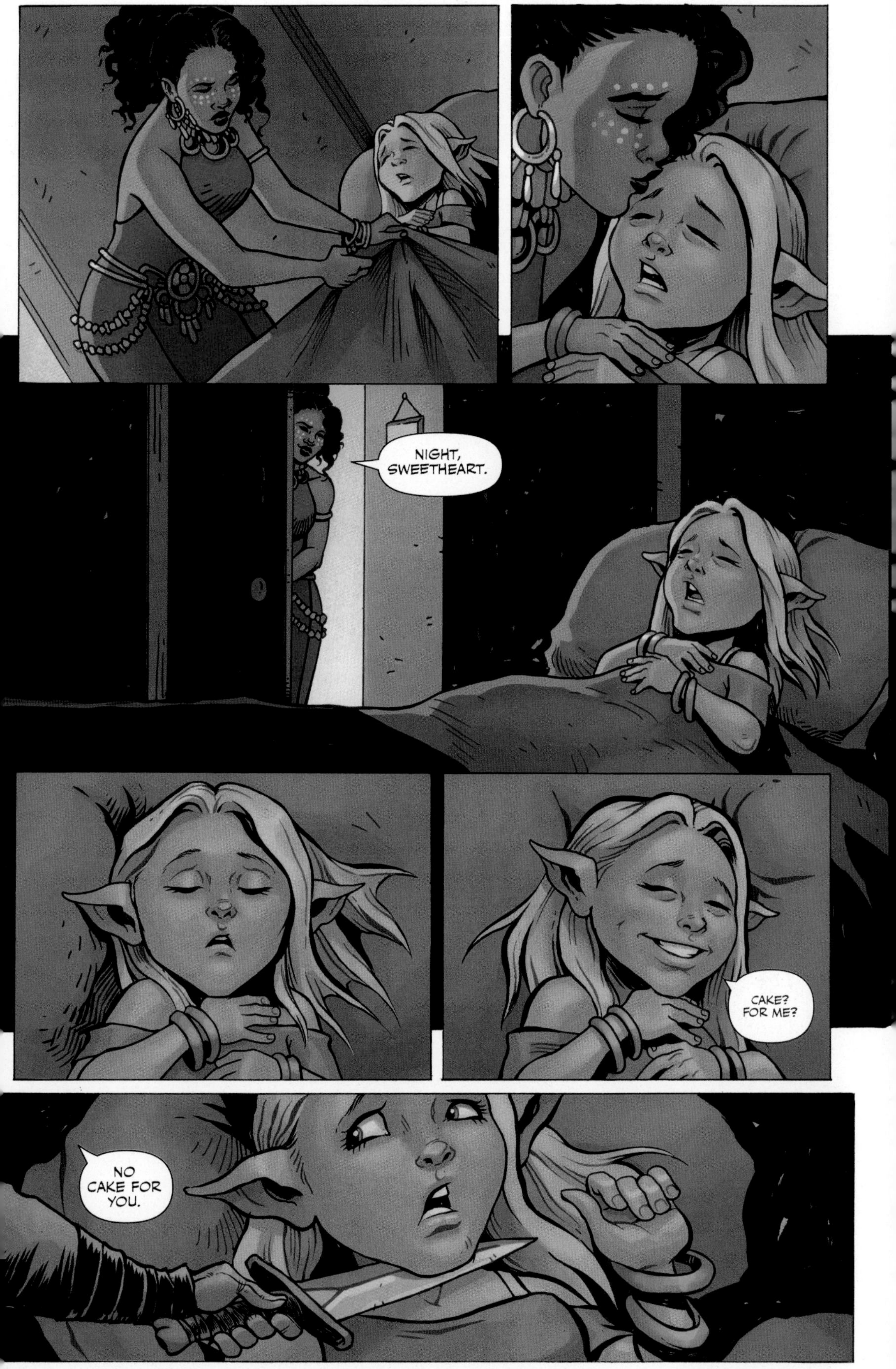
NIGHT, SWEETHEART.
CAKE? FOR ME?
NO CAKE FOR YOU.

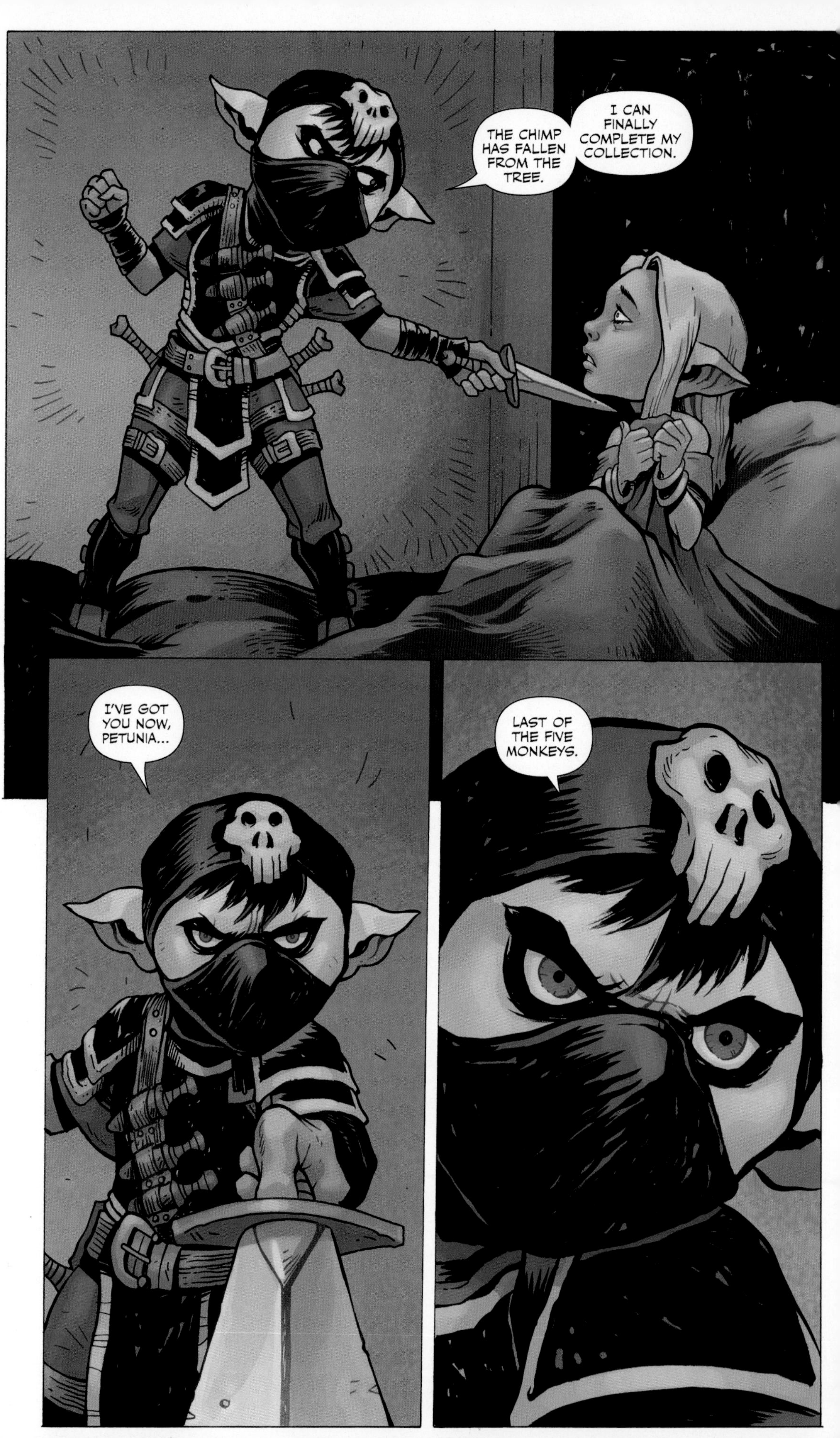
THE CHIMP HAS FALLEN FROM THE TREE.
I CAN FINALLY COMPLETE MY COLLECTION.
I'VE GOT YOU NOW, PETUNIA...
LAST OF THE FIVE MONKEYS.

CHAPTER TWELVE

TESS 2016

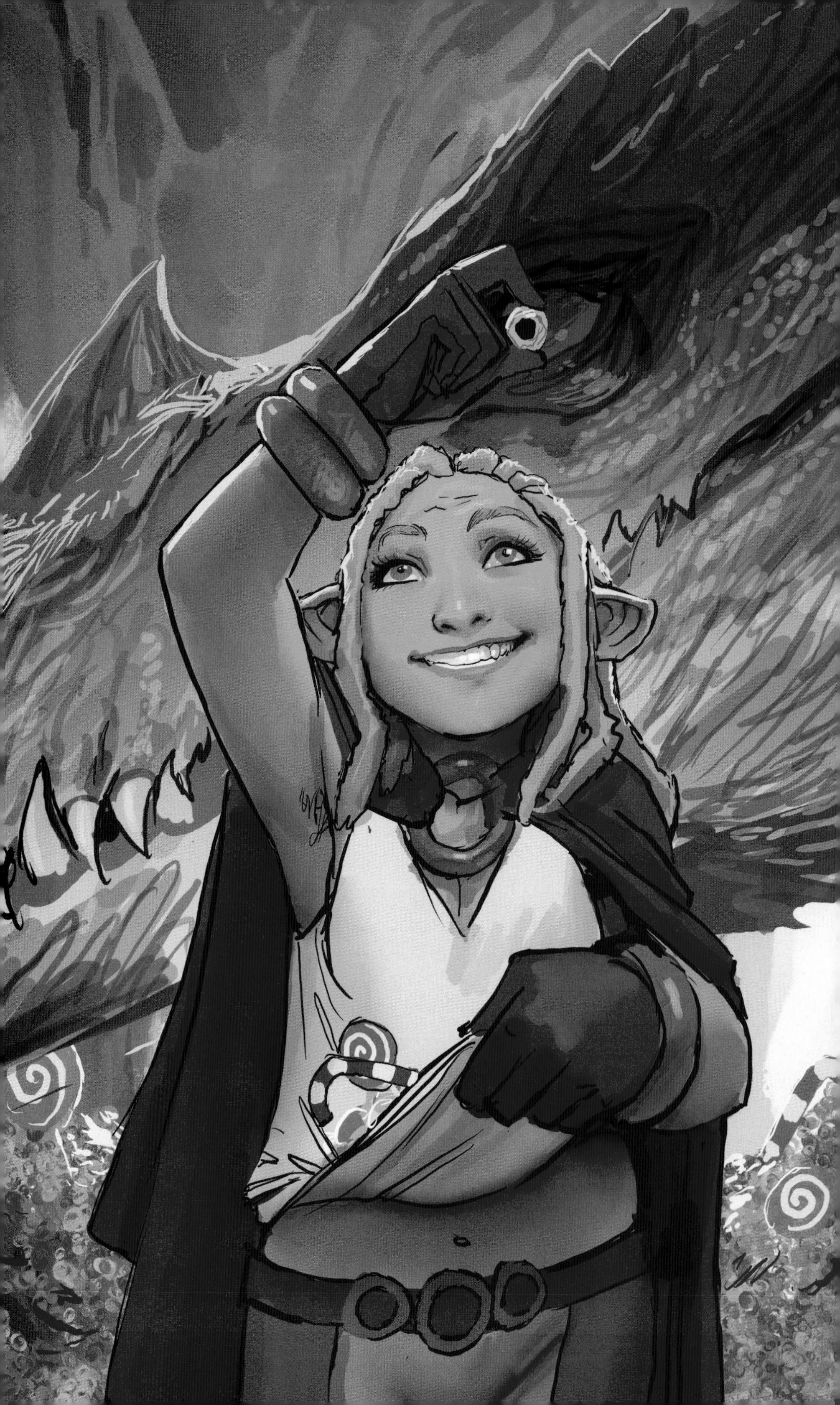

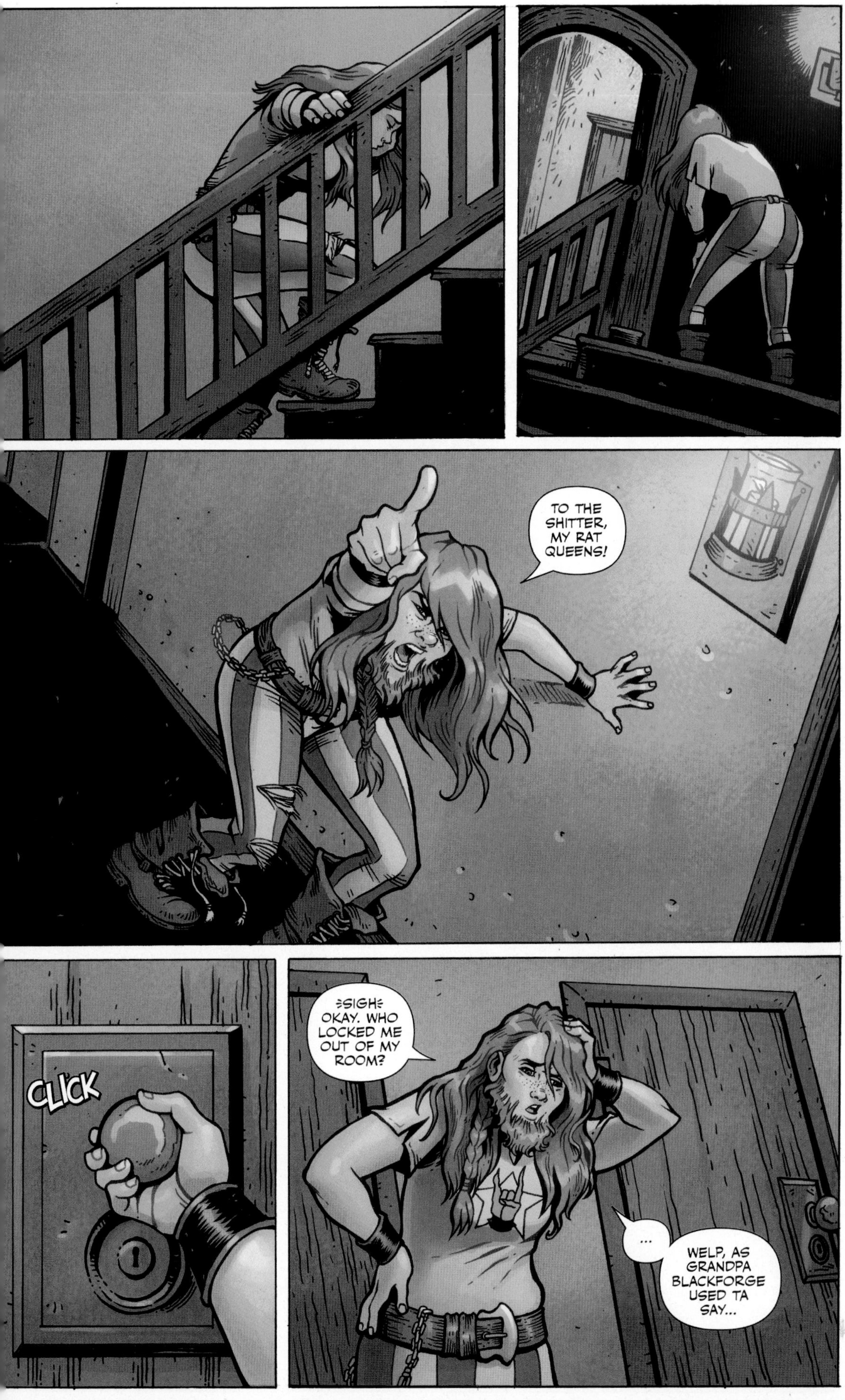
TO THE SHITTER, MY RAT QUEENS!
CLICK
≡SIGH≡ OKAY. WHO LOCKED ME OUT OF MY ROOM?
...
WELP, AS GRANDPA BLACKFORGE USED TA SAY...

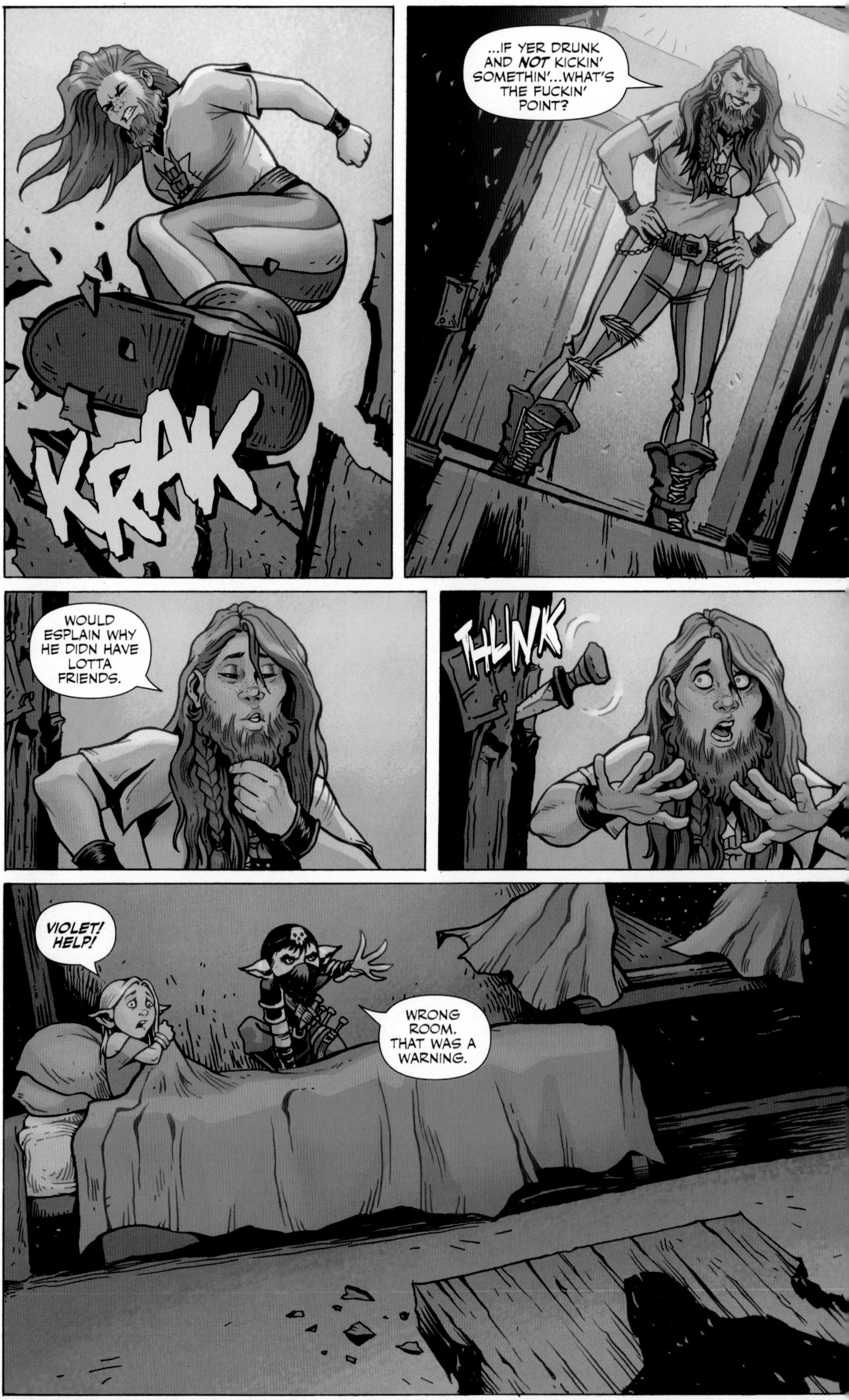
KRAK
...IF YER DRUNK AND NOT KICKIN' SOMETHIN'...WHAT'S THE FUCKIN' POINT?
WOULD ESPLAIN WHY HE DIDN HAVE LOTTA FRIENDS.
THUNK
VIOLET! HELP!
WRONG ROOM. THAT WAS A WARNING.

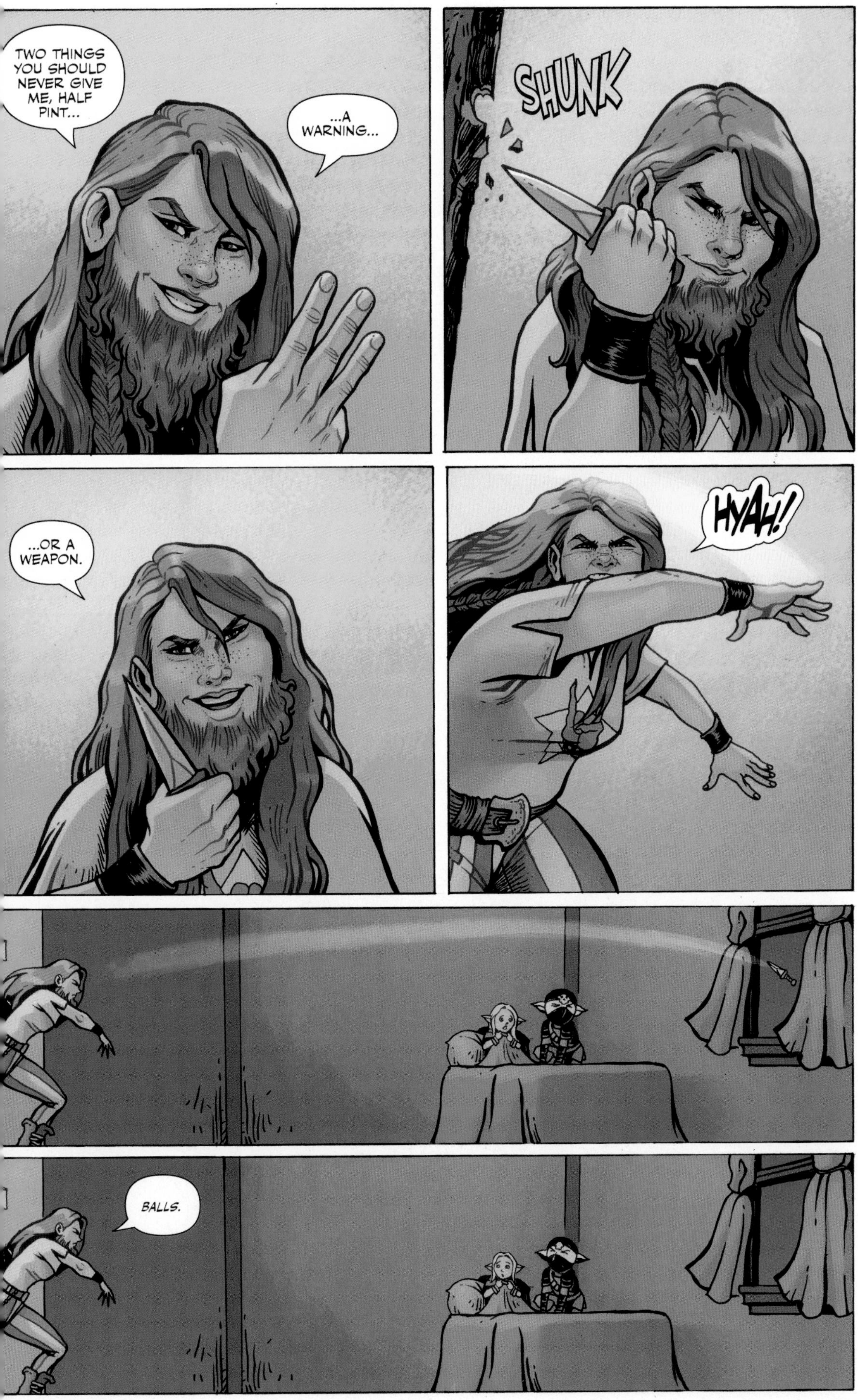
TWO THINGS YOU SHOULD NEVER GIVE ME, HALF PINT...
...A WARNING...
SHUNK
...OR A WEAPON.
HYAH!
BALLS.

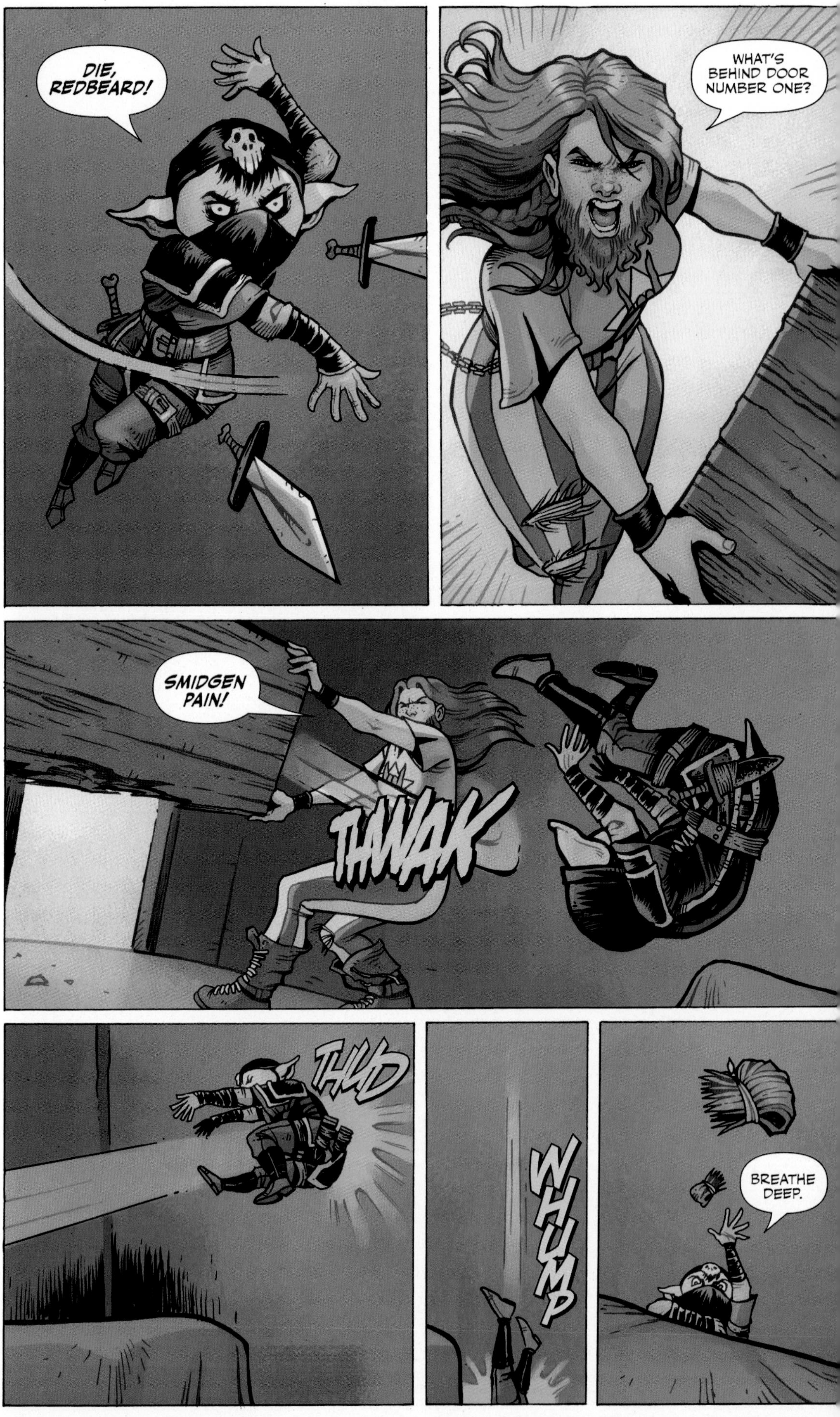
DIE, REDBEARD!
WHAT'S BEHIND DOOR NUMBER ONE?
SMIDGEN PAIN!
THWAK
THUD
WHUMP
BREATHE DEEP.

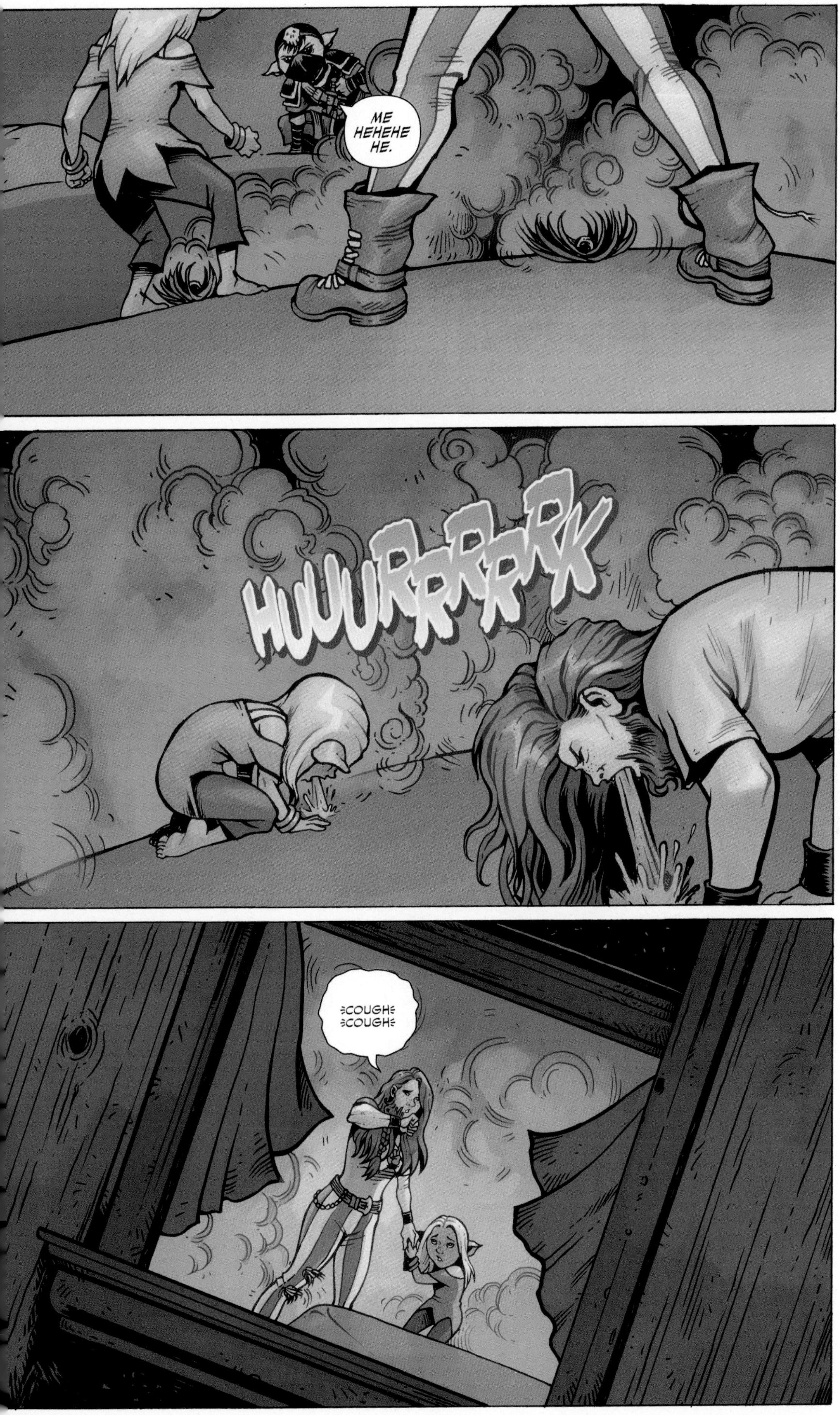
ME HEHEHE HE.
HUUURRRRRK
≡COUGH≡ ≡COUGH≡

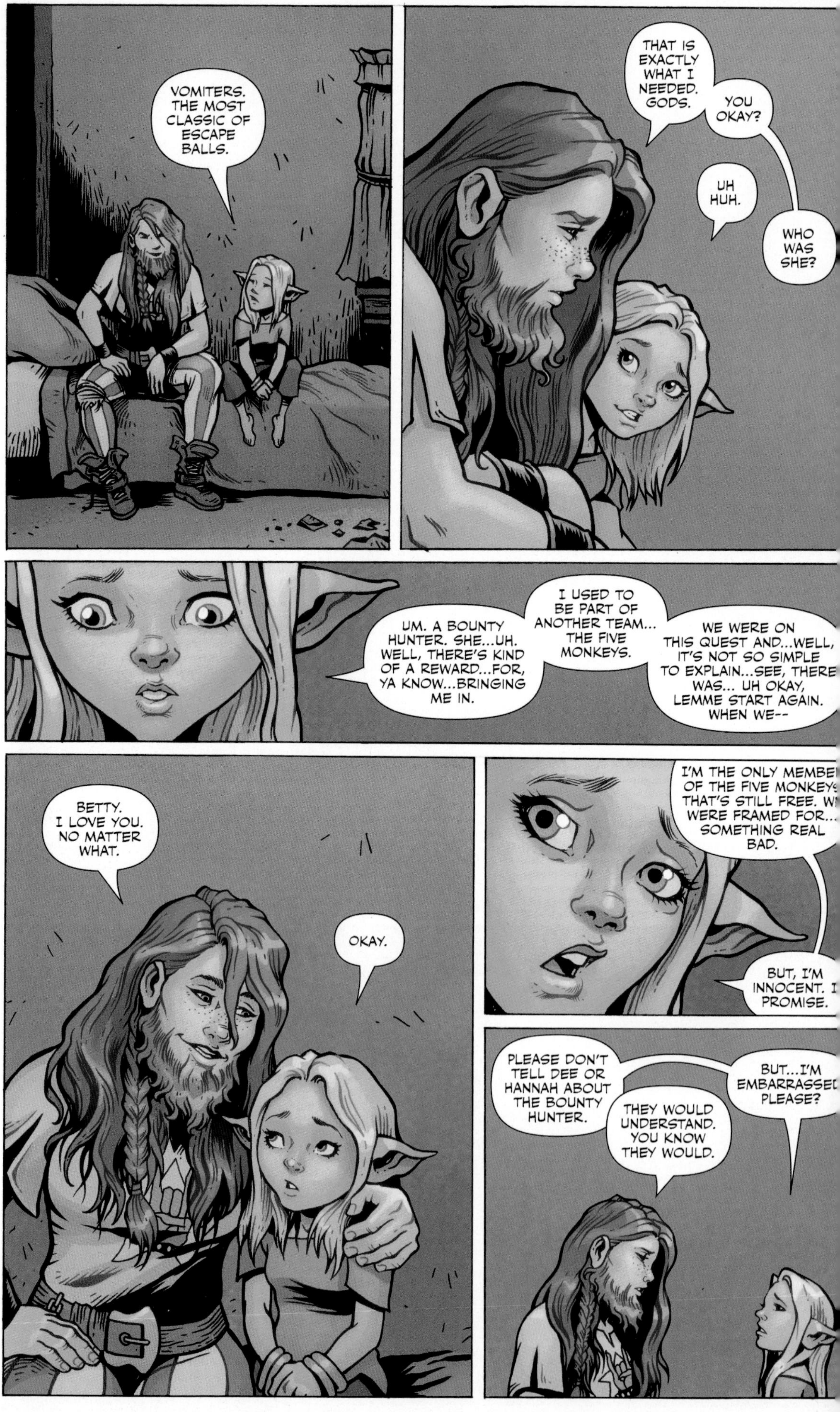
VOMITERS. THE MOST CLASSIC OF ESCAPE BALLS.
THAT IS EXACTLY WHAT I NEEDED. GODS.
YOU OKAY?
UH HUH.
WHO WAS SHE?
UM. A BOUNTY HUNTER. SHE...UH. WELL, THERE'S KIND OF A REWARD...FOR, YA KNOW...BRINGING ME IN.
I USED TO BE PART OF ANOTHER TEAM... THE FIVE MONKEYS.
WE WERE ON THIS QUEST AND...WELL, IT'S NOT SO SIMPLE TO EXPLAIN...SEE, THERE WAS... UH OKAY, LEMME START AGAIN. WHEN WE--
BETTY. I LOVE YOU. NO MATTER WHAT.
OKAY.
I'M THE ONLY MEMBE OF THE FIVE MONKEYS THAT'S STILL FREE. W WERE FRAMED FOR... SOMETHING REAL BAD.
BUT, I'M INNOCENT. I PROMISE.
PLEASE DON'T TELL DEE OR HANNAH ABOUT THE BOUNTY HUNTER.
THEY WOULD UNDERSTAND. YOU KNOW THEY WOULD.
BUT...I'M EMBARRASSE PLEASE?

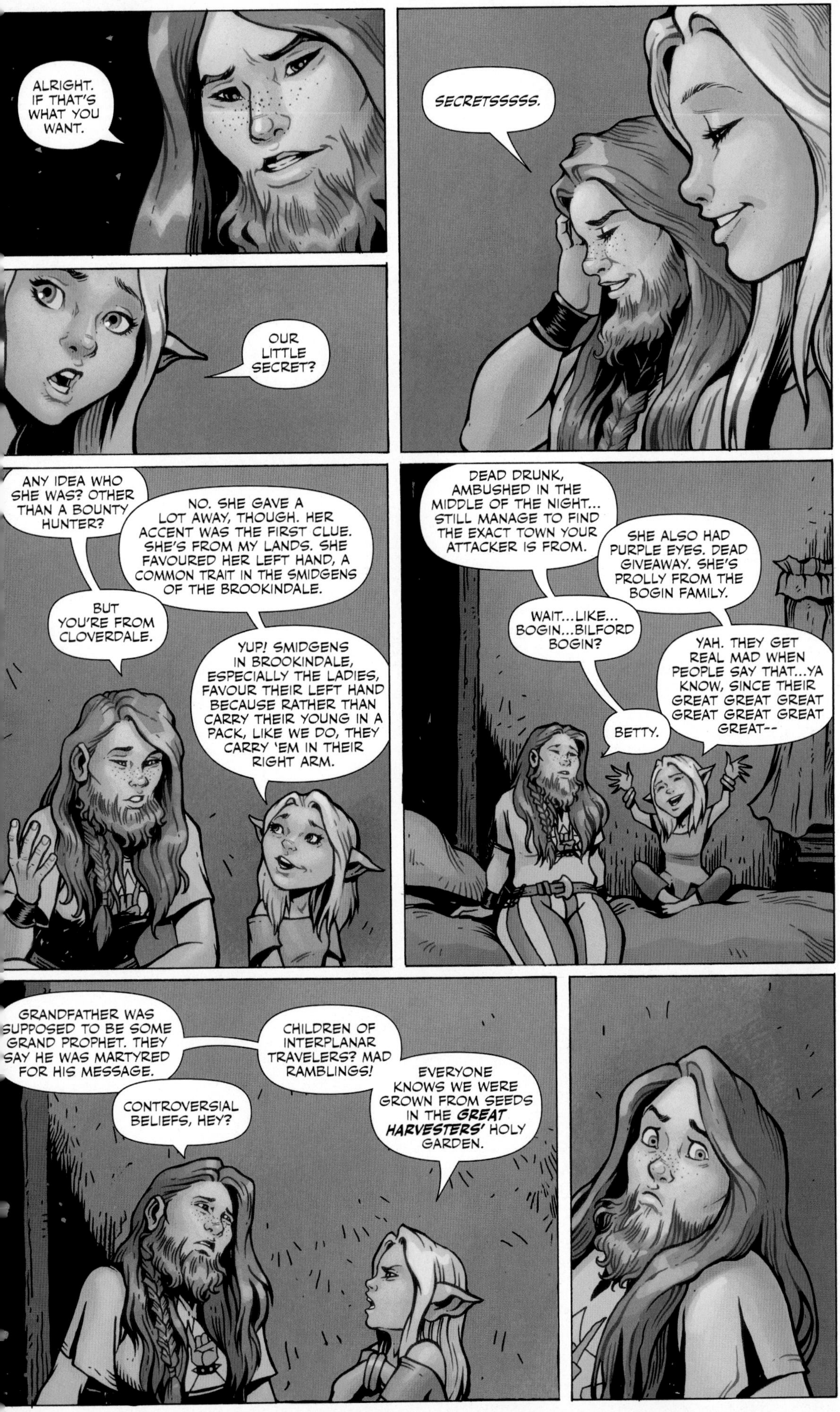

ALRIGHT. IF THAT'S WHAT YOU WANT.
SECRETSSSSS.
OUR LITTLE SECRET?
ANY IDEA WHO SHE WAS? OTHER THAN A BOUNTY HUNTER?
NO. SHE GAVE A LOT AWAY, THOUGH. HER ACCENT WAS THE FIRST CLUE. SHE'S FROM MY LANDS. SHE FAVOURED HER LEFT HAND, A COMMON TRAIT IN THE SMIDGENS OF THE BROOKINDALE.
BUT YOU'RE FROM CLOVERDALE.
YUP! SMIDGENS IN BROOKINDALE, ESPECIALLY THE LADIES, FAVOUR THEIR LEFT HAND BECAUSE RATHER THAN CARRY THEIR YOUNG IN A PACK, LIKE WE DO, THEY CARRY 'EM IN THEIR RIGHT ARM.
DEAD DRUNK, AMBUSHED IN THE MIDDLE OF THE NIGHT... STILL MANAGE TO FIND THE EXACT TOWN YOUR ATTACKER IS FROM.
SHE ALSO HAD PURPLE EYES. DEAD GIVEAWAY. SHE'S PROLLY FROM THE BOGIN FAMILY.
WAIT...LIKE... BOGIN...BILFORD BOGIN?
YAH. THEY GET REAL MAD WHEN PEOPLE SAY THAT...YA KNOW, SINCE THEIR GREAT GREAT GREAT GREAT GREAT GREAT GREAT--
BETTY.
GRANDFATHER WAS SUPPOSED TO BE SOME GRAND PROPHET. THEY SAY HE WAS MARTYRED FOR HIS MESSAGE.
CONTROVERSIAL BELIEFS, HEY?
CHILDREN OF INTERPLANAR TRAVELERS? MAD RAMBLINGS!
EVERYONE KNOWS WE WERE GROWN FROM SEEDS IN THE GREAT HARVESTERS' HOLY GARDEN.

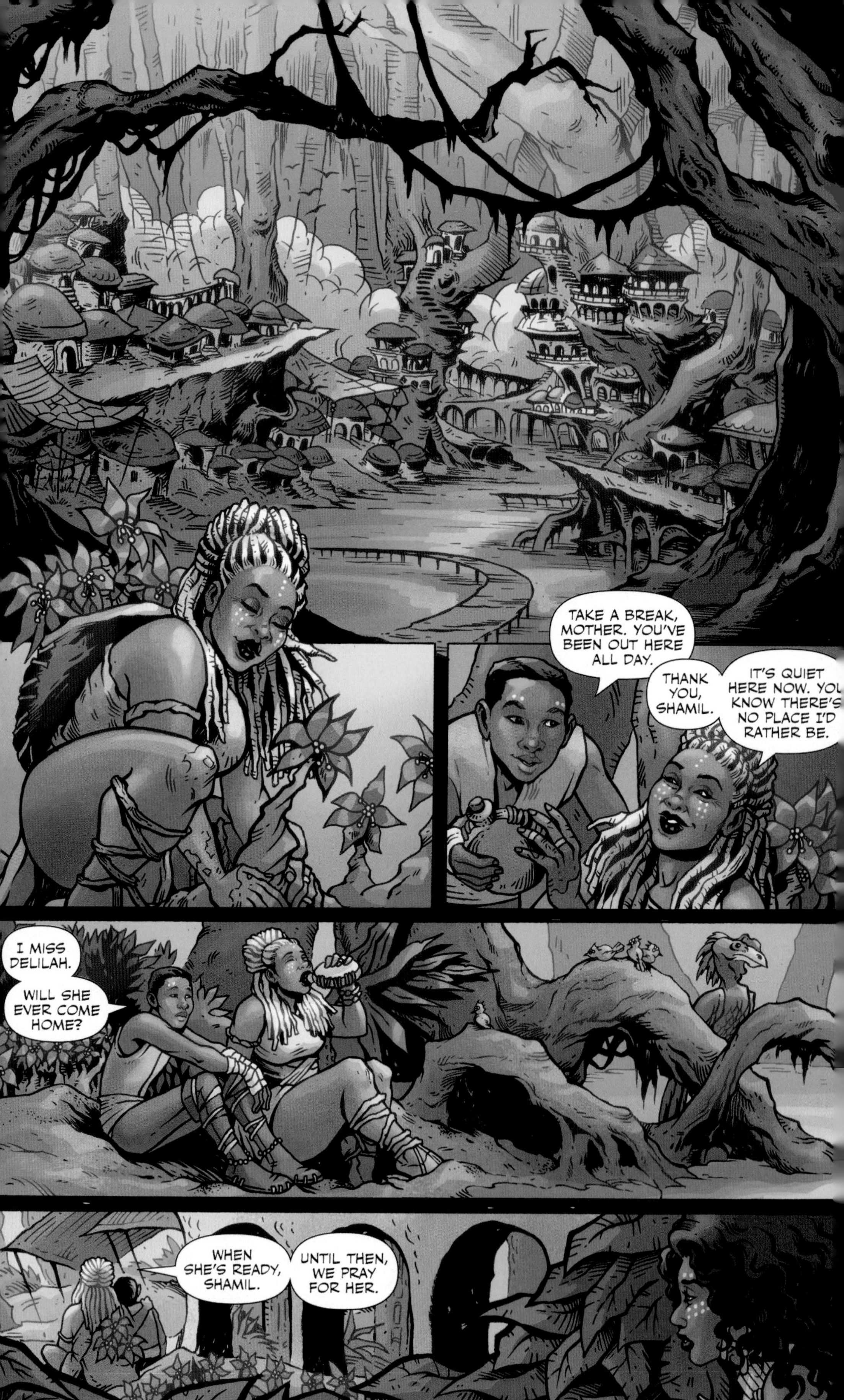
TAKE A BREAK, MOTHER. YOU'VE BEEN OUT HERE ALL DAY.
THANK YOU, SHAMIL.
IT'S QUIET HERE NOW. YOU KNOW THERE'S NO PLACE I'D RATHER BE.
I MISS DELILAH.
WILL SHE EVER COME HOME?
WHEN SHE'S READY, SHAMIL.
UNTIL THEN, WE PRAY FOR HER.

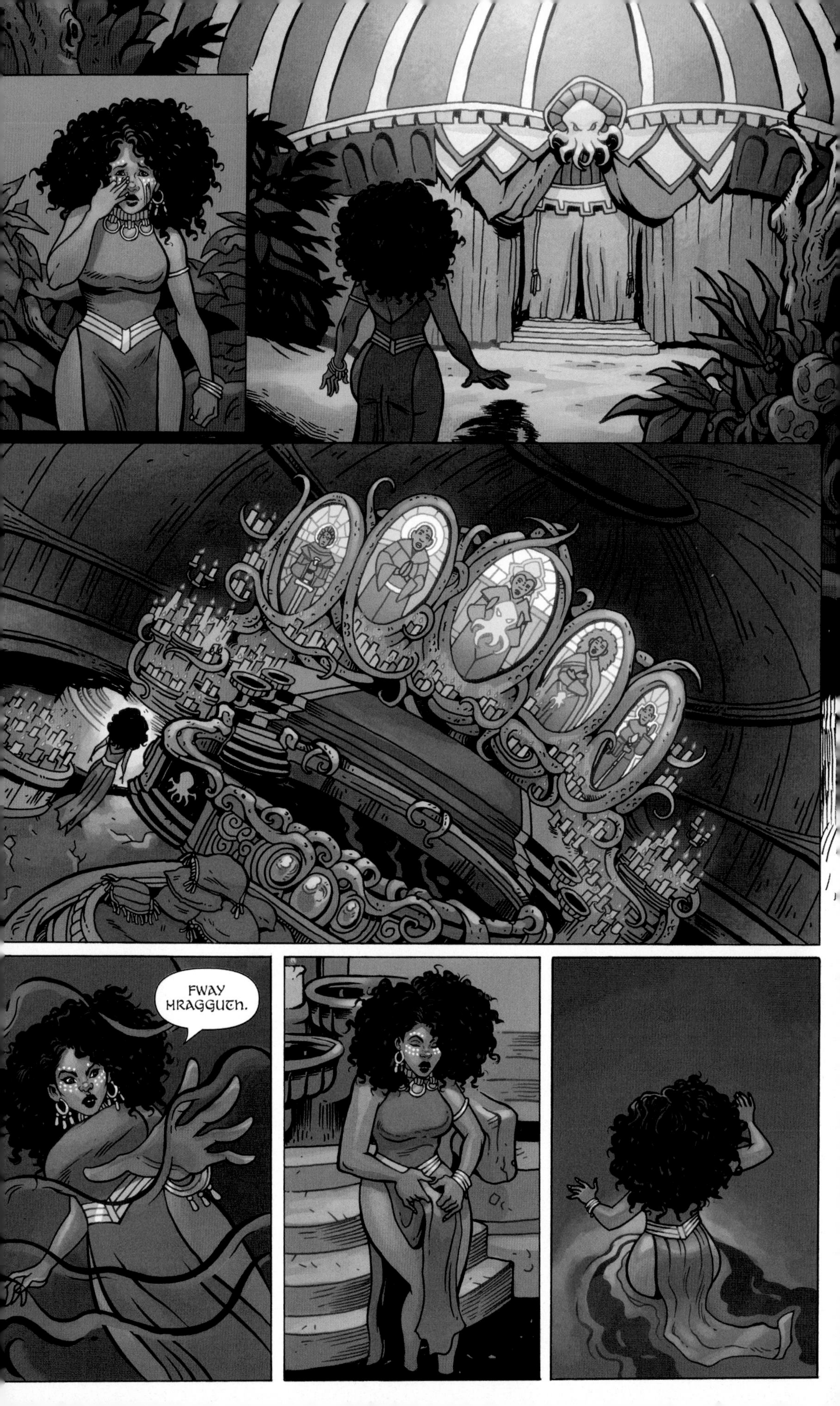
FWAY
HRAGGUTH.

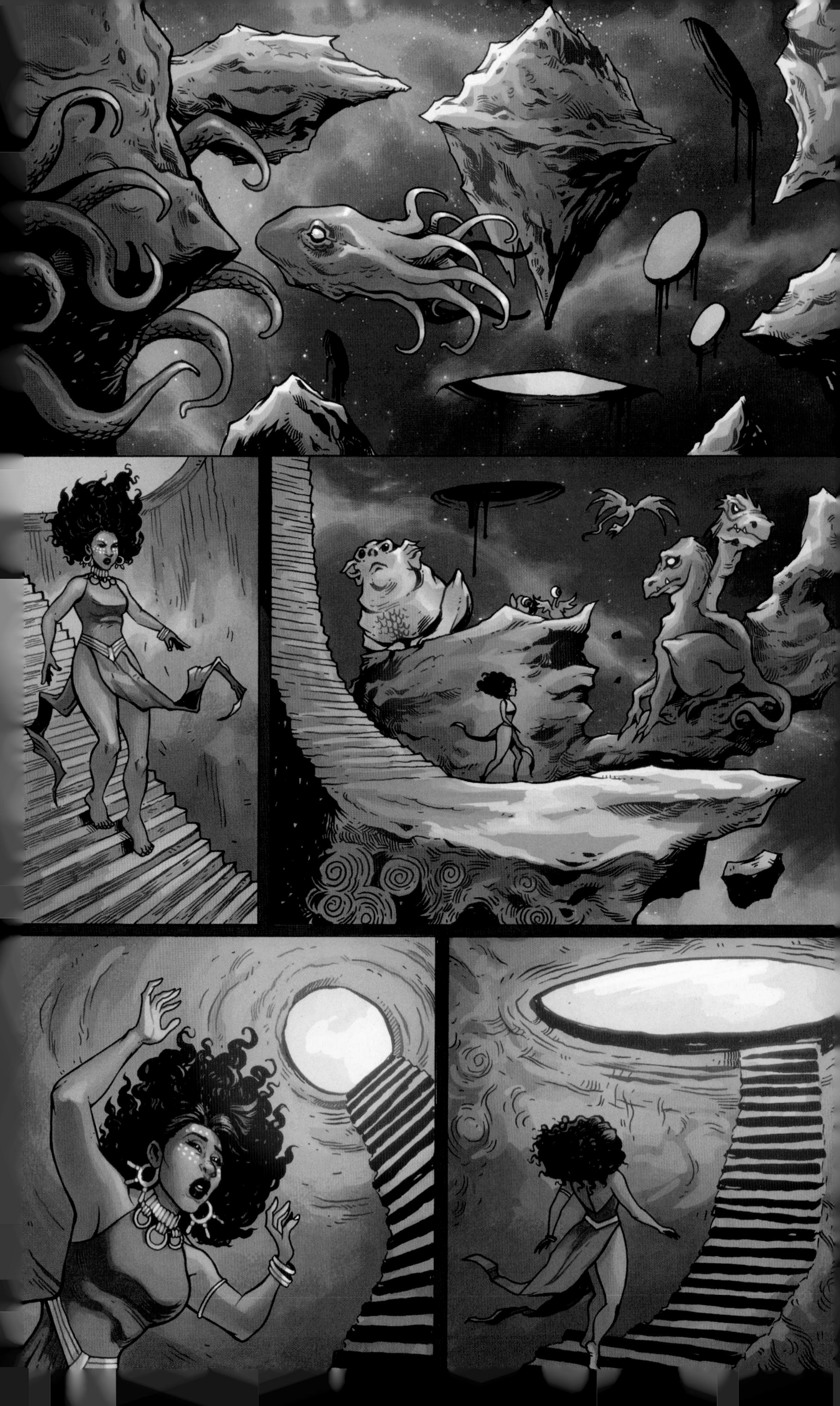

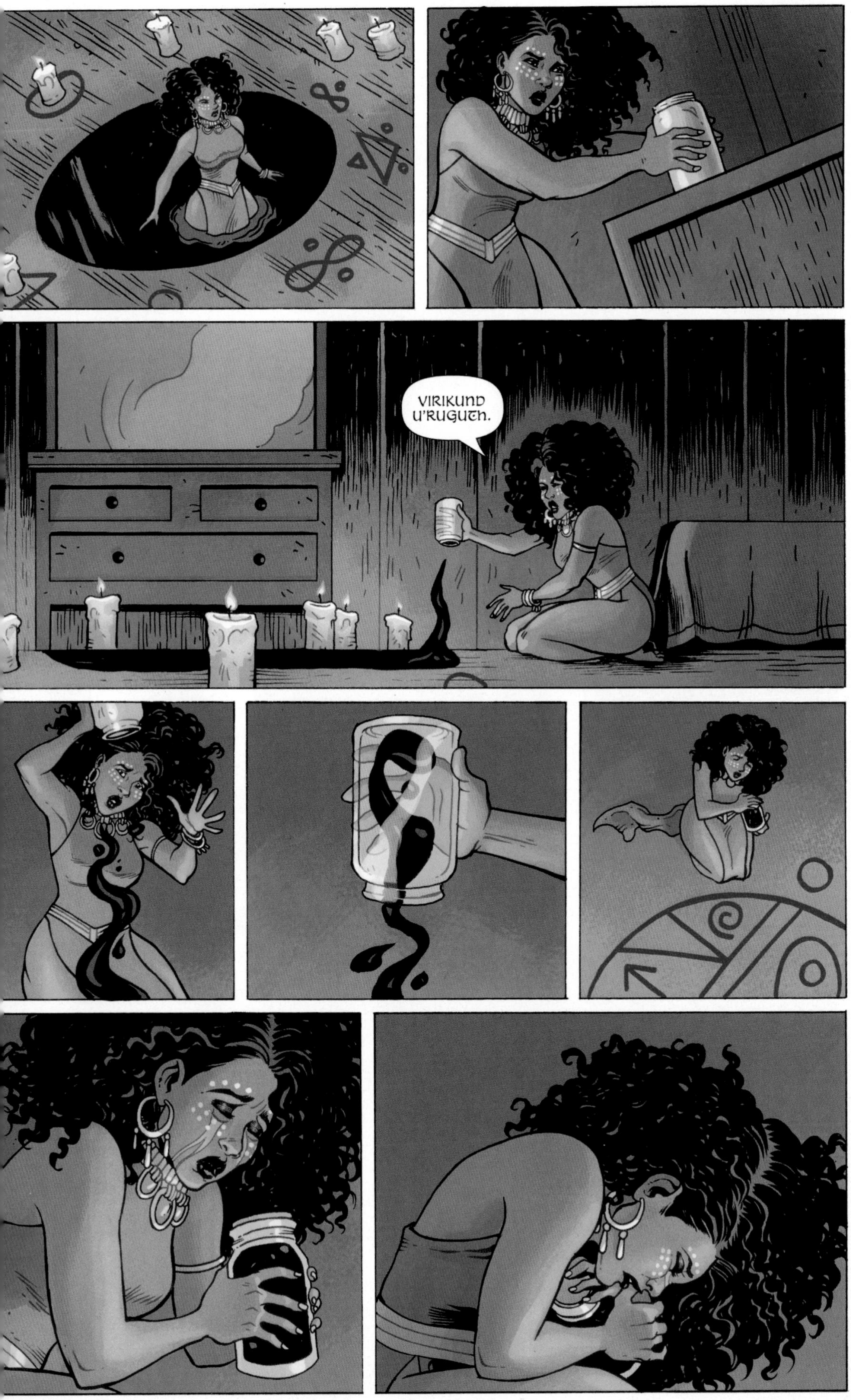
VIRIKUND U'RUGUTH.

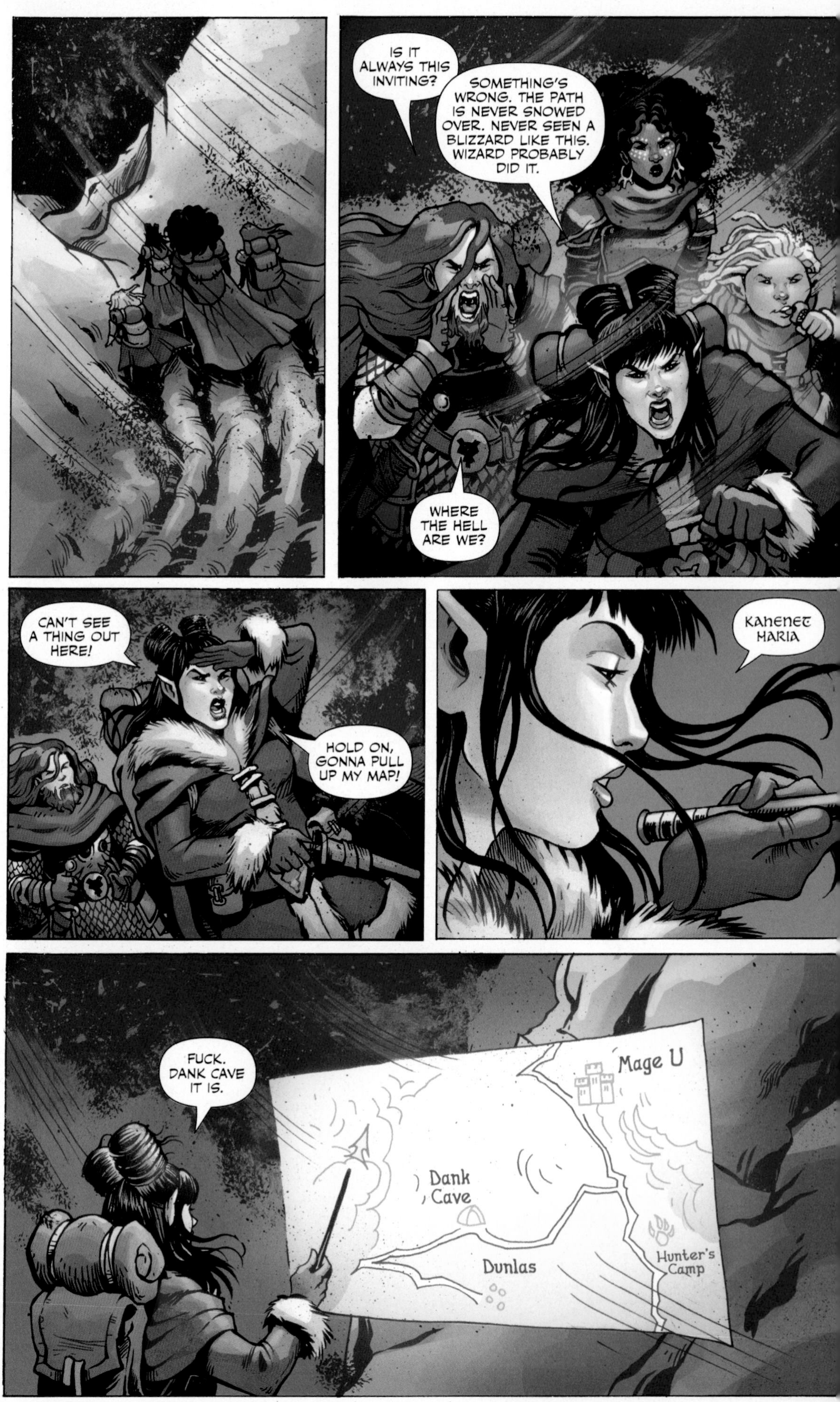
IS IT ALWAYS THIS INVITING?
SOMETHING'S WRONG. THE PATH IS NEVER SNOWED OVER. NEVER SEEN A BLIZZARD LIKE THIS. WIZARD PROBABLY DID IT.
WHERE THE HELL ARE WE?
CAN'T SEE A THING OUT HERE!
HOLD ON, GONNA PULL UP MY MAP!
KAHENET MARIA
FUCK. DANK CAVE IT IS.
Mage U
Dank Cave
Dunlas
Hunter's Camp

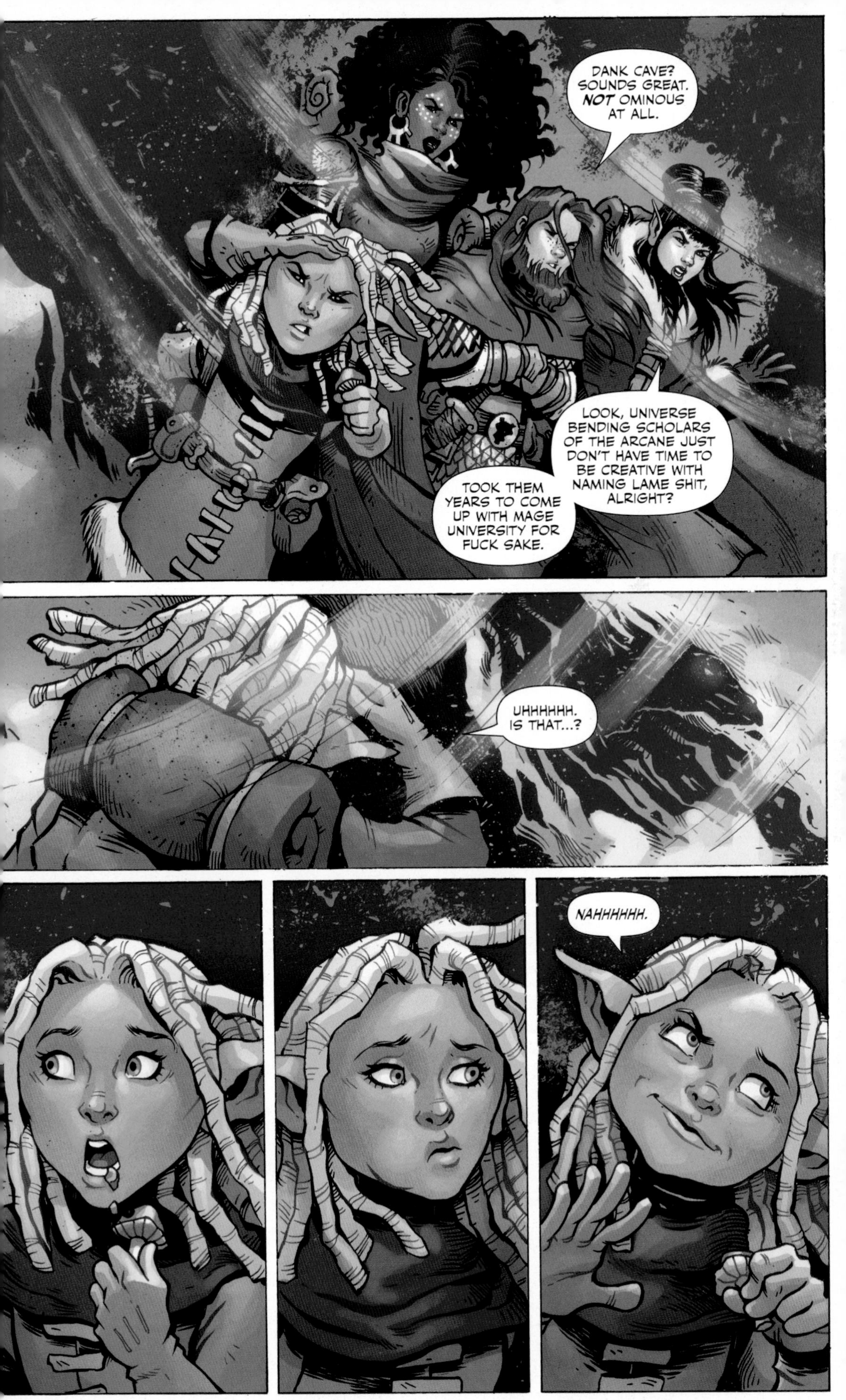
DANK CAVE? SOUNDS GREAT. *NOT* OMINOUS AT ALL.
LOOK, UNIVERSE BENDING SCHOLARS OF THE ARCANE JUST DON'T HAVE TIME TO BE CREATIVE WITH NAMING LAME SHIT, ALRIGHT?
TOOK THEM YEARS TO COME UP WITH MAGE UNIVERSITY FOR FUCK SAKE.
UHHHHHH. IS THAT...?
NAHHHHHH.

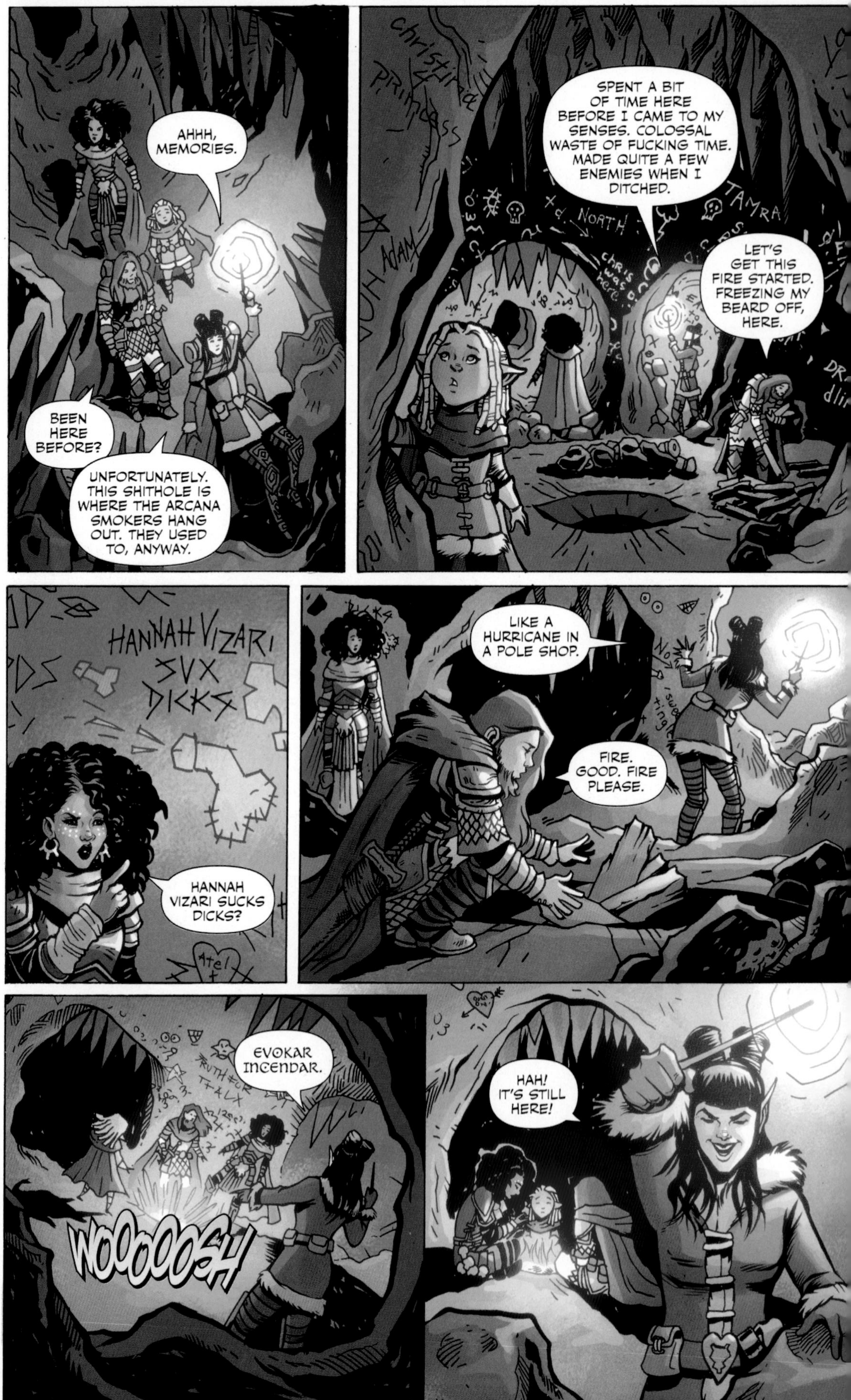
AHHH, MEMORIES.
BEEN HERE BEFORE?
UNFORTUNATELY. THIS SHITHOLE IS WHERE THE ARCANA SMOKERS HANG OUT. THEY USED TO, ANYWAY.
SPENT A BIT OF TIME HERE BEFORE I CAME TO MY SENSES. COLOSSAL WASTE OF FUCKING TIME. MADE QUITE A FEW ENEMIES WHEN I DITCHED.
LET'S GET THIS FIRE STARTED. FREEZING MY BEARD OFF, HERE.
HANNAH VIZARI SUX DICKS
HANNAH VIZARI SUCKS DICKS?
LIKE A HURRICANE IN A POLE SHOP.
FIRE. GOOD. FIRE PLEASE.
EVOKAR INCENDAR.
WOOOOOSH
HAH! IT'S STILL HERE!

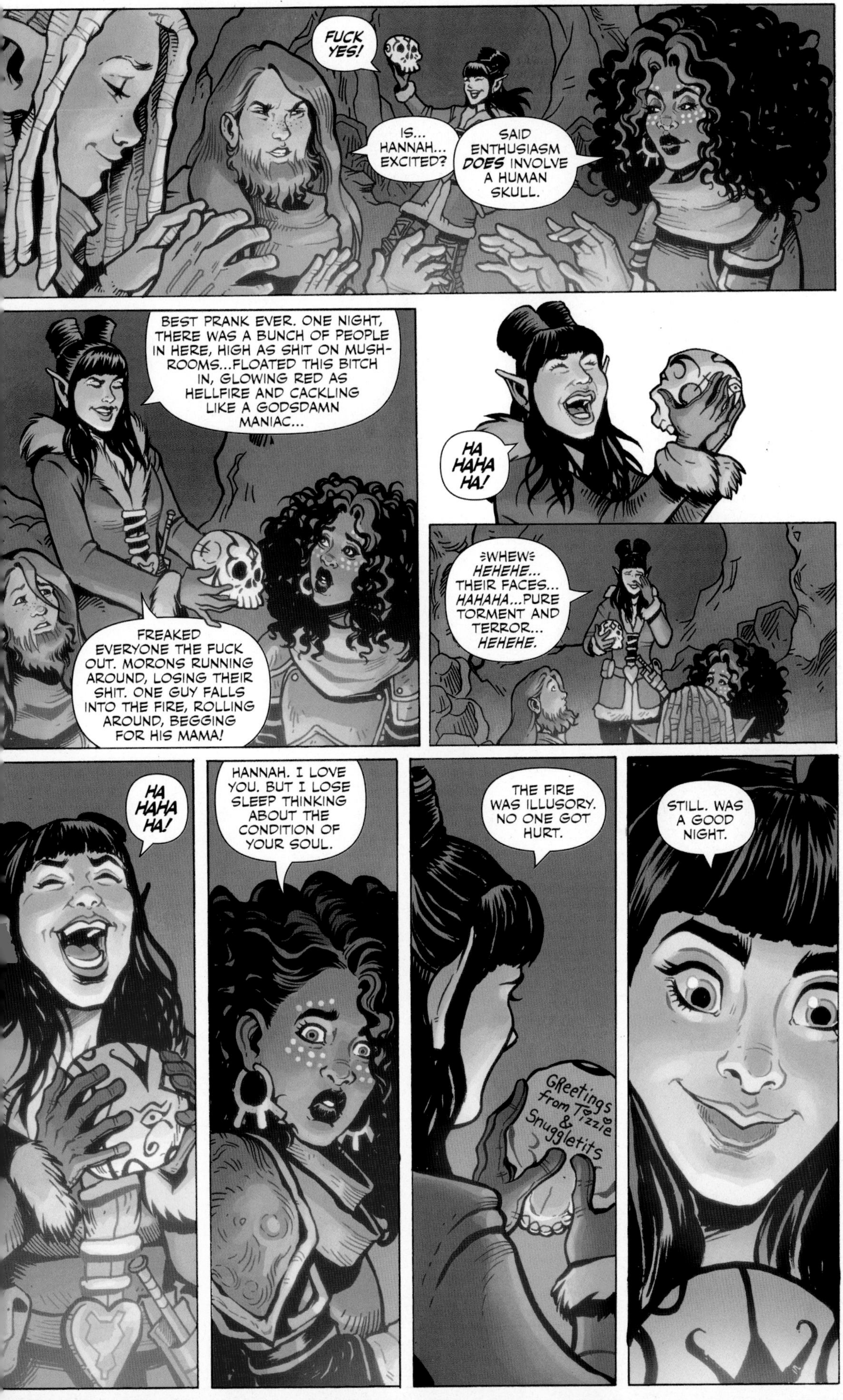
FUCK YES!
IS... HANNAH... EXCITED?
SAID ENTHUSIASM DOES INVOLVE A HUMAN SKULL.
BEST PRANK EVER. ONE NIGHT, THERE WAS A BUNCH OF PEOPLE IN HERE, HIGH AS SHIT ON MUSH-ROOMS...FLOATED THIS BITCH IN, GLOWING RED AS HELLFIRE AND CACKLING LIKE A GODSDAMN MANIAC...
FREAKED EVERYONE THE FUCK OUT. MORONS RUNNING AROUND, LOSING THEIR SHIT. ONE GUY FALLS INTO THE FIRE, ROLLING AROUND, BEGGING FOR HIS MAMA!
HA HAHA HA!
WHEW HEHEHE... THEIR FACES... HAHAHA...PURE TORMENT AND TERROR... HEHEHE.
HA HAHA HA!
HANNAH. I LOVE YOU. BUT I LOSE SLEEP THINKING ABOUT THE CONDITION OF YOUR SOUL.
THE FIRE WAS ILLUSORY. NO ONE GOT HURT.
Greetings from Tizzie & Snuggletits
STILL. WAS A GOOD NIGHT.

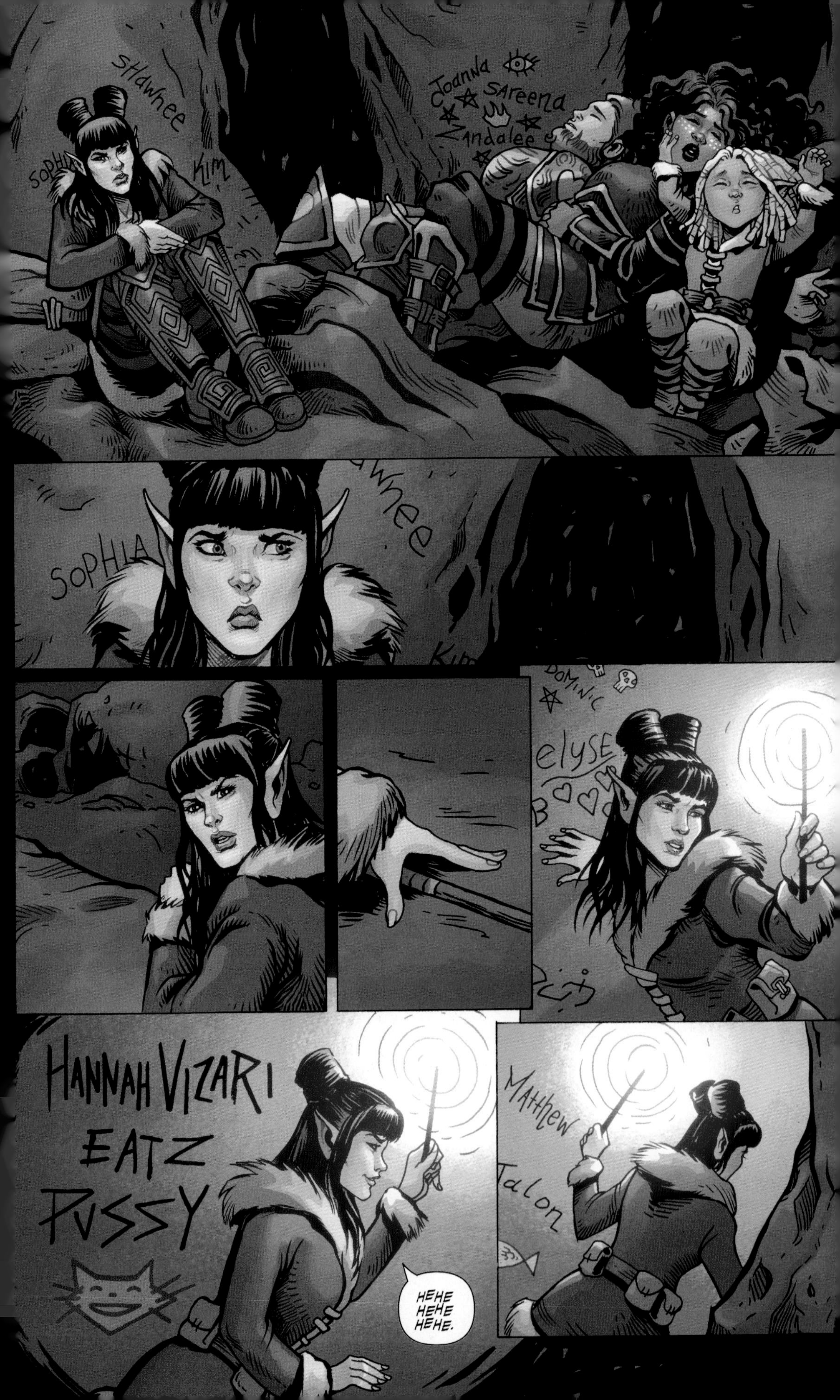
Shawnee
SOPHIA
KIM
Joanna
Sareena
Zandalee
SOPHIA
awnee
DOMINIC
elyse
HANNAH VIZARI
EATZ
PUSSY
HEHE HEHE HEHE.
Matthew
Talon

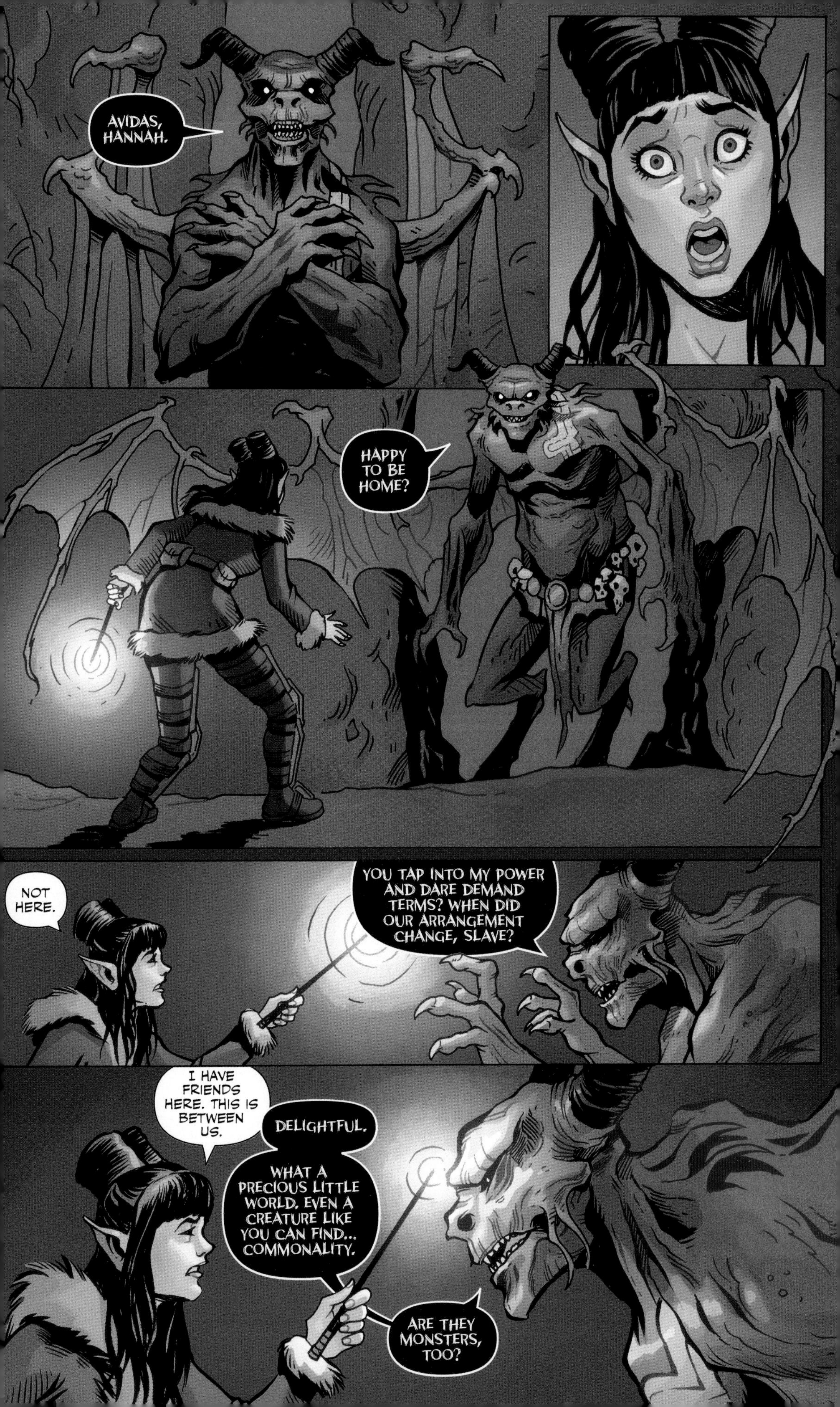

AVIDAS, HANNAH.
HAPPY TO BE HOME?
NOT HERE.
YOU TAP INTO MY POWER AND DARE DEMAND TERMS? WHEN DID OUR ARRANGEMENT CHANGE, SLAVE?
I HAVE FRIENDS HERE. THIS IS BETWEEN US.
DELIGHTFUL.
WHAT A PRECIOUS LITTLE WORLD. EVEN A CREATURE LIKE YOU CAN FIND... COMMONALITY.
ARE THEY MONSTERS, TOO?

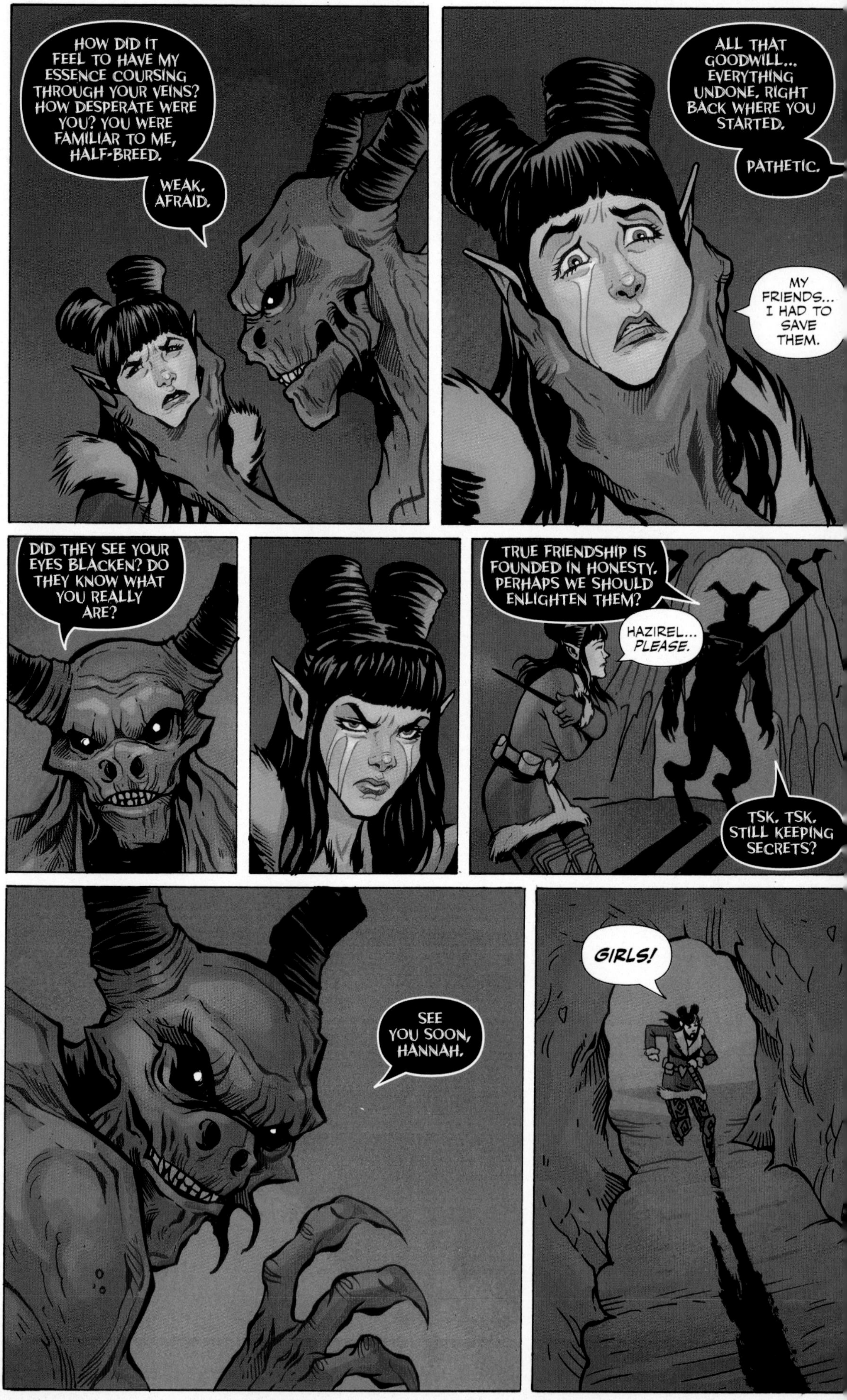
HOW DID IT FEEL TO HAVE MY ESSENCE COURSING THROUGH YOUR VEINS? HOW DESPERATE WERE YOU? YOU WERE FAMILIAR TO ME, HALF-BREED.
WEAK. AFRAID.
ALL THAT GOODWILL... EVERYTHING UNDONE. RIGHT BACK WHERE YOU STARTED.
PATHETIC.
MY FRIENDS... I HAD TO SAVE THEM.
DID THEY SEE YOUR EYES BLACKEN? DO THEY KNOW WHAT YOU REALLY ARE?
TRUE FRIENDSHIP IS FOUNDED IN HONESTY. PERHAPS WE SHOULD ENLIGHTEN THEM?
HAZIREL... *PLEASE.*
TSK. TSK. STILL KEEPING SECRETS?
SEE YOU SOON, HANNAH.
GIRLS!

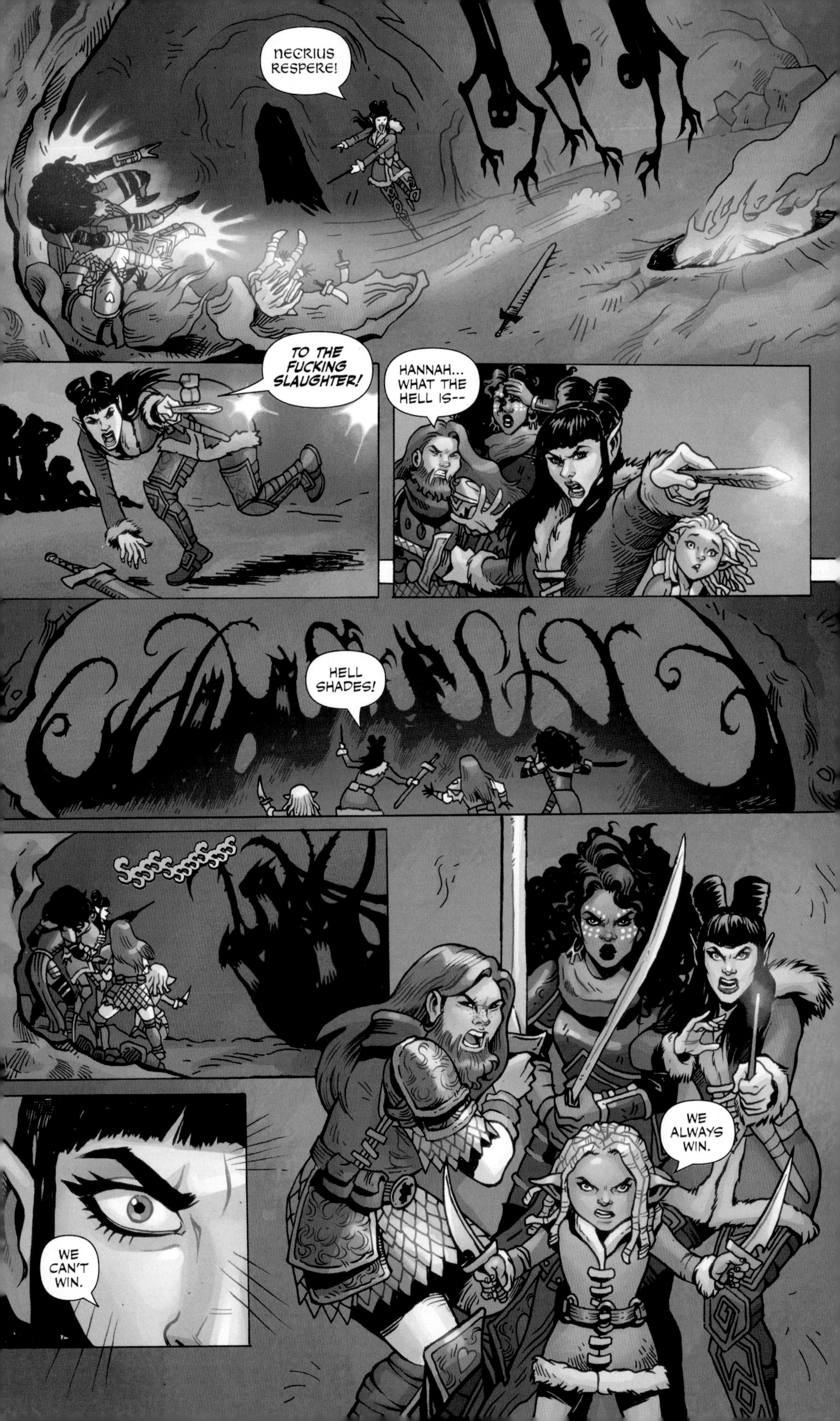

NECRIUS RESPERE!
TO THE FUCKING SLAUGHTER!
HANNAH... WHAT THE HELL IS--
HELL SHADES!
SSSSSSSSSS
WE CAN'T WIN.
WE ALWAYS WIN.

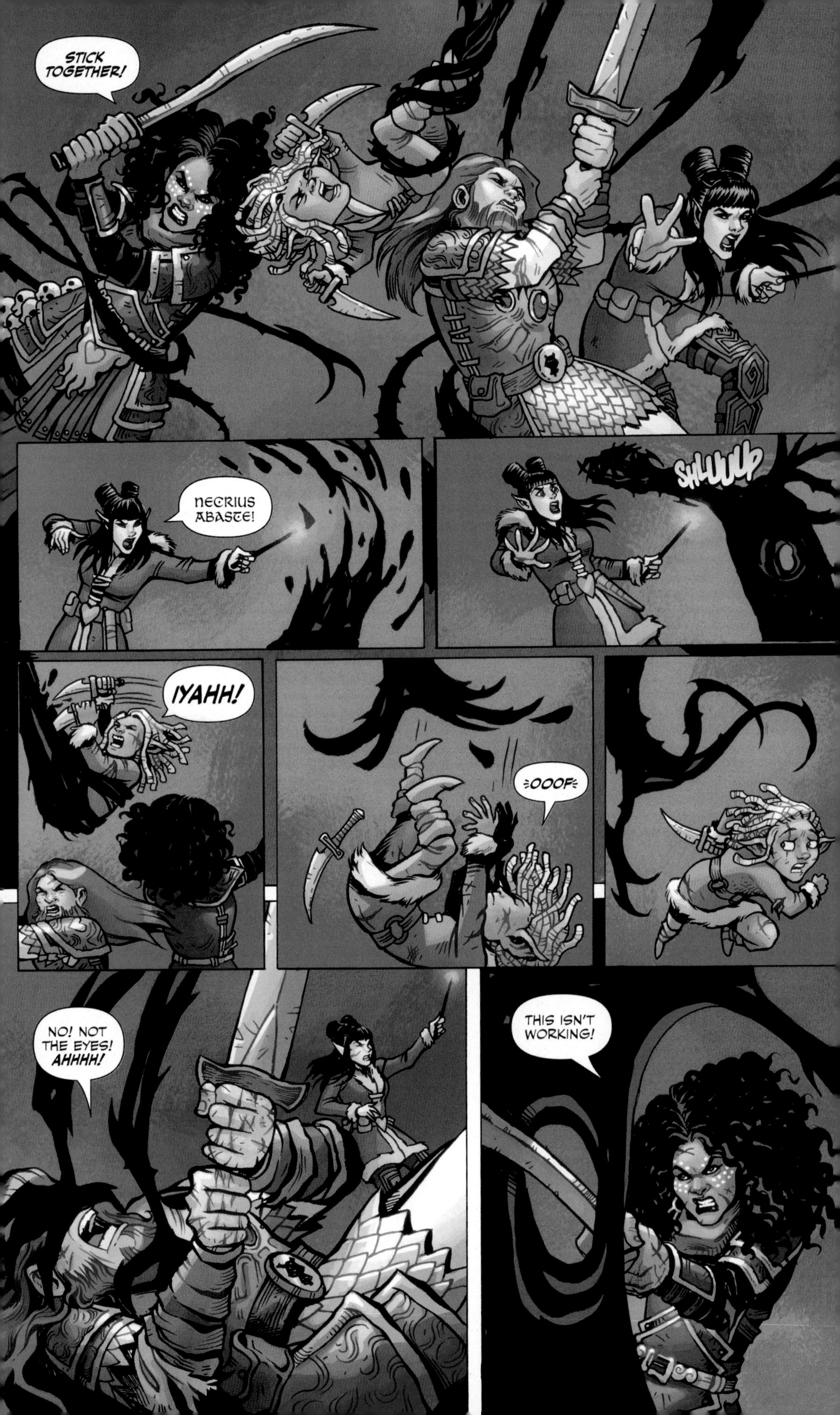
STICK TOGETHER!
NECRIUS ABASTE!
SHLUUUP
IYAHH!
OOOF
NO! NOT THE EYES! AHHHH!
THIS ISN'T WORKING!

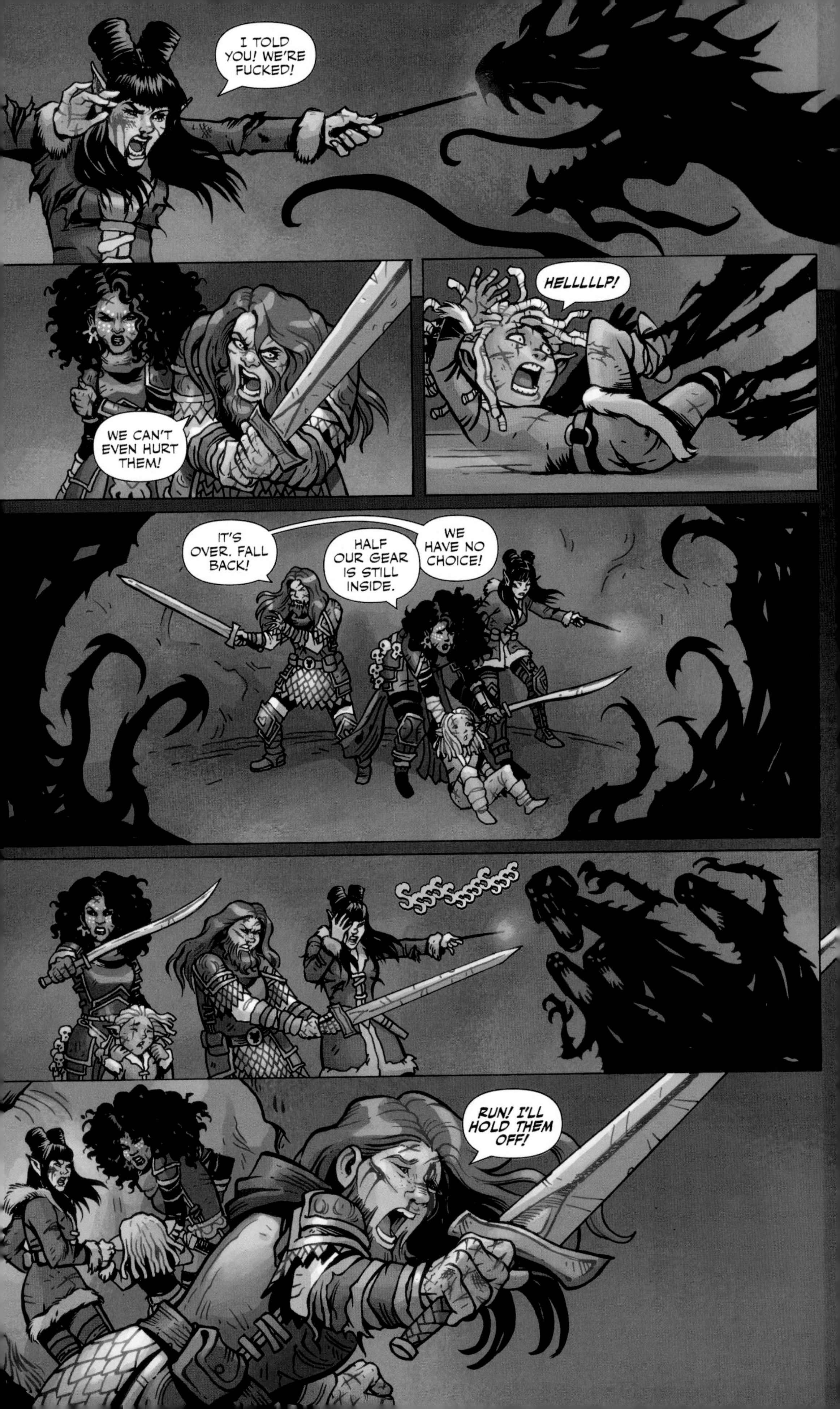
I TOLD YOU! WE'RE FUCKED!
WE CAN'T EVEN HURT THEM!
HELLLLLLP!
IT'S OVER. FALL BACK!
HALF OUR GEAR IS STILL INSIDE.
WE HAVE NO CHOICE!
SSSSSSSSSS
RUN! I'LL HOLD THEM OFF!

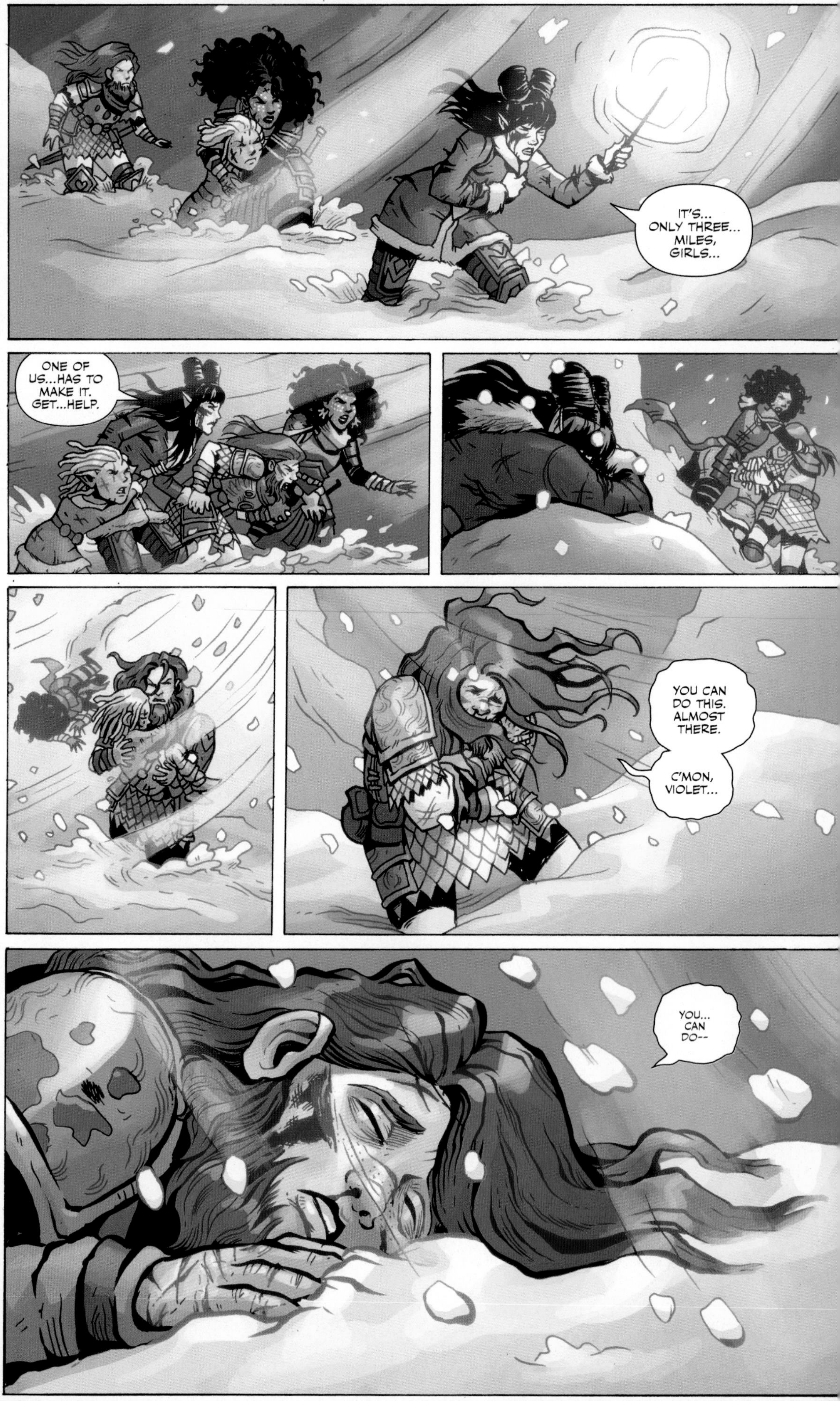
IT'S... ONLY THREE... MILES, GIRLS...
ONE OF US...HAS TO MAKE IT. GET...HELP.
YOU CAN DO THIS. ALMOST THERE.
C'MON, VIOLET...
YOU... CAN DO--

CHAPTER THIRTEEN

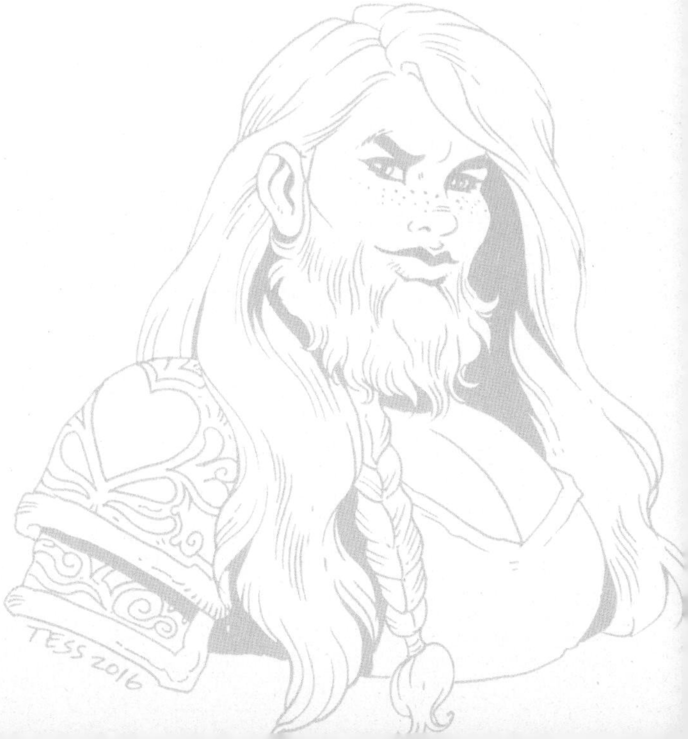
TESS 2016

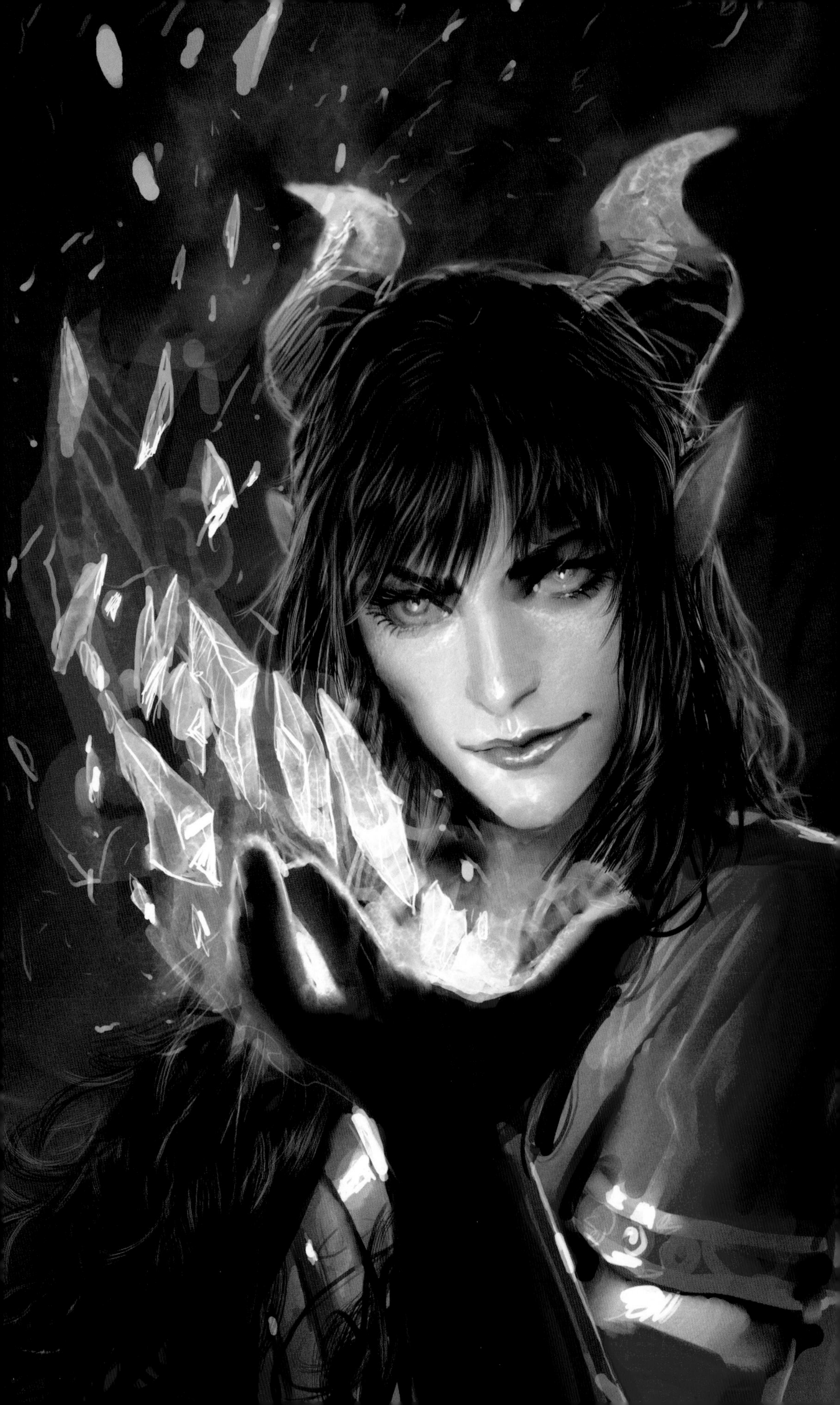

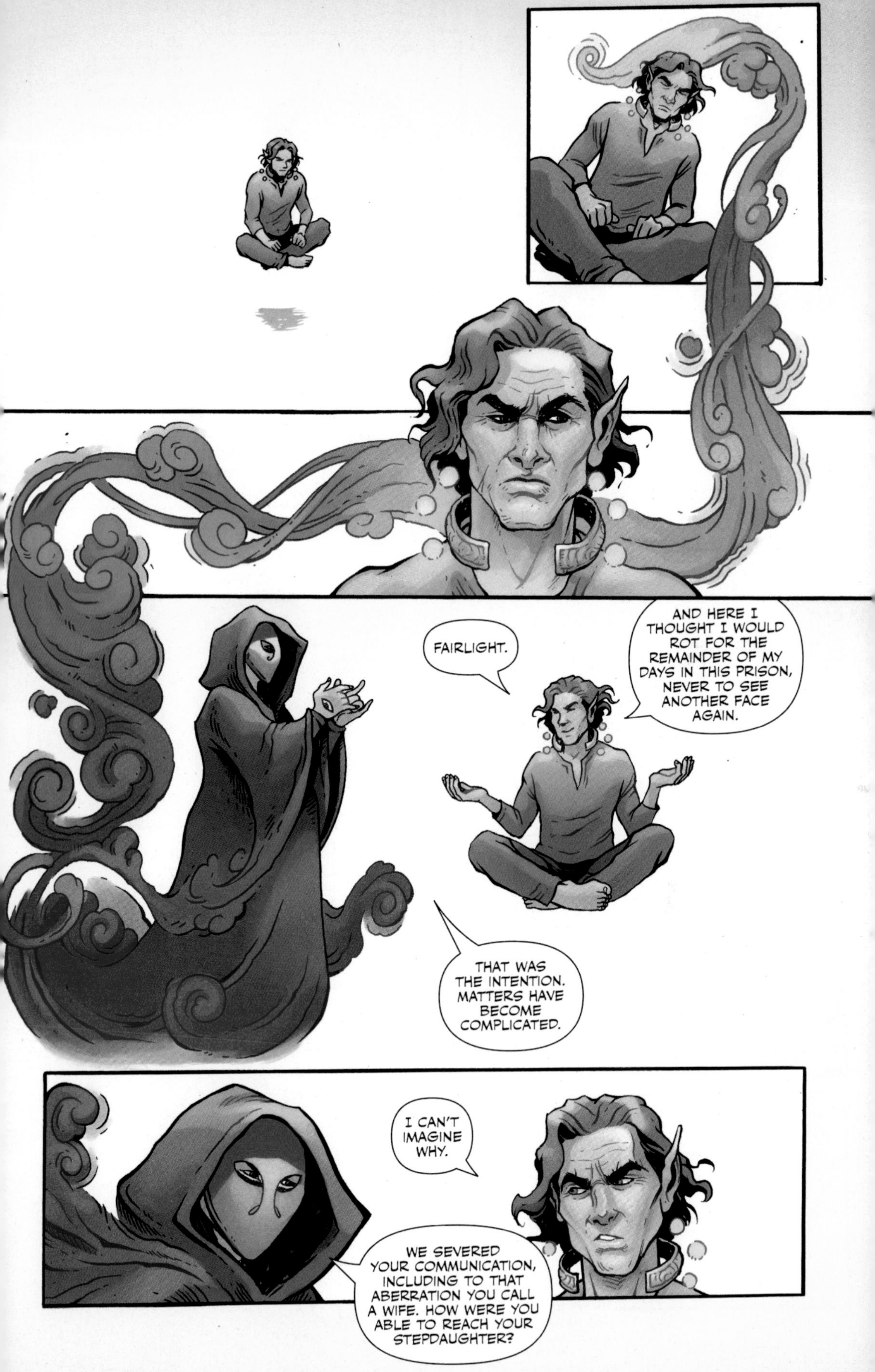
FAIRLIGHT.
AND HERE I THOUGHT I WOULD ROT FOR THE REMAINDER OF MY DAYS IN THIS PRISON, NEVER TO SEE ANOTHER FACE AGAIN.
THAT WAS THE INTENTION. MATTERS HAVE BECOME COMPLICATED.
I CAN'T IMAGINE WHY.
WE SEVERED YOUR COMMUNICATION, INCLUDING TO THAT ABERRATION YOU CALL A WIFE. HOW WERE YOU ABLE TO REACH YOUR STEPDAUGHTER?

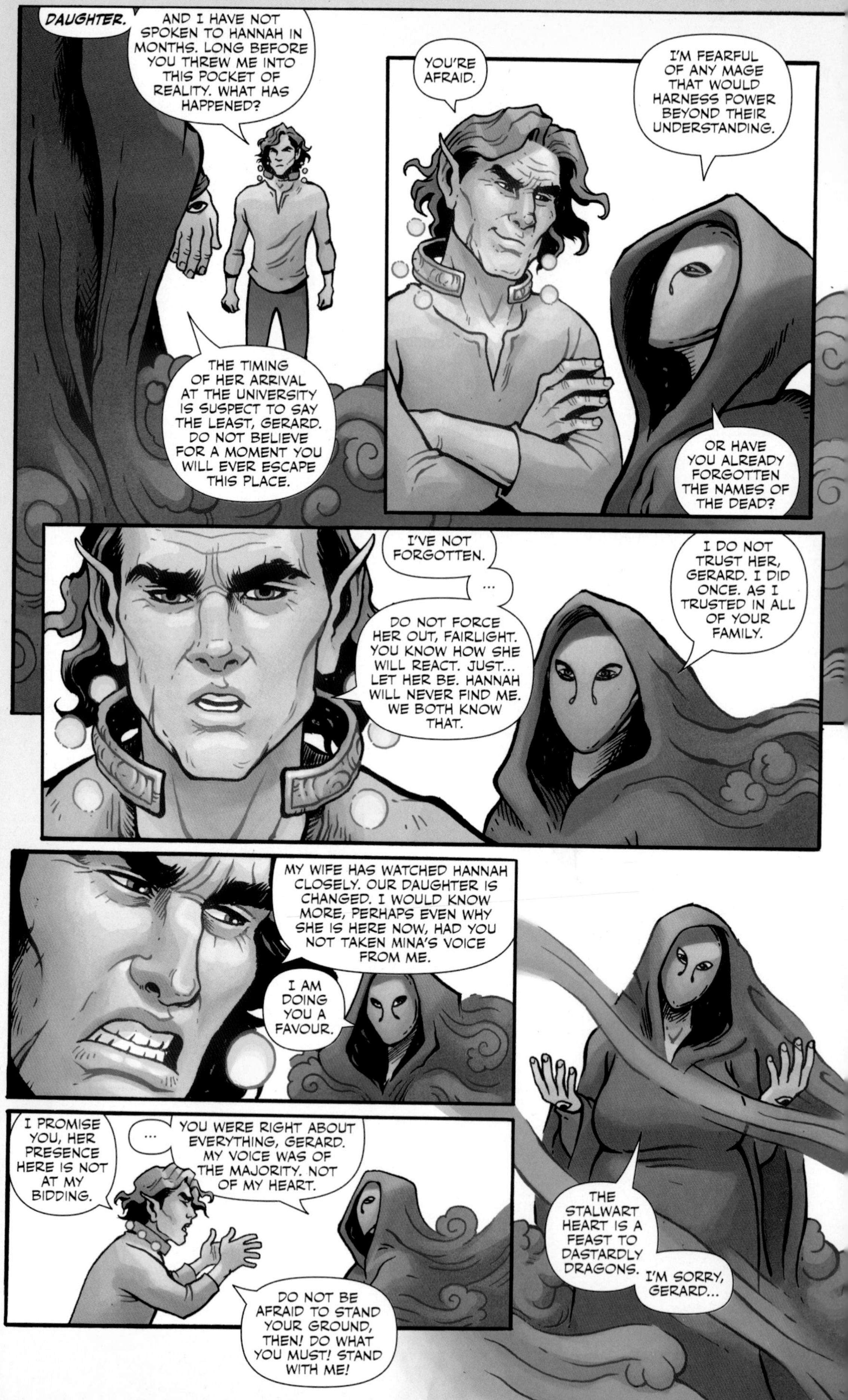
DAUGHTER.
AND I HAVE NOT SPOKEN TO HANNAH IN MONTHS. LONG BEFORE YOU THREW ME INTO THIS POCKET OF REALITY. WHAT HAS HAPPENED?
THE TIMING OF HER ARRIVAL AT THE UNIVERSITY IS SUSPECT TO SAY THE LEAST, GERARD. DO NOT BELIEVE FOR A MOMENT YOU WILL EVER ESCAPE THIS PLACE.
YOU'RE AFRAID.
I'M FEARFUL OF ANY MAGE THAT WOULD HARNESS POWER BEYOND THEIR UNDERSTANDING.
OR HAVE YOU ALREADY FORGOTTEN THE NAMES OF THE DEAD?
I'VE NOT FORGOTTEN.
...
DO NOT FORCE HER OUT, FAIRLIGHT. YOU KNOW HOW SHE WILL REACT. JUST... LET HER BE. HANNAH WILL NEVER FIND ME. WE BOTH KNOW THAT.
I DO NOT TRUST HER, GERARD. I DID ONCE. AS I TRUSTED IN ALL OF YOUR FAMILY.
MY WIFE HAS WATCHED HANNAH CLOSELY. OUR DAUGHTER IS CHANGED. I WOULD KNOW MORE, PERHAPS EVEN WHY SHE IS HERE NOW, HAD YOU NOT TAKEN MINA'S VOICE FROM ME.
I AM DOING YOU A FAVOUR.
I PROMISE YOU, HER PRESENCE HERE IS NOT AT MY BIDDING.
...
YOU WERE RIGHT ABOUT EVERYTHING, GERARD. MY VOICE WAS OF THE MAJORITY. NOT OF MY HEART.
DO NOT BE AFRAID TO STAND YOUR GROUND, THEN! DO WHAT YOU MUST! STAND WITH ME!
THE STALWART HEART IS A FEAST TO DASTARDLY DRAGONS.
I'M SORRY, GERARD...

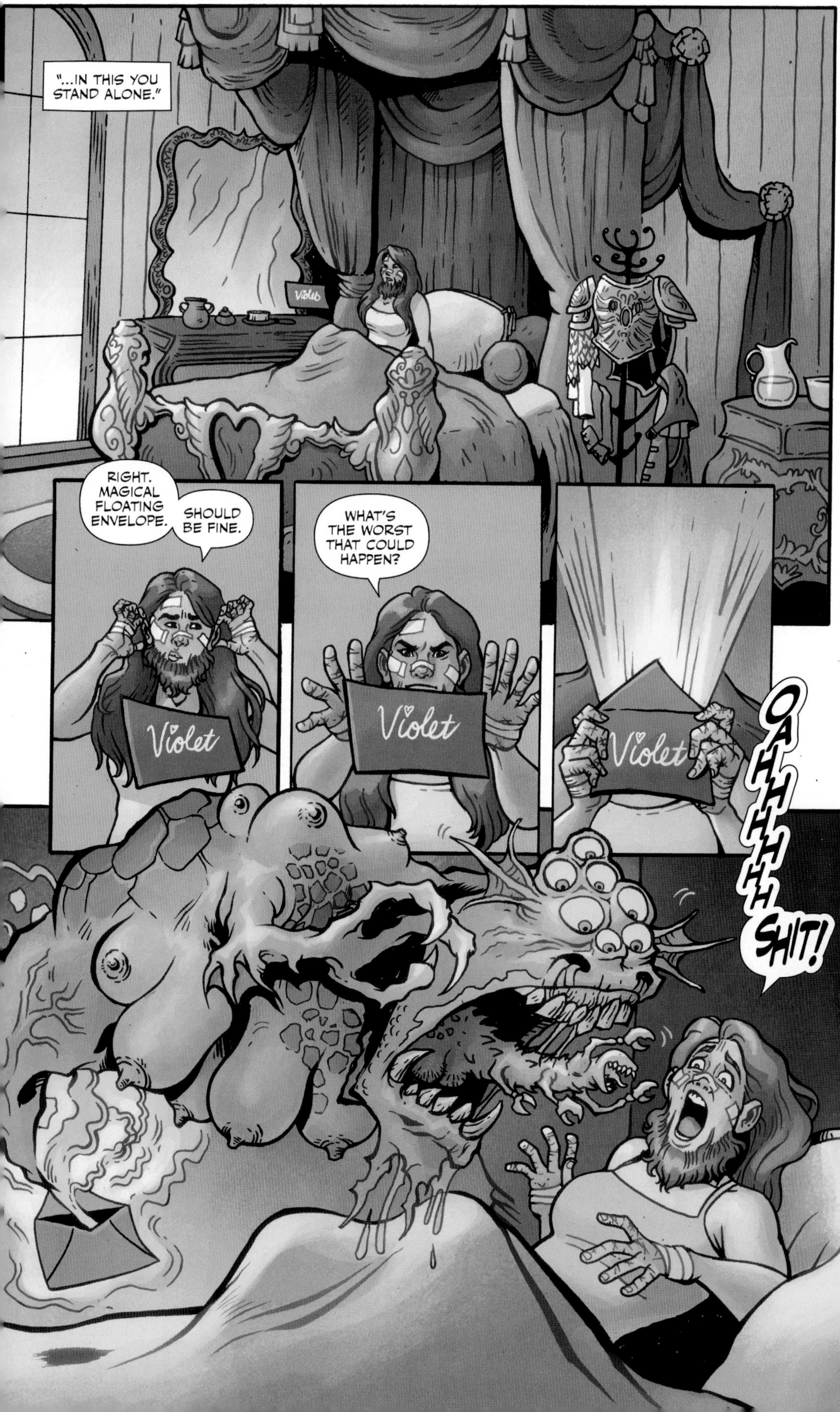
"...IN THIS YOU STAND ALONE."
Violet
RIGHT. MAGICAL FLOATING ENVELOPE.
SHOULD BE FINE.
Violet
WHAT'S THE WORST THAT COULD HAPPEN?
Violet
Violet
OAHHHHHHH SHIT!

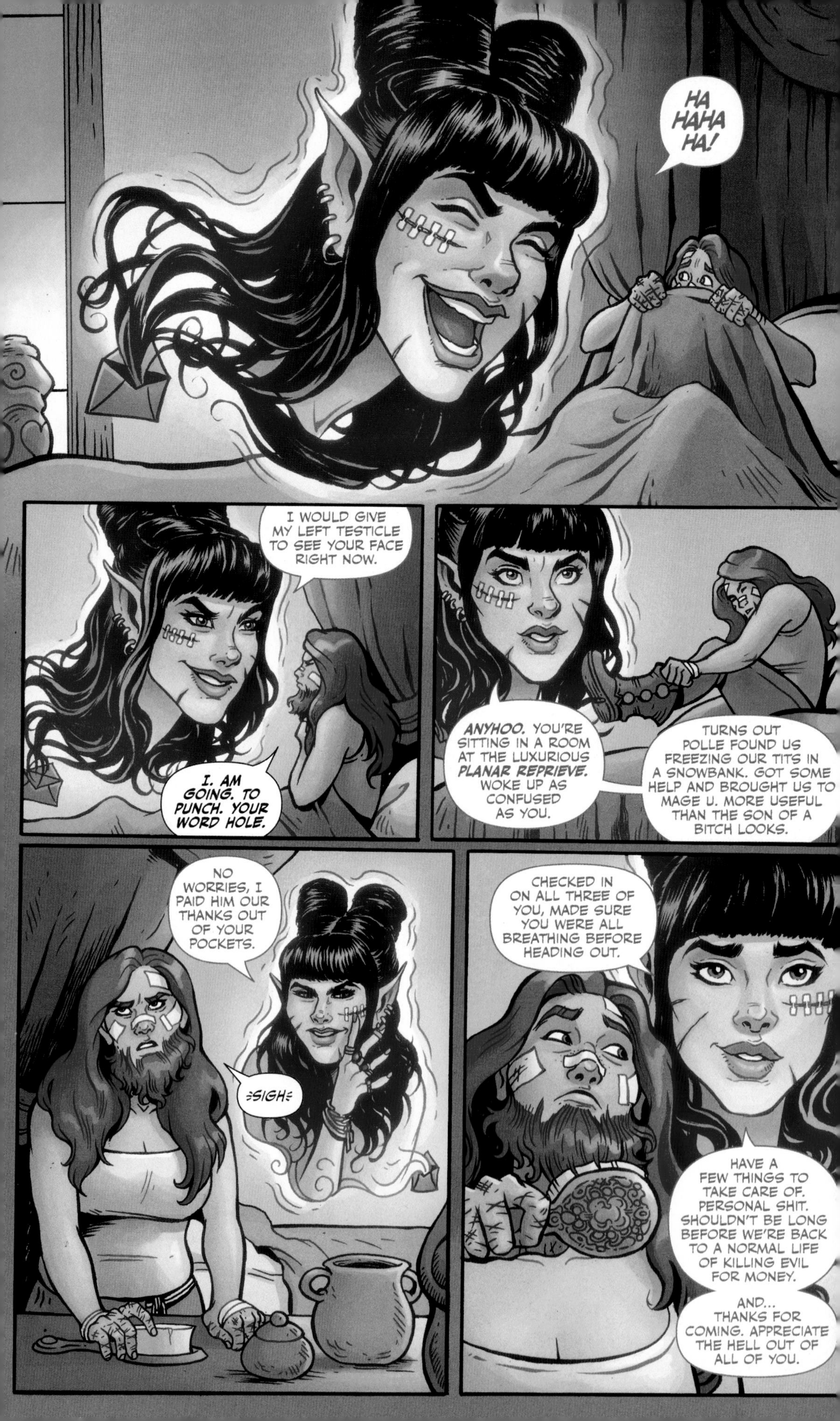
HA HAHAHA!
I WOULD GIVE MY LEFT TESTICLE TO SEE YOUR FACE RIGHT NOW.
I. AM GOING. TO PUNCH. YOUR WORD HOLE.
ANYHOO. YOU'RE SITTING IN A ROOM AT THE LUXURIOUS PLANAR REPRIEVE. WOKE UP AS CONFUSED AS YOU.
TURNS OUT POLLE FOUND US FREEZING OUR TITS IN A SNOWBANK. GOT SOME HELP AND BROUGHT US TO MAGE U. MORE USEFUL THAN THE SON OF A BITCH LOOKS.
NO WORRIES, I PAID HIM OUR THANKS OUT OF YOUR POCKETS.
SIGH
CHECKED IN ON ALL THREE OF YOU, MADE SURE YOU WERE ALL BREATHING BEFORE HEADING OUT.
HAVE A FEW THINGS TO TAKE CARE OF. PERSONAL SHIT. SHOULDN'T BE LONG BEFORE WE'RE BACK TO A NORMAL LIFE OF KILLING EVIL FOR MONEY.
AND... THANKS FOR COMING. APPRECIATE THE HELL OUT OF ALL OF YOU.

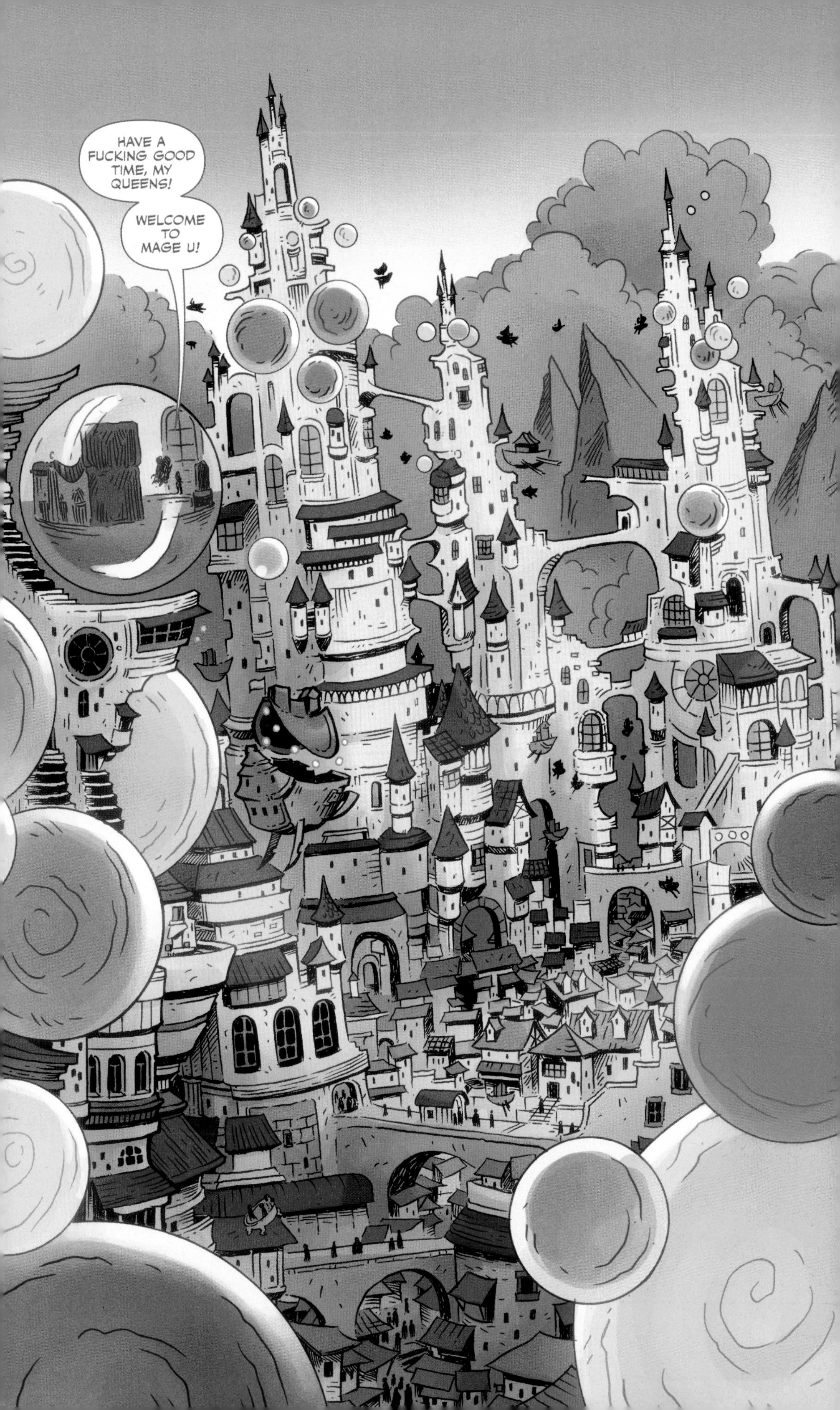
HAVE A FUCKING GOOD TIME, MY QUEENS!
WELCOME TO MAGE U!

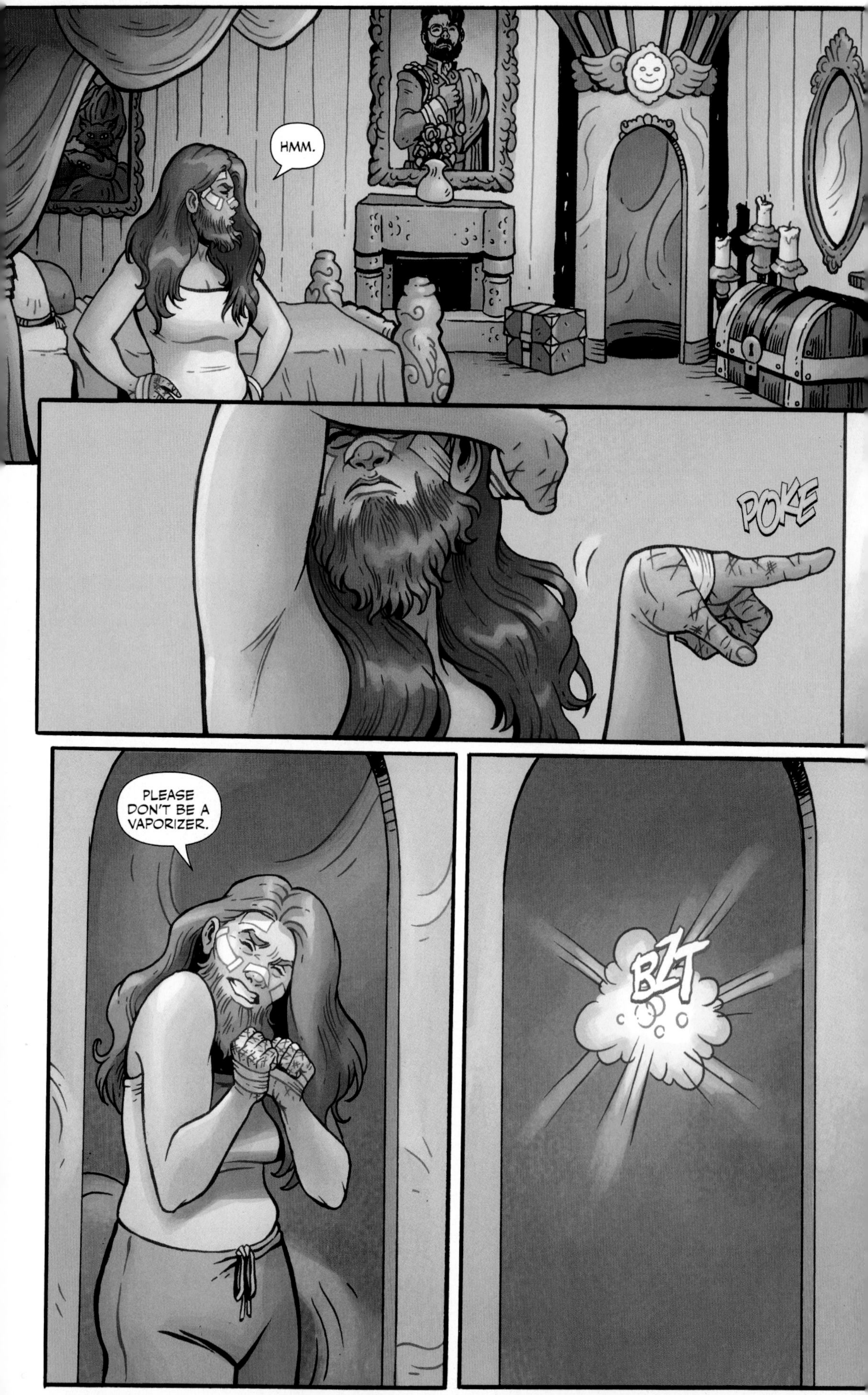
HMM.
POKE
PLEASE DON'T BE A VAPORIZER.
BZT

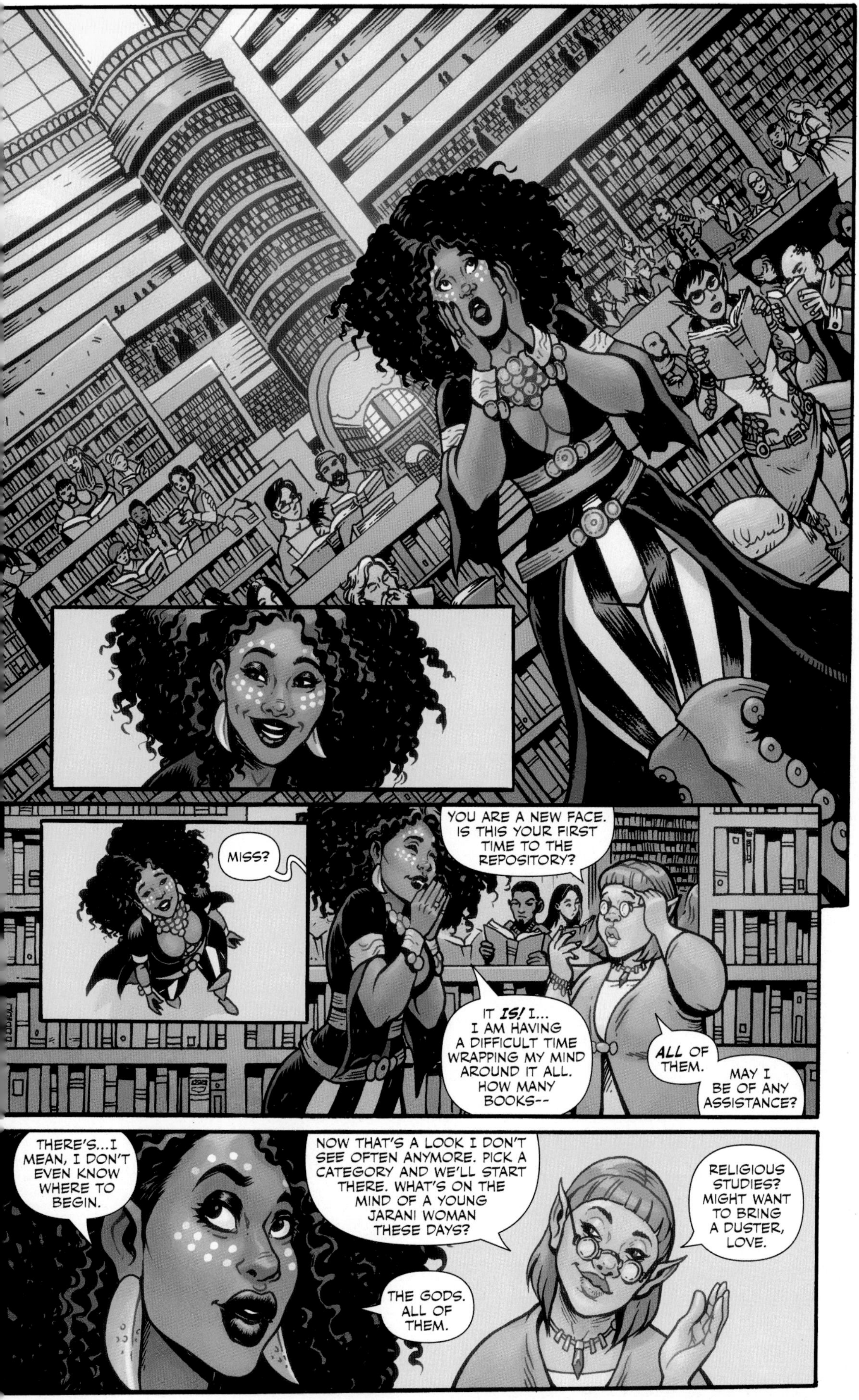
MISS?
YOU ARE A NEW FACE. IS THIS YOUR FIRST TIME TO THE REPOSITORY?
IT IS! I... I AM HAVING A DIFFICULT TIME WRAPPING MY MIND AROUND IT ALL. HOW MANY BOOKS--
ALL OF THEM.
MAY I BE OF ANY ASSISTANCE?
THERE'S...I MEAN, I DON'T EVEN KNOW WHERE TO BEGIN.
NOW THAT'S A LOOK I DON'T SEE OFTEN ANYMORE. PICK A CATEGORY AND WE'LL START THERE. WHAT'S ON THE MIND OF A YOUNG JARANI WOMAN THESE DAYS?
THE GODS. ALL OF THEM.
RELIGIOUS STUDIES? MIGHT WANT TO BRING A DUSTER, LOVE.

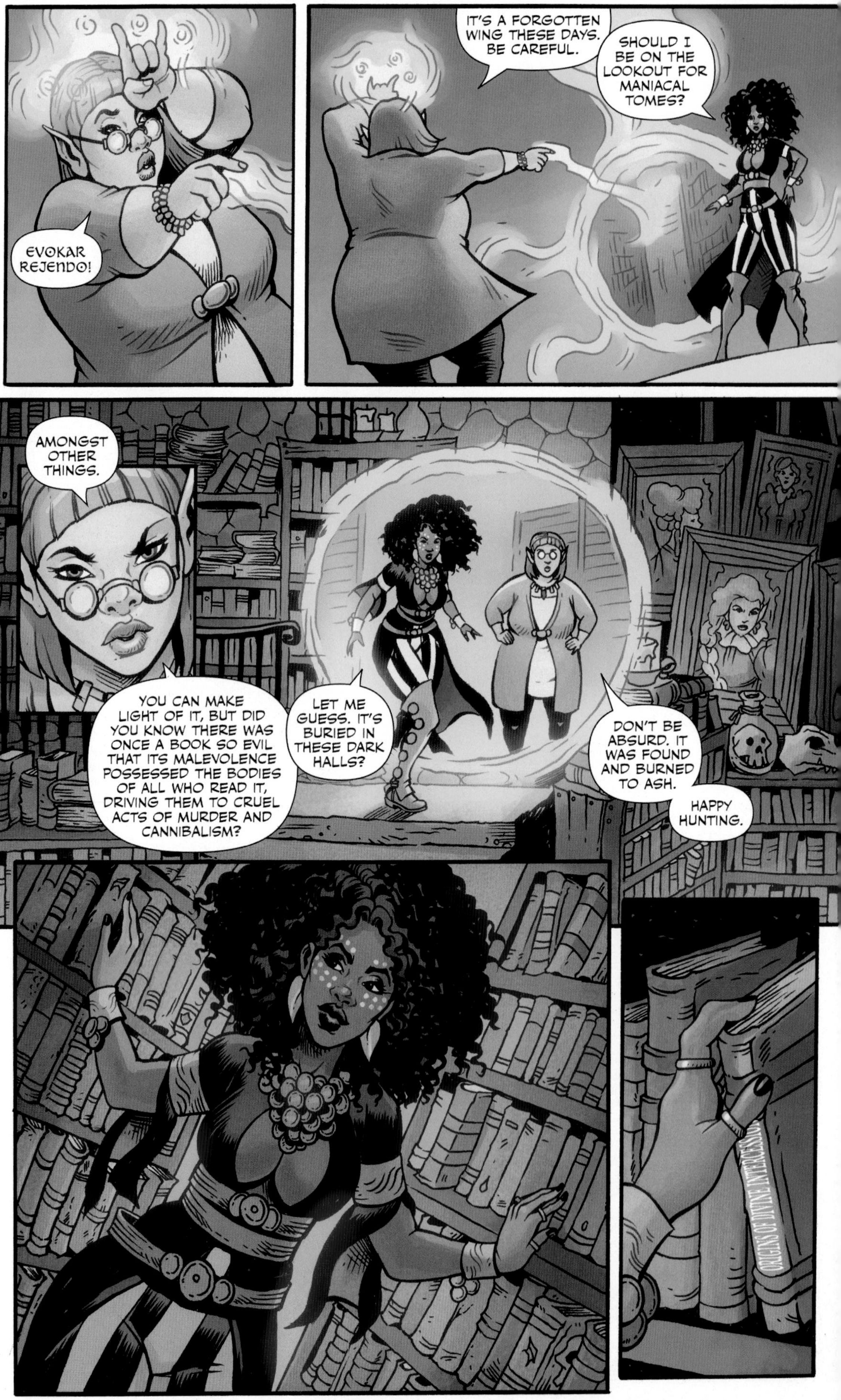

EVOKAR REJENDO!
IT'S A FORGOTTEN WING THESE DAYS. BE CAREFUL.
SHOULD I BE ON THE LOOKOUT FOR MANIACAL TOMES?
AMONGST OTHER THINGS.
YOU CAN MAKE LIGHT OF IT, BUT DID YOU KNOW THERE WAS ONCE A BOOK SO EVIL THAT ITS MALEVOLENCE POSSESSED THE BODIES OF ALL WHO READ IT, DRIVING THEM TO CRUEL ACTS OF MURDER AND CANNIBALISM?
LET ME GUESS. IT'S BURIED IN THESE DARK HALLS?
DON'T BE ABSURD. IT WAS FOUND AND BURNED TO ASH.
HAPPY HUNTING.
ORIGINS OF DIVINE INTERCESSION

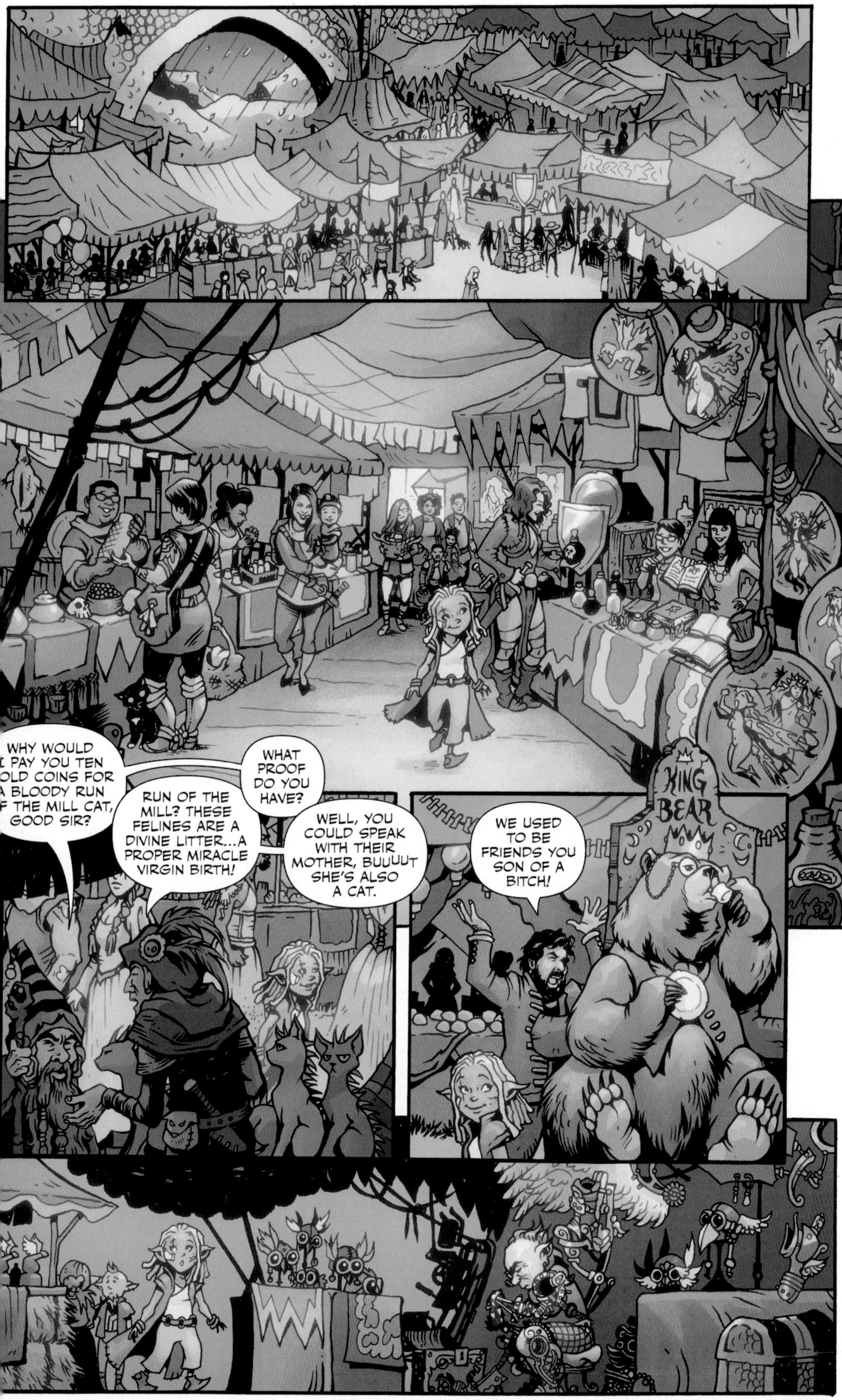

WHY WOULD PAY YOU TEN OLD COINS FOR A BLOODY RUN THE MILL CAT, GOOD SIR?
WHAT PROOF DO YOU HAVE?
RUN OF THE MILL? THESE FELINES ARE A DIVINE LITTER...A PROPER MIRACLE VIRGIN BIRTH!
WELL, YOU COULD SPEAK WITH THEIR MOTHER, BUUUUT SHE'S ALSO A CAT.
KING BEAR
WE USED TO BE FRIENDS YOU SON OF A BITCH!

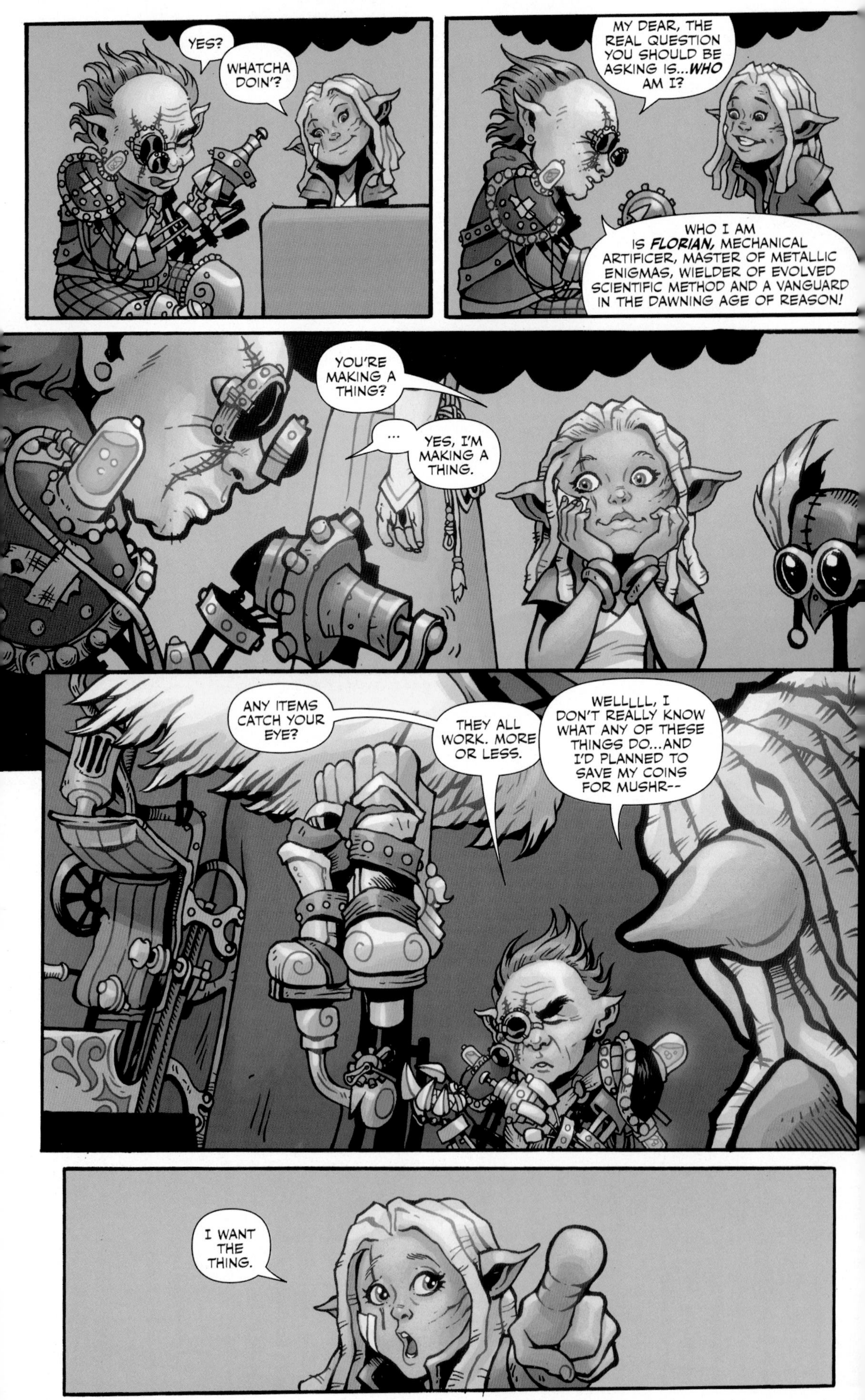
YES?
WHATCHA DOIN'?
MY DEAR, THE REAL QUESTION YOU SHOULD BE ASKING IS...WHO AM I?
WHO I AM IS FLORIAN, MECHANICAL ARTIFICER, MASTER OF METALLIC ENIGMAS, WIELDER OF EVOLVED SCIENTIFIC METHOD AND A VANGUARD IN THE DAWNING AGE OF REASON!
YOU'RE MAKING A THING?
...
YES, I'M MAKING A THING.
ANY ITEMS CATCH YOUR EYE?
THEY ALL WORK. MORE OR LESS.
WELLLLL, I DON'T REALLY KNOW WHAT ANY OF THESE THINGS DO...AND I'D PLANNED TO SAVE MY COINS FOR MUSHR--
I WANT THE THING.

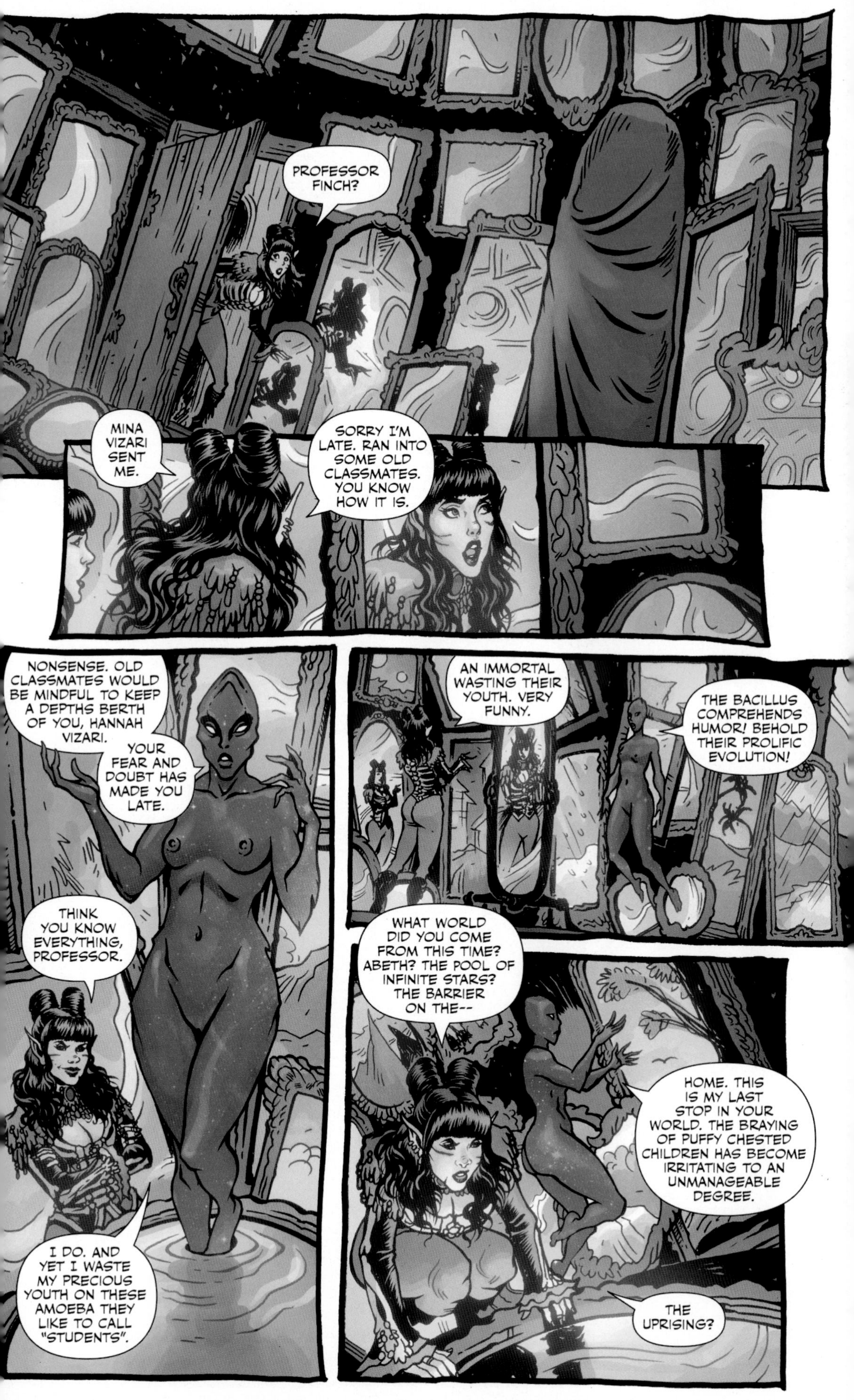
PROFESSOR FINCH?
MINA VIZARI SENT ME.
SORRY I'M LATE. RAN INTO SOME OLD CLASSMATES. YOU KNOW HOW IT IS.
NONSENSE. OLD CLASSMATES WOULD BE MINDFUL TO KEEP A DEPTHS BERTH OF YOU, HANNAH VIZARI.
YOUR FEAR AND DOUBT HAS MADE YOU LATE.
THINK YOU KNOW EVERYTHING, PROFESSOR.
I DO. AND YET I WASTE MY PRECIOUS YOUTH ON THESE AMOEBA THEY LIKE TO CALL "STUDENTS".
AN IMMORTAL WASTING THEIR YOUTH. VERY FUNNY.
THE BACILLUS COMPREHENDS HUMOR! BEHOLD THEIR PROLIFIC EVOLUTION!
WHAT WORLD DID YOU COME FROM THIS TIME? ABETH? THE POOL OF INFINITE STARS? THE BARRIER ON THE--
HOME. THIS IS MY LAST STOP IN YOUR WORLD. THE BRAYING OF PUFFY CHESTED CHILDREN HAS BECOME IRRITATING TO AN UNMANAGEABLE DEGREE.
THE UPRISING?

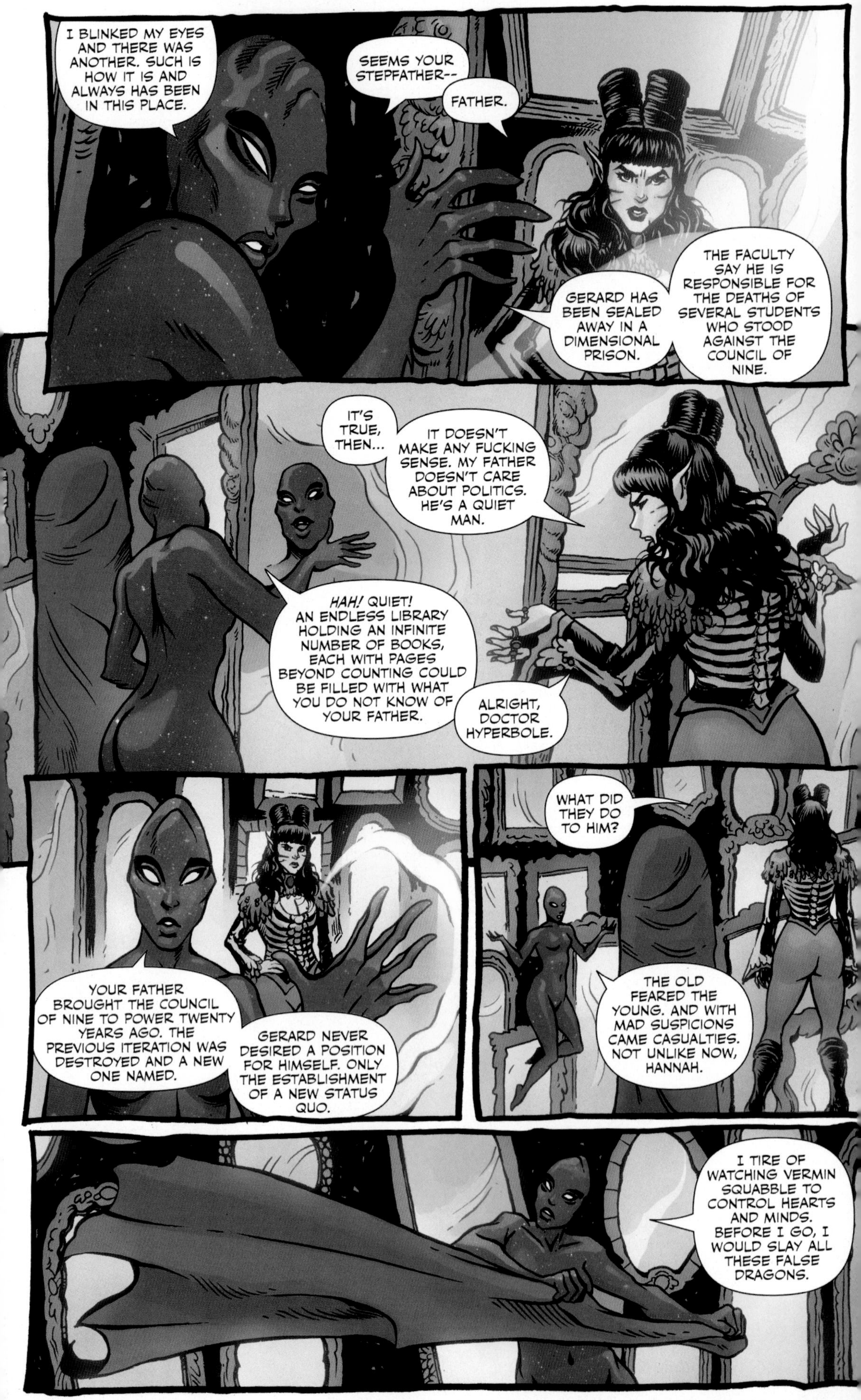
I BLINKED MY EYES AND THERE WAS ANOTHER. SUCH IS HOW IT IS AND ALWAYS HAS BEEN IN THIS PLACE.
SEEMS YOUR STEPFATHER--
FATHER.
GERARD HAS BEEN SEALED AWAY IN A DIMENSIONAL PRISON.
THE FACULTY SAY HE IS RESPONSIBLE FOR THE DEATHS OF SEVERAL STUDENTS WHO STOOD AGAINST THE COUNCIL OF NINE.
IT'S TRUE, THEN...
IT DOESN'T MAKE ANY FUCKING SENSE. MY FATHER DOESN'T CARE ABOUT POLITICS. HE'S A QUIET MAN.
HAH! QUIET! AN ENDLESS LIBRARY HOLDING AN INFINITE NUMBER OF BOOKS, EACH WITH PAGES BEYOND COUNTING COULD BE FILLED WITH WHAT YOU DO NOT KNOW OF YOUR FATHER.
ALRIGHT, DOCTOR HYPERBOLE.
YOUR FATHER BROUGHT THE COUNCIL OF NINE TO POWER TWENTY YEARS AGO. THE PREVIOUS ITERATION WAS DESTROYED AND A NEW ONE NAMED.
GERARD NEVER DESIRED A POSITION FOR HIMSELF. ONLY THE ESTABLISHMENT OF A NEW STATUS QUO.
WHAT DID THEY DO TO HIM?
THE OLD FEARED THE YOUNG. AND WITH MAD SUSPICIONS CAME CASUALTIES. NOT UNLIKE NOW, HANNAH.
I TIRE OF WATCHING VERMIN SQUABBLE TO CONTROL HEARTS AND MINDS. BEFORE I GO, I WOULD SLAY ALL THESE FALSE DRAGONS.

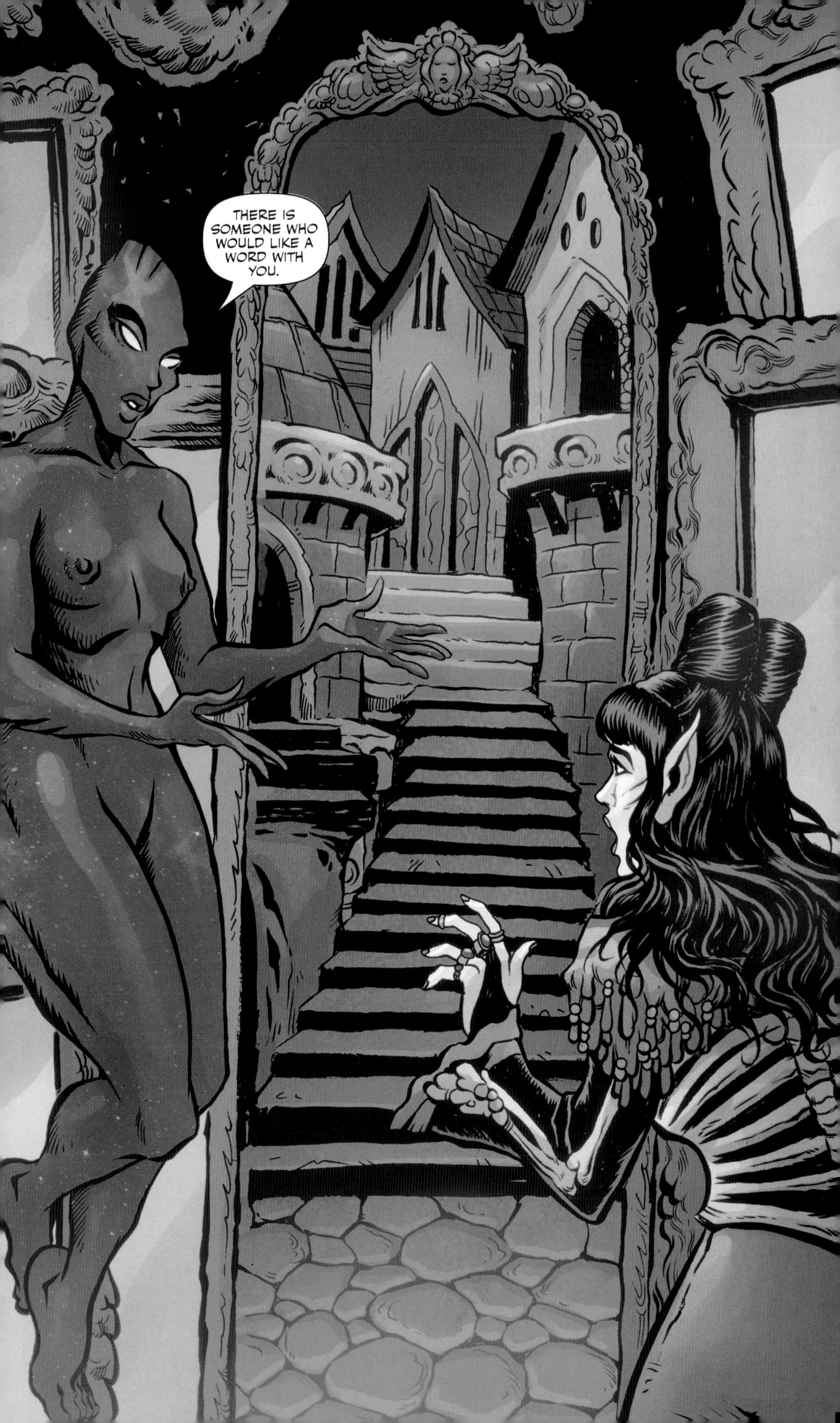
THERE IS SOMEONE WHO WOULD LIKE A WORD WITH YOU.

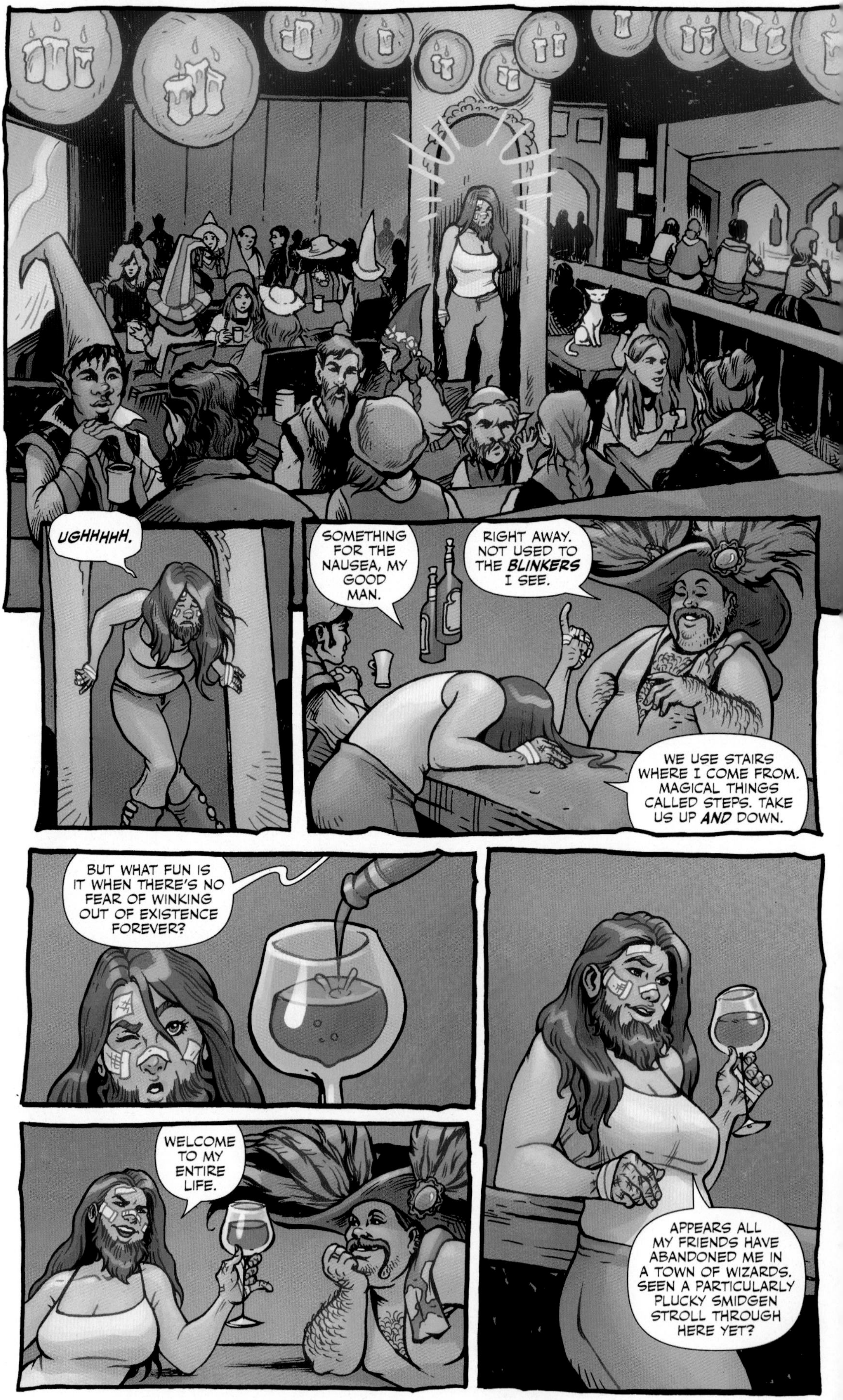
UGHHHHH.
SOMETHING FOR THE NAUSEA, MY GOOD MAN.
RIGHT AWAY. NOT USED TO THE BLINKERS I SEE.
WE USE STAIRS WHERE I COME FROM. MAGICAL THINGS CALLED STEPS. TAKE US UP AND DOWN.
BUT WHAT FUN IS IT WHEN THERE'S NO FEAR OF WINKING OUT OF EXISTENCE FOREVER?
WELCOME TO MY ENTIRE LIFE.
APPEARS ALL MY FRIENDS HAVE ABANDONED ME IN A TOWN OF WIZARDS. SEEN A PARTICULARLY PLUCKY SMIDGEN STROLL THROUGH HERE YET?

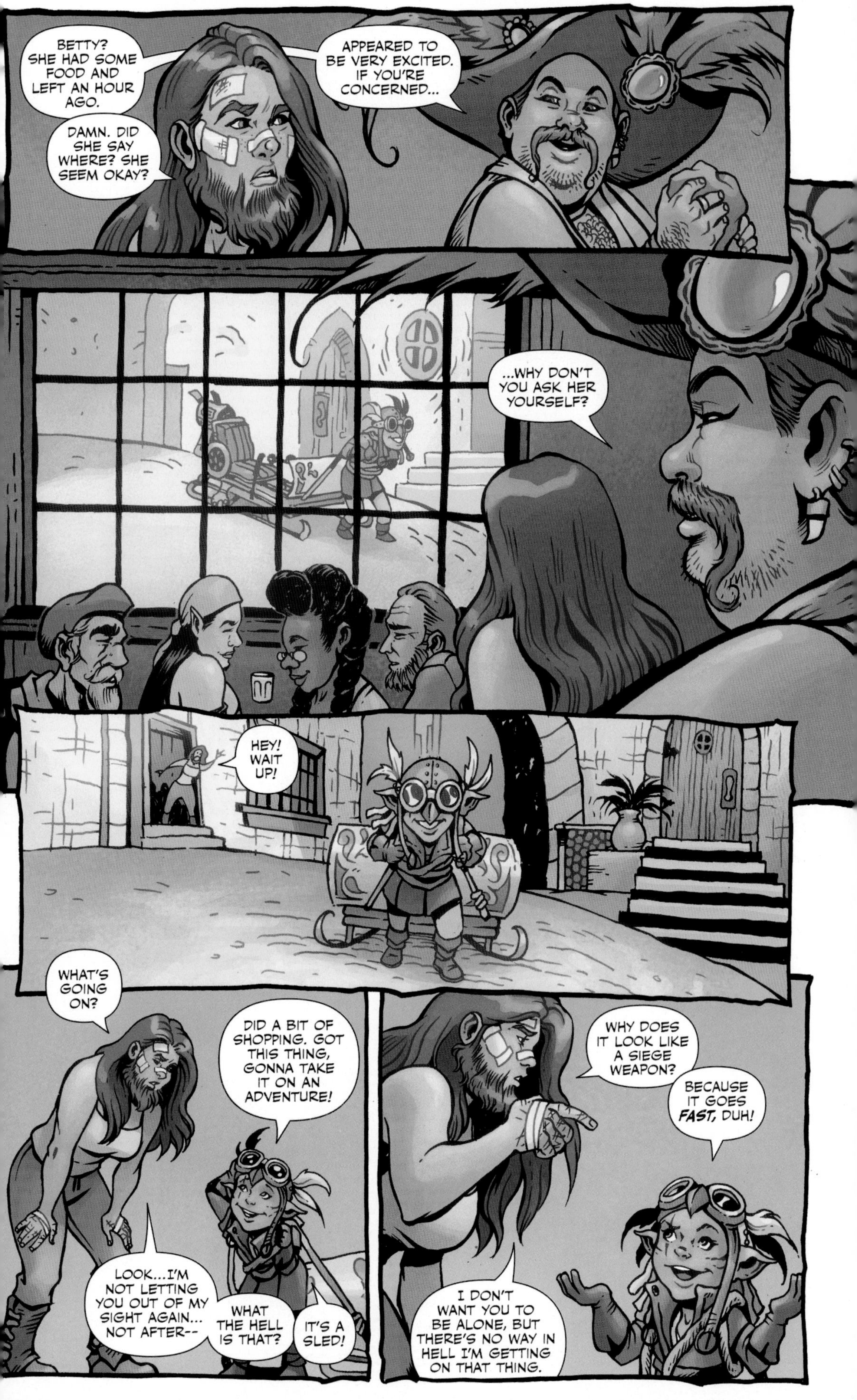
BETTY? SHE HAD SOME FOOD AND LEFT AN HOUR AGO.
DAMN. DID SHE SAY WHERE? SHE SEEM OKAY?
APPEARED TO BE VERY EXCITED. IF YOU'RE CONCERNED...
...WHY DON'T YOU ASK HER YOURSELF?
HEY! WAIT UP!
WHAT'S GOING ON?
DID A BIT OF SHOPPING. GOT THIS THING, GONNA TAKE IT ON AN ADVENTURE!
LOOK...I'M NOT LETTING YOU OUT OF MY SIGHT AGAIN... NOT AFTER--
WHAT THE HELL IS THAT?
IT'S A SLED!
WHY DOES IT LOOK LIKE A SIEGE WEAPON?
BECAUSE IT GOES *FAST,* DUH!
I DON'T WANT YOU TO BE ALONE, BUT THERE'S NO WAY IN HELL I'M GETTING ON THAT THING.

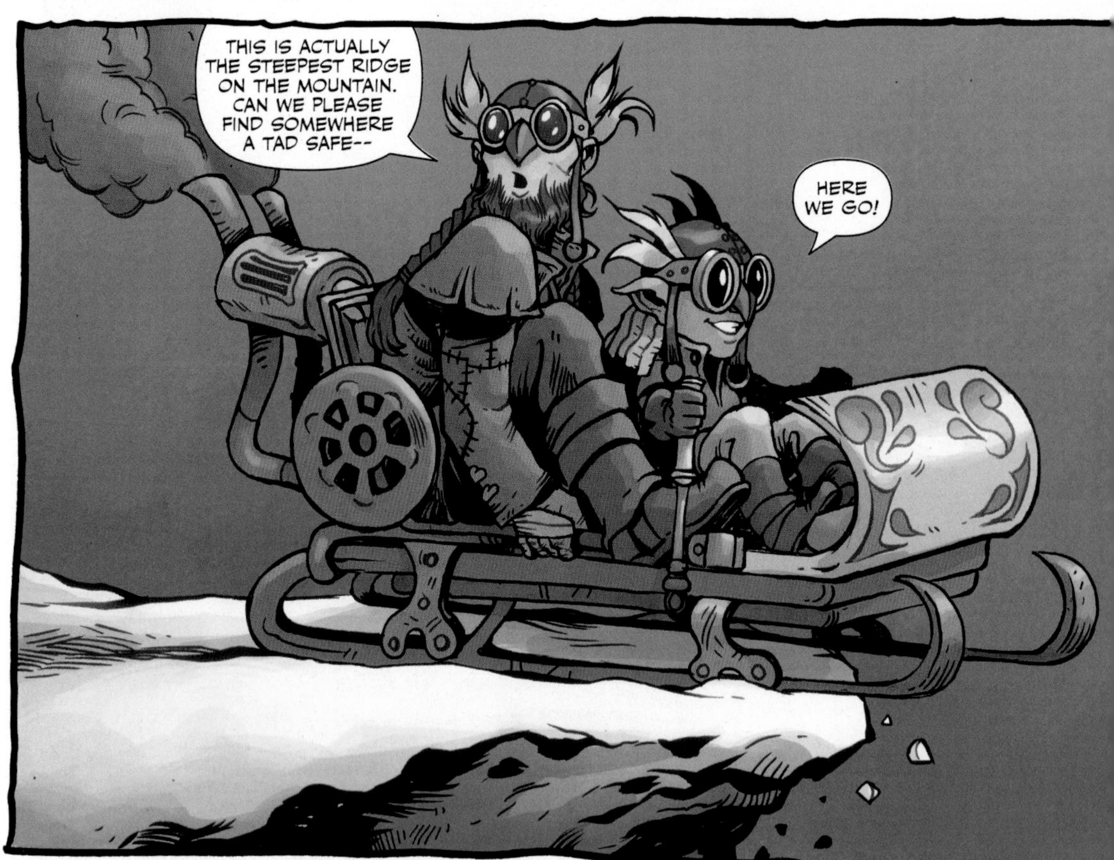
THIS IS ACTUALLY THE STEEPEST RIDGE ON THE MOUNTAIN. CAN WE PLEASE FIND SOMEWHERE A TAD SAFE--
HERE WE GO!

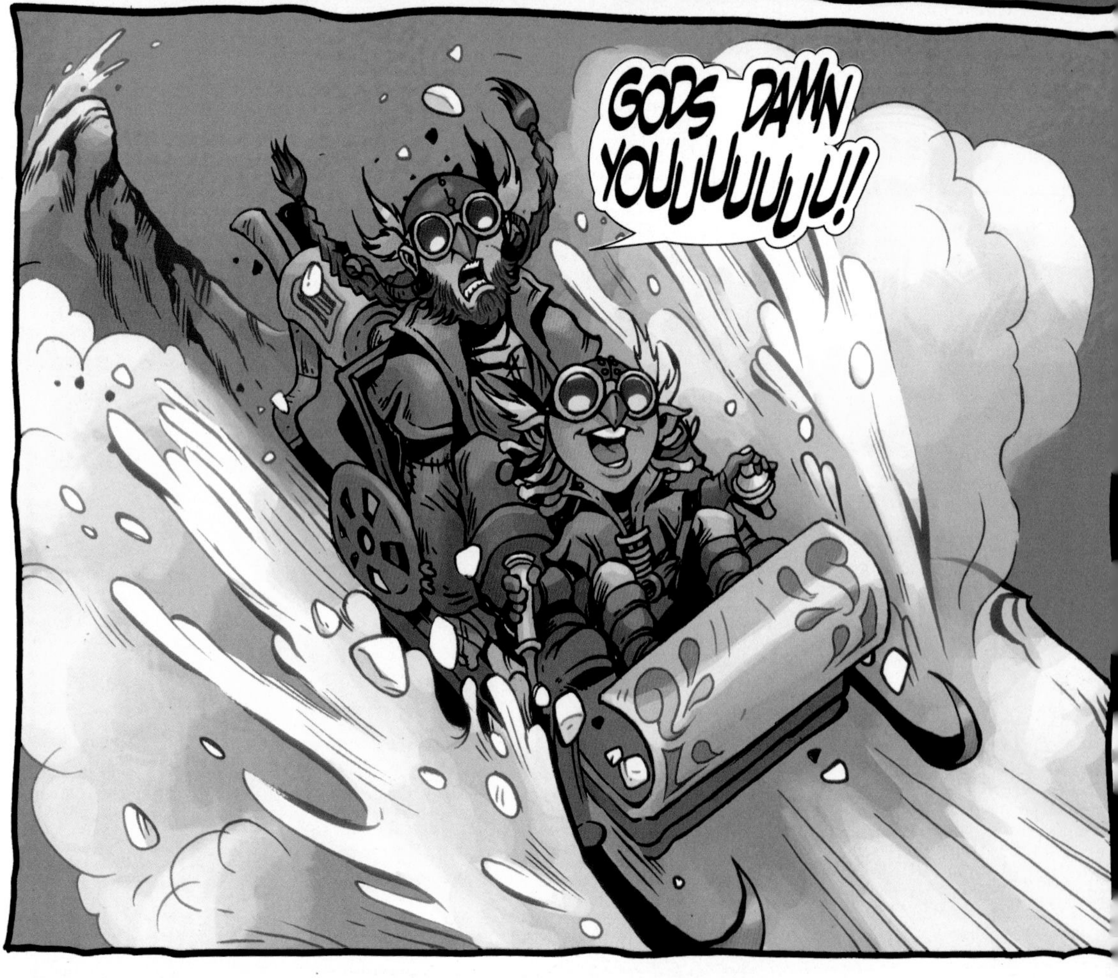
GODS DAMN YOUUUUUUU!

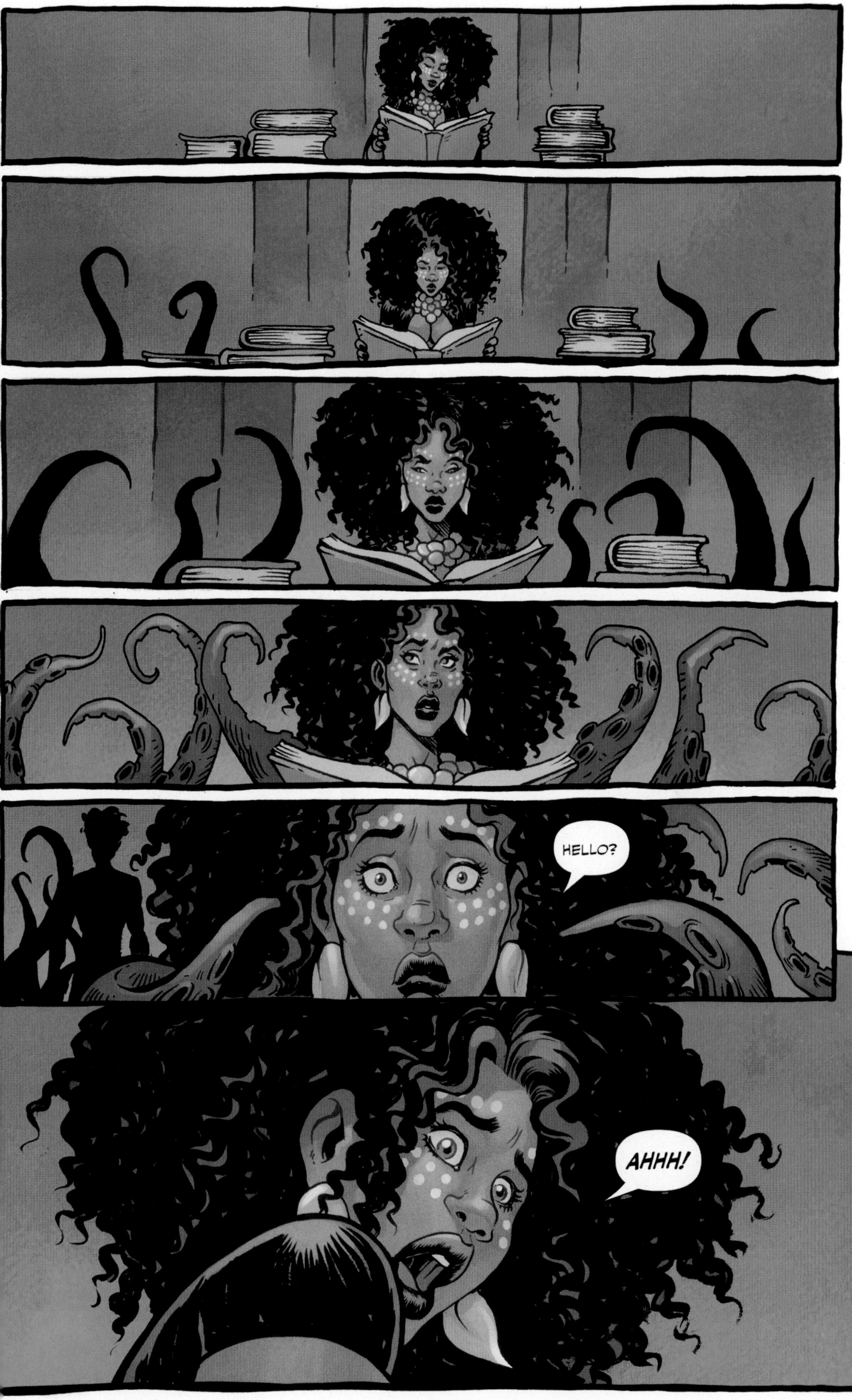
HELLO?
AHHH!

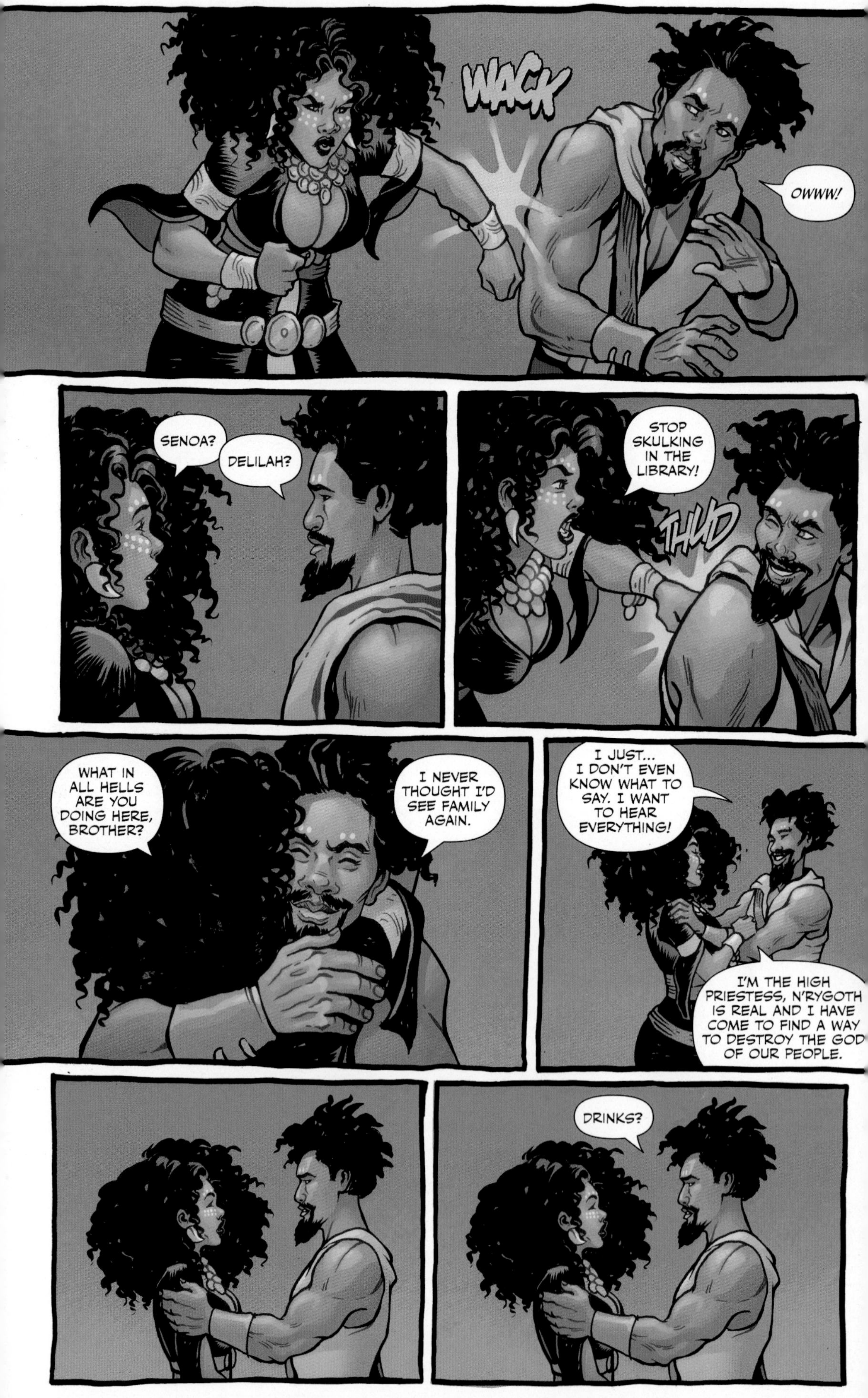
WACK
OWWW!
SENOA?
DELILAH?
STOP SKULKING IN THE LIBRARY!
THUD
WHAT IN ALL HELLS ARE YOU DOING HERE, BROTHER?
I NEVER THOUGHT I'D SEE FAMILY AGAIN.
I JUST... I DON'T EVEN KNOW WHAT TO SAY. I WANT TO HEAR EVERYTHING!
I'M THE HIGH PRIESTESS, N'RYGOTH IS REAL AND I HAVE COME TO FIND A WAY TO DESTROY THE GOD OF OUR PEOPLE.
DRINKS?

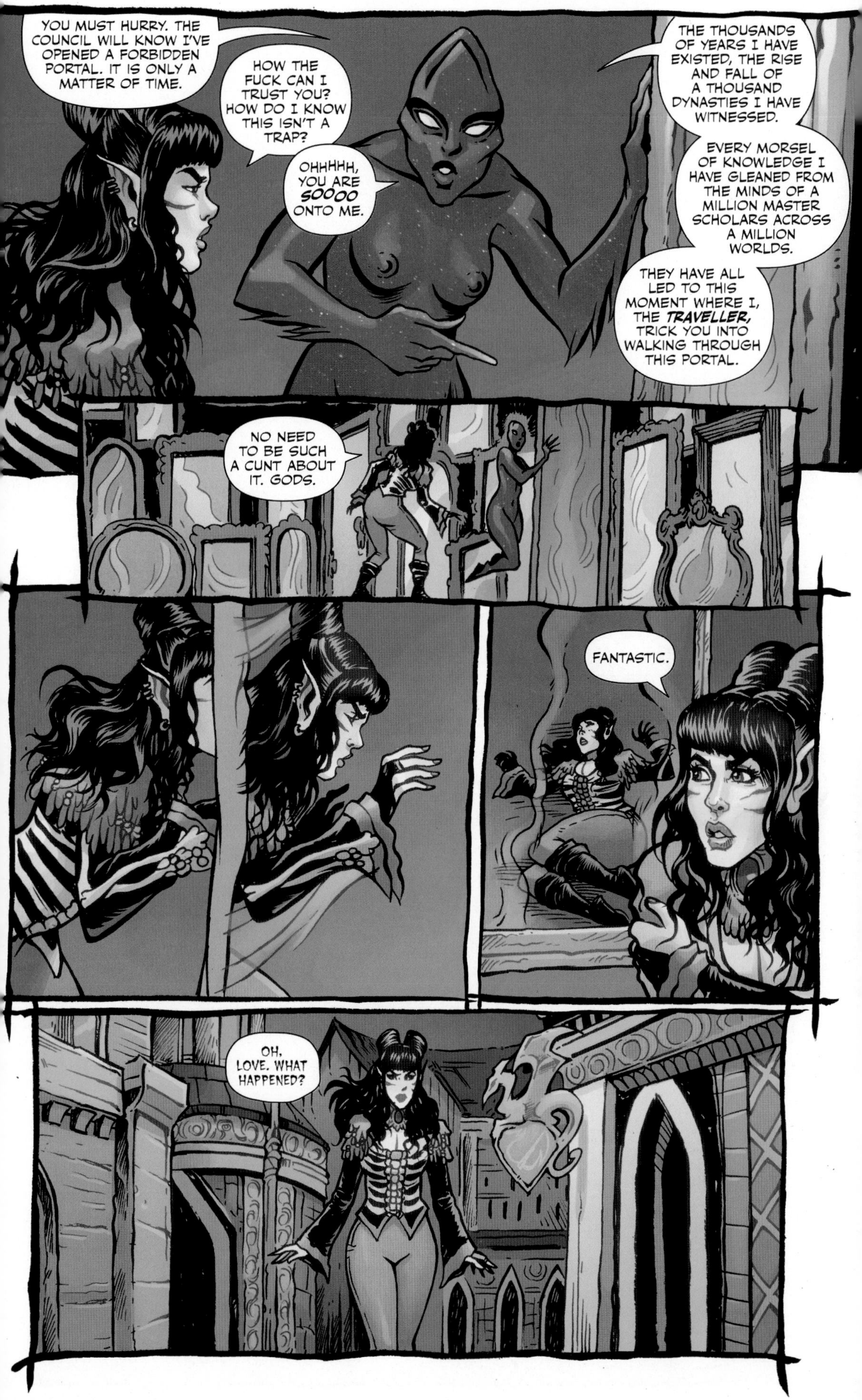
YOU MUST HURRY. THE COUNCIL WILL KNOW I'VE OPENED A FORBIDDEN PORTAL. IT IS ONLY A MATTER OF TIME.
HOW THE FUCK CAN I TRUST YOU? HOW DO I KNOW THIS ISN'T A TRAP?
OHHHHH, YOU ARE SOOOO ONTO ME.
THE THOUSANDS OF YEARS I HAVE EXISTED, THE RISE AND FALL OF A THOUSAND DYNASTIES I HAVE WITNESSED.
EVERY MORSEL OF KNOWLEDGE I HAVE GLEANED FROM THE MINDS OF A MILLION MASTER SCHOLARS ACROSS A MILLION WORLDS.
THEY HAVE ALL LED TO THIS MOMENT WHERE I, THE TRAVELLER, TRICK YOU INTO WALKING THROUGH THIS PORTAL.
NO NEED TO BE SUCH A CUNT ABOUT IT. GODS.
FANTASTIC.
OH, LOVE. WHAT HAPPENED?

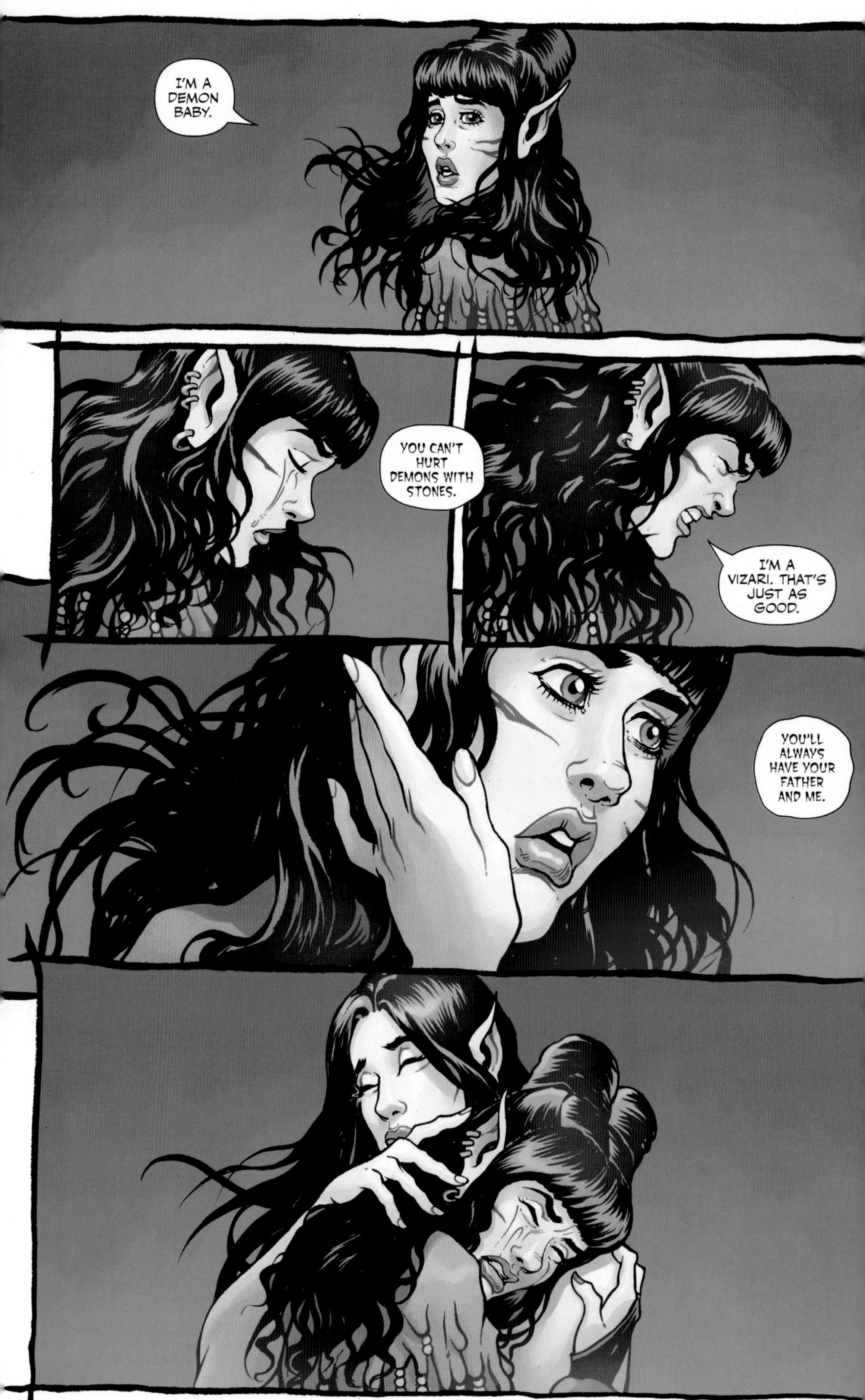
I'M A DEMON BABY.
YOU CAN'T HURT DEMONS WITH STONES.
I'M A VIZARI. THAT'S JUST AS GOOD.
YOU'LL ALWAYS HAVE YOUR FATHER AND ME.

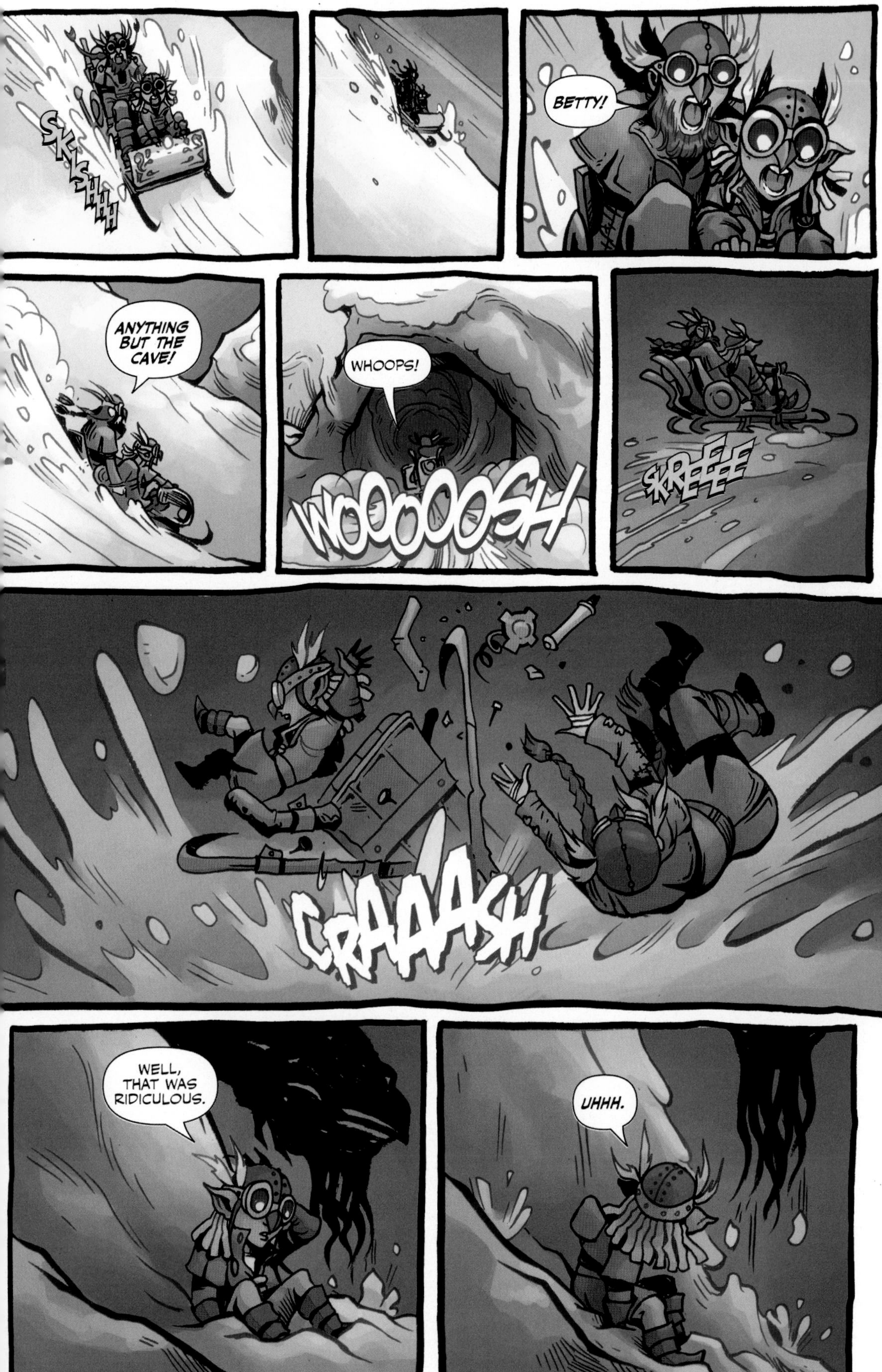
SKISHHH
BETTY!
ANYTHING BUT THE CAVE!
WHOOPS!
WOOOOOSH
SKREEEE
CRAAASH
WELL, THAT WAS RIDICULOUS.
UHHH.

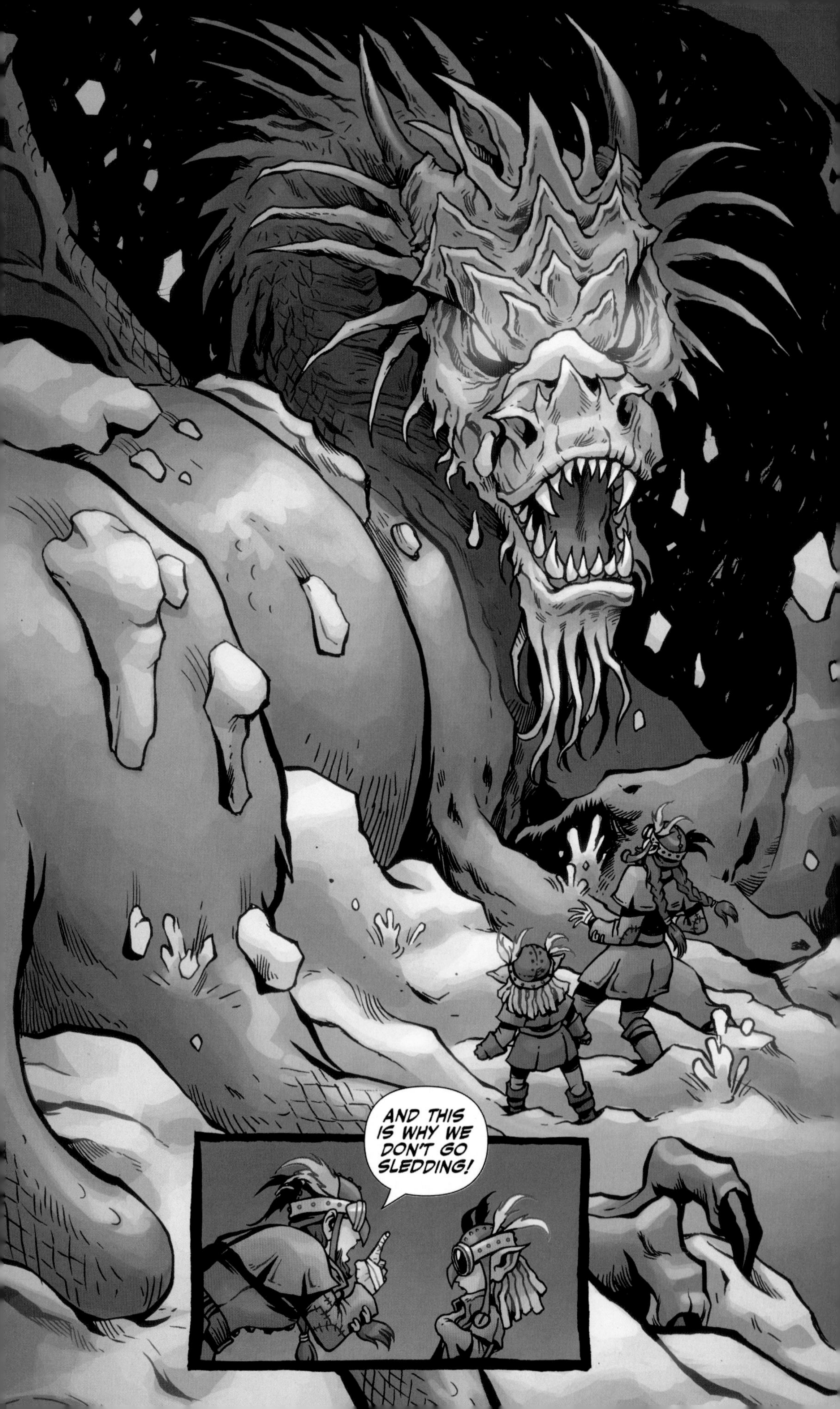
AND THIS IS WHY WE DON'T GO SLEDDING!

CHAPTER FOURTEEN

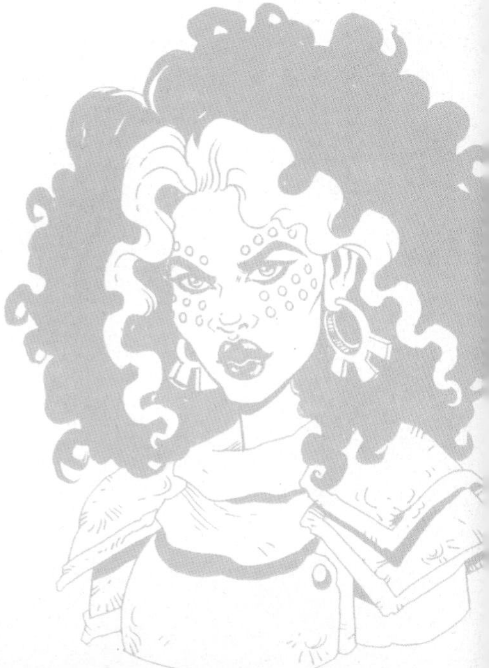
TESS 2016

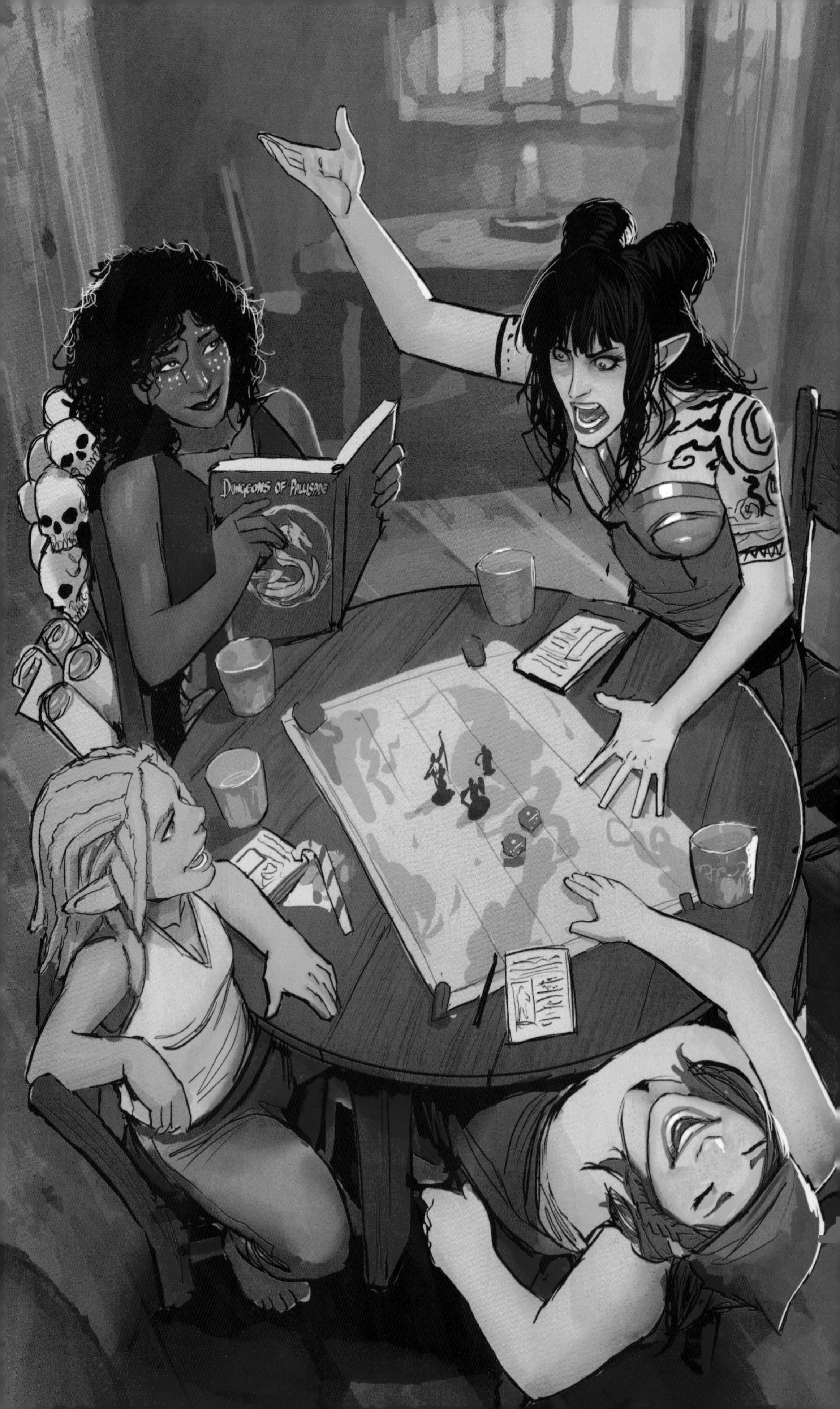
DUNGEONS OF PALLISADE

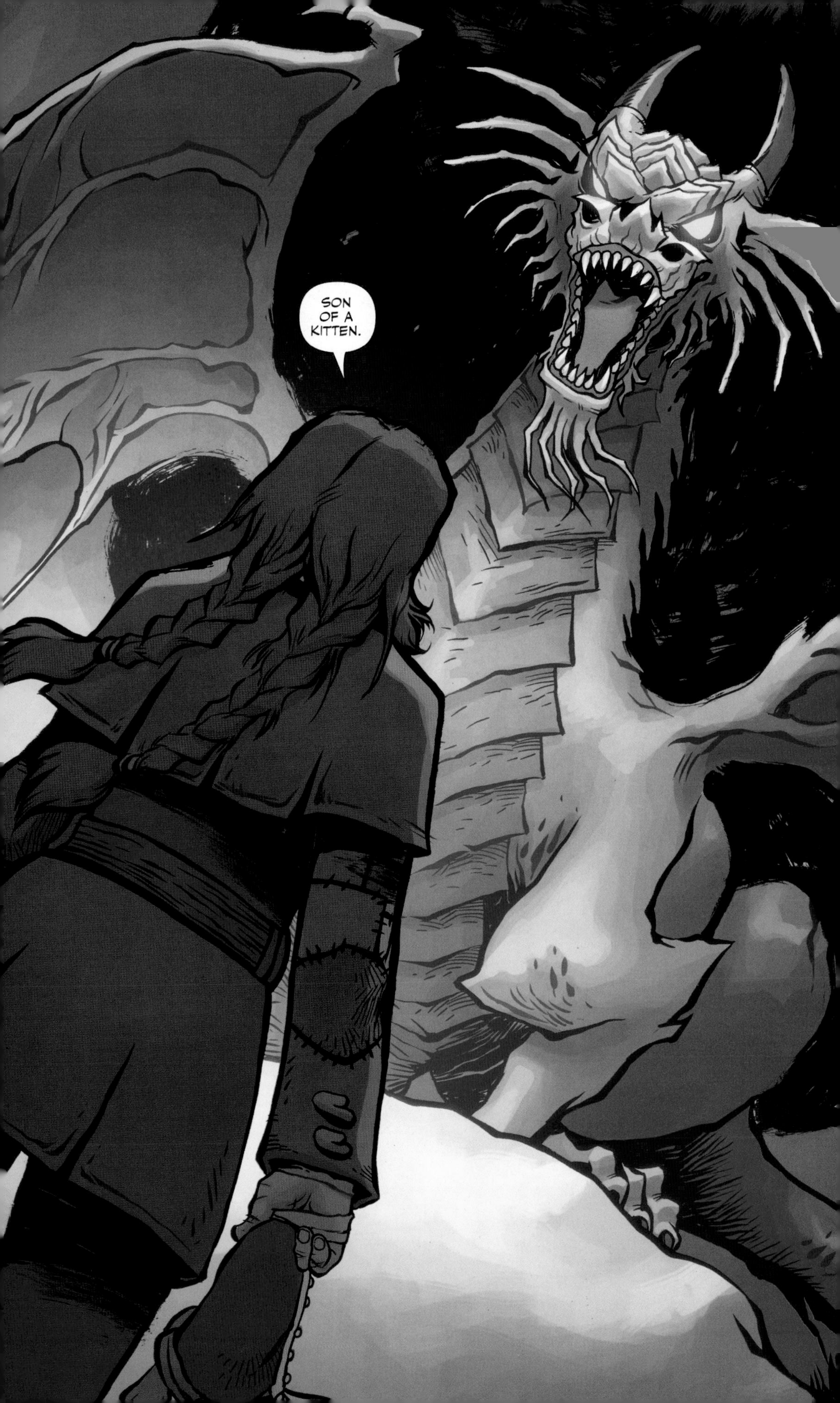
SON OF A KITTEN.

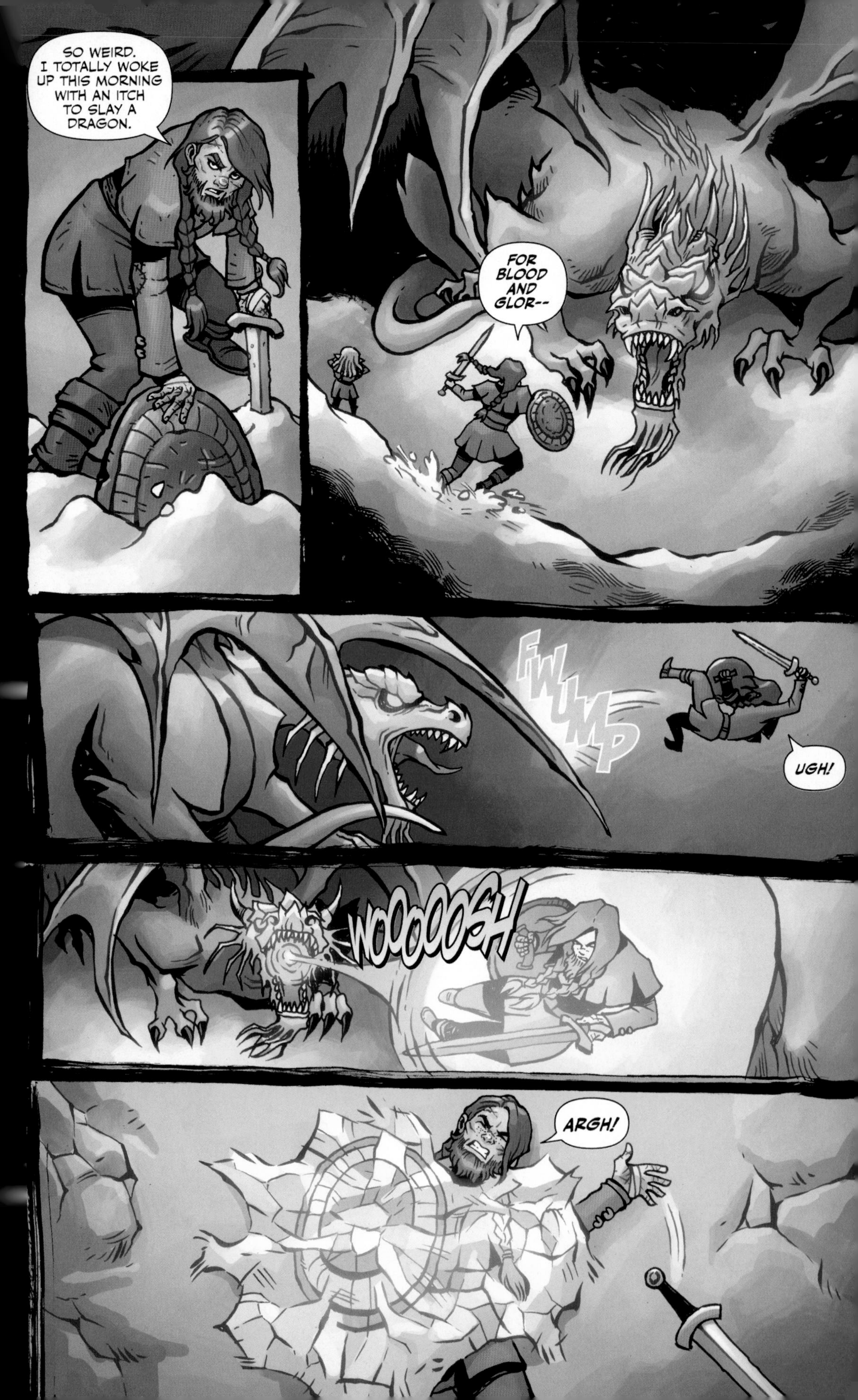
SO WEIRD. I TOTALLY WOKE UP THIS MORNING WITH AN ITCH TO SLAY A DRAGON.
FOR BLOOD AND GLOR--
FWUMP
UGH!
WOOOOOSH
ARGH!

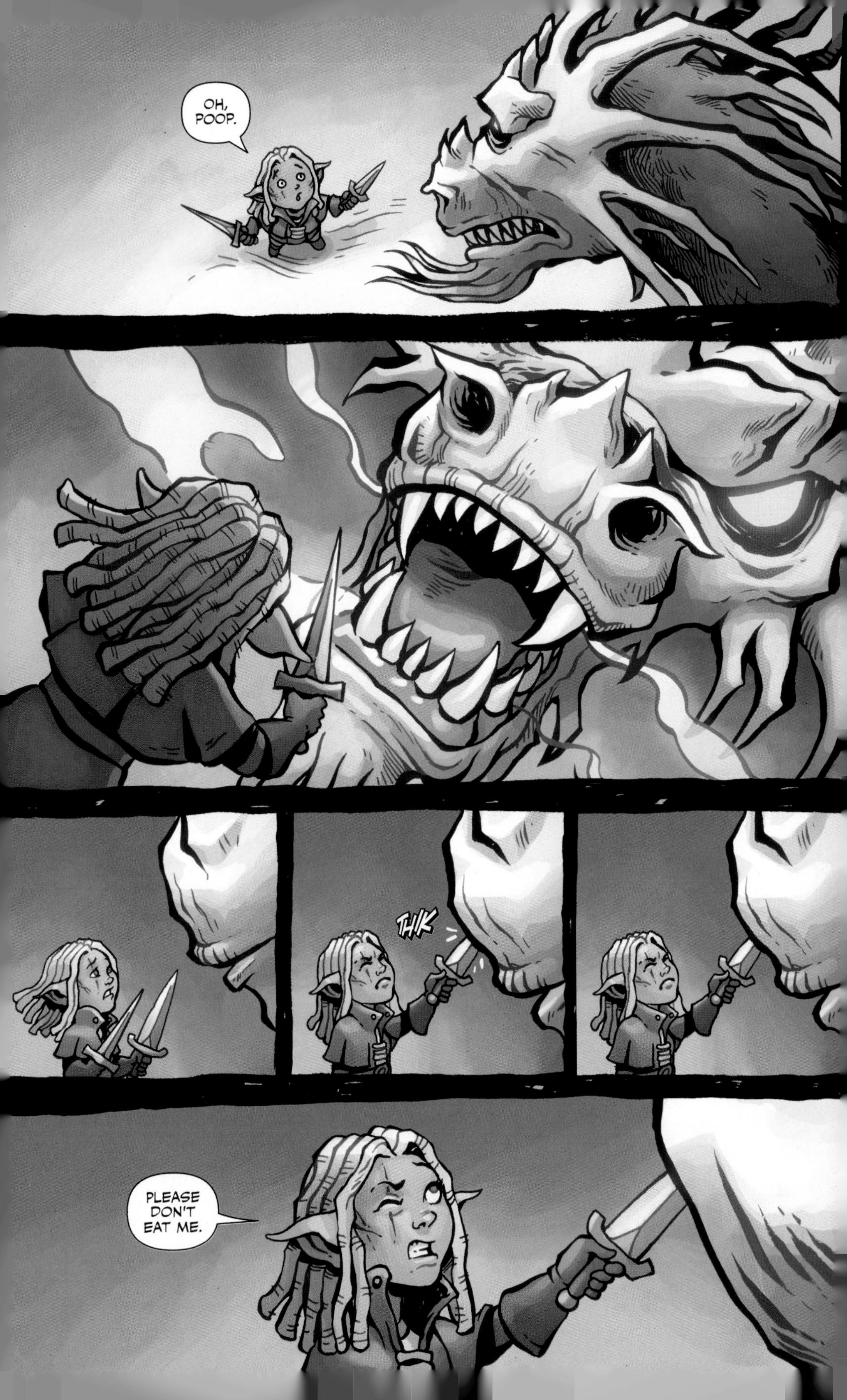
OH, POOP.
THIK
PLEASE DON'T EAT ME.

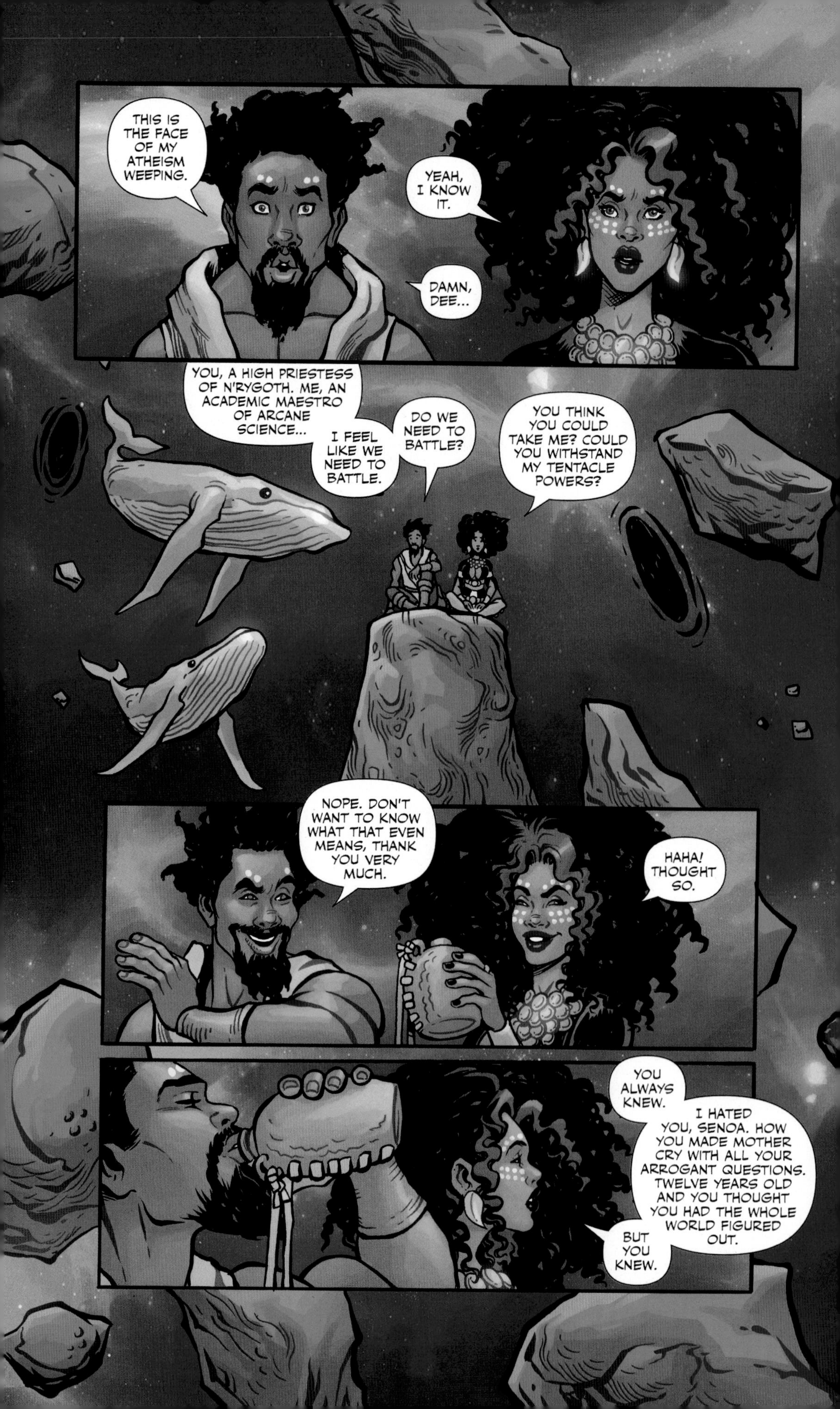

THIS IS THE FACE OF MY ATHEISM WEEPING.
YEAH, I KNOW IT.
DAMN, DEE...
YOU, A HIGH PRIESTESS OF N'RYGOTH. ME, AN ACADEMIC MAESTRO OF ARCANE SCIENCE...
I FEEL LIKE WE NEED TO BATTLE.
DO WE NEED TO BATTLE?
YOU THINK YOU COULD TAKE ME? COULD YOU WITHSTAND MY TENTACLE POWERS?
NOPE. DON'T WANT TO KNOW WHAT THAT EVEN MEANS, THANK YOU VERY MUCH.
HAHA! THOUGHT SO.
YOU ALWAYS KNEW.
I HATED YOU, SENOA. HOW YOU MADE MOTHER CRY WITH ALL YOUR ARROGANT QUESTIONS. TWELVE YEARS OLD AND YOU THOUGHT YOU HAD THE WHOLE WORLD FIGURED OUT.
BUT YOU KNEW.

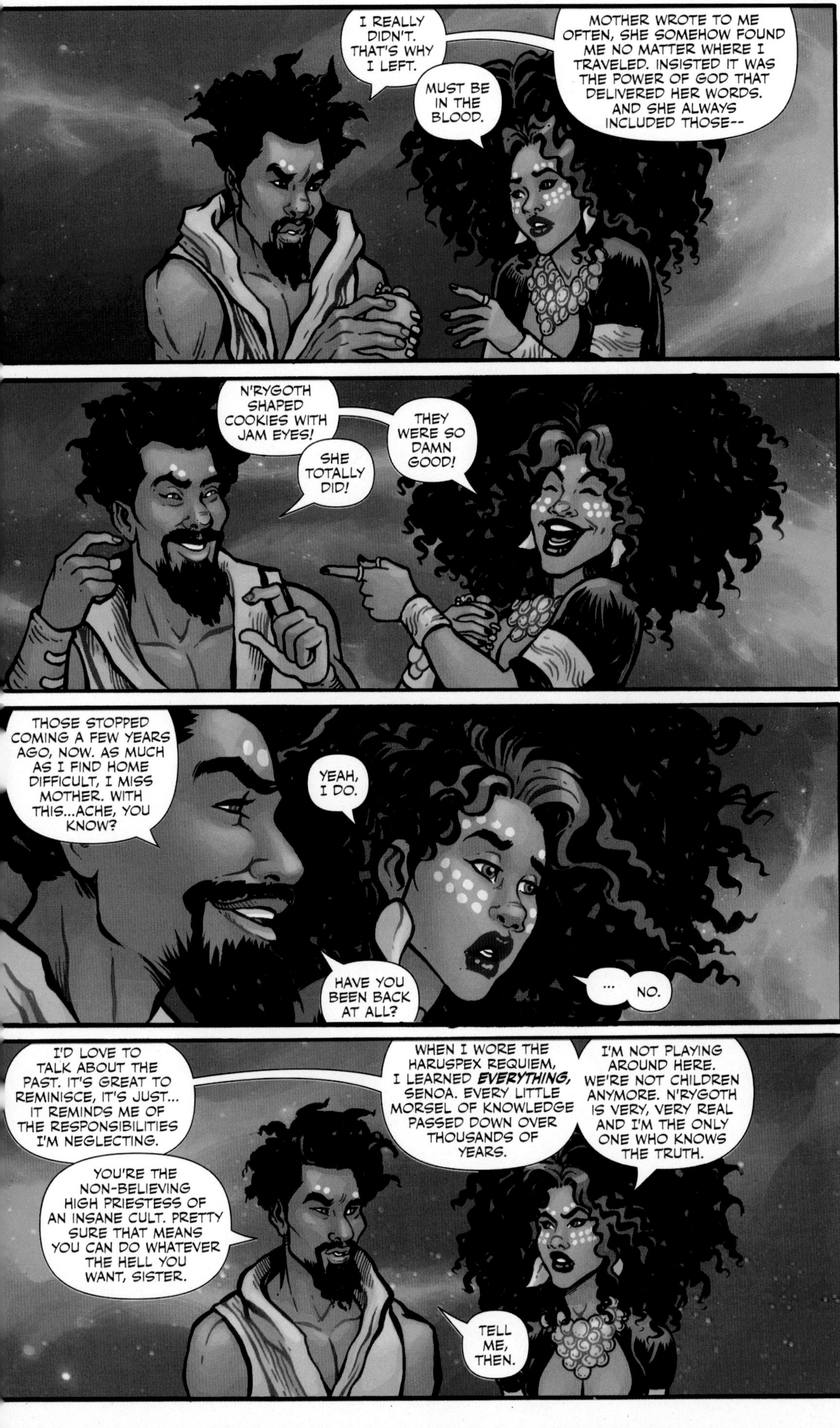
I REALLY DIDN'T. THAT'S WHY I LEFT.
MUST BE IN THE BLOOD.
MOTHER WROTE TO ME OFTEN, SHE SOMEHOW FOUND ME NO MATTER WHERE I TRAVELED. INSISTED IT WAS THE POWER OF GOD THAT DELIVERED HER WORDS. AND SHE ALWAYS INCLUDED THOSE--
N'RYGOTH SHAPED COOKIES WITH JAM EYES!
SHE TOTALLY DID!
THEY WERE SO DAMN GOOD!
THOSE STOPPED COMING A FEW YEARS AGO, NOW. AS MUCH AS I FIND HOME DIFFICULT, I MISS MOTHER. WITH THIS...ACHE, YOU KNOW?
YEAH, I DO.
HAVE YOU BEEN BACK AT ALL?
...
NO.
I'D LOVE TO TALK ABOUT THE PAST. IT'S GREAT TO REMINISCE, IT'S JUST... IT REMINDS ME OF THE RESPONSIBILITIES I'M NEGLECTING.
YOU'RE THE NON-BELIEVING HIGH PRIESTESS OF AN INSANE CULT. PRETTY SURE THAT MEANS YOU CAN DO WHATEVER THE HELL YOU WANT, SISTER.
WHEN I WORE THE HARUSPEX REQUIEM, I LEARNED *EVERYTHING,* SENOA. EVERY LITTLE MORSEL OF KNOWLEDGE PASSED DOWN OVER THOUSANDS OF YEARS.
I'M NOT PLAYING AROUND HERE. WE'RE NOT CHILDREN ANYMORE. N'RYGOTH IS VERY, VERY REAL AND I'M THE ONLY ONE WHO KNOWS THE TRUTH.
TELL ME, THEN.

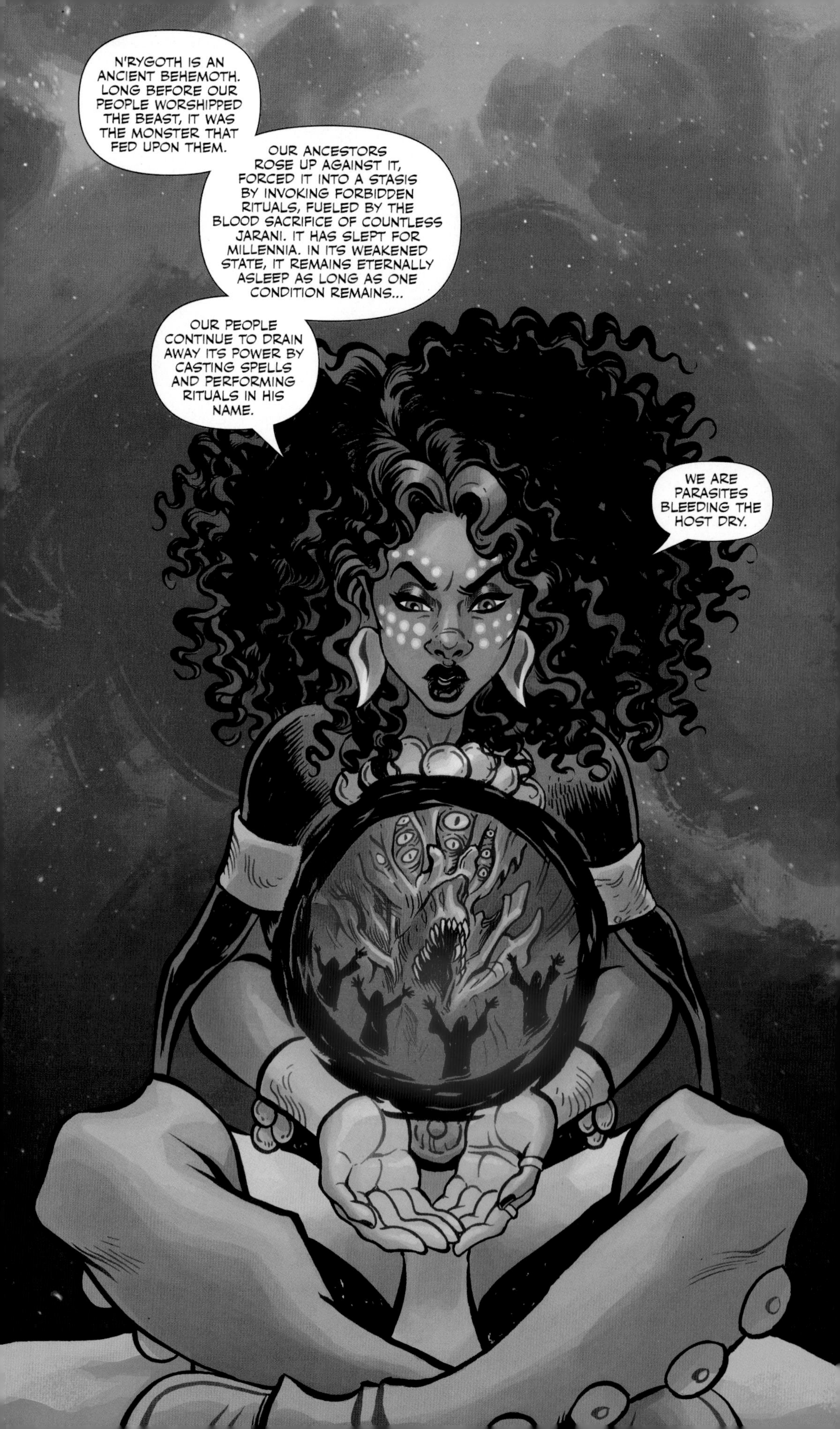
N'RYGOTH IS AN ANCIENT BEHEMOTH. LONG BEFORE OUR PEOPLE WORSHIPPED THE BEAST, IT WAS THE MONSTER THAT FED UPON THEM.
OUR ANCESTORS ROSE UP AGAINST IT, FORCED IT INTO A STASIS BY INVOKING FORBIDDEN RITUALS, FUELED BY THE BLOOD SACRIFICE OF COUNTLESS JARANI. IT HAS SLEPT FOR MILLENNIA. IN ITS WEAKENED STATE, IT REMAINS ETERNALLY ASLEEP AS LONG AS ONE CONDITION REMAINS...
OUR PEOPLE CONTINUE TO DRAIN AWAY ITS POWER BY CASTING SPELLS AND PERFORMING RITUALS IN HIS NAME.
WE ARE PARASITES BLEEDING THE HOST DRY.

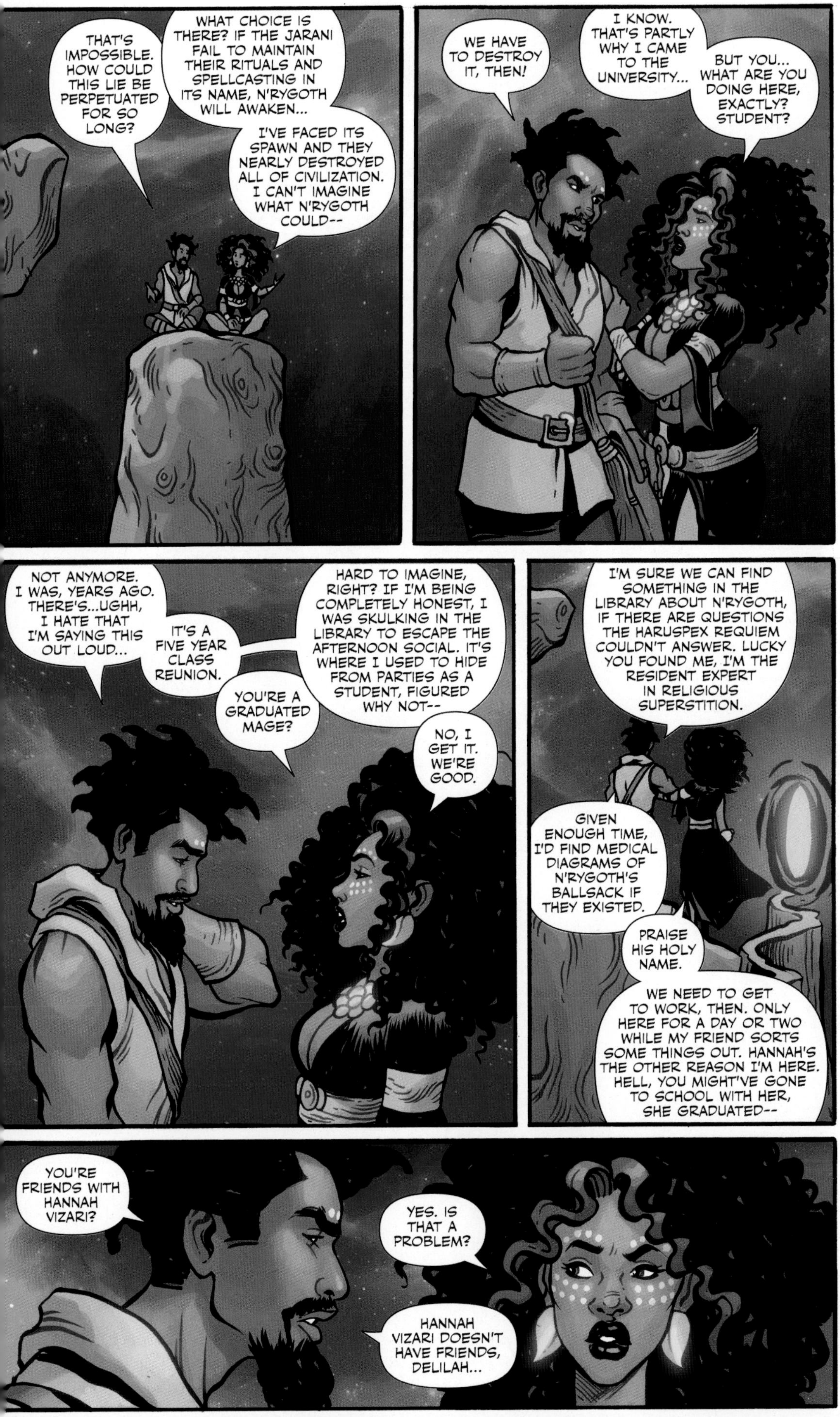
THAT'S IMPOSSIBLE. HOW COULD THIS LIE BE PERPETUATED FOR SO LONG?
WHAT CHOICE IS THERE? IF THE JARANI FAIL TO MAINTAIN THEIR RITUALS AND SPELLCASTING IN ITS NAME, N'RYGOTH WILL AWAKEN...
I'VE FACED ITS SPAWN AND THEY NEARLY DESTROYED ALL OF CIVILIZATION. I CAN'T IMAGINE WHAT N'RYGOTH COULD--
WE HAVE TO DESTROY IT, THEN!
I KNOW. THAT'S PARTLY WHY I CAME TO THE UNIVERSITY...
BUT YOU... WHAT ARE YOU DOING HERE, EXACTLY? STUDENT?
NOT ANYMORE. I WAS, YEARS AGO. THERE'S...UGHH, I HATE THAT I'M SAYING THIS OUT LOUD...
IT'S A FIVE YEAR CLASS REUNION.
YOU'RE A GRADUATED MAGE?
HARD TO IMAGINE, RIGHT? IF I'M BEING COMPLETELY HONEST, I WAS SKULKING IN THE LIBRARY TO ESCAPE THE AFTERNOON SOCIAL. IT'S WHERE I USED TO HIDE FROM PARTIES AS A STUDENT, FIGURED WHY NOT--
NO, I GET IT. WE'RE GOOD.
I'M SURE WE CAN FIND SOMETHING IN THE LIBRARY ABOUT N'RYGOTH, IF THERE ARE QUESTIONS THE HARUSPEX REQUIEM COULDN'T ANSWER. LUCKY YOU FOUND ME, I'M THE RESIDENT EXPERT IN RELIGIOUS SUPERSTITION.
GIVEN ENOUGH TIME, I'D FIND MEDICAL DIAGRAMS OF N'RYGOTH'S BALLSACK IF THEY EXISTED.
PRAISE HIS HOLY NAME.
WE NEED TO GET TO WORK, THEN. ONLY HERE FOR A DAY OR TWO WHILE MY FRIEND SORTS SOME THINGS OUT. HANNAH'S THE OTHER REASON I'M HERE. HELL, YOU MIGHT'VE GONE TO SCHOOL WITH HER, SHE GRADUATED--
YOU'RE FRIENDS WITH HANNAH VIZARI?
YES. IS THAT A PROBLEM?
HANNAH VIZARI DOESN'T HAVE FRIENDS, DELILAH...

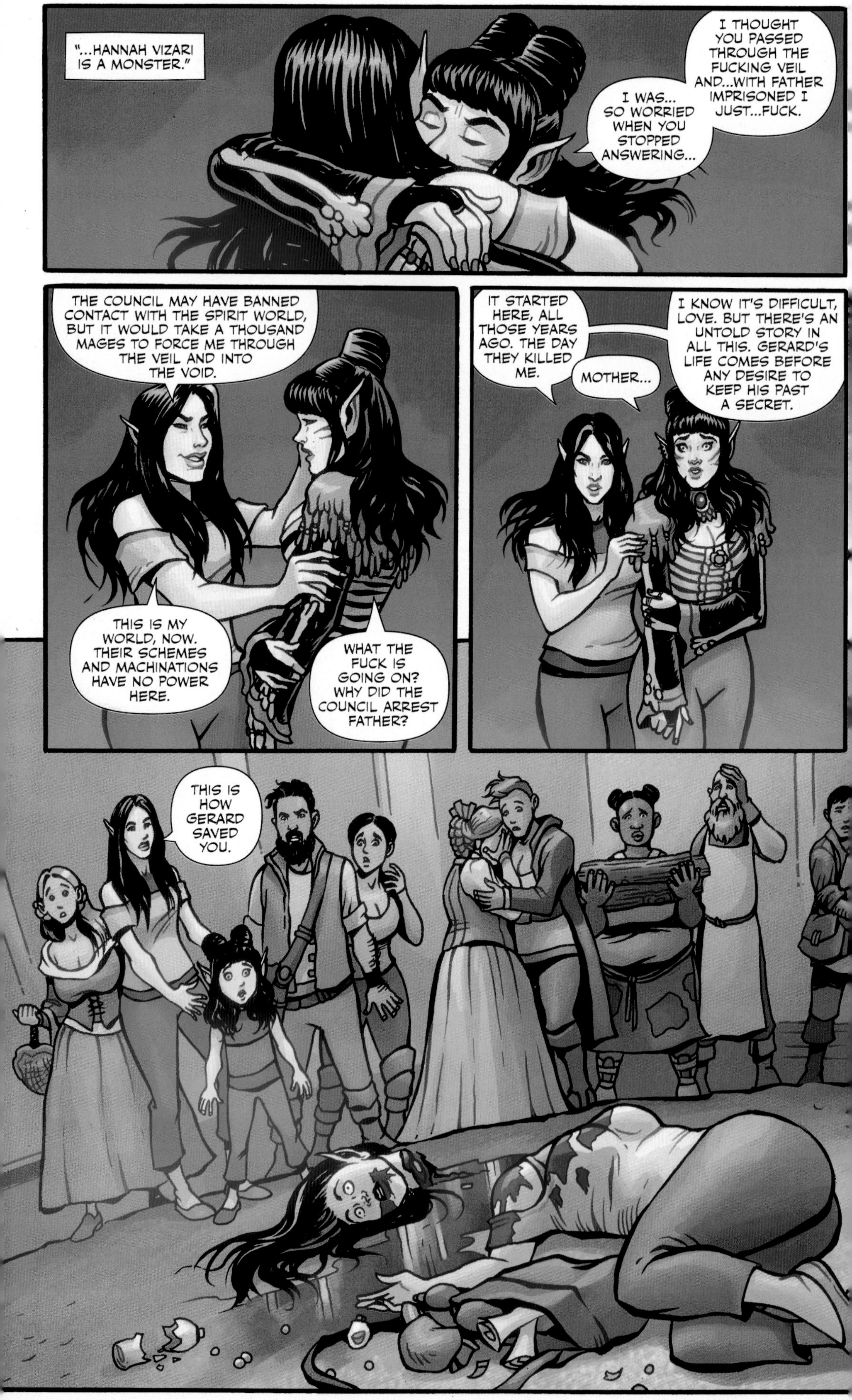

"...HANNAH VIZARI IS A MONSTER."
I WAS... SO WORRIED WHEN YOU STOPPED ANSWERING...
I THOUGHT YOU PASSED THROUGH THE FUCKING VEIL AND...WITH FATHER IMPRISONED I JUST...FUCK.
THE COUNCIL MAY HAVE BANNED CONTACT WITH THE SPIRIT WORLD, BUT IT WOULD TAKE A THOUSAND MAGES TO FORCE ME THROUGH THE VEIL AND INTO THE VOID.
THIS IS MY WORLD, NOW. THEIR SCHEMES AND MACHINATIONS HAVE NO POWER HERE.
WHAT THE FUCK IS GOING ON? WHY DID THE COUNCIL ARREST FATHER?
I KNOW IT'S DIFFICULT, LOVE. BUT THERE'S AN UNTOLD STORY IN ALL THIS. GERARD'S LIFE COMES BEFORE ANY DESIRE TO KEEP HIS PAST A SECRET.
MOTHER...
IT STARTED HERE, ALL THOSE YEARS AGO. THE DAY THEY KILLED ME.
THIS IS HOW GERARD SAVED YOU.

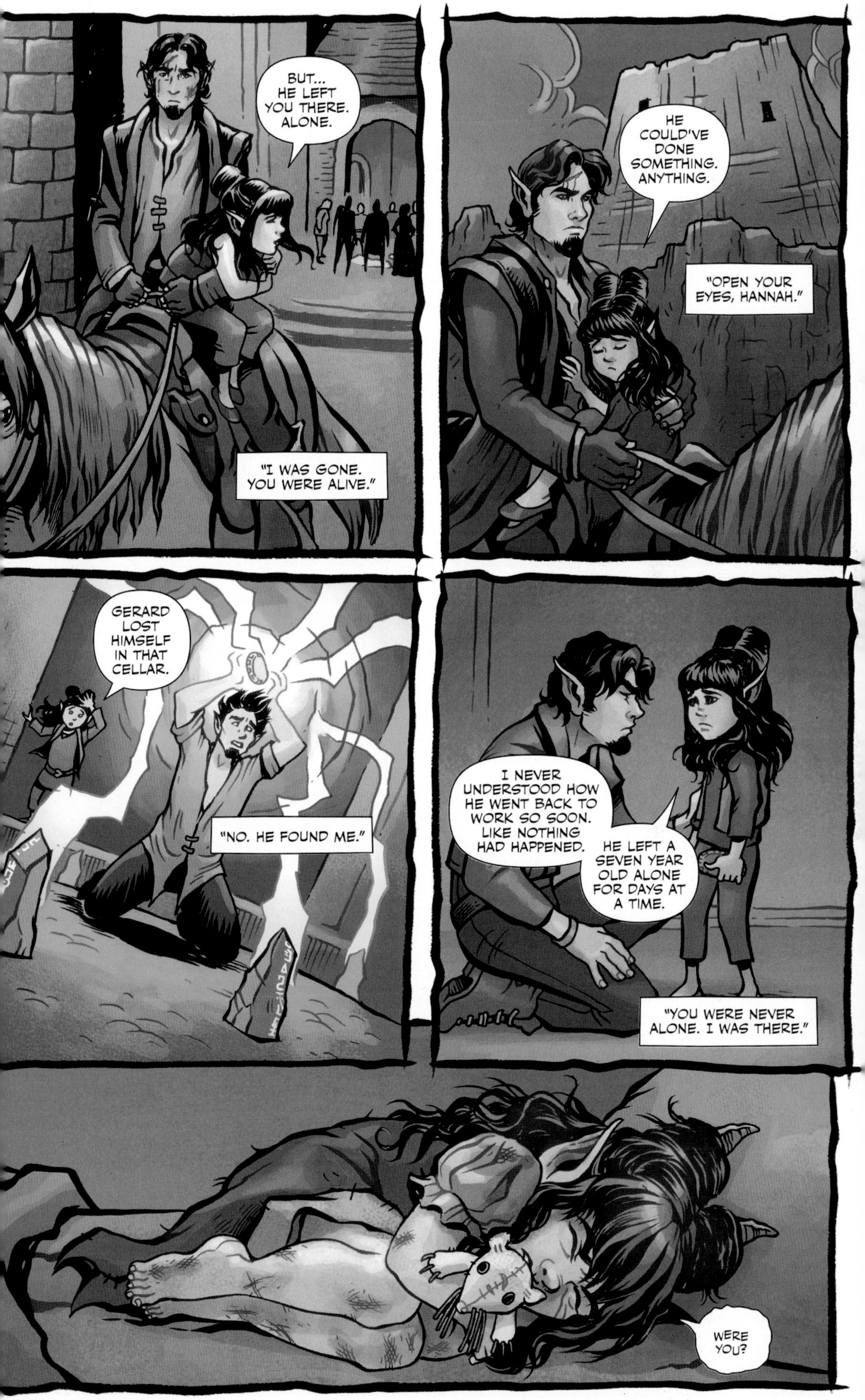
BUT... HE LEFT YOU THERE. ALONE.
"I WAS GONE. YOU WERE ALIVE."
HE COULD'VE DONE SOMETHING. ANYTHING.
"OPEN YOUR EYES, HANNAH."
GERARD LOST HIMSELF IN THAT CELLAR.
"NO. HE FOUND ME."
I NEVER UNDERSTOOD HOW HE WENT BACK TO WORK SO SOON. LIKE NOTHING HAD HAPPENED.
HE LEFT A SEVEN YEAR OLD ALONE FOR DAYS AT A TIME.
"YOU WERE NEVER ALONE. I WAS THERE."
WERE YOU?

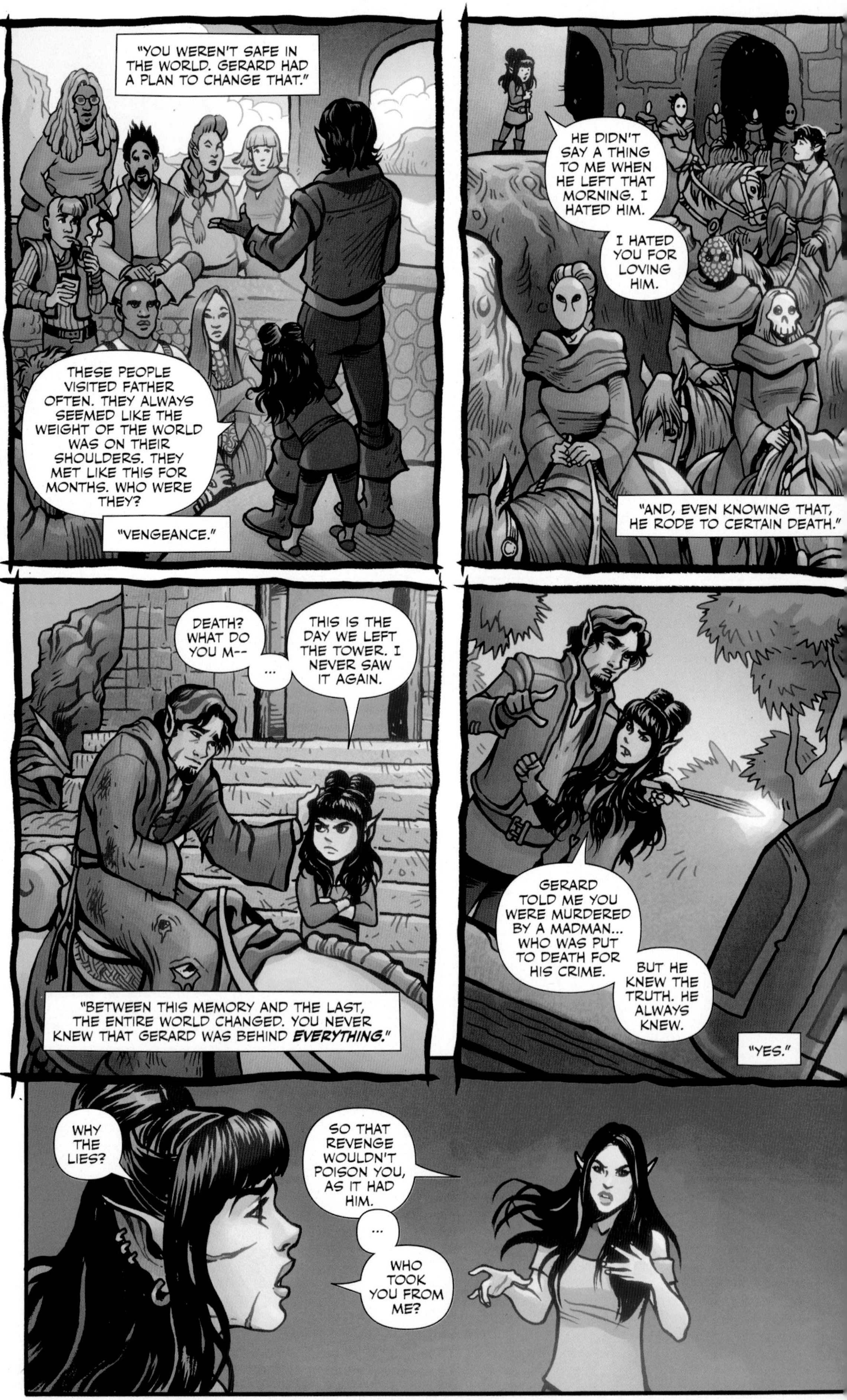
"YOU WEREN'T SAFE IN THE WORLD. GERARD HAD A PLAN TO CHANGE THAT."
THESE PEOPLE VISITED FATHER OFTEN. THEY ALWAYS SEEMED LIKE THE WEIGHT OF THE WORLD WAS ON THEIR SHOULDERS. THEY MET LIKE THIS FOR MONTHS. WHO WERE THEY?
"VENGEANCE."
HE DIDN'T SAY A THING TO ME WHEN HE LEFT THAT MORNING. I HATED HIM.
I HATED YOU FOR LOVING HIM.
"AND, EVEN KNOWING THAT, HE RODE TO CERTAIN DEATH."
DEATH? WHAT DO YOU M--
...
THIS IS THE DAY WE LEFT THE TOWER. I NEVER SAW IT AGAIN.
"BETWEEN THIS MEMORY AND THE LAST, THE ENTIRE WORLD CHANGED. YOU NEVER KNEW THAT GERARD WAS BEHIND *EVERYTHING.*"
GERARD TOLD ME YOU WERE MURDERED BY A MADMAN... WHO WAS PUT TO DEATH FOR HIS CRIME.
BUT HE KNEW THE TRUTH. HE ALWAYS KNEW.
"YES."
WHY THE LIES?
SO THAT REVENGE WOULDN'T POISON YOU, AS IT HAD HIM.
...
WHO TOOK YOU FROM ME?

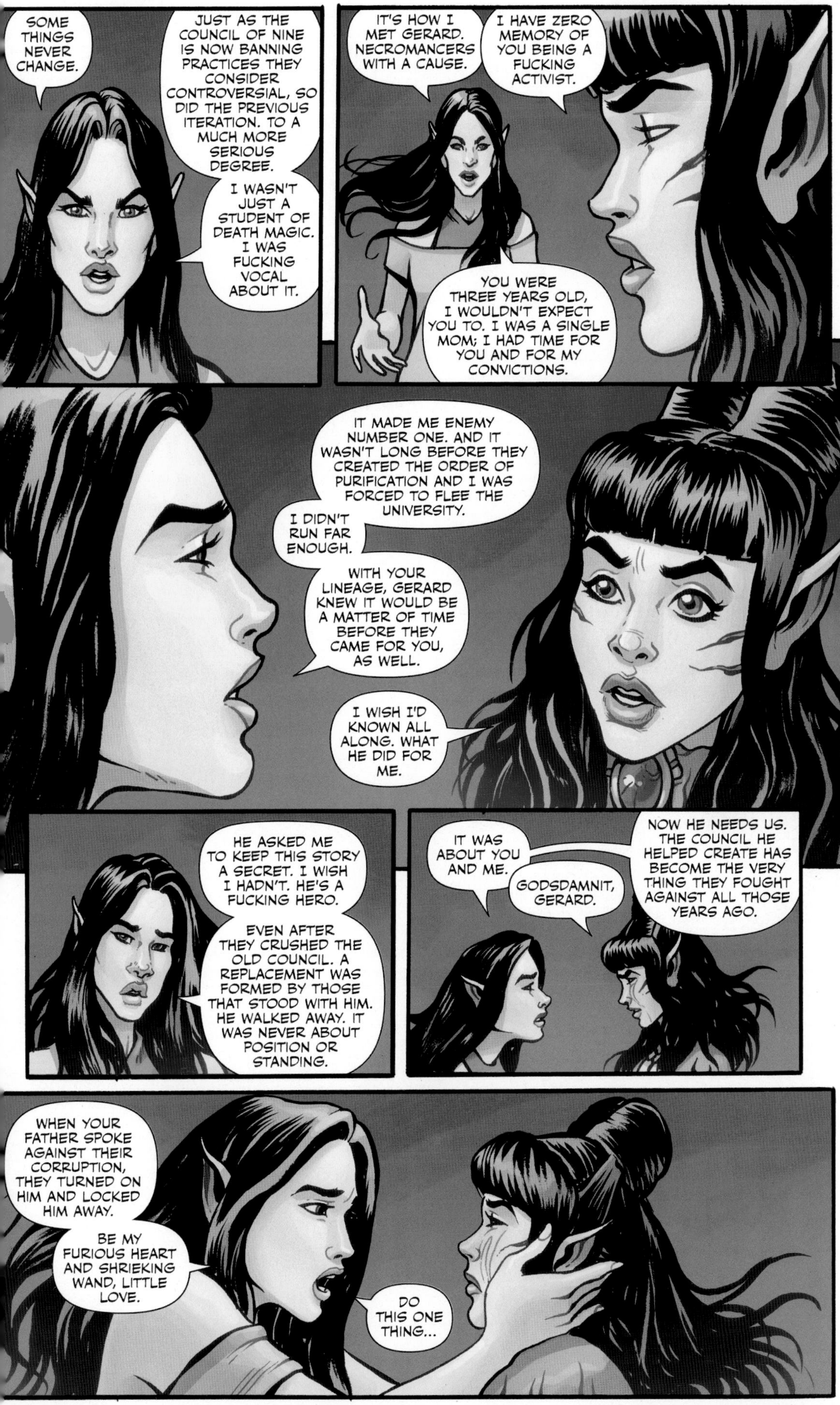
SOME THINGS NEVER CHANGE.
JUST AS THE COUNCIL OF NINE IS NOW BANNING PRACTICES THEY CONSIDER CONTROVERSIAL, SO DID THE PREVIOUS ITERATION. TO A MUCH MORE SERIOUS DEGREE.
I WASN'T JUST A STUDENT OF DEATH MAGIC. I WAS FUCKING VOCAL ABOUT IT.
IT'S HOW I MET GERARD. NECROMANCERS WITH A CAUSE.
I HAVE ZERO MEMORY OF YOU BEING A FUCKING ACTIVIST.
YOU WERE THREE YEARS OLD, I WOULDN'T EXPECT YOU TO. I WAS A SINGLE MOM; I HAD TIME FOR YOU AND FOR MY CONVICTIONS.
IT MADE ME ENEMY NUMBER ONE. AND IT WASN'T LONG BEFORE THEY CREATED THE ORDER OF PURIFICATION AND I WAS FORCED TO FLEE THE UNIVERSITY.
I DIDN'T RUN FAR ENOUGH.
WITH YOUR LINEAGE, GERARD KNEW IT WOULD BE A MATTER OF TIME BEFORE THEY CAME FOR YOU, AS WELL.
I WISH I'D KNOWN ALL ALONG. WHAT HE DID FOR ME.
HE ASKED ME TO KEEP THIS STORY A SECRET. I WISH I HADN'T. HE'S A FUCKING HERO.
EVEN AFTER THEY CRUSHED THE OLD COUNCIL. A REPLACEMENT WAS FORMED BY THOSE THAT STOOD WITH HIM. HE WALKED AWAY. IT WAS NEVER ABOUT POSITION OR STANDING.
IT WAS ABOUT YOU AND ME.
GODSDAMNIT, GERARD.
NOW HE NEEDS US. THE COUNCIL HE HELPED CREATE HAS BECOME THE VERY THING THEY FOUGHT AGAINST ALL THOSE YEARS AGO.
WHEN YOUR FATHER SPOKE AGAINST THEIR CORRUPTION, THEY TURNED ON HIM AND LOCKED HIM AWAY.
BE MY FURIOUS HEART AND SHRIEKING WAND, LITTLE LOVE.
DO THIS ONE THING...

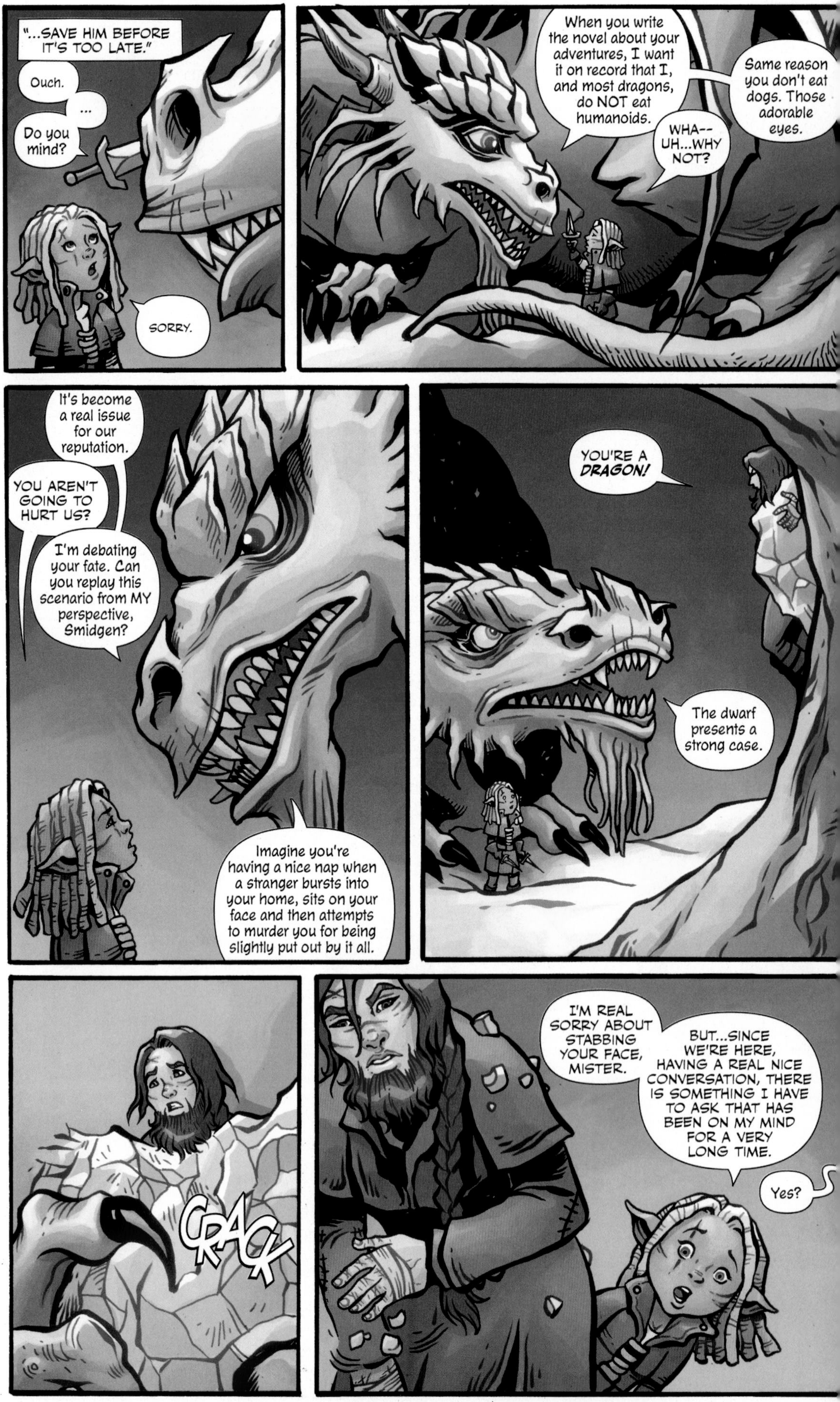
"...SAVE HIM BEFORE IT'S TOO LATE."
Ouch.
...
Do you mind?
SORRY.
When you write the novel about your adventures, I want it on record that I, and most dragons, do NOT eat humanoids.
WHA-- UH...WHY NOT?
Same reason you don't eat dogs. Those adorable eyes.
It's become a real issue for our reputation.
YOU AREN'T GOING TO HURT US?
I'm debating your fate. Can you replay this scenario from MY perspective, Smidgen?
Imagine you're having a nice nap when a stranger bursts into your home, sits on your face and then attempts to murder you for being slightly put out by it all.
YOU'RE A DRAGON!
The dwarf presents a strong case.
CRACK
I'M REAL SORRY ABOUT STABBING YOUR FACE, MISTER.
BUT...SINCE WE'RE HERE, HAVING A REAL NICE CONVERSATION, THERE IS SOMETHING I HAVE TO ASK THAT HAS BEEN ON MY MIND FOR A VERY LONG TIME.
Yes?

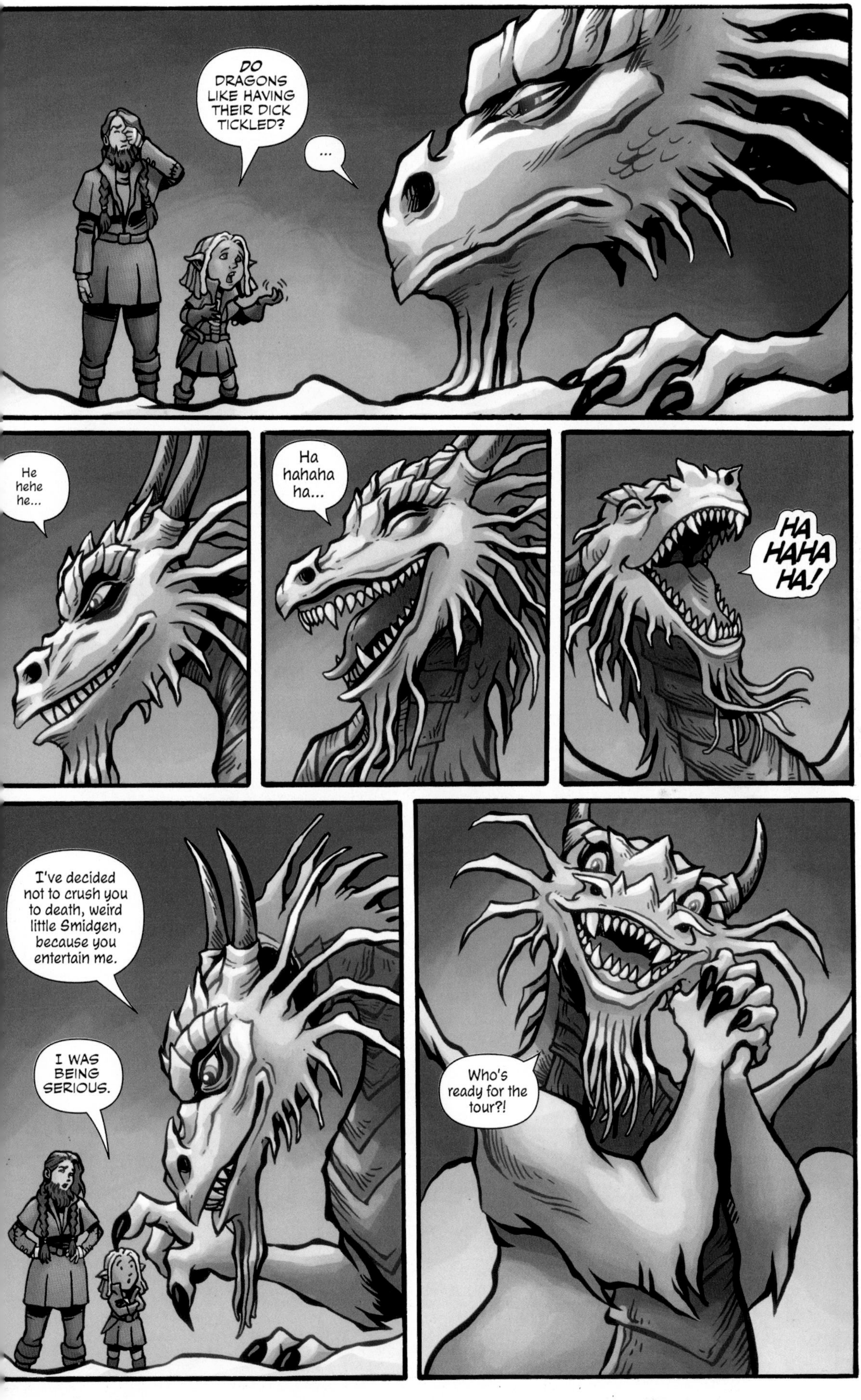
DO DRAGONS LIKE HAVING THEIR DICK TICKLED?
...
He hehe he...
Ha hahaha ha...
HA HAHA HA!
I've decided not to crush you to death, weird little Smidgen, because you entertain me.
I WAS BEING SERIOUS.
Who's ready for the tour?!

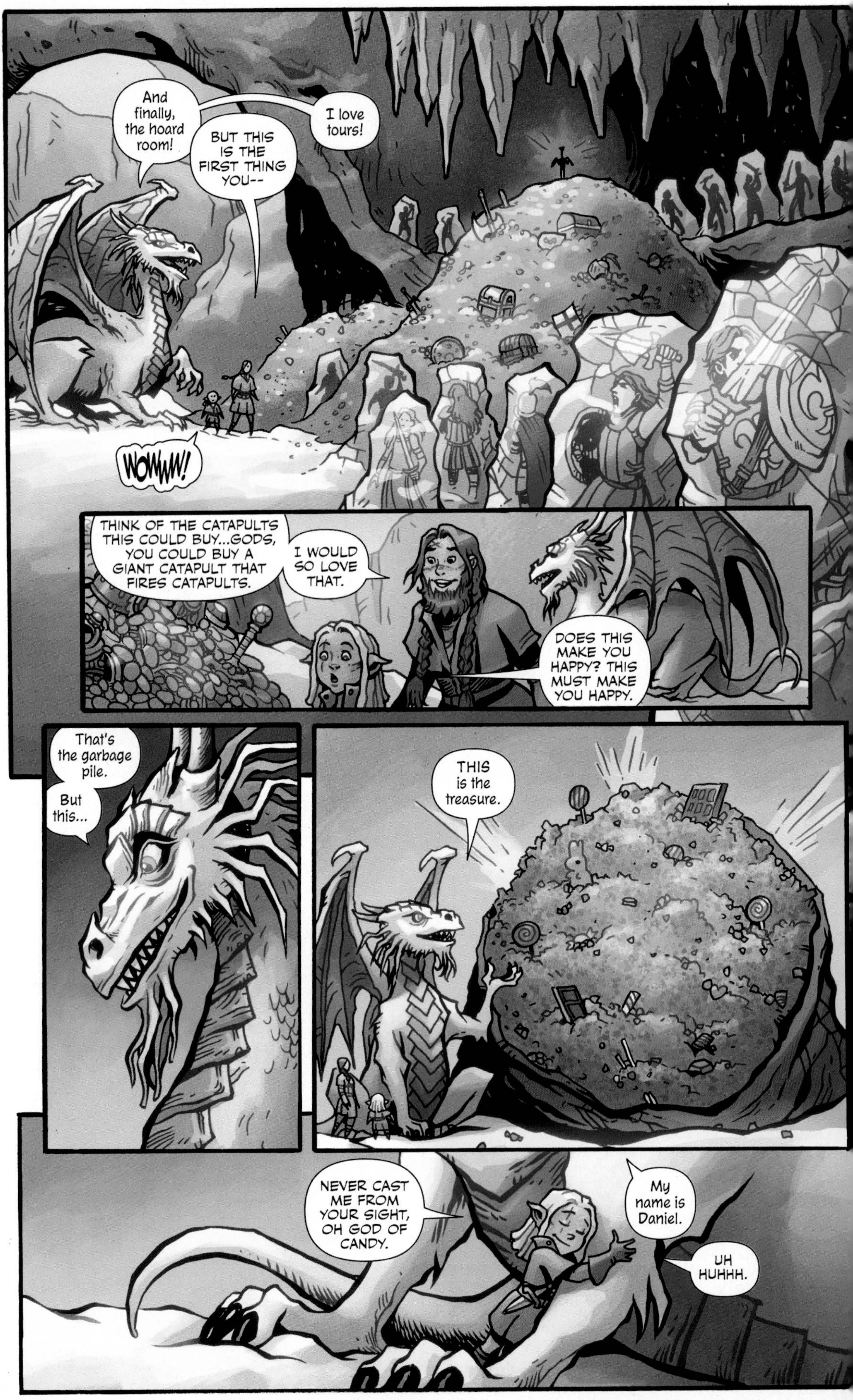
And finally, the hoard room!
BUT THIS IS THE FIRST THING YOU--
I love tours!
WOWWW!
THINK OF THE CATAPULTS THIS COULD BUY...GODS, YOU COULD BUY A GIANT CATAPULT THAT FIRES CATAPULTS.
I WOULD SO LOVE THAT.
DOES THIS MAKE YOU HAPPY? THIS MUST MAKE YOU HAPPY.
That's the garbage pile.
But this...
THIS is the treasure.
NEVER CAST ME FROM YOUR SIGHT, OH GOD OF CANDY.
My name is Daniel.
UH HUHHH.

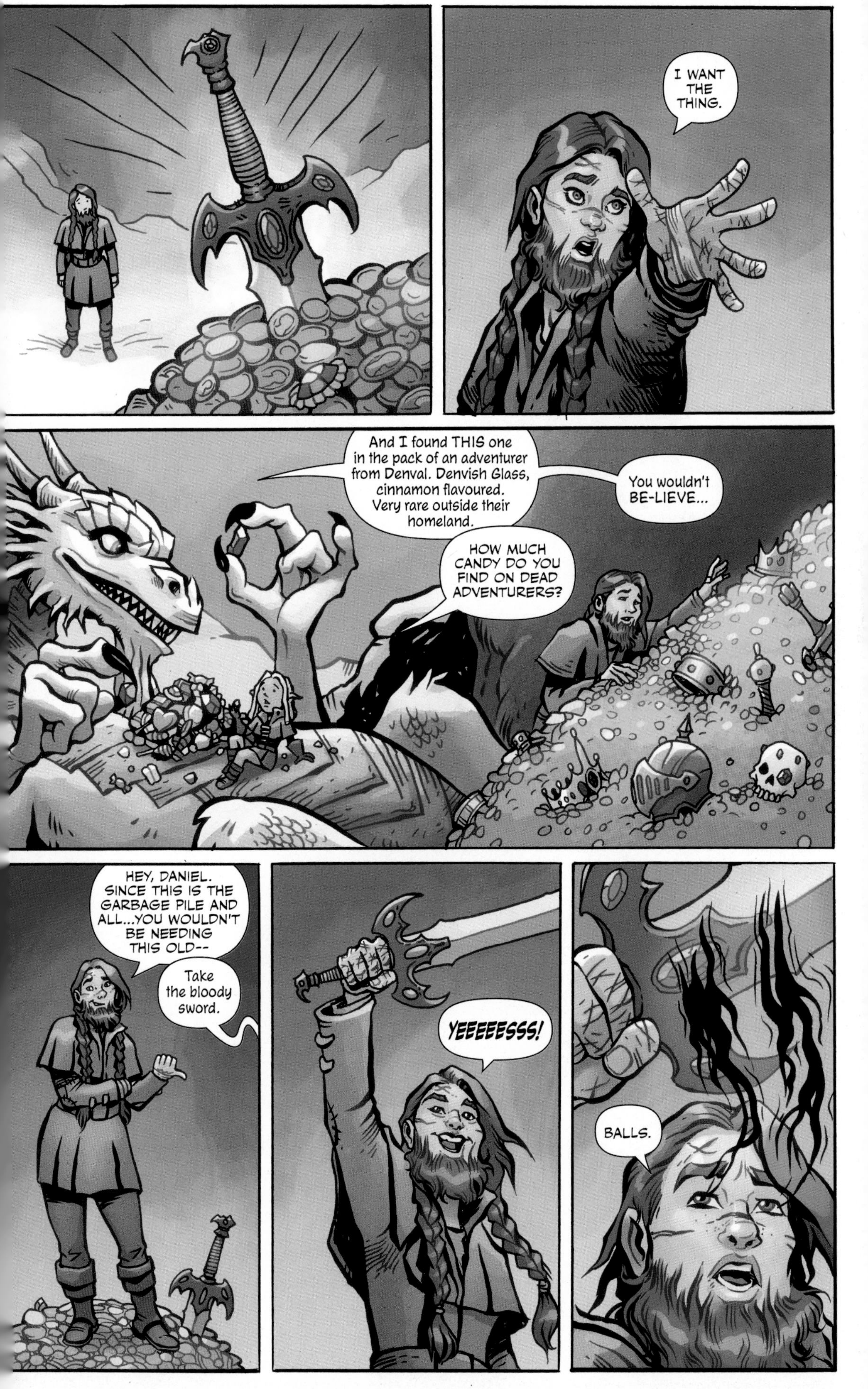
I WANT THE THING.
And I found THIS one in the pack of an adventurer from Denval. Denvish Glass, cinnamon flavoured. Very rare outside their homeland.
You wouldn't BE-LIEVE...
HOW MUCH CANDY DO YOU FIND ON DEAD ADVENTURERS?
HEY, DANIEL. SINCE THIS IS THE GARBAGE PILE AND ALL...YOU WOULDN'T BE NEEDING THIS OLD--
Take the bloody sword.
YEEEEESSS!
BALLS.

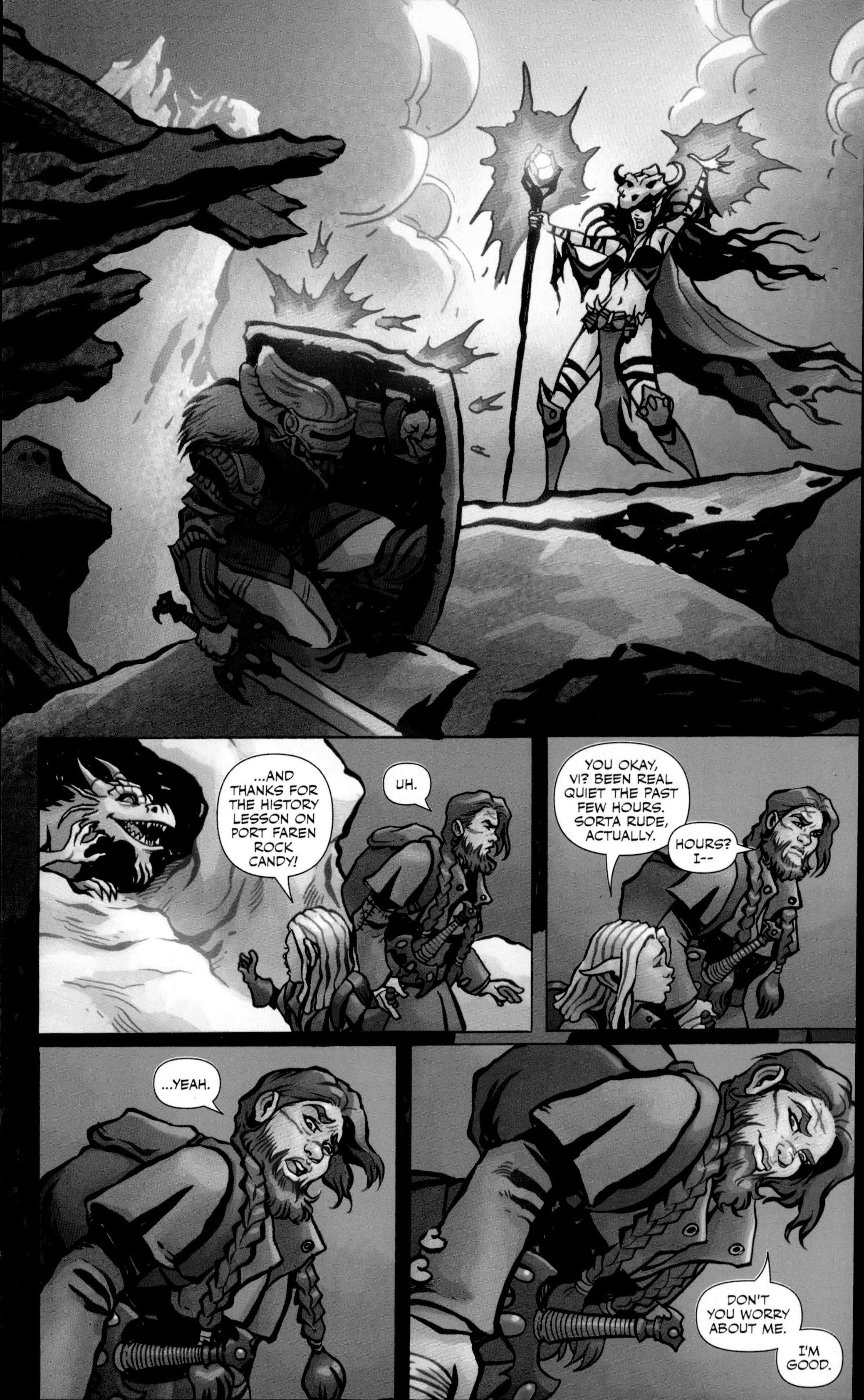
...AND THANKS FOR THE HISTORY LESSON ON PORT FAREN ROCK CANDY!
UH.
YOU OKAY, VI? BEEN REAL QUIET THE PAST FEW HOURS. SORTA RUDE, ACTUALLY.
HOURS? I--
...YEAH.
DON'T YOU WORRY ABOUT ME.
I'M GOOD.

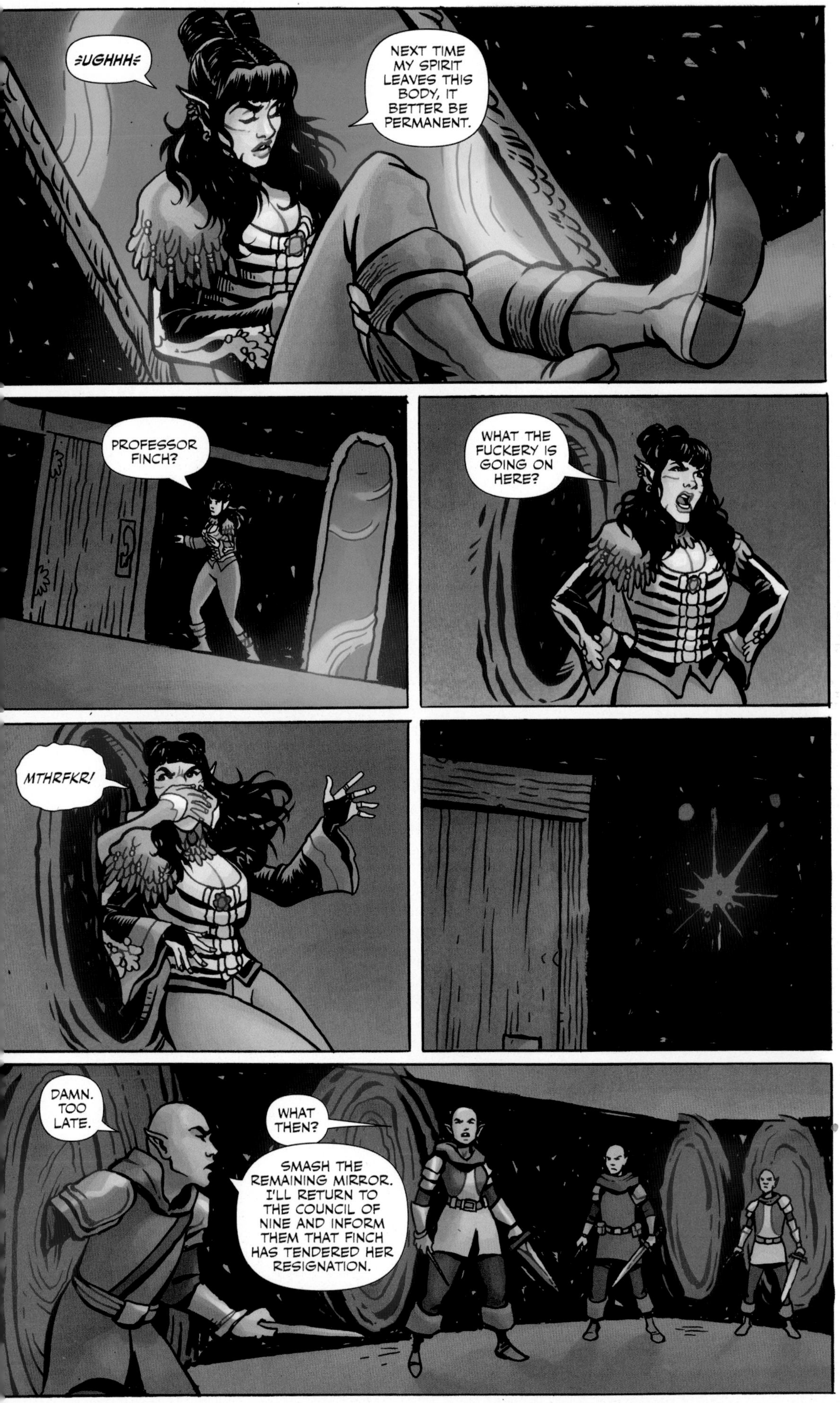

≠UGHHH≠
NEXT TIME MY SPIRIT LEAVES THIS BODY, IT BETTER BE PERMANENT.
PROFESSOR FINCH?
WHAT THE FUCKERY IS GOING ON HERE?
MTHRFKR!
DAMN. TOO LATE.
WHAT THEN?
SMASH THE REMAINING MIRROR. I'LL RETURN TO THE COUNCIL OF NINE AND INFORM THEM THAT FINCH HAS TENDERED HER RESIGNATION.

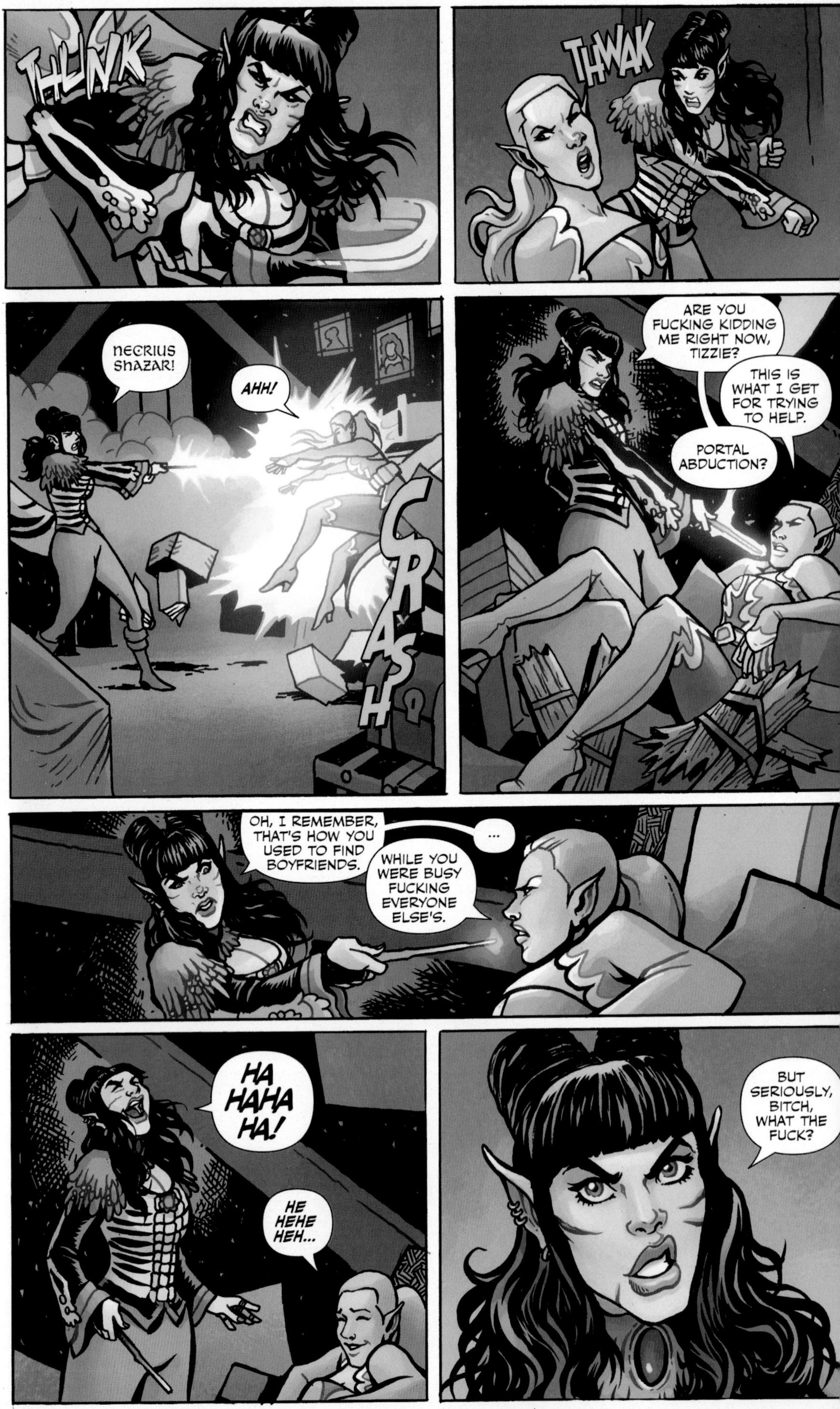
THUNK
THWAK
NECRIUS SHAZAR!
AHH!
CRASH
ARE YOU FUCKING KIDDING ME RIGHT NOW, TIZZIE?
THIS IS WHAT I GET FOR TRYING TO HELP.
PORTAL ABDUCTION?
OH, I REMEMBER, THAT'S HOW YOU USED TO FIND BOYFRIENDS.
...
WHILE YOU WERE BUSY FUCKING EVERYONE ELSE'S.
HA HAHAHA HA!
HE HEHE HEH...
BUT SERIOUSLY, BITCH, WHAT THE FUCK?

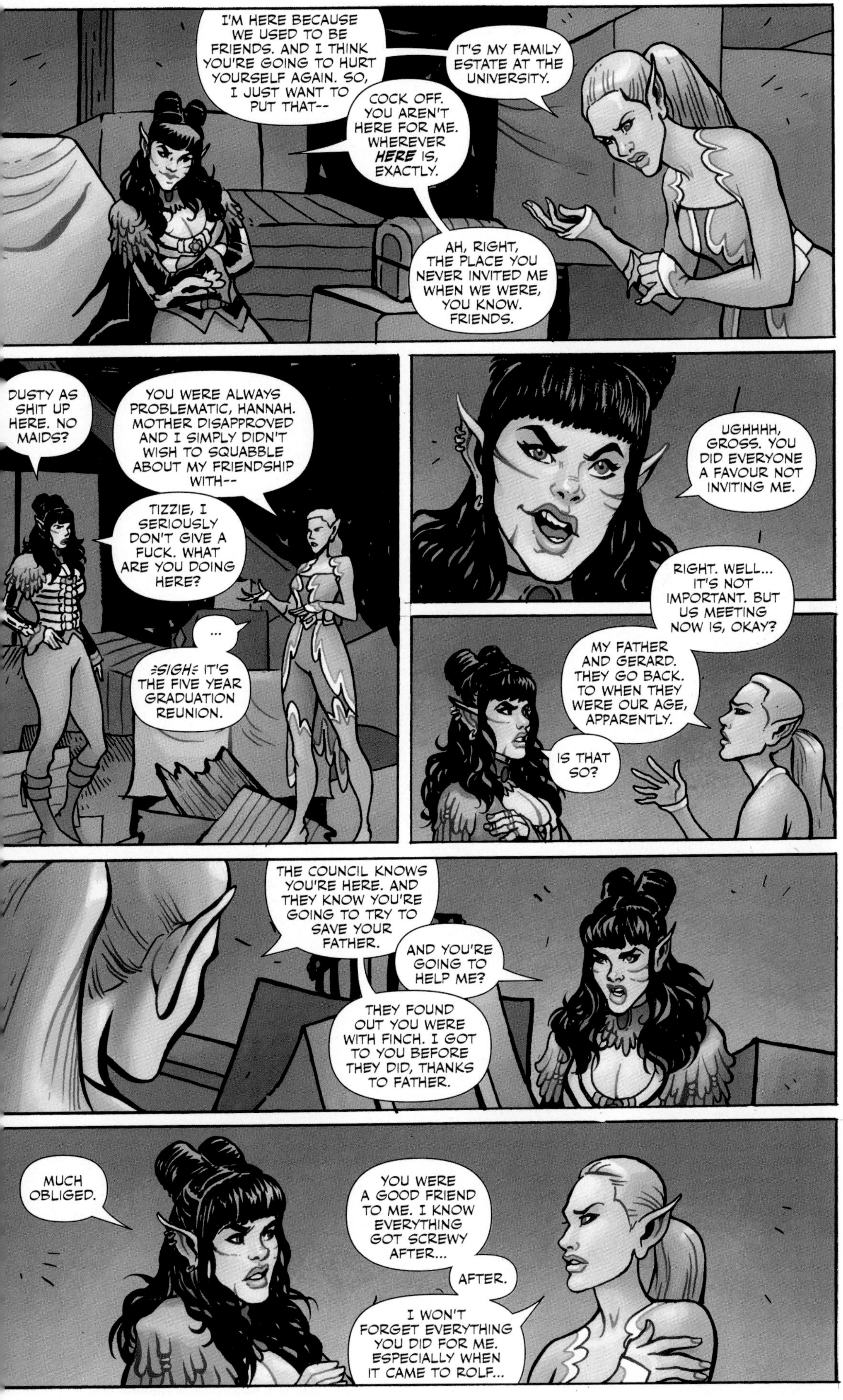
I'M HERE BECAUSE WE USED TO BE FRIENDS. AND I THINK YOU'RE GOING TO HURT YOURSELF AGAIN. SO, I JUST WANT TO PUT THAT--
IT'S MY FAMILY ESTATE AT THE UNIVERSITY.
COCK OFF. YOU AREN'T HERE FOR ME. WHEREVER *HERE* IS, EXACTLY.
AH, RIGHT, THE PLACE YOU NEVER INVITED ME WHEN WE WERE, YOU KNOW. FRIENDS.
DUSTY AS SHIT UP HERE. NO MAIDS?
YOU WERE ALWAYS PROBLEMATIC, HANNAH. MOTHER DISAPPROVED AND I SIMPLY DIDN'T WISH TO SQUABBLE ABOUT MY FRIENDSHIP WITH--
TIZZIE, I SERIOUSLY DON'T GIVE A FUCK. WHAT ARE YOU DOING HERE?
...
SIGH IT'S THE FIVE YEAR GRADUATION REUNION.
UGHHHH, GROSS. YOU DID EVERYONE A FAVOUR NOT INVITING ME.
RIGHT. WELL... IT'S NOT IMPORTANT. BUT US MEETING NOW IS, OKAY?
MY FATHER AND GERARD. THEY GO BACK. TO WHEN THEY WERE OUR AGE, APPARENTLY.
IS THAT SO?
THE COUNCIL KNOWS YOU'RE HERE. AND THEY KNOW YOU'RE GOING TO TRY TO SAVE YOUR FATHER.
AND YOU'RE GOING TO HELP ME?
THEY FOUND OUT YOU WERE WITH FINCH. I GOT TO YOU BEFORE THEY DID, THANKS TO FATHER.
MUCH OBLIGED.
YOU WERE A GOOD FRIEND TO ME. I KNOW EVERYTHING GOT SCREWY AFTER...
AFTER.
I WON'T FORGET EVERYTHING YOU DID FOR ME. ESPECIALLY WHEN IT CAME TO ROLF...

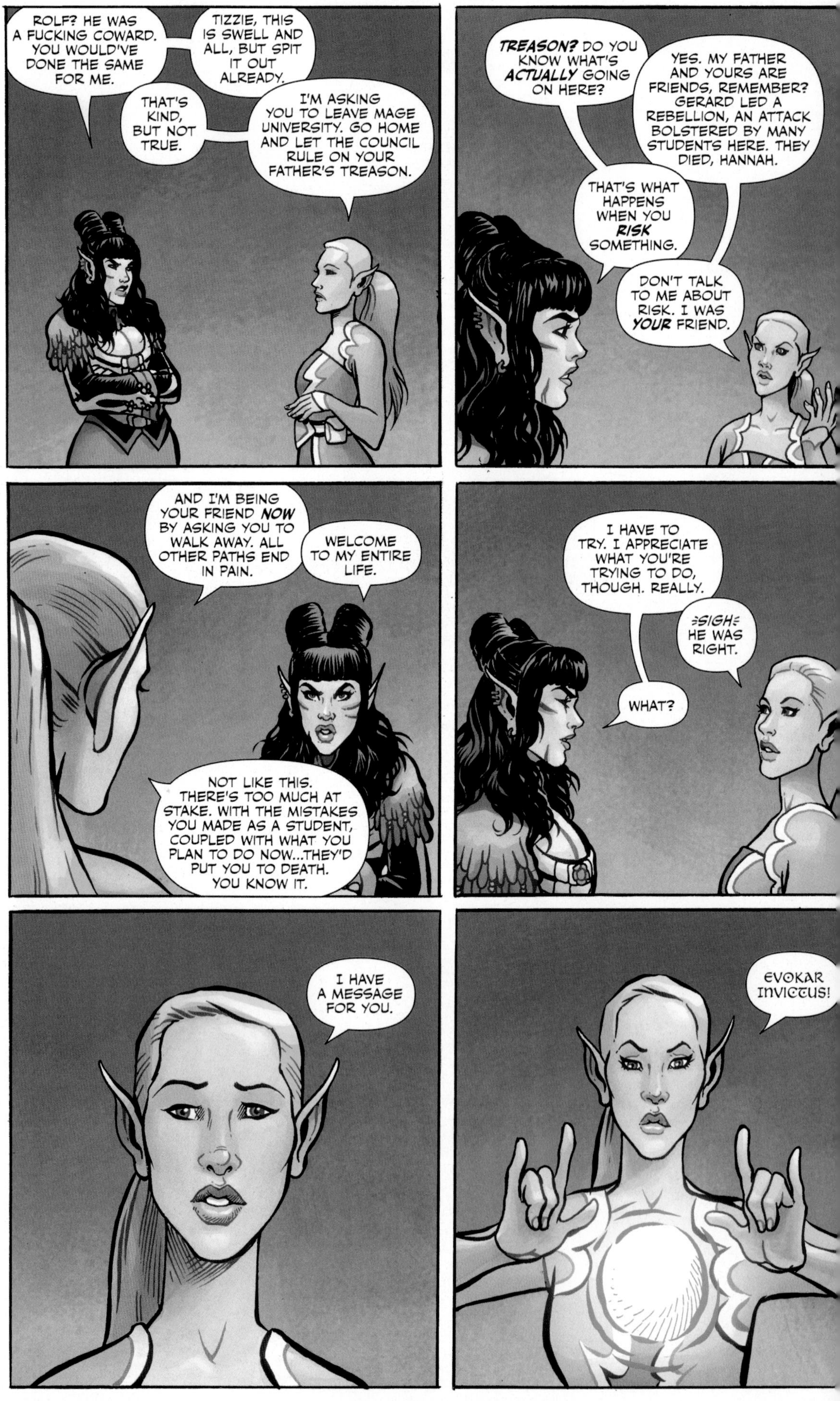
ROLF? HE WAS A FUCKING COWARD. YOU WOULD'VE DONE THE SAME FOR ME.
TIZZIE, THIS IS SWELL AND ALL, BUT SPIT IT OUT ALREADY.
THAT'S KIND, BUT NOT TRUE.
I'M ASKING YOU TO LEAVE MAGE UNIVERSITY. GO HOME AND LET THE COUNCIL RULE ON YOUR FATHER'S TREASON.
TREASON? DO YOU KNOW WHAT'S ACTUALLY GOING ON HERE?
YES. MY FATHER AND YOURS ARE FRIENDS, REMEMBER? GERARD LED A REBELLION, AN ATTACK BOLSTERED BY MANY STUDENTS HERE. THEY DIED, HANNAH.
THAT'S WHAT HAPPENS WHEN YOU RISK SOMETHING.
DON'T TALK TO ME ABOUT RISK. I WAS YOUR FRIEND.
AND I'M BEING YOUR FRIEND NOW BY ASKING YOU TO WALK AWAY. ALL OTHER PATHS END IN PAIN.
WELCOME TO MY ENTIRE LIFE.
NOT LIKE THIS. THERE'S TOO MUCH AT STAKE. WITH THE MISTAKES YOU MADE AS A STUDENT, COUPLED WITH WHAT YOU PLAN TO DO NOW...THEY'D PUT YOU TO DEATH. YOU KNOW IT.
I HAVE TO TRY. I APPRECIATE WHAT YOU'RE TRYING TO DO, THOUGH. REALLY.
SIGH HE WAS RIGHT.
WHAT?
I HAVE A MESSAGE FOR YOU.
EVOKAR INVICTUS!

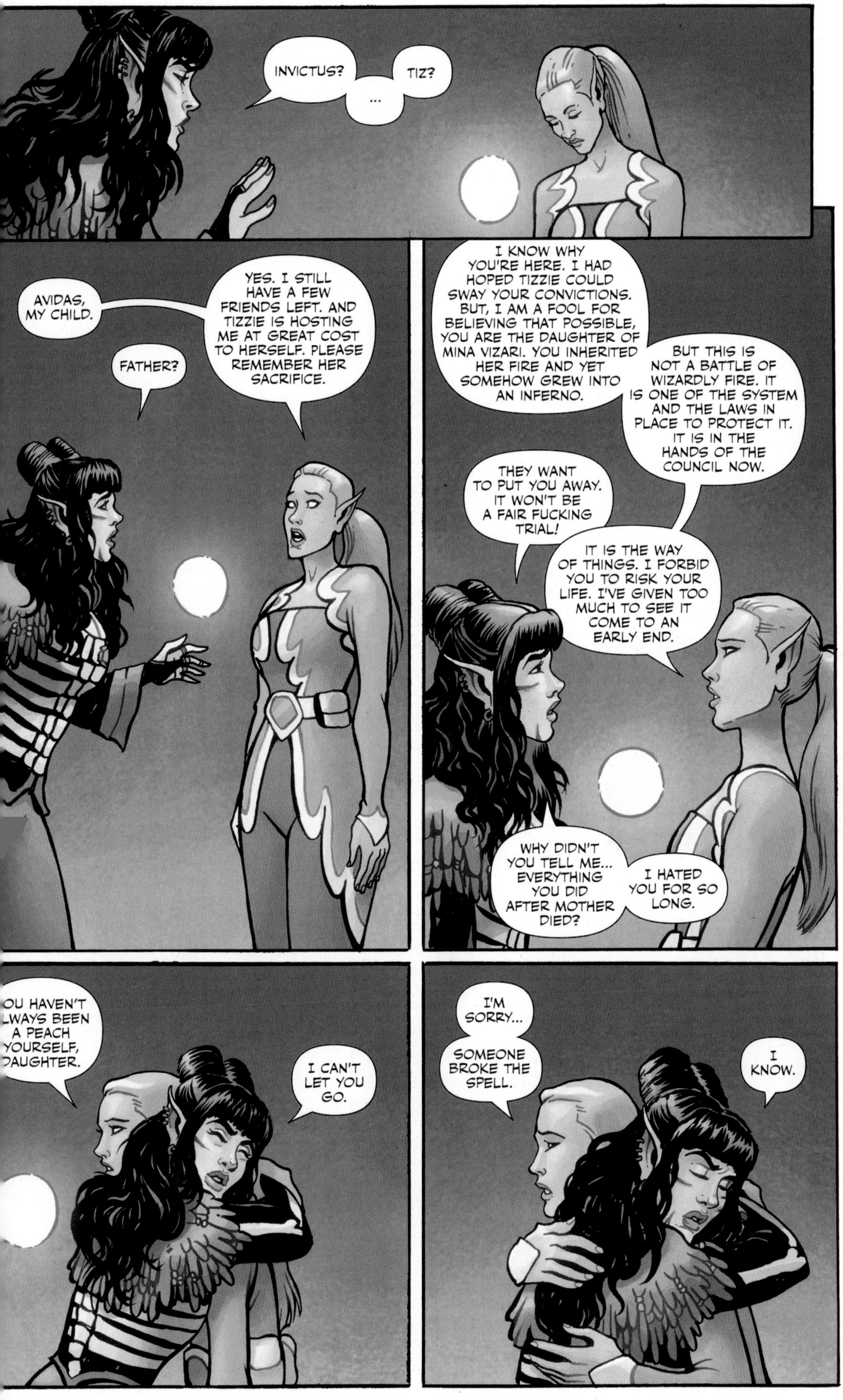
INVICTUS?
...
TIZ?
AVIDAS, MY CHILD.
FATHER?
YES. I STILL HAVE A FEW FRIENDS LEFT. AND TIZZIE IS HOSTING ME AT GREAT COST TO HERSELF. PLEASE REMEMBER HER SACRIFICE.
I KNOW WHY YOU'RE HERE. I HAD HOPED TIZZIE COULD SWAY YOUR CONVICTIONS. BUT, I AM A FOOL FOR BELIEVING THAT POSSIBLE, YOU ARE THE DAUGHTER OF MINA VIZARI. YOU INHERITED HER FIRE AND YET SOMEHOW GREW INTO AN INFERNO.
BUT THIS IS NOT A BATTLE OF WIZARDLY FIRE. IT IS ONE OF THE SYSTEM AND THE LAWS IN PLACE TO PROTECT IT. IT IS IN THE HANDS OF THE COUNCIL NOW.
THEY WANT TO PUT YOU AWAY. IT WON'T BE A FAIR FUCKING TRIAL!
IT IS THE WAY OF THINGS. I FORBID YOU TO RISK YOUR LIFE. I'VE GIVEN TOO MUCH TO SEE IT COME TO AN EARLY END.
WHY DIDN'T YOU TELL ME... EVERYTHING YOU DID AFTER MOTHER DIED?
I HATED YOU FOR SO LONG.
OU HAVEN'T LWAYS BEEN A PEACH YOURSELF, DAUGHTER.
I CAN'T LET YOU GO.
I'M SORRY...
SOMEONE BROKE THE SPELL.
I KNOW.

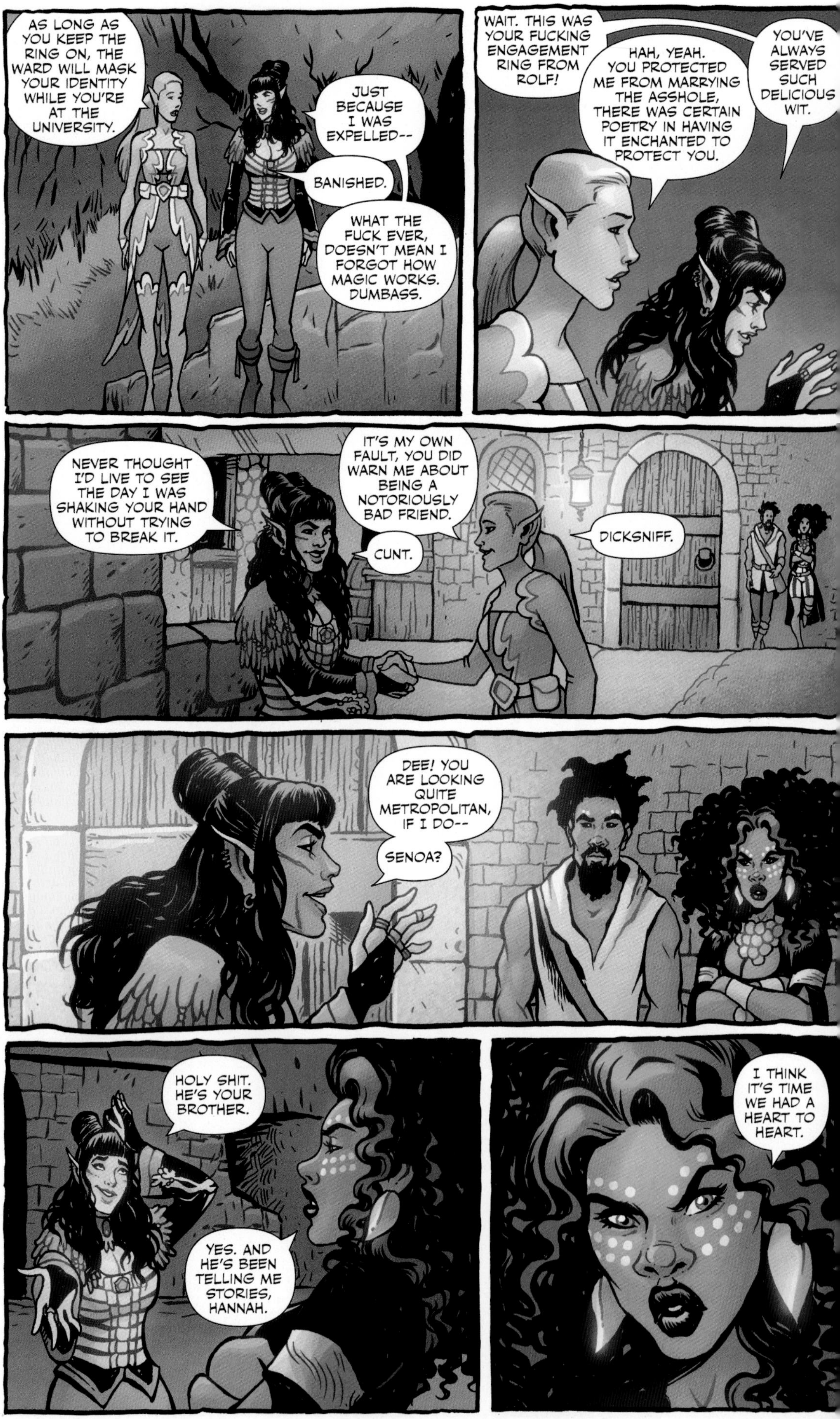
AS LONG AS YOU KEEP THE RING ON, THE WARD WILL MASK YOUR IDENTITY WHILE YOU'RE AT THE UNIVERSITY.
JUST BECAUSE I WAS EXPELLED--
BANISHED.
WHAT THE FUCK EVER, DOESN'T MEAN I FORGOT HOW MAGIC WORKS. DUMBASS.
WAIT. THIS WAS YOUR FUCKING ENGAGEMENT RING FROM ROLF!
HAH, YEAH. YOU PROTECTED ME FROM MARRYING THE ASSHOLE, THERE WAS CERTAIN POETRY IN HAVING IT ENCHANTED TO PROTECT YOU.
YOU'VE ALWAYS SERVED SUCH DELICIOUS WIT.
NEVER THOUGHT I'D LIVE TO SEE THE DAY I WAS SHAKING YOUR HAND WITHOUT TRYING TO BREAK IT.
IT'S MY OWN FAULT, YOU DID WARN ME ABOUT BEING A NOTORIOUSLY BAD FRIEND.
CUNT.
DICKSNIFF.
DEE! YOU ARE LOOKING QUITE METROPOLITAN, IF I DO--
SENOA?
HOLY SHIT. HE'S YOUR BROTHER.
YES. AND HE'S BEEN TELLING ME STORIES, HANNAH.
I THINK IT'S TIME WE HAD A HEART TO HEART.

CHAPTER FIFTEEN

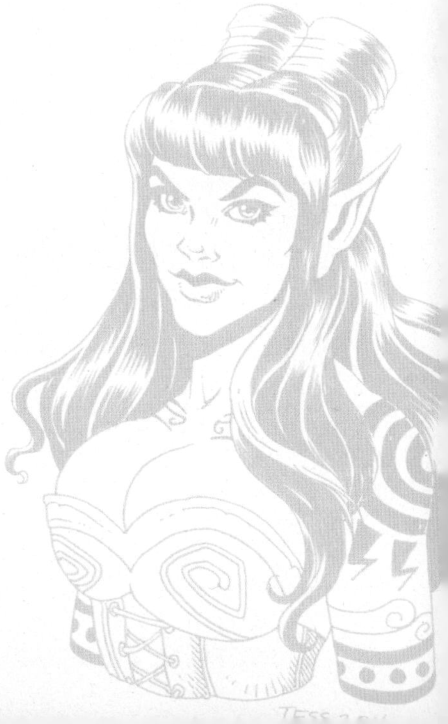

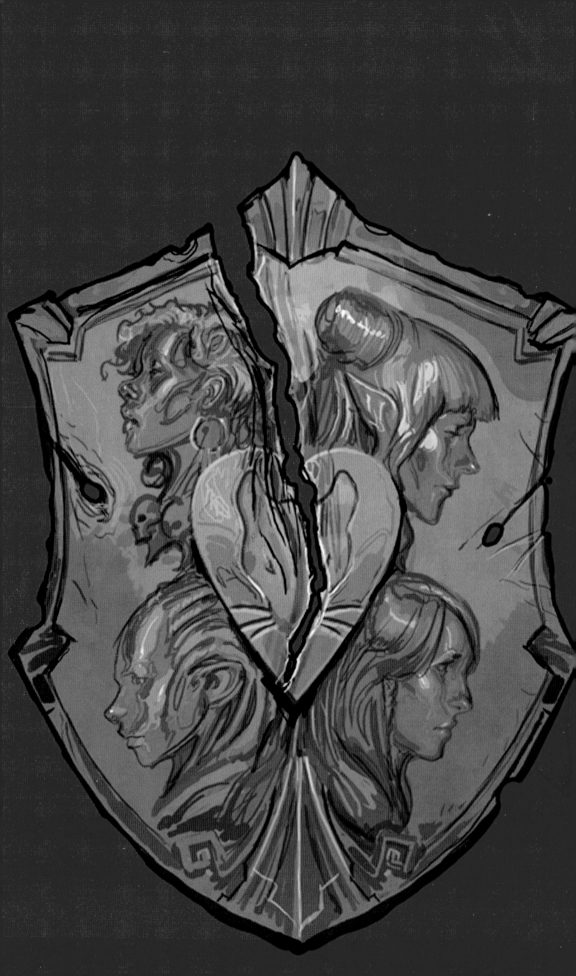

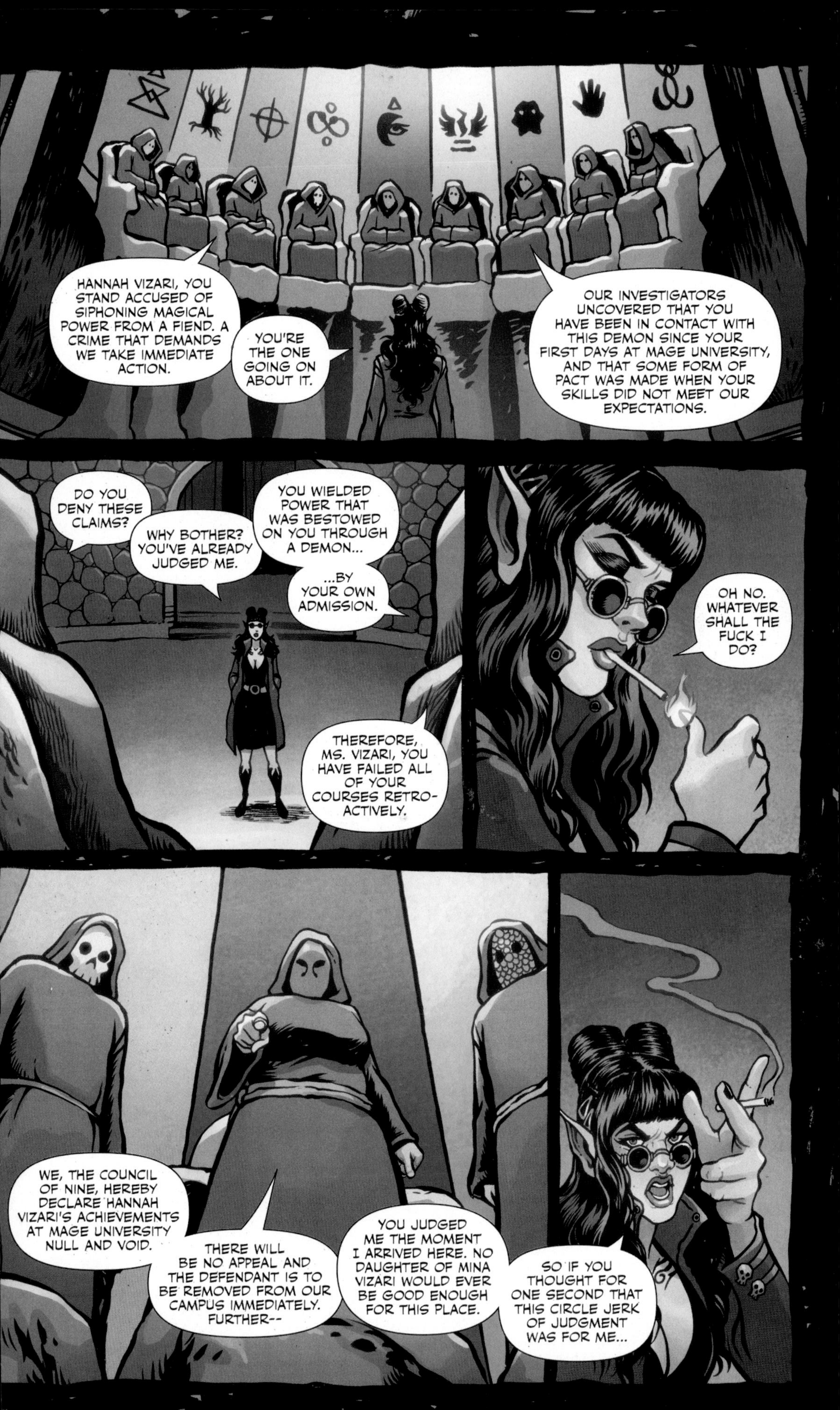
HANNAH VIZARI, YOU STAND ACCUSED OF SIPHONING MAGICAL POWER FROM A FIEND. A CRIME THAT DEMANDS WE TAKE IMMEDIATE ACTION.
YOU'RE THE ONE GOING ON ABOUT IT.
OUR INVESTIGATORS UNCOVERED THAT YOU HAVE BEEN IN CONTACT WITH THIS DEMON SINCE YOUR FIRST DAYS AT MAGE UNIVERSITY, AND THAT SOME FORM OF PACT WAS MADE WHEN YOUR SKILLS DID NOT MEET OUR EXPECTATIONS.
DO YOU DENY THESE CLAIMS?
WHY BOTHER? YOU'VE ALREADY JUDGED ME.
YOU WIELDED POWER THAT WAS BESTOWED ON YOU THROUGH A DEMON...
...BY YOUR OWN ADMISSION.
THEREFORE, MS. VIZARI, YOU HAVE FAILED ALL OF YOUR COURSES RETRO-ACTIVELY.
OH NO. WHATEVER SHALL THE FUCK I DO?
WE, THE COUNCIL OF NINE, HEREBY DECLARE HANNAH VIZARI'S ACHIEVEMENTS AT MAGE UNIVERSITY NULL AND VOID.
THERE WILL BE NO APPEAL AND THE DEFENDANT IS TO BE REMOVED FROM OUR CAMPUS IMMEDIATELY. FURTHER--
YOU JUDGED ME THE MOMENT I ARRIVED HERE. NO DAUGHTER OF MINA VIZARI WOULD EVER BE GOOD ENOUGH FOR THIS PLACE.
SO IF YOU THOUGHT FOR ONE SECOND THAT THIS CIRCLE JERK OF JUDGMENT WAS FOR ME...

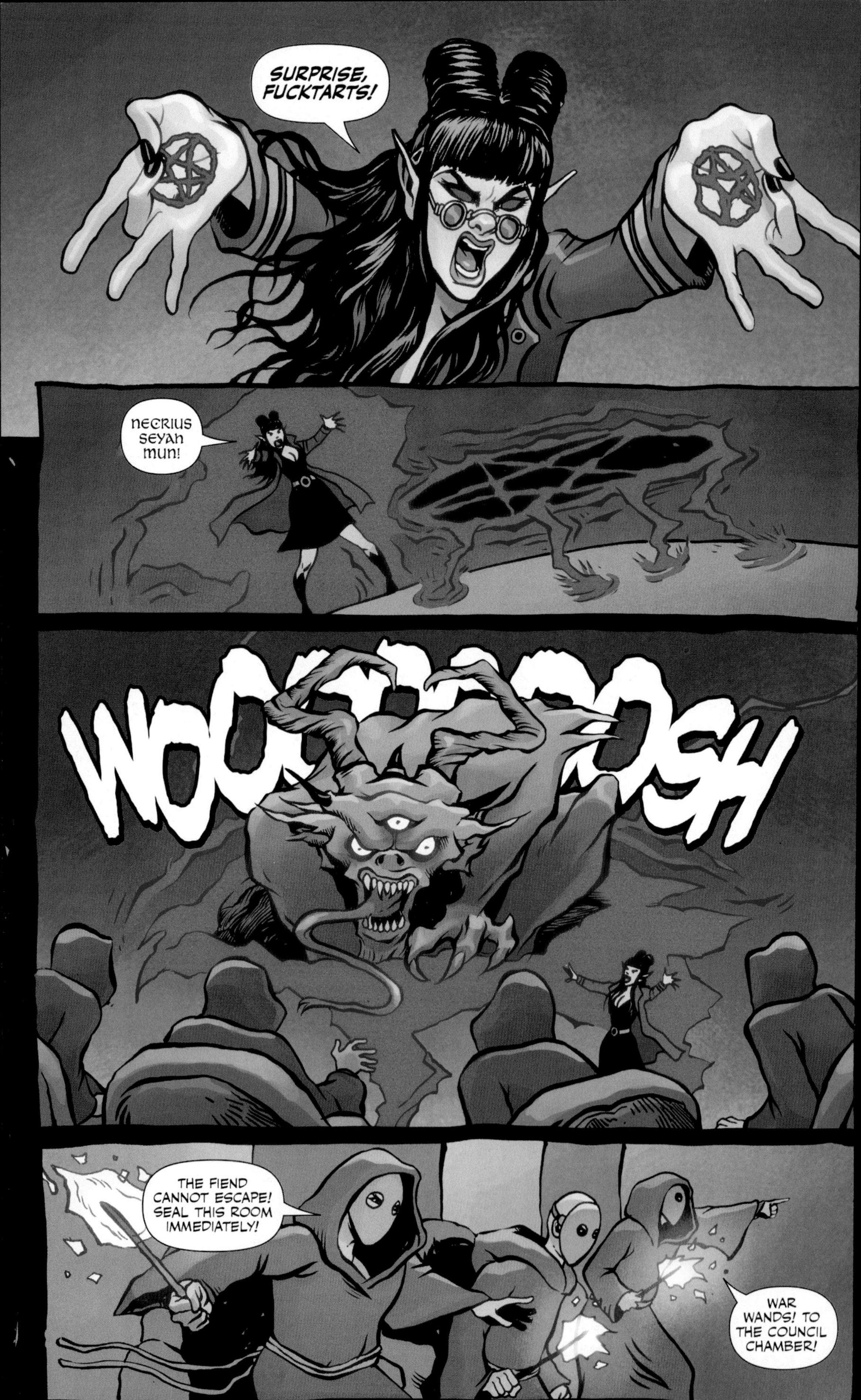
SURPRISE, FUCKTARTS!
NECRIUS SEYAH MUN!
WOOOOOOOSH
THE FIEND CANNOT ESCAPE! SEAL THIS ROOM IMMEDIATELY!
WAR WANDS! TO THE COUNCIL CHAMBER!

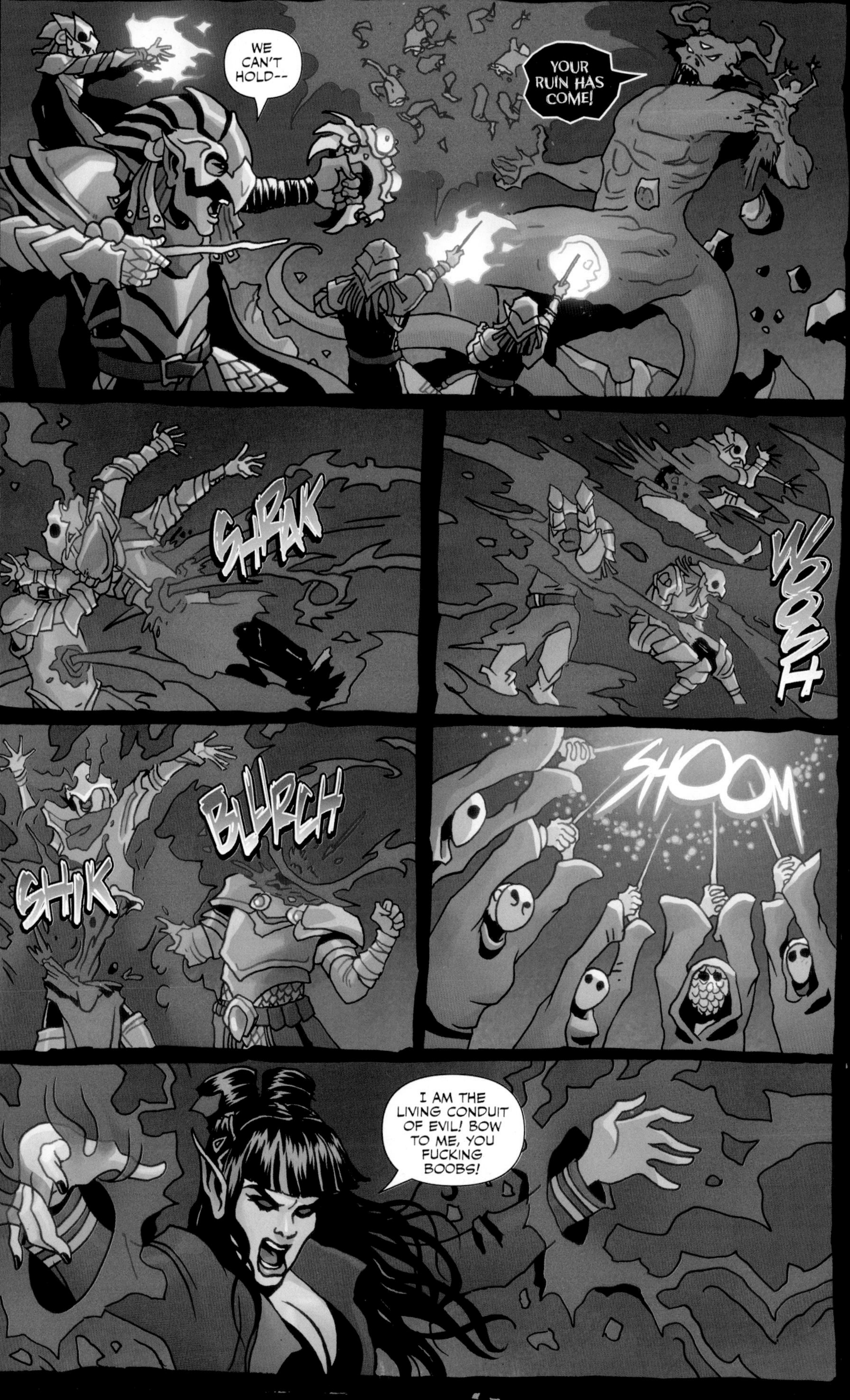
WE CAN'T HOLD--
YOUR RUIN HAS COME!
SHRAK
WOOSH
SHIK
BLURCH
SHOOM
I AM THE LIVING CONDUIT OF EVIL! BOW TO ME, YOU FUCKING BOOBS!

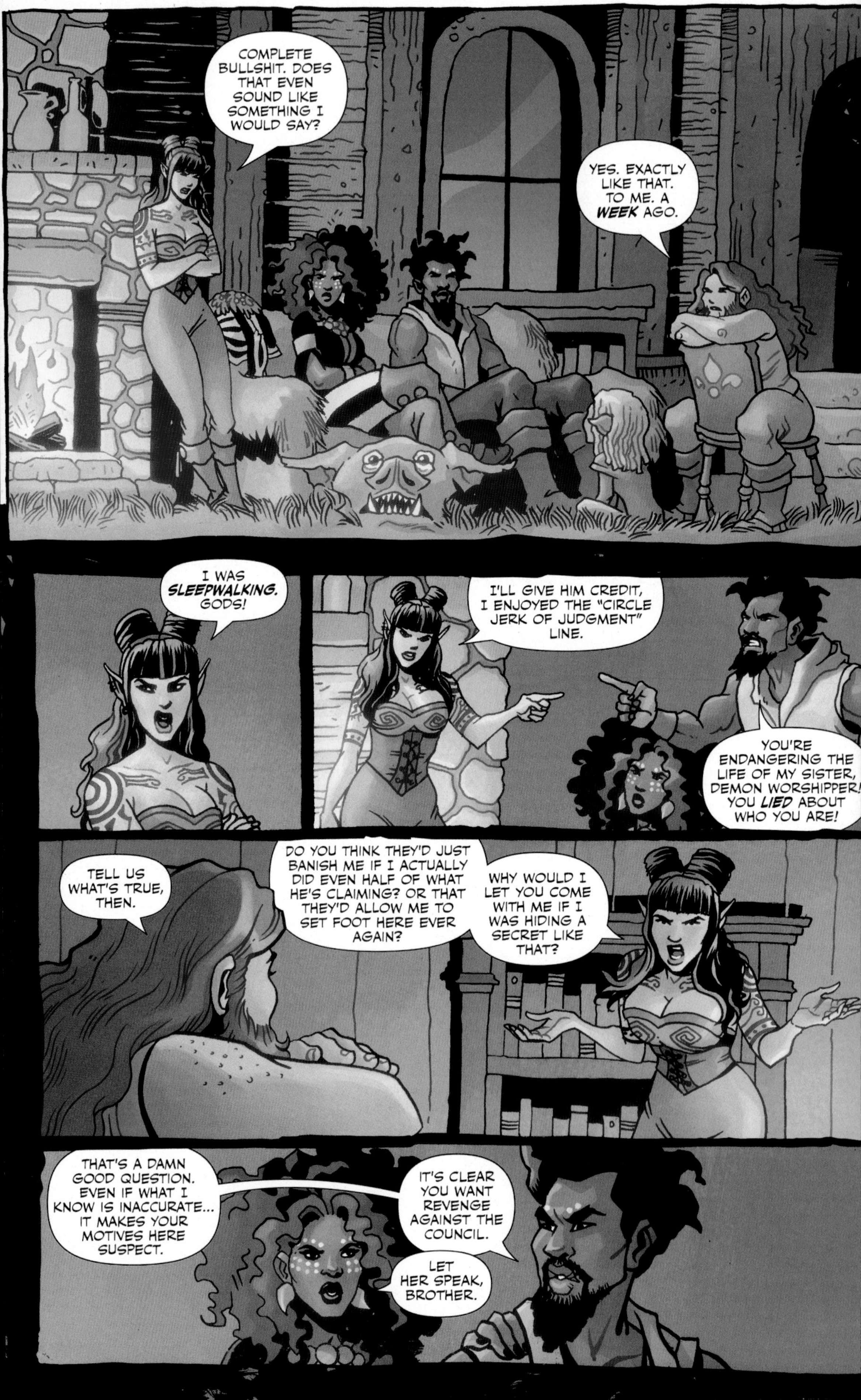
COMPLETE BULLSHIT. DOES THAT EVEN SOUND LIKE SOMETHING I WOULD SAY?
YES. EXACTLY LIKE THAT. TO ME. A **WEEK** AGO.
I WAS **SLEEPWALKING.** GODS!
I'LL GIVE HIM CREDIT, I ENJOYED THE "CIRCLE JERK OF JUDGMENT" LINE.
YOU'RE ENDANGERING THE LIFE OF MY SISTER, DEMON WORSHIPPER! YOU **LIED** ABOUT WHO YOU ARE!
TELL US WHAT'S TRUE, THEN.
DO YOU THINK THEY'D JUST BANISH ME IF I ACTUALLY DID EVEN HALF OF WHAT HE'S CLAIMING? OR THAT THEY'D ALLOW ME TO SET FOOT HERE EVER AGAIN?
WHY WOULD I LET YOU COME WITH ME IF I WAS HIDING A SECRET LIKE THAT?
THAT'S A DAMN GOOD QUESTION. EVEN IF WHAT I KNOW IS INACCURATE... IT MAKES YOUR MOTIVES HERE SUSPECT.
IT'S CLEAR YOU WANT REVENGE AGAINST THE COUNCIL.
LET HER SPEAK, BROTHER.

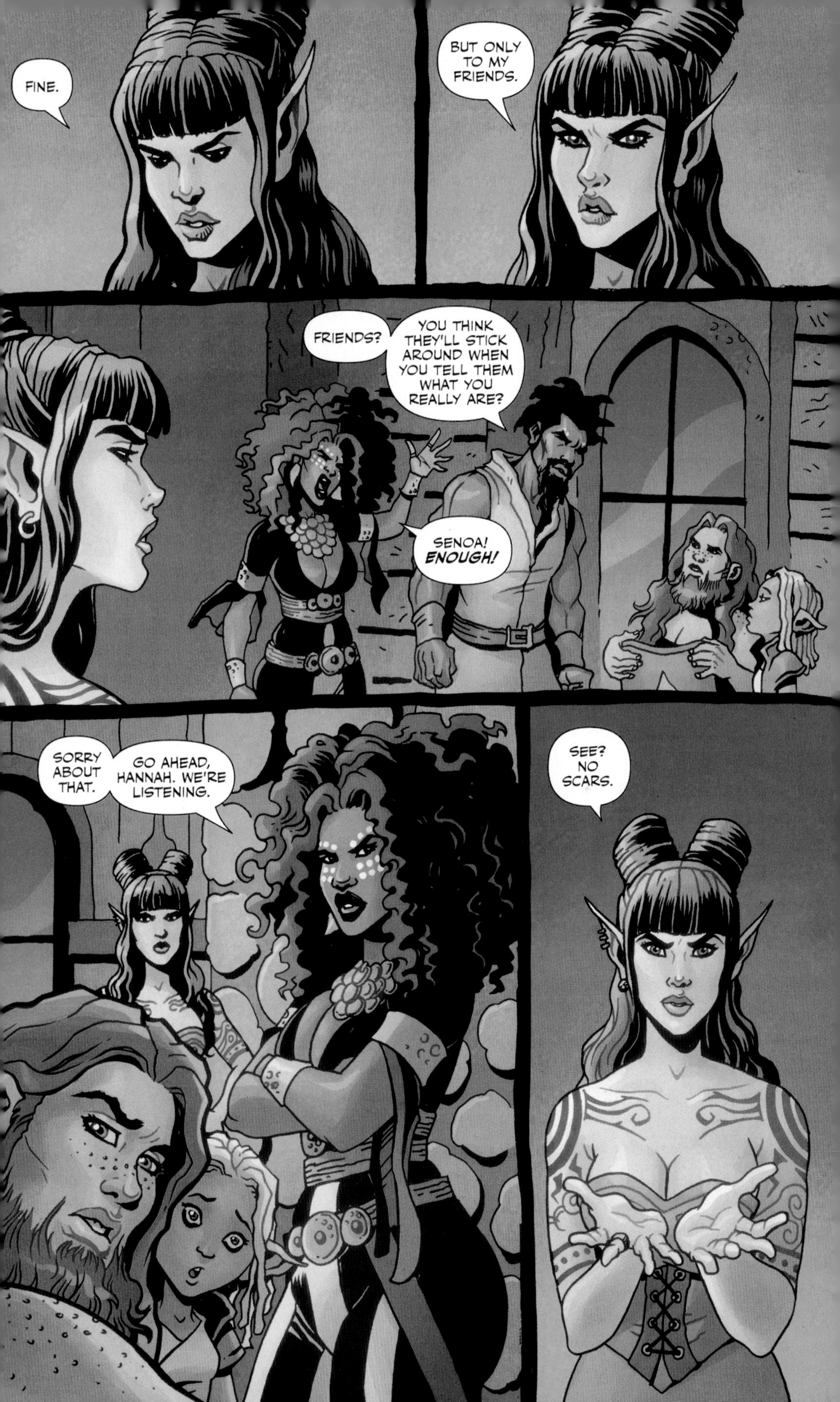
FINE.
BUT ONLY TO MY FRIENDS.
FRIENDS?
YOU THINK THEY'LL STICK AROUND WHEN YOU TELL THEM WHAT YOU REALLY ARE?
SENOA! ***ENOUGH!***
SORRY ABOUT THAT.
GO AHEAD, HANNAH. WE'RE LISTENING.
SEE? NO SCARS.

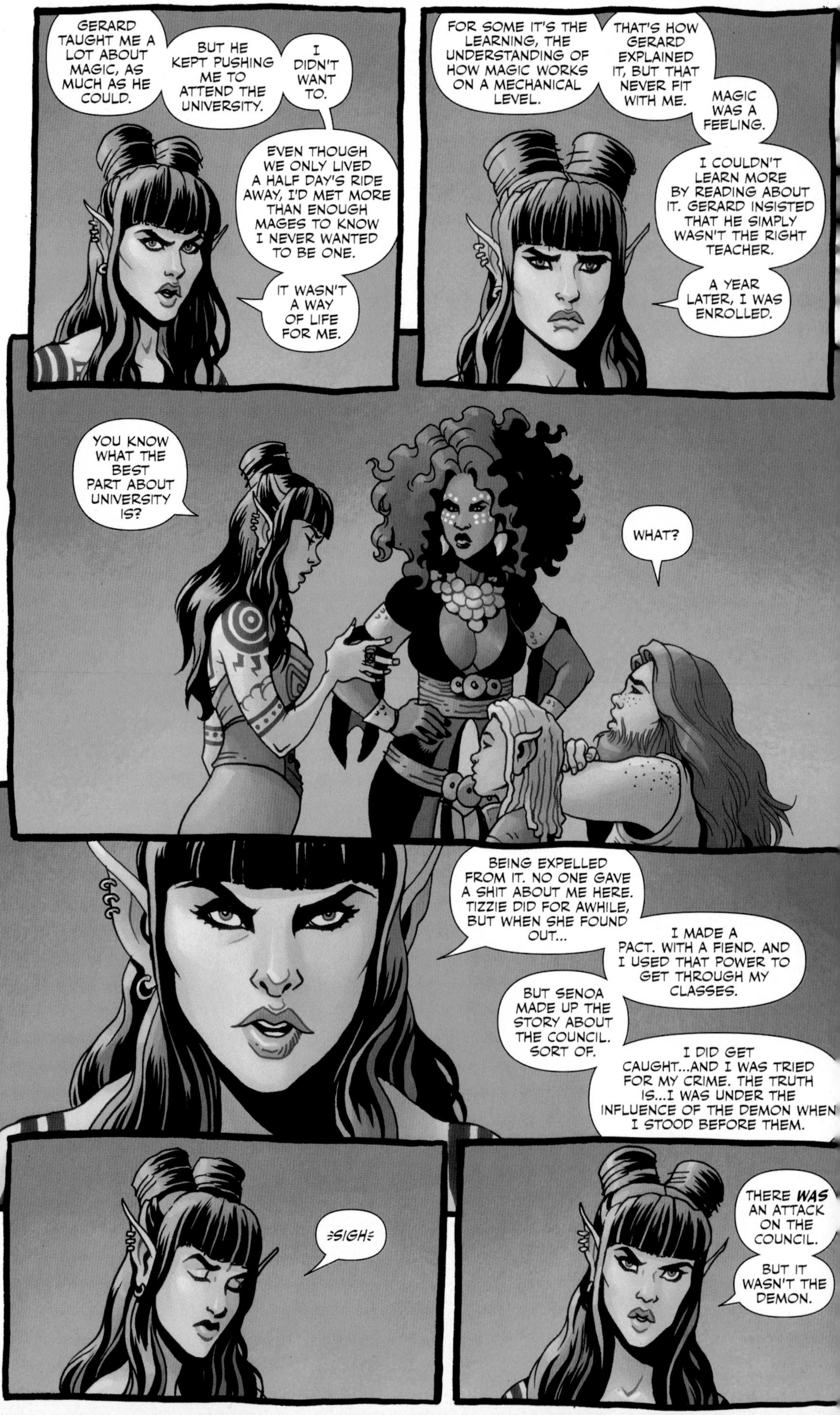
GERARD TAUGHT ME A LOT ABOUT MAGIC, AS MUCH AS HE COULD.
BUT HE KEPT PUSHING ME TO ATTEND THE UNIVERSITY.
I DIDN'T WANT TO.
EVEN THOUGH WE ONLY LIVED A HALF DAY'S RIDE AWAY, I'D MET MORE THAN ENOUGH MAGES TO KNOW I NEVER WANTED TO BE ONE.
IT WASN'T A WAY OF LIFE FOR ME.
FOR SOME IT'S THE LEARNING, THE UNDERSTANDING OF HOW MAGIC WORKS ON A MECHANICAL LEVEL.
THAT'S HOW GERARD EXPLAINED IT, BUT THAT NEVER FIT WITH ME.
MAGIC WAS A FEELING.
I COULDN'T LEARN MORE BY READING ABOUT IT. GERARD INSISTED THAT HE SIMPLY WASN'T THE RIGHT TEACHER.
A YEAR LATER, I WAS ENROLLED.
YOU KNOW WHAT THE BEST PART ABOUT UNIVERSITY IS?
WHAT?
BEING EXPELLED FROM IT. NO ONE GAVE A SHIT ABOUT ME HERE. TIZZIE DID FOR AWHILE, BUT WHEN SHE FOUND OUT...
I MADE A PACT. WITH A FIEND. AND I USED THAT POWER TO GET THROUGH MY CLASSES.
BUT SENOA MADE UP THE STORY ABOUT THE COUNCIL. SORT OF.
I DID GET CAUGHT...AND I WAS TRIED FOR MY CRIME. THE TRUTH IS...I WAS UNDER THE INFLUENCE OF THE DEMON WHEN I STOOD BEFORE THEM.
SIGH
THERE ***WAS*** AN ATTACK ON THE COUNCIL.
BUT IT WASN'T THE DEMON.

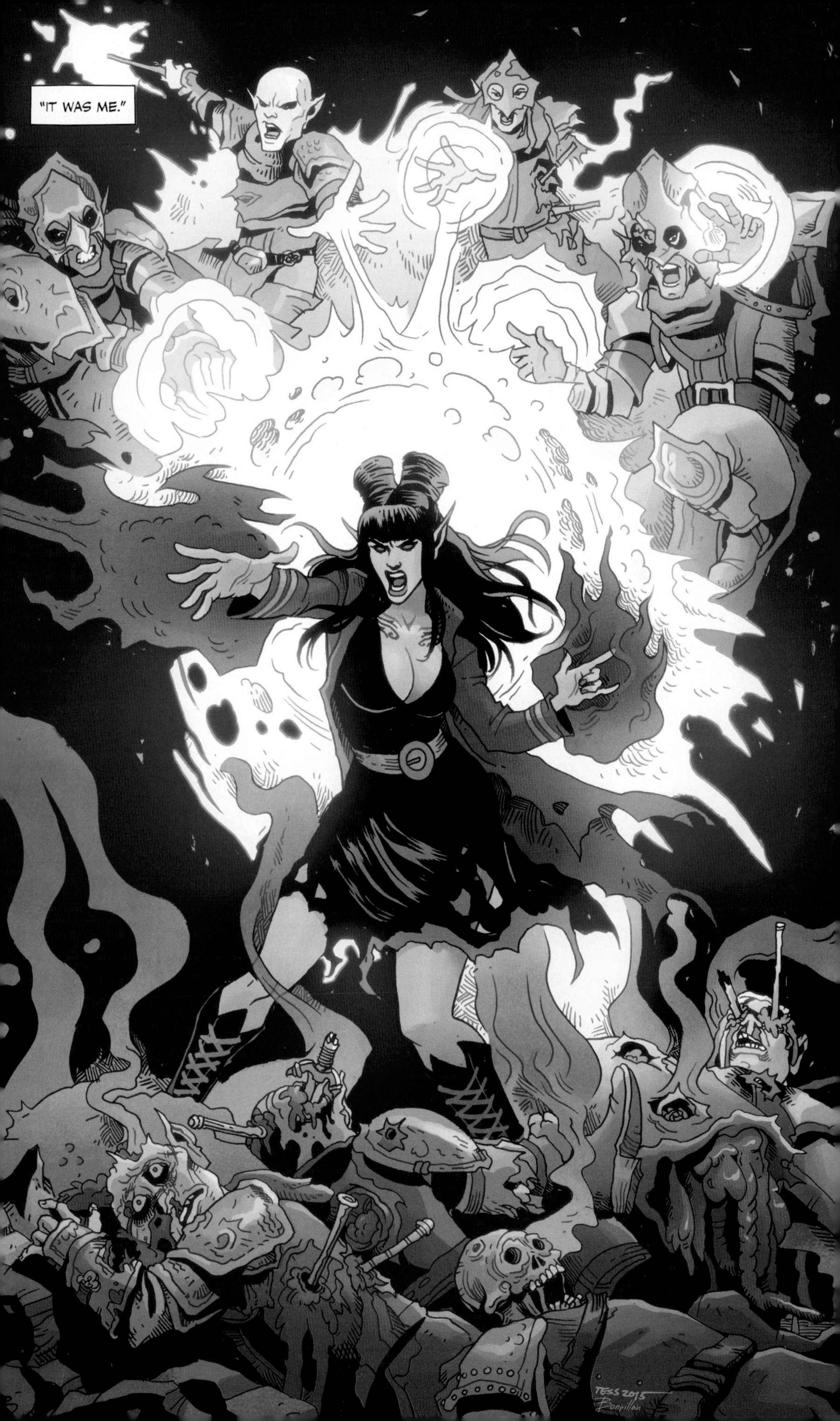
"IT WAS ME."
TESS 2015
Bonvillain

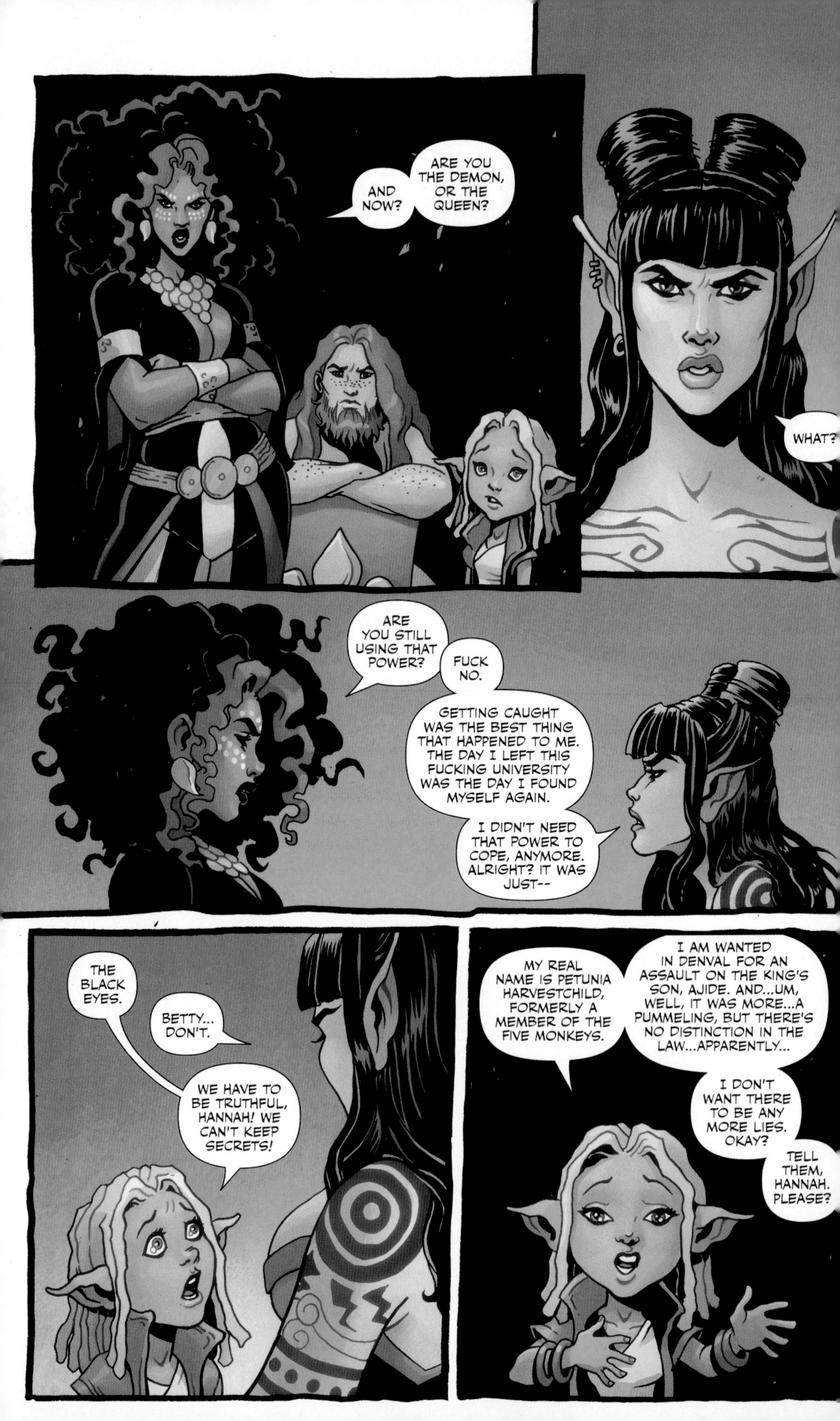
AND NOW?
ARE YOU THE DEMON, OR THE QUEEN?
WHAT?
ARE YOU STILL USING THAT POWER?
FUCK NO.
GETTING CAUGHT WAS THE BEST THING THAT HAPPENED TO ME. THE DAY I LEFT THIS FUCKING UNIVERSITY WAS THE DAY I FOUND MYSELF AGAIN.
I DIDN'T NEED THAT POWER TO COPE, ANYMORE. ALRIGHT? IT WAS JUST--
THE BLACK EYES.
BETTY... DON'T.
WE HAVE TO BE TRUTHFUL, HANNAH! WE CAN'T KEEP SECRETS!
MY REAL NAME IS PETUNIA HARVESTCHILD, FORMERLY A MEMBER OF THE FIVE MONKEYS.
I AM WANTED IN DENVAL FOR AN ASSAULT ON THE KING'S SON, AJIDE. AND...UM, WELL, IT WAS MORE...A PUMMELING, BUT THERE'S NO DISTINCTION IN THE LAW...APPARENTLY...
I DON'T WANT THERE TO BE ANY MORE LIES. OKAY?
TELL THEM, HANNAH. PLEASE?

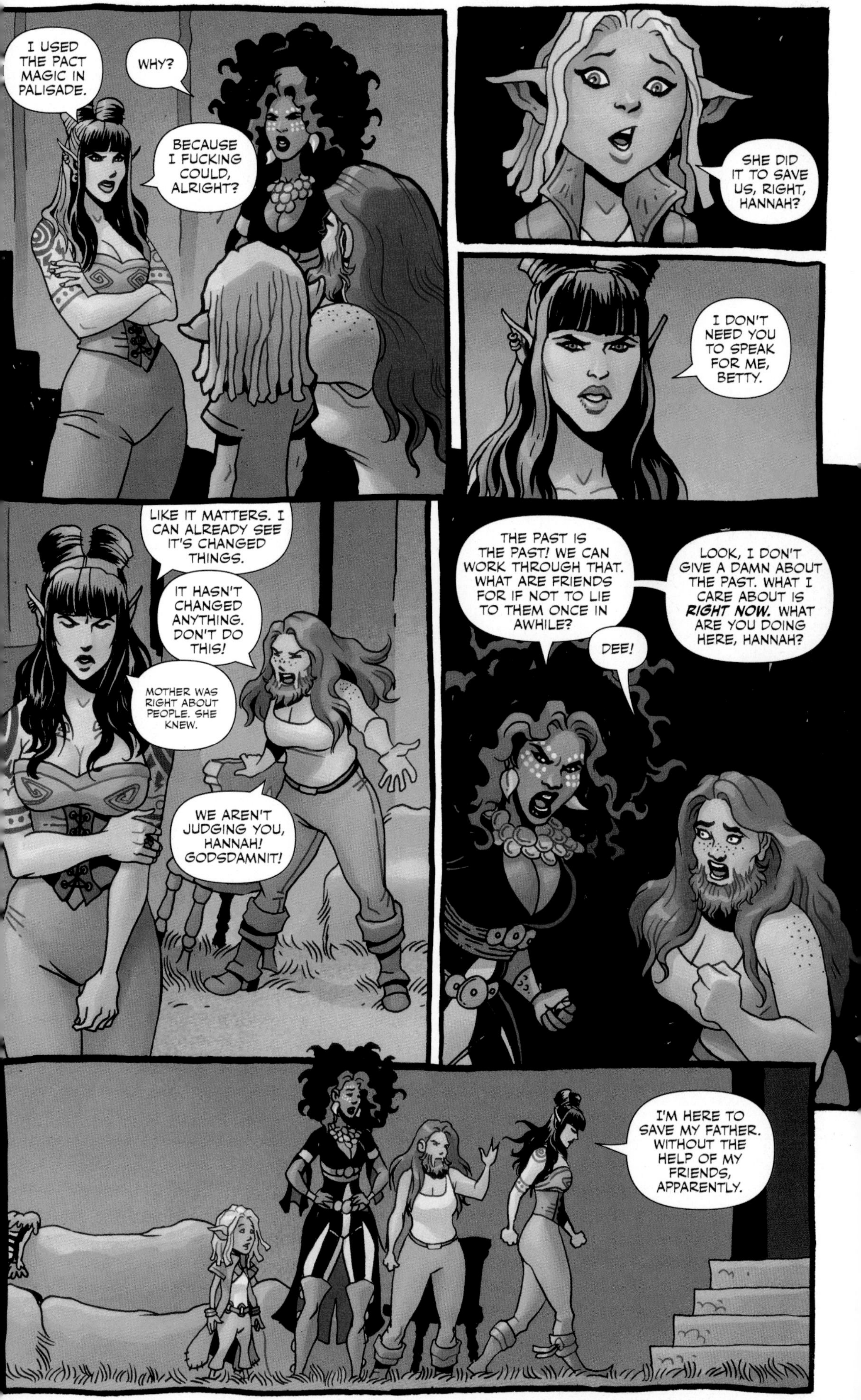

I USED THE PACT MAGIC IN PALISADE.
WHY?
BECAUSE I FUCKING COULD, ALRIGHT?
SHE DID IT TO SAVE US, RIGHT, HANNAH?
I DON'T NEED YOU TO SPEAK FOR ME, BETTY.
LIKE IT MATTERS. I CAN ALREADY SEE IT'S CHANGED THINGS.
IT HASN'T CHANGED ANYTHING. DON'T DO THIS!
MOTHER WAS RIGHT ABOUT PEOPLE. SHE KNEW.
WE AREN'T JUDGING YOU, HANNAH! GODSDAMNIT!
THE PAST IS THE PAST! WE CAN WORK THROUGH THAT. WHAT ARE FRIENDS FOR IF NOT TO LIE TO THEM ONCE IN AWHILE?
DEE!
LOOK, I DON'T GIVE A DAMN ABOUT THE PAST. WHAT I CARE ABOUT IS ***RIGHT NOW.*** WHAT ARE YOU DOING HERE, HANNAH?
I'M HERE TO SAVE MY FATHER. WITHOUT THE HELP OF MY FRIENDS, APPARENTLY.

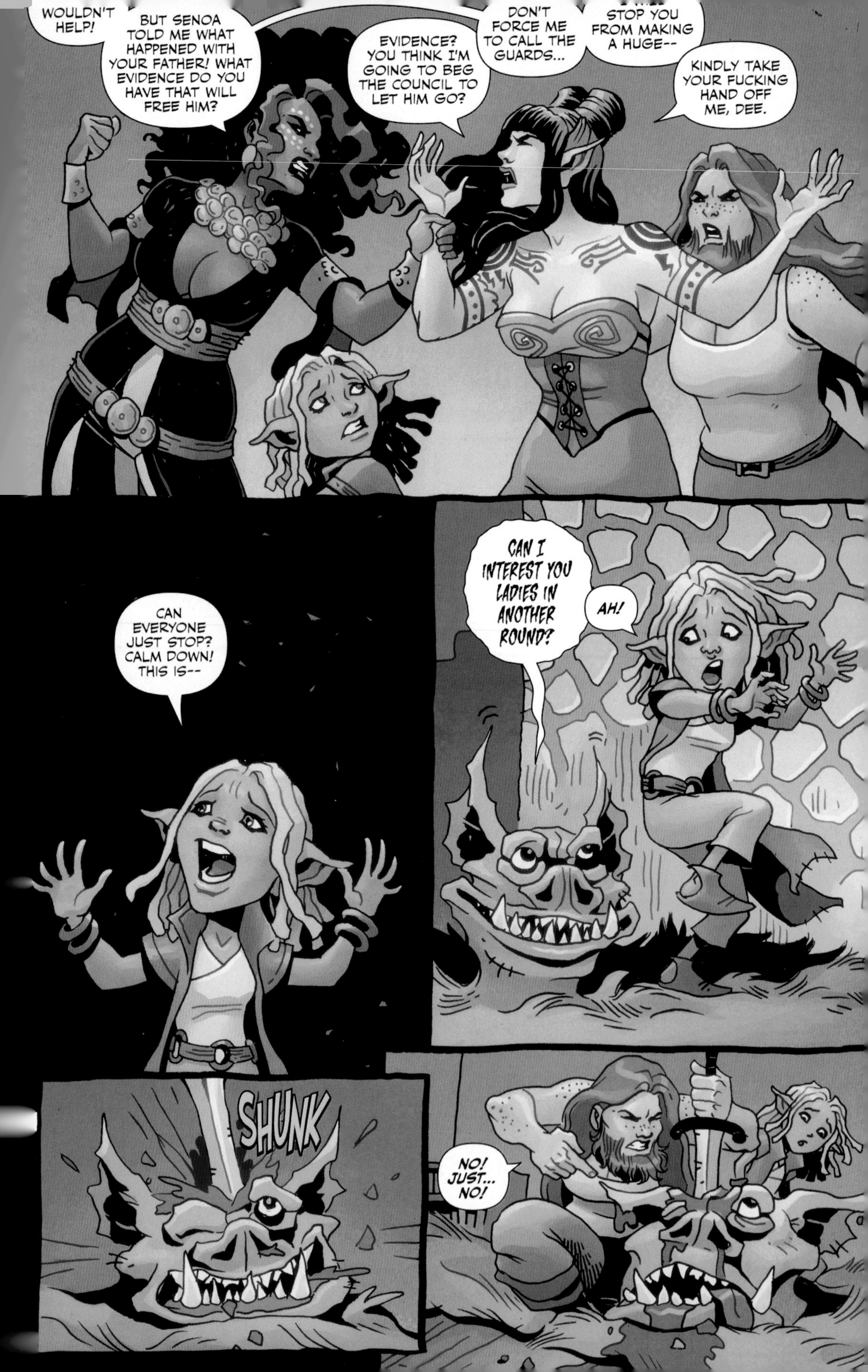

WOULDN'T HELP!
BUT SENOA TOLD ME WHAT HAPPENED WITH YOUR FATHER! WHAT EVIDENCE DO YOU HAVE THAT WILL FREE HIM?
EVIDENCE? YOU THINK I'M GOING TO BEG THE COUNCIL TO LET HIM GO?
DON'T FORCE ME TO CALL THE GUARDS...
STOP YOU FROM MAKING A HUGE--
KINDLY TAKE YOUR FUCKING HAND OFF ME, DEE.
CAN EVERYONE JUST STOP? CALM DOWN! THIS IS--
CAN I INTEREST YOU LADIES IN ANOTHER ROUND?
AH!
SHUNK
NO! JUST... NO!

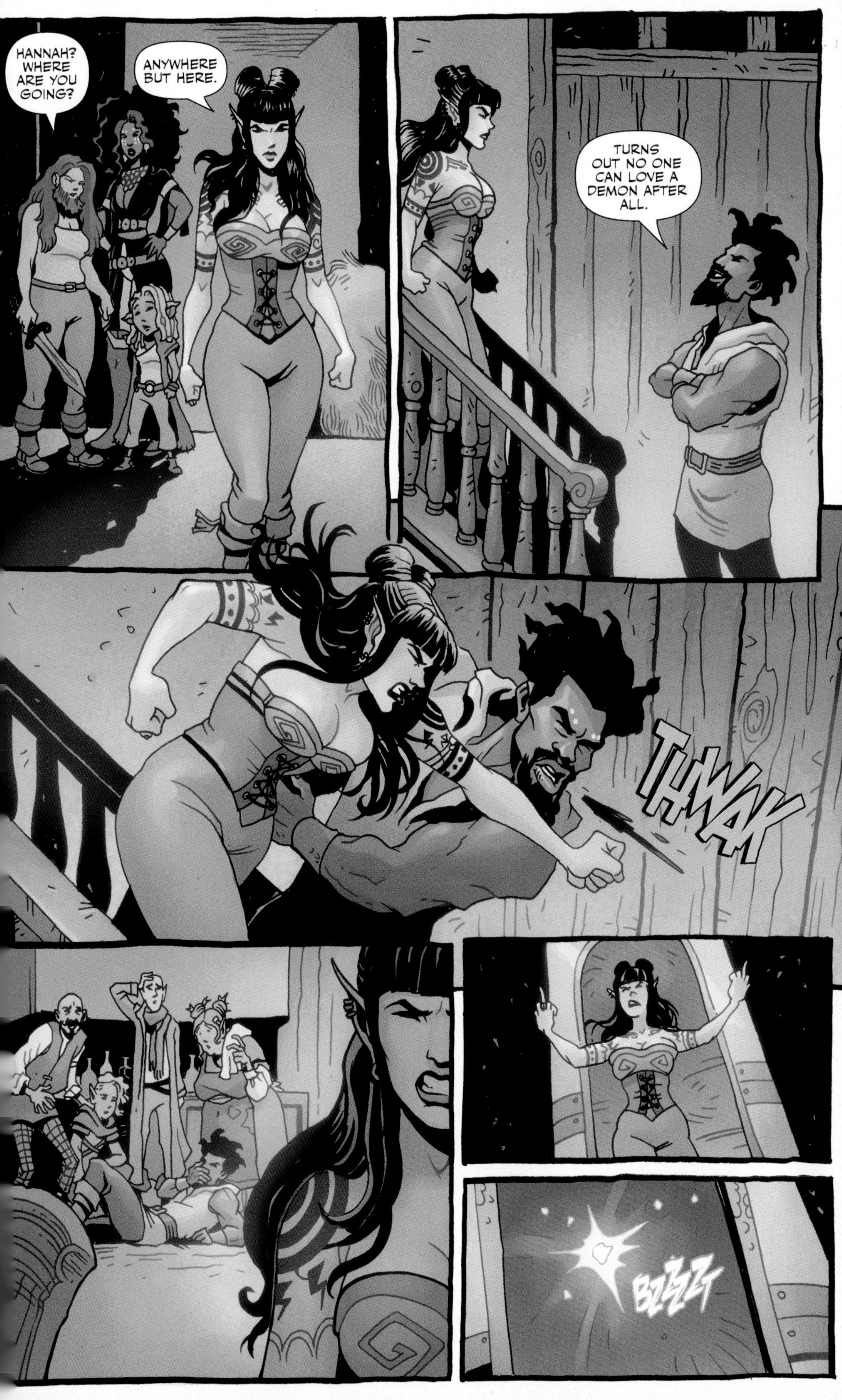

HANNAH? WHERE ARE YOU GOING?
ANYWHERE BUT HERE.
TURNS OUT NO ONE CAN LOVE A DEMON AFTER ALL.
THWAK
BZZZZT

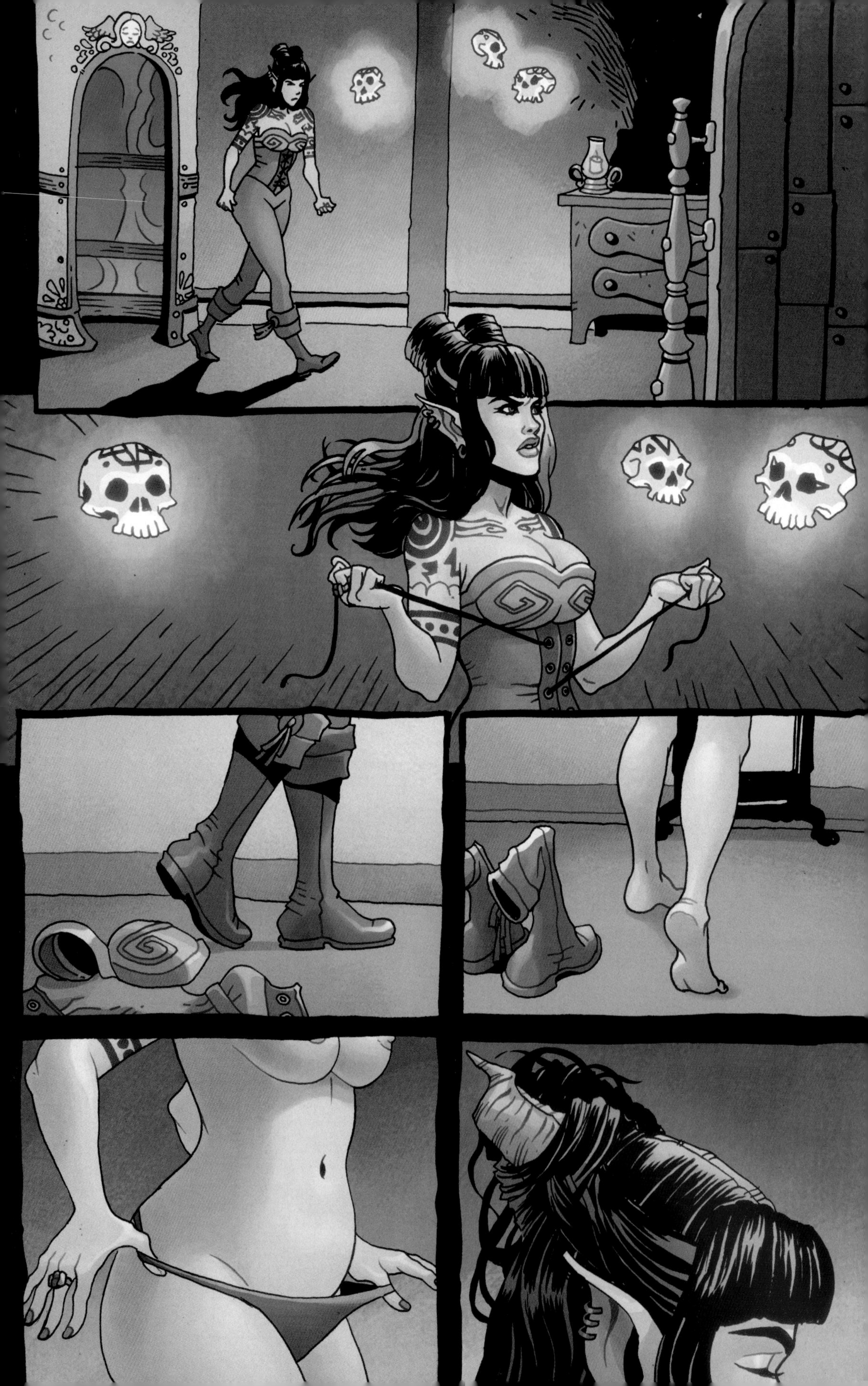

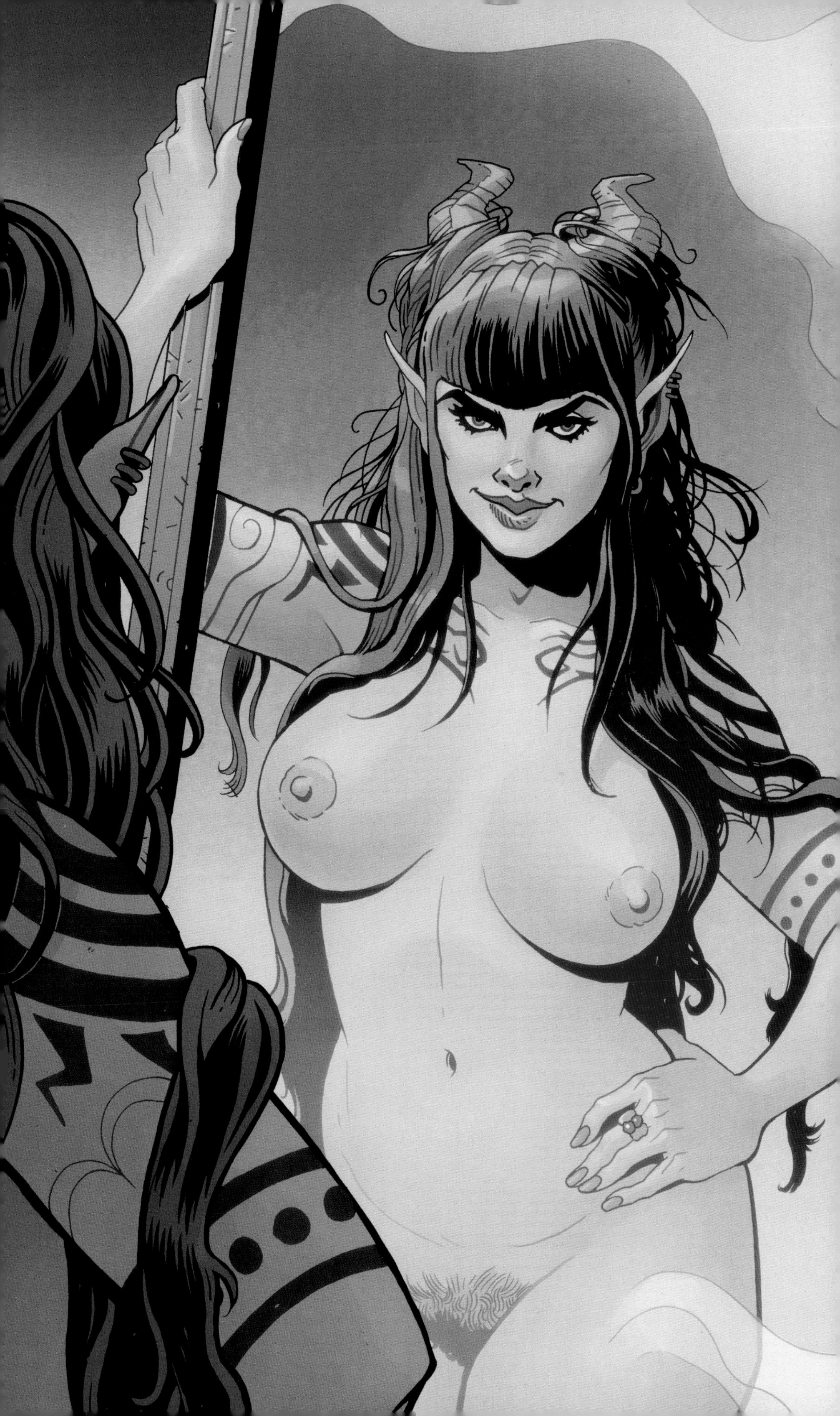

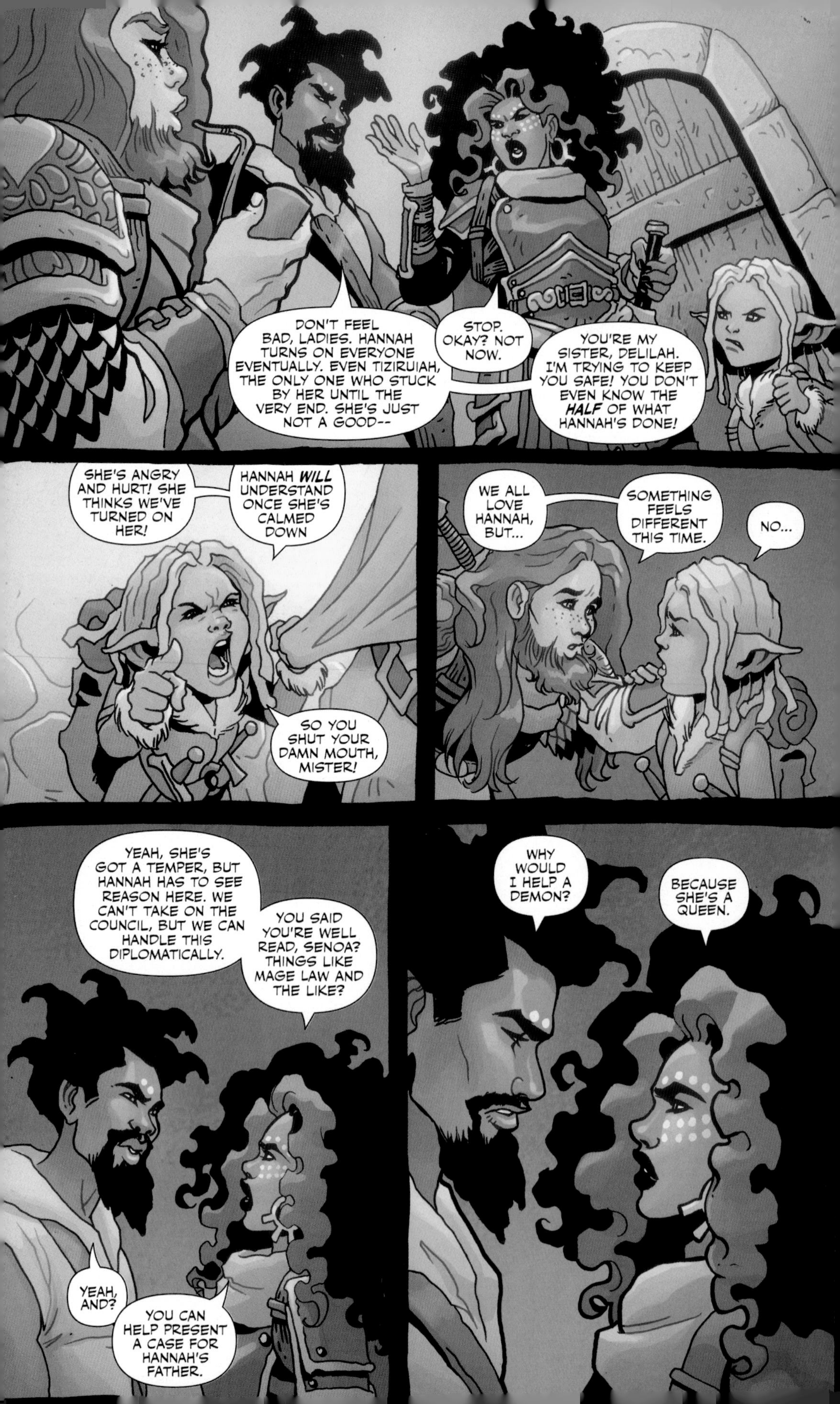
DON'T FEEL BAD, LADIES. HANNAH TURNS ON EVERYONE EVENTUALLY. EVEN TIZIRUIAH, THE ONLY ONE WHO STUCK BY HER UNTIL THE VERY END. SHE'S JUST NOT A GOOD--
STOP. OKAY? NOT NOW.
YOU'RE MY SISTER, DELILAH. I'M TRYING TO KEEP YOU SAFE! YOU DON'T EVEN KNOW THE *HALF* OF WHAT HANNAH'S DONE!
SHE'S ANGRY AND HURT! SHE THINKS WE'VE TURNED ON HER!
HANNAH *WILL* UNDERSTAND ONCE SHE'S CALMED DOWN
SO YOU SHUT YOUR DAMN MOUTH, MISTER!
WE ALL LOVE HANNAH, BUT...
SOMETHING FEELS DIFFERENT THIS TIME.
NO...
YEAH, SHE'S GOT A TEMPER, BUT HANNAH HAS TO SEE REASON HERE. WE CAN'T TAKE ON THE COUNCIL, BUT WE CAN HANDLE THIS DIPLOMATICALLY.
YOU SAID YOU'RE WELL READ, SENOA? THINGS LIKE MAGE LAW AND THE LIKE?
YEAH, AND?
YOU CAN HELP PRESENT A CASE FOR HANNAH'S FATHER.
WHY WOULD I HELP A DEMON?
BECAUSE SHE'S A QUEEN.

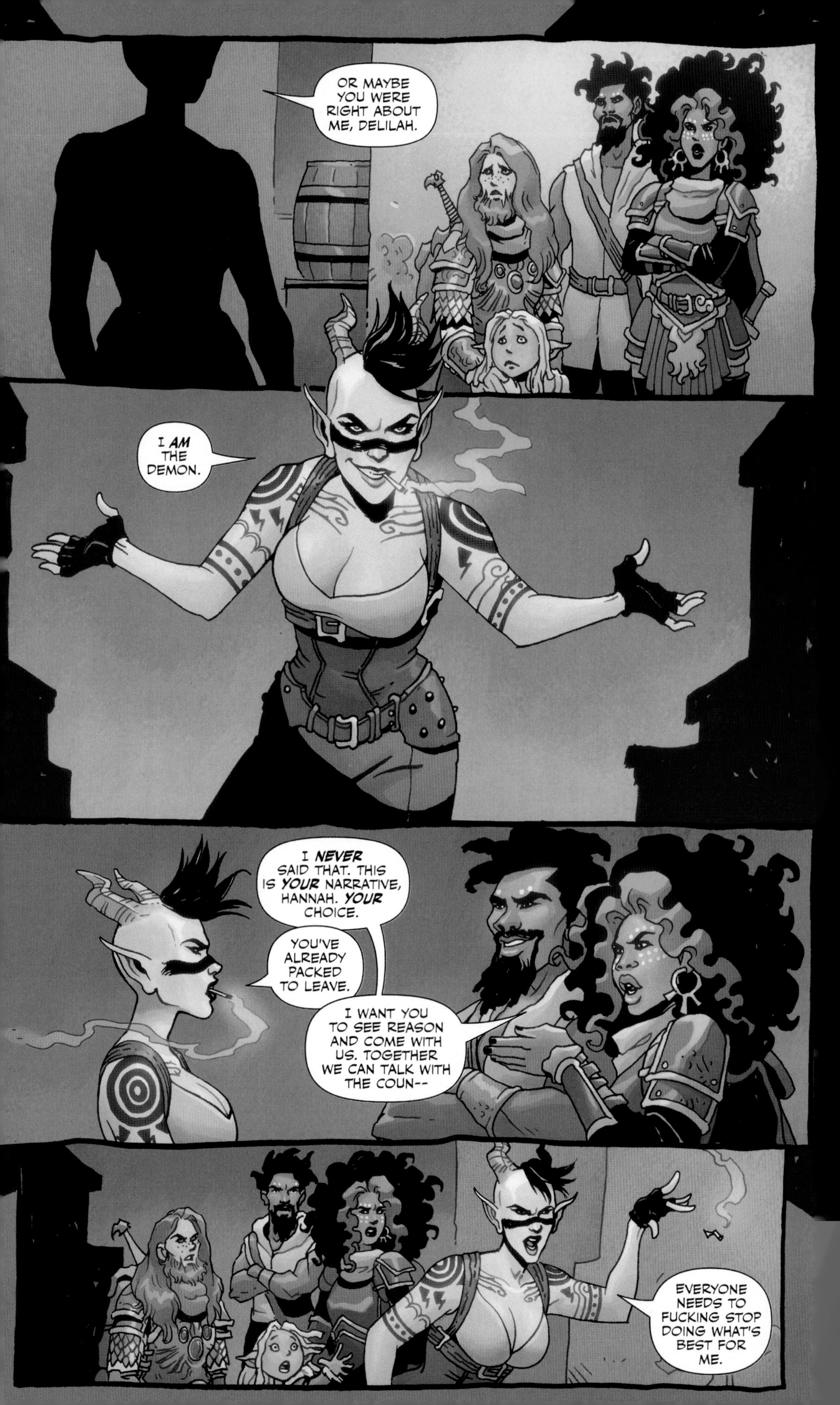
OR MAYBE YOU WERE RIGHT ABOUT ME, DELILAH.
I *AM* THE DEMON.
I *NEVER* SAID THAT. THIS IS *YOUR* NARRATIVE, HANNAH. *YOUR* CHOICE.
YOU'VE ALREADY PACKED TO LEAVE.
I WANT YOU TO SEE REASON AND COME WITH US. TOGETHER WE CAN TALK WITH THE COUN--
EVERYONE NEEDS TO FUCKING STOP DOING WHAT'S BEST FOR ME.

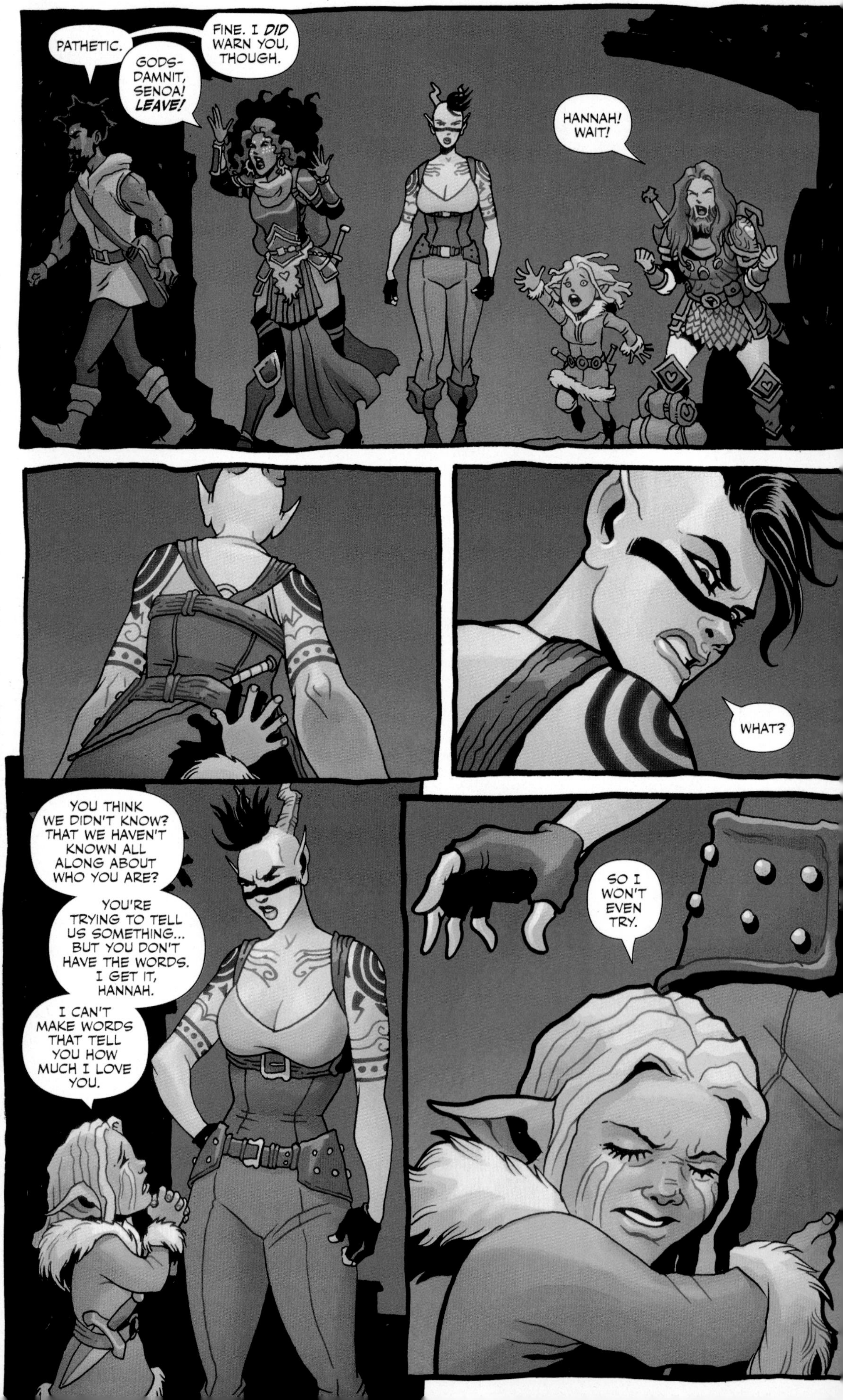
PATHETIC.
FINE. I *DID* WARN YOU, THOUGH.
GODS-DAMNIT, SENOA! ***LEAVE!***
HANNAH! WAIT!
WHAT?
YOU THINK WE DIDN'T KNOW? THAT WE HAVEN'T KNOWN ALL ALONG ABOUT WHO YOU ARE?
YOU'RE TRYING TO TELL US SOMETHING... BUT YOU DON'T HAVE THE WORDS. I GET IT, HANNAH.
I CAN'T MAKE WORDS THAT TELL YOU HOW MUCH I LOVE YOU.
SO I WON'T EVEN TRY.

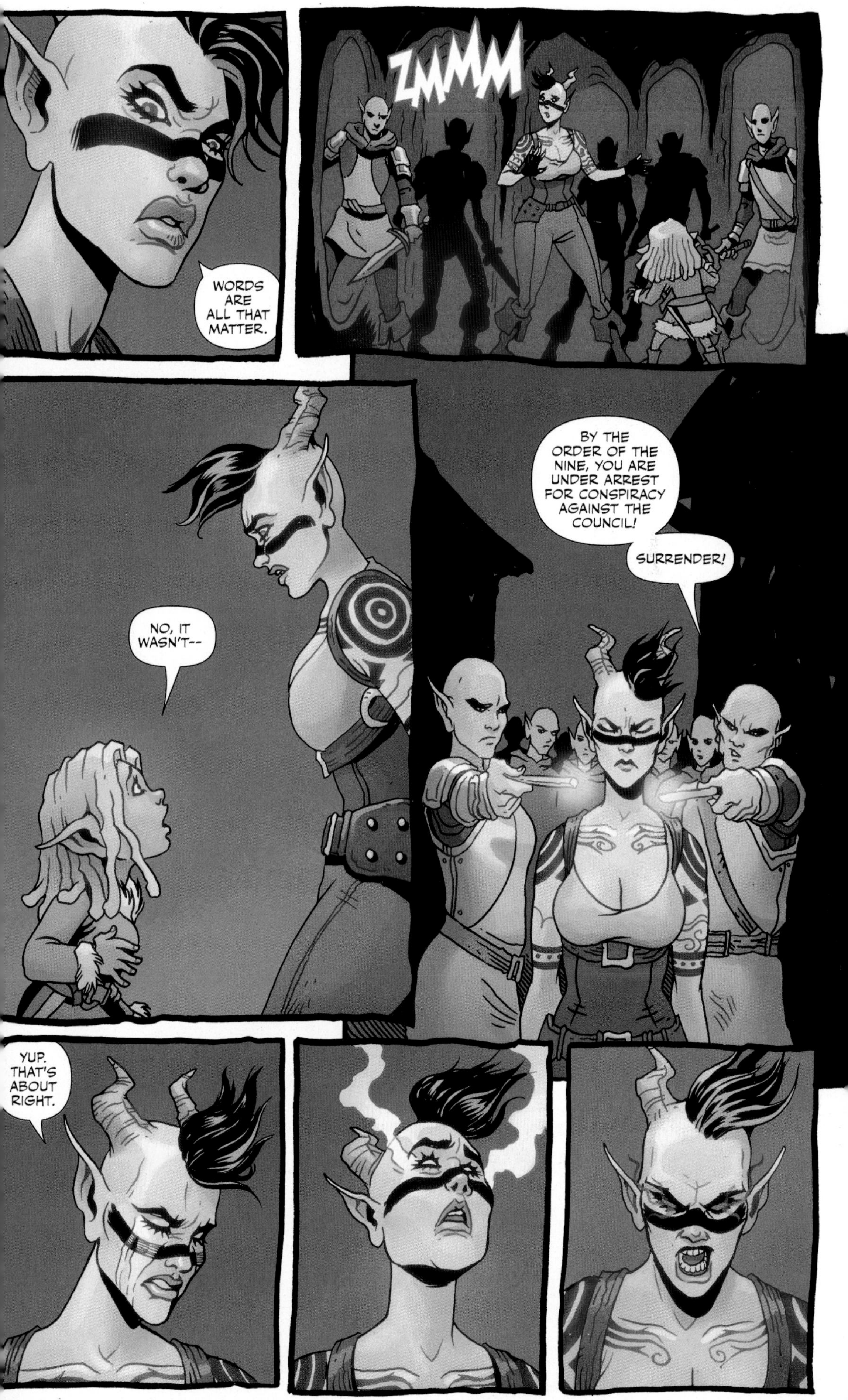
WORDS ARE ALL THAT MATTER.
ZMMM
NO, IT WASN'T--
BY THE ORDER OF THE NINE, YOU ARE UNDER ARREST FOR CONSPIRACY AGAINST THE COUNCIL!
SURRENDER!
YUP. THAT'S ABOUT RIGHT.

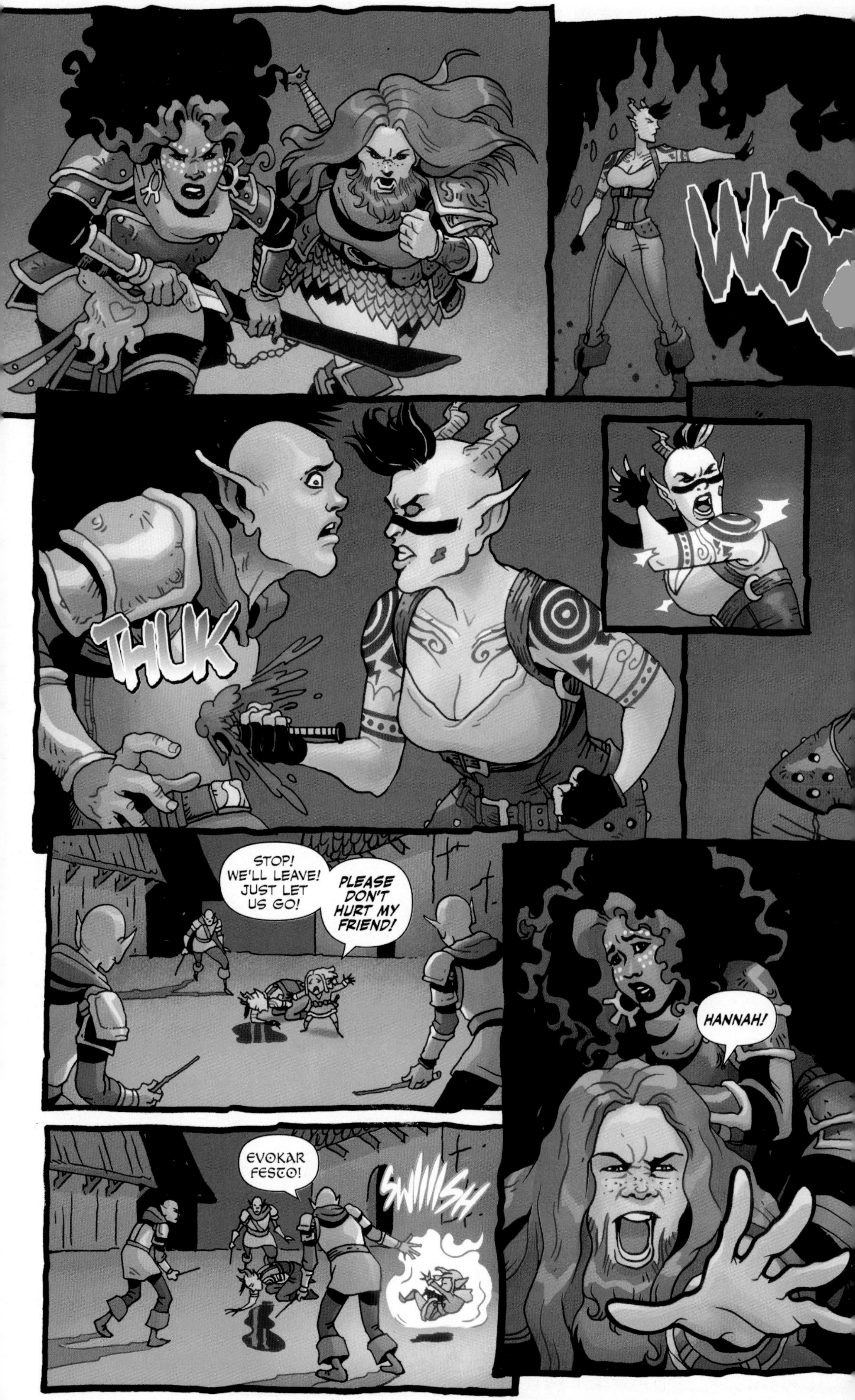
WOO
THUK
STOP! WE'LL LEAVE! JUST LET US GO!
PLEASE DON'T HURT MY FRIEND!
EVOKAR FESTO!
SWIIIISH
HANNAH!

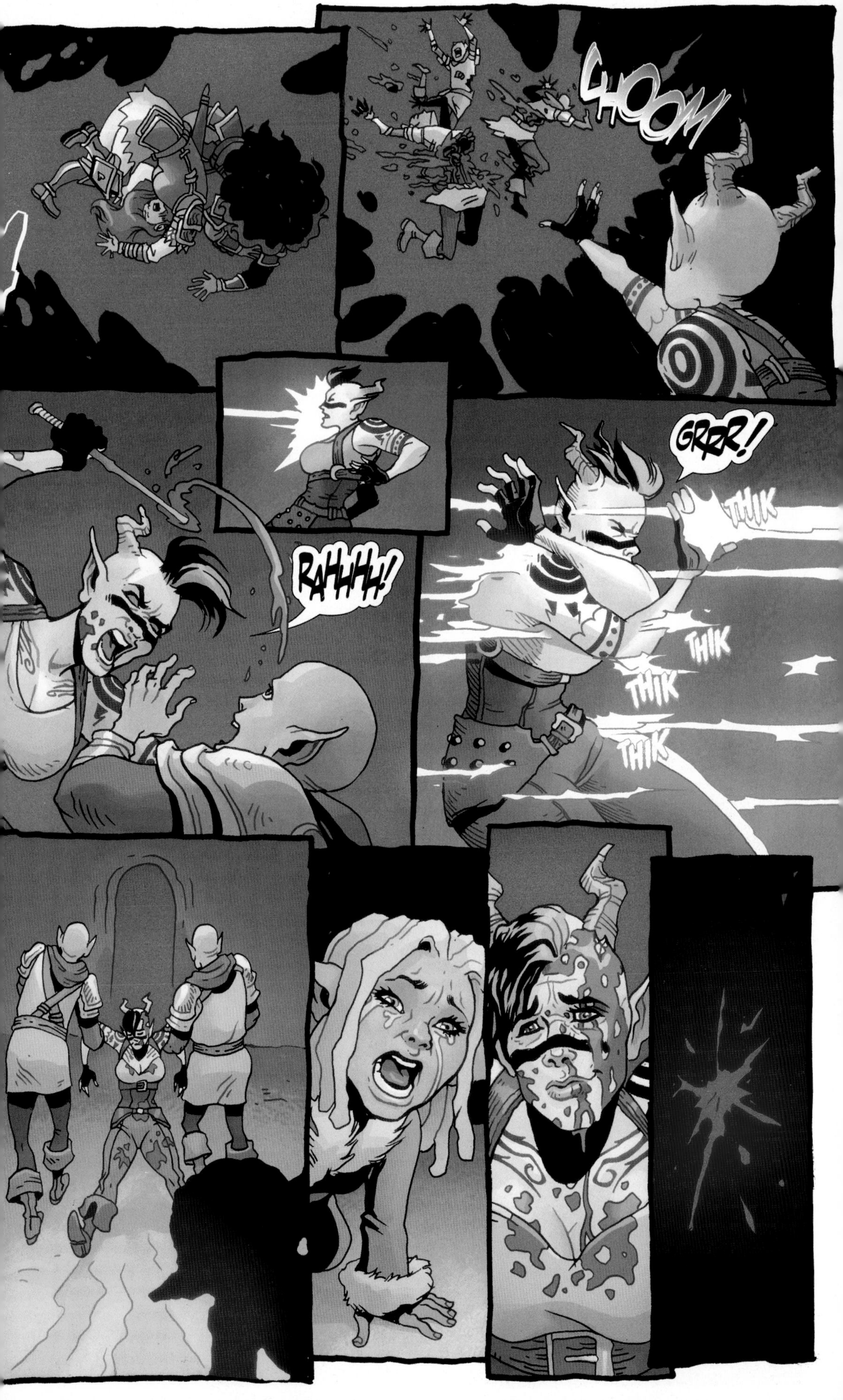
CHOOM
RAHHHH!
GRRR!
THIK
THIK
THIK
THIK

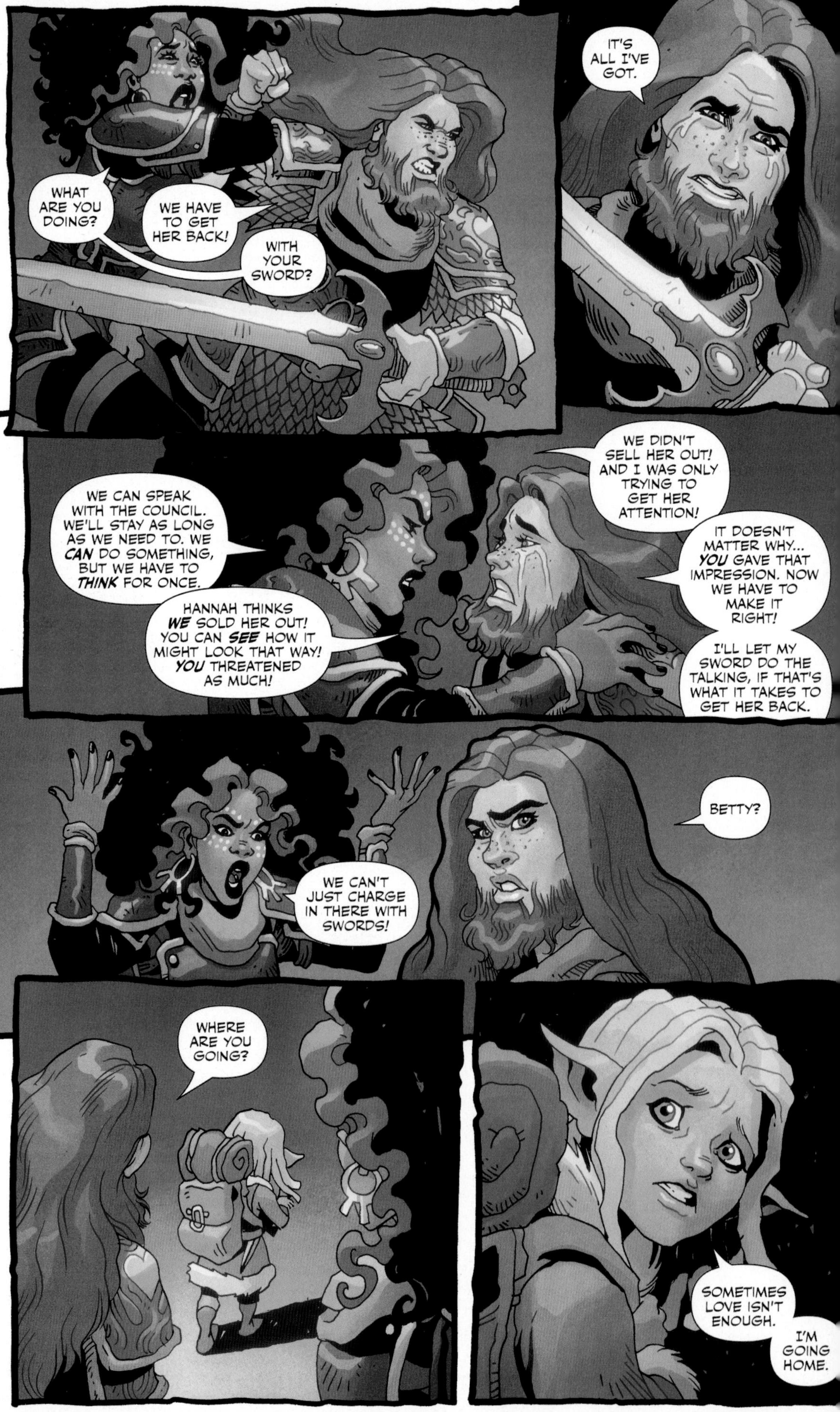

WHAT ARE YOU DOING?
WE HAVE TO GET HER BACK!
WITH YOUR SWORD?
IT'S ALL I'VE GOT.
WE CAN SPEAK WITH THE COUNCIL. WE'LL STAY AS LONG AS WE NEED TO. WE *CAN* DO SOMETHING, BUT WE HAVE TO *THINK* FOR ONCE.
HANNAH THINKS *WE* SOLD HER OUT! YOU CAN *SEE* HOW IT MIGHT LOOK THAT WAY! *YOU* THREATENED AS MUCH!
WE DIDN'T SELL HER OUT! AND I WAS ONLY TRYING TO GET HER ATTENTION!
IT DOESN'T MATTER WHY... *YOU* GAVE THAT IMPRESSION. NOW WE HAVE TO MAKE IT RIGHT!
I'LL LET MY SWORD DO THE TALKING, IF THAT'S WHAT IT TAKES TO GET HER BACK.
WE CAN'T JUST CHARGE IN THERE WITH SWORDS!
BETTY?
WHERE ARE YOU GOING?
SOMETIMES LOVE ISN'T ENOUGH.
I'M GOING HOME.

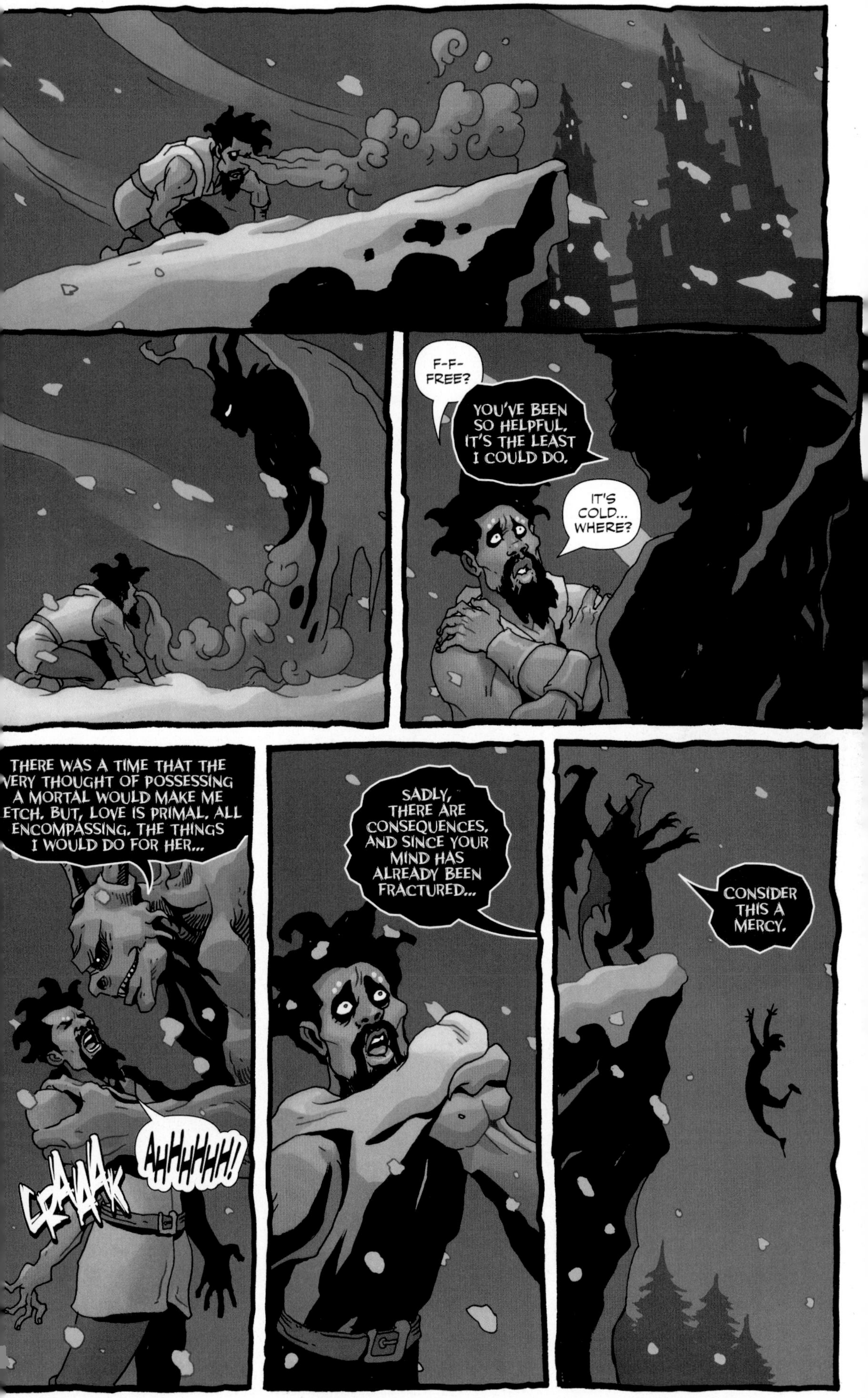
F-F-FREE?
YOU'VE BEEN SO HELPFUL, IT'S THE LEAST I COULD DO.
IT'S COLD... WHERE?
THERE WAS A TIME THAT THE VERY THOUGHT OF POSSESSING A MORTAL WOULD MAKE ME ETCH. BUT, LOVE IS PRIMAL, ALL ENCOMPASSING. THE THINGS I WOULD DO FOR HER...
CRAAAK
AHHHHHH!
SADLY, THERE ARE CONSEQUENCES, AND SINCE YOUR MIND HAS ALREADY BEEN FRACTURED...
CONSIDER THIS A MERCY.

Months later.

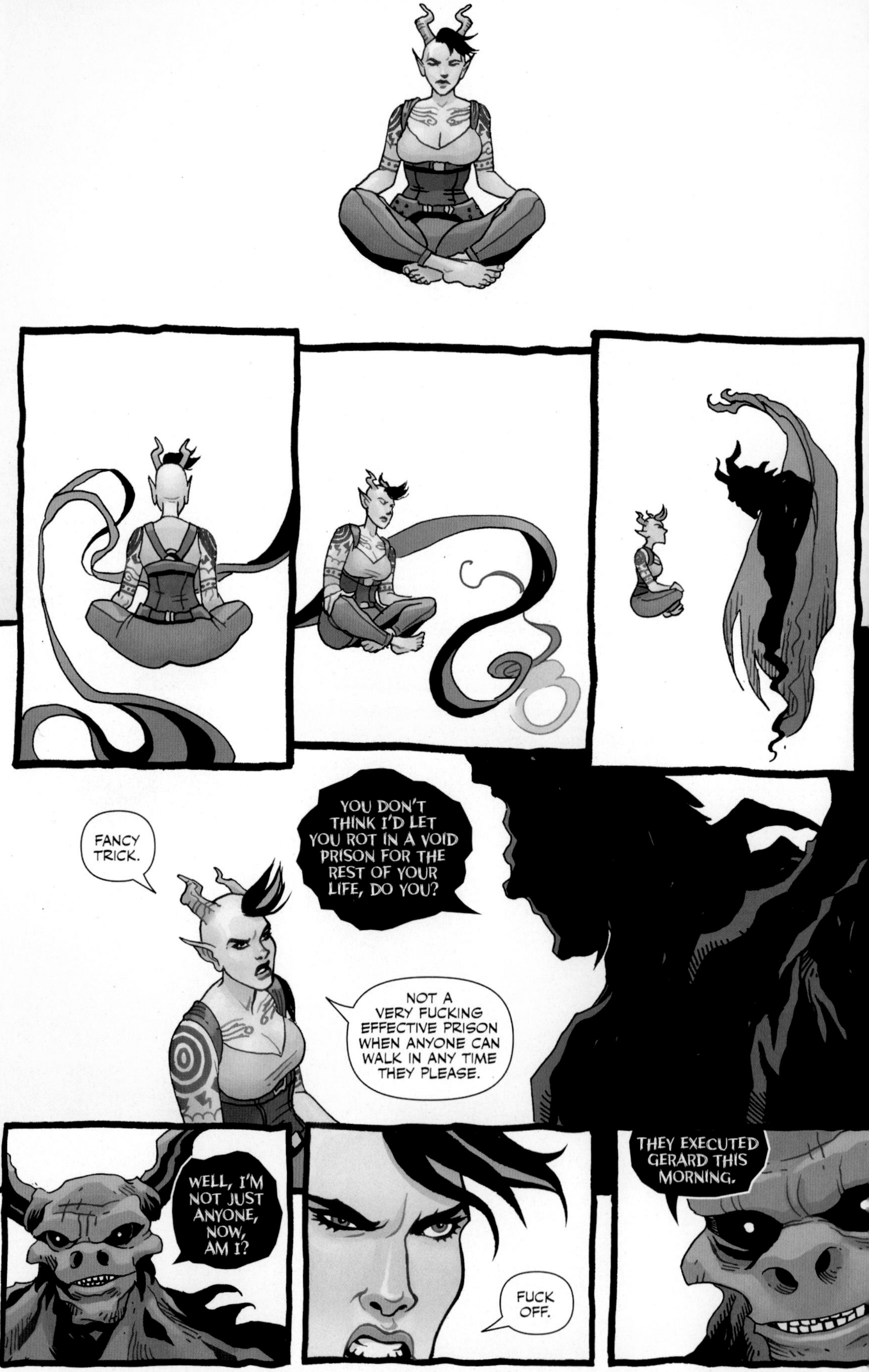

FANCY TRICK.
YOU DON'T THINK I'D LET YOU ROT IN A VOID PRISON FOR THE REST OF YOUR LIFE, DO YOU?
NOT A VERY FUCKING EFFECTIVE PRISON WHEN ANYONE CAN WALK IN ANY TIME THEY PLEASE.
WELL, I'M NOT JUST ANYONE, NOW, AM I?
FUCK OFF.
THEY EXECUTED GERARD THIS MORNING.

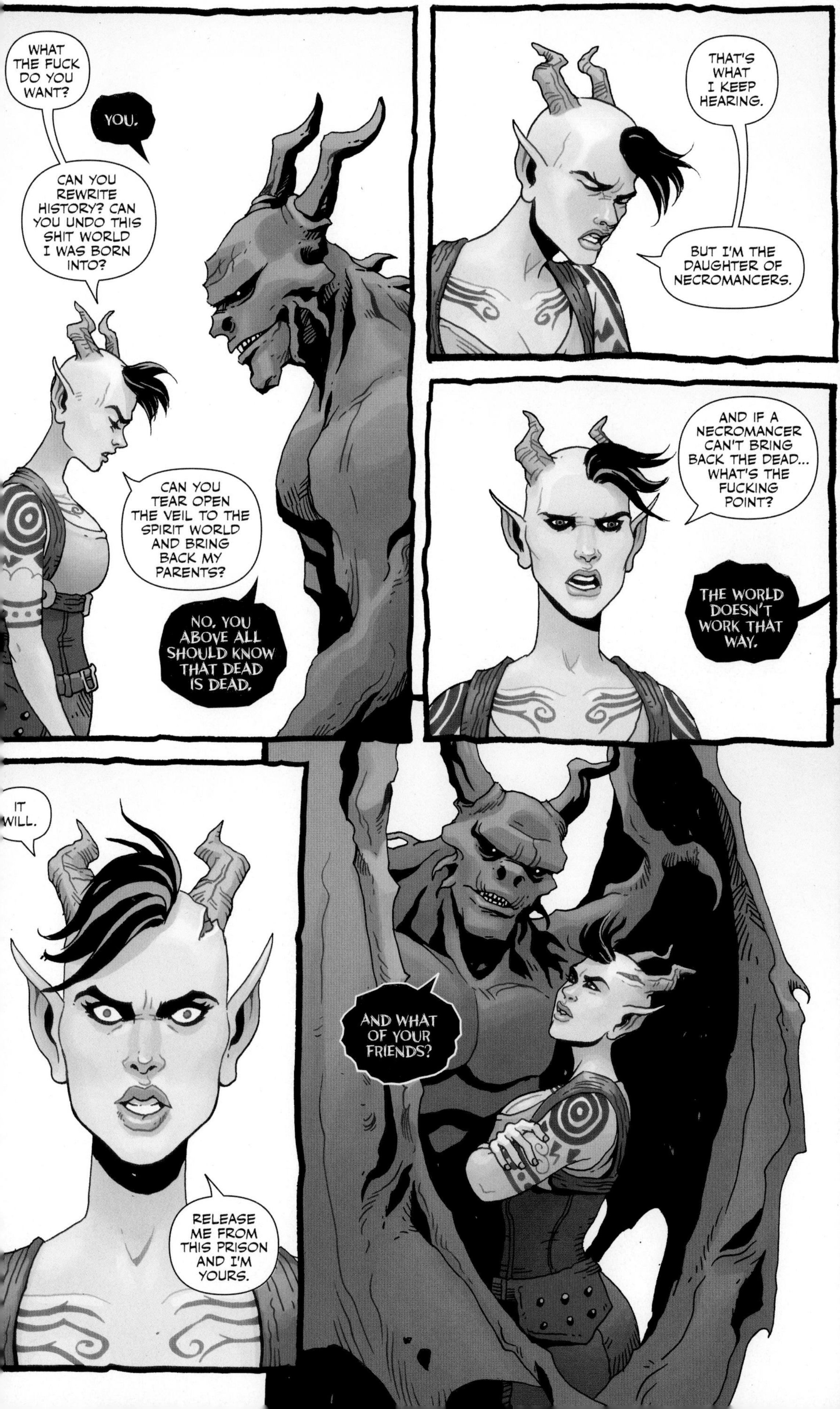
WHAT THE FUCK DO YOU WANT?
YOU.
CAN YOU REWRITE HISTORY? CAN YOU UNDO THIS SHIT WORLD I WAS BORN INTO?
CAN YOU TEAR OPEN THE VEIL TO THE SPIRIT WORLD AND BRING BACK MY PARENTS?
NO, YOU ABOVE ALL SHOULD KNOW THAT DEAD IS DEAD.
THAT'S WHAT I KEEP HEARING.
BUT I'M THE DAUGHTER OF NECROMANCERS.
AND IF A NECROMANCER CAN'T BRING BACK THE DEAD... WHAT'S THE FUCKING POINT?
THE WORLD DOESN'T WORK THAT WAY.
IT WILL.
RELEASE ME FROM THIS PRISON AND I'M YOURS.
AND WHAT OF YOUR FRIENDS?

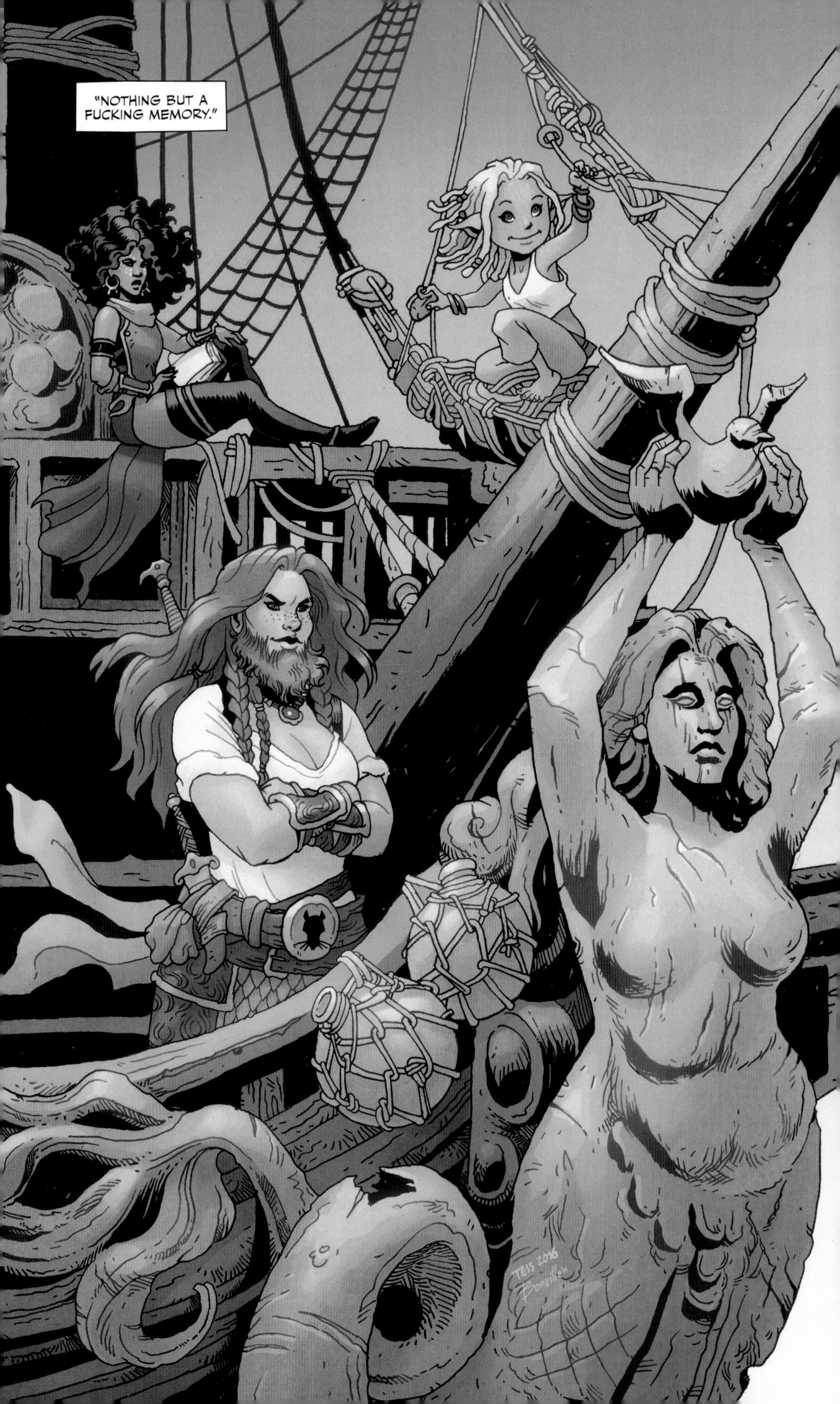
"NOTHING BUT A
FUCKING MEMORY."
TESS 2016
Bonvillain

BRAGA SPECIAL

KURTIS J. WIEBE
story

TESS FOWLER
art/cover

KELLY FITZPATRICK
colors

ED BRISSON
letters

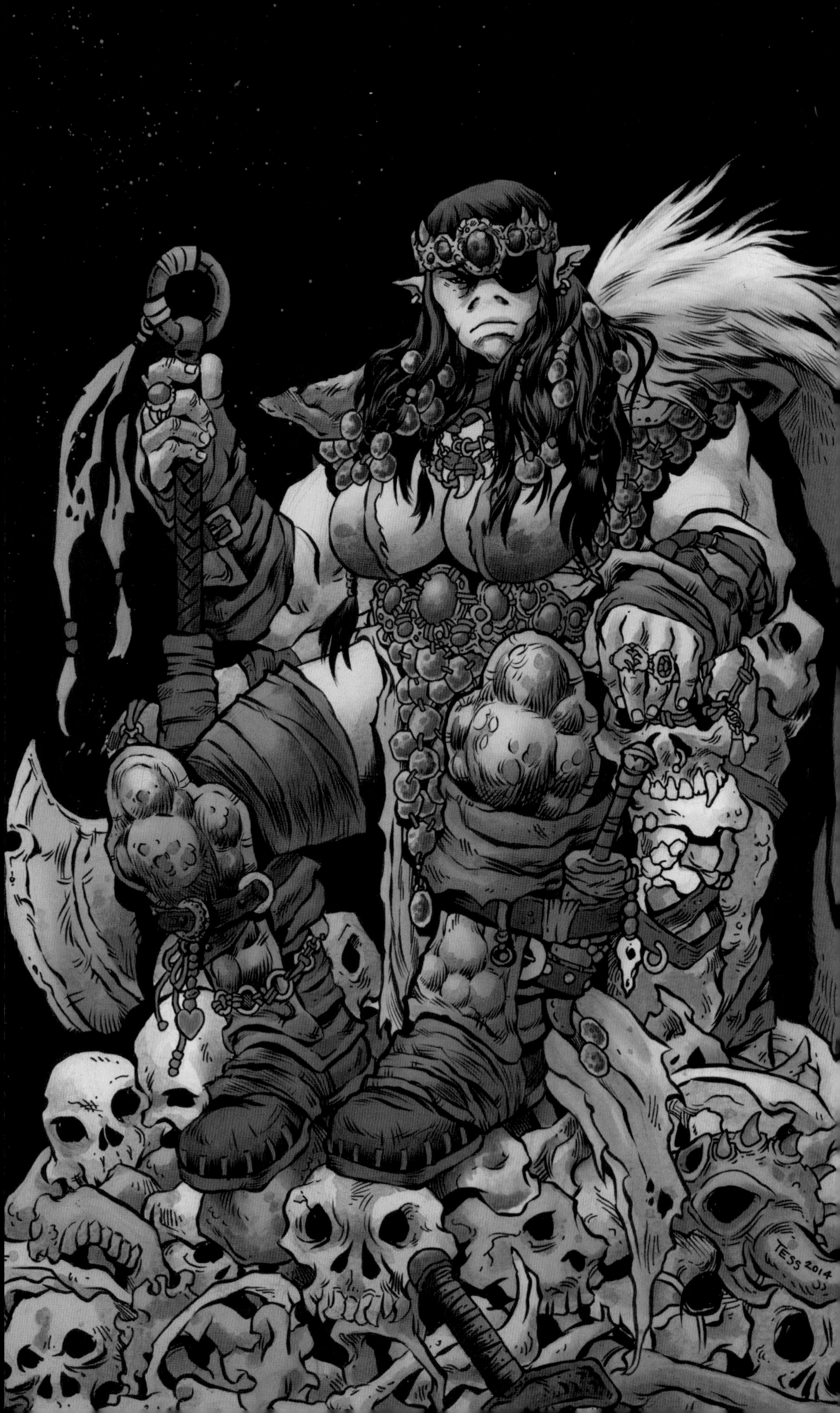
TESS 2014

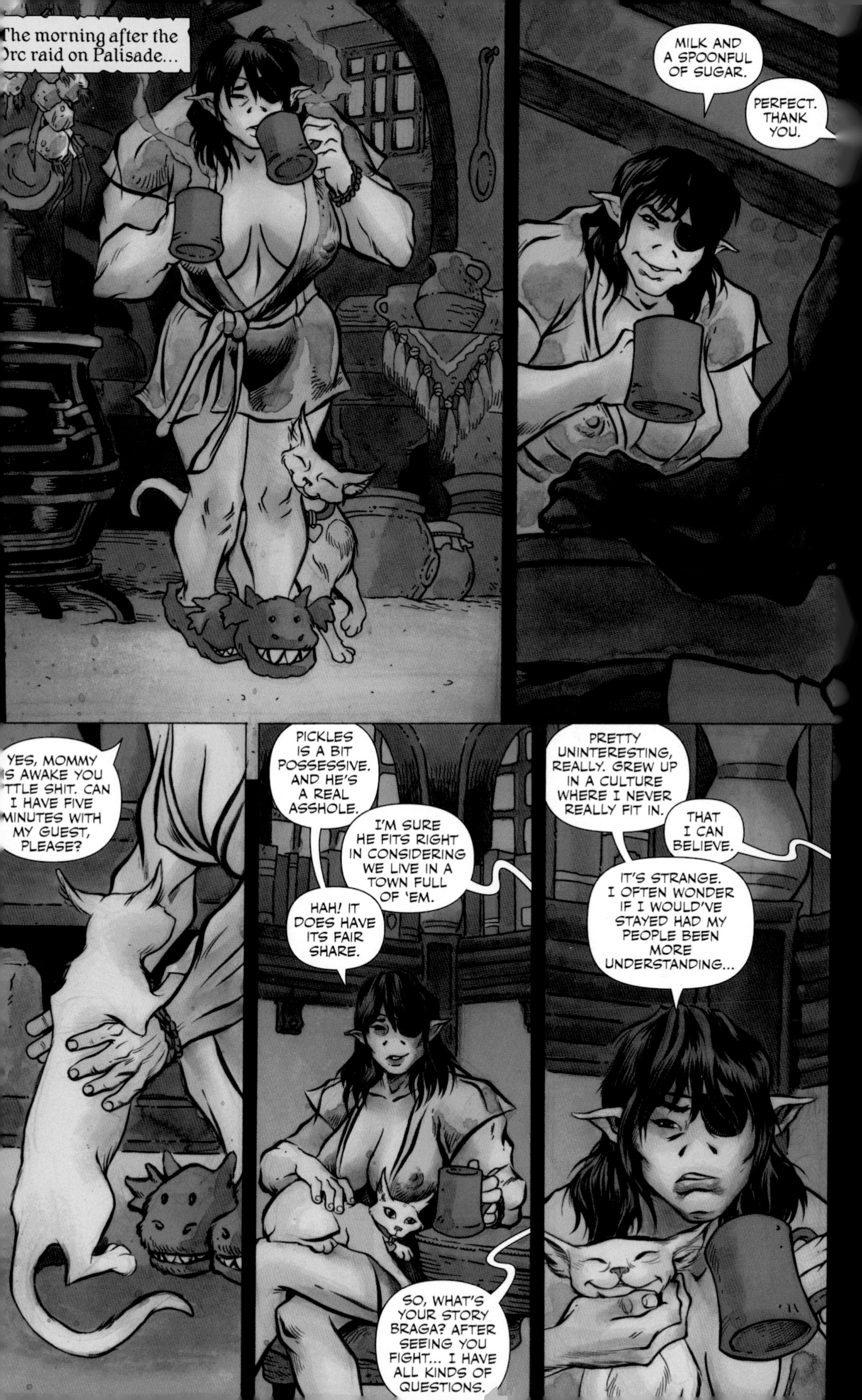
The morning after the Orc raid on Palisade…
MILK AND A SPOONFUL OF SUGAR.
PERFECT. THANK YOU.
YES, MOMMY S AWAKE YOU TTLE SHIT. CAN I HAVE FIVE MINUTES WITH MY GUEST, PLEASE?
PICKLES IS A BIT POSSESSIVE. AND HE'S A REAL ASSHOLE.
I'M SURE HE FITS RIGHT IN CONSIDERING WE LIVE IN A TOWN FULL OF 'EM.
HAH! IT DOES HAVE ITS FAIR SHARE.
SO, WHAT'S YOUR STORY BRAGA? AFTER SEEING YOU FIGHT… I HAVE ALL KINDS OF QUESTIONS.
PRETTY UNINTERESTING, REALLY. GREW UP IN A CULTURE WHERE I NEVER REALLY FIT IN.
THAT I CAN BELIEVE.
IT'S STRANGE. I OFTEN WONDER IF I WOULD'VE STAYED HAD MY PEOPLE BEEN MORE UNDERSTANDING…

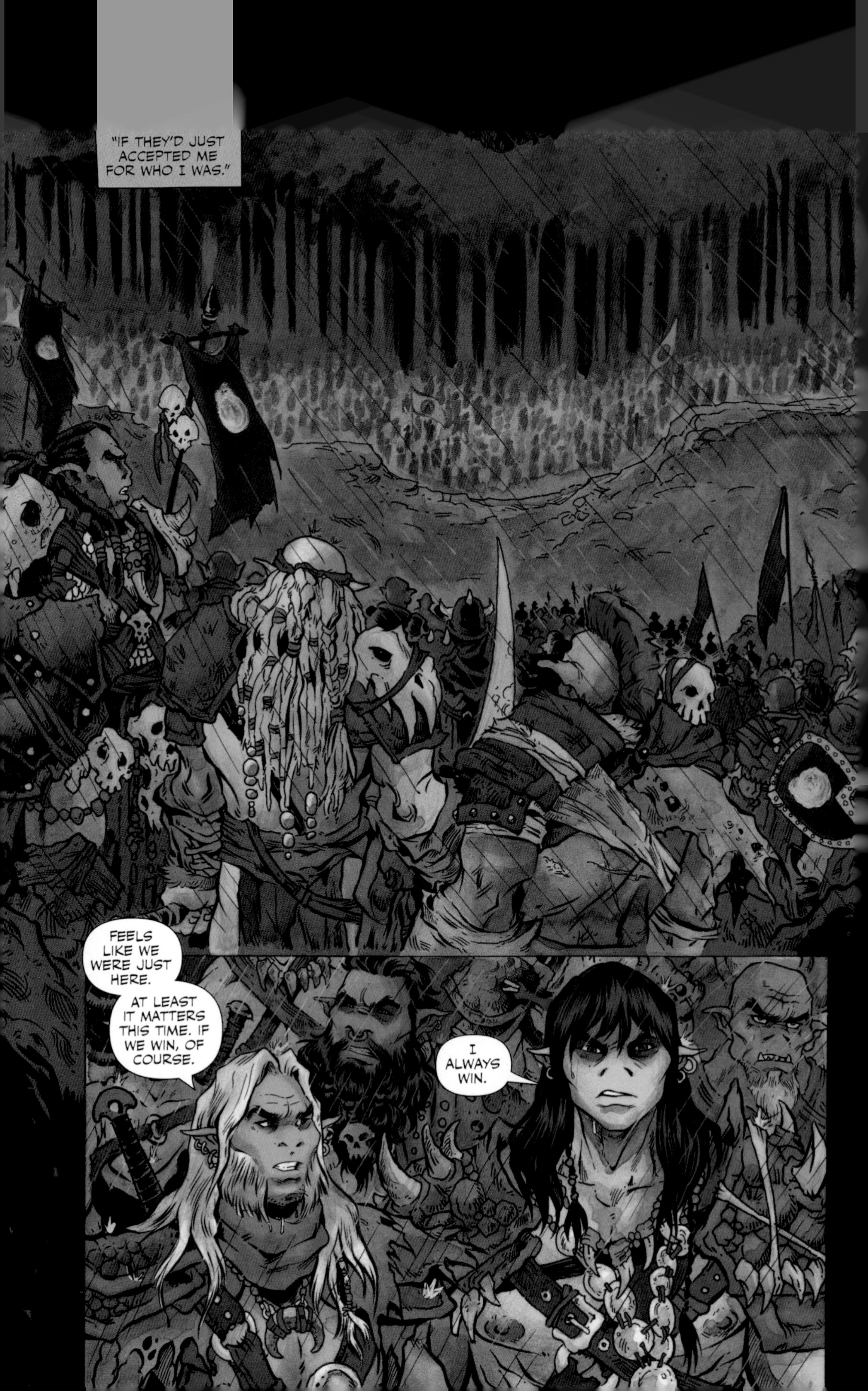
"IF THEY'D JUST ACCEPTED ME FOR WHO I WAS."
FEELS LIKE WE WERE JUST HERE.
AT LEAST IT MATTERS THIS TIME. IF WE WIN, OF COURSE.
I ALWAYS WIN.

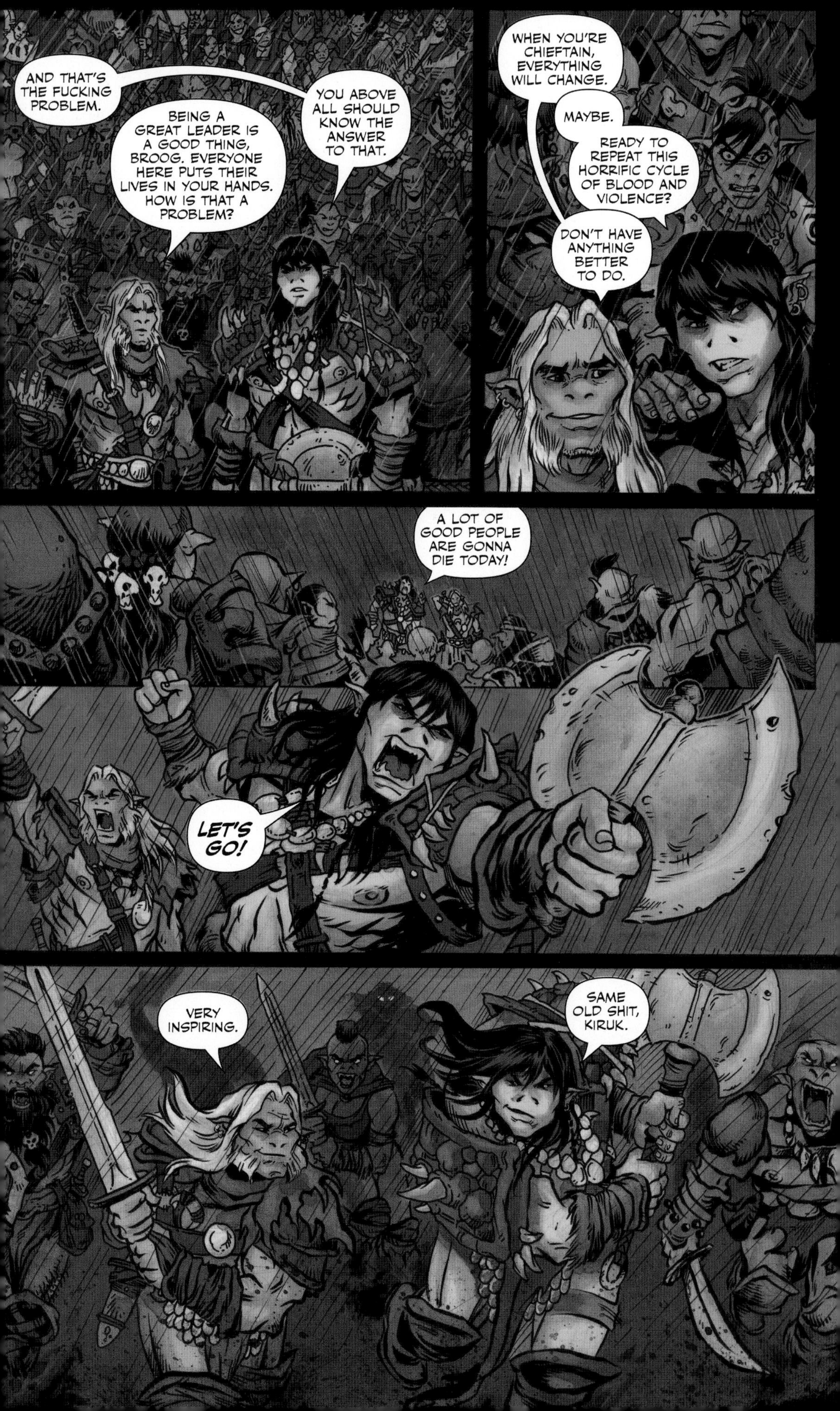
AND THAT'S THE FUCKING PROBLEM.
BEING A GREAT LEADER IS A GOOD THING, BROOG. EVERYONE HERE PUTS THEIR LIVES IN YOUR HANDS. HOW IS THAT A PROBLEM?
YOU ABOVE ALL SHOULD KNOW THE ANSWER TO THAT.
WHEN YOU'RE CHIEFTAIN, EVERYTHING WILL CHANGE.
MAYBE.
READY TO REPEAT THIS HORRIFIC CYCLE OF BLOOD AND VIOLENCE?
DON'T HAVE ANYTHING BETTER TO DO.
A LOT OF GOOD PEOPLE ARE GONNA DIE TODAY!
LET'S GO!
VERY INSPIRING.
SAME OLD SHIT, KIRUK.

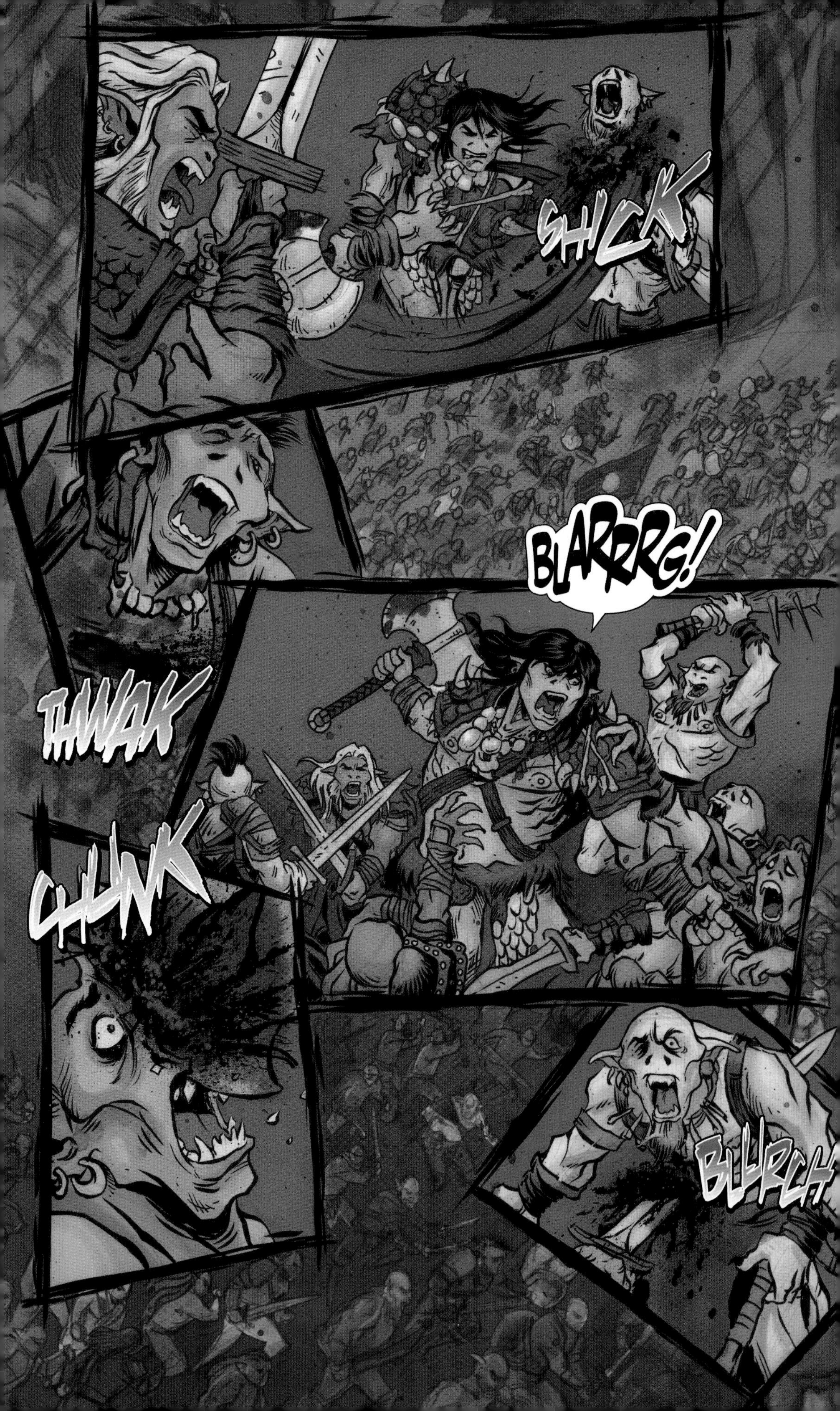
SHICK
BLARRRG!
THWAK
CHUNK
BLURCH

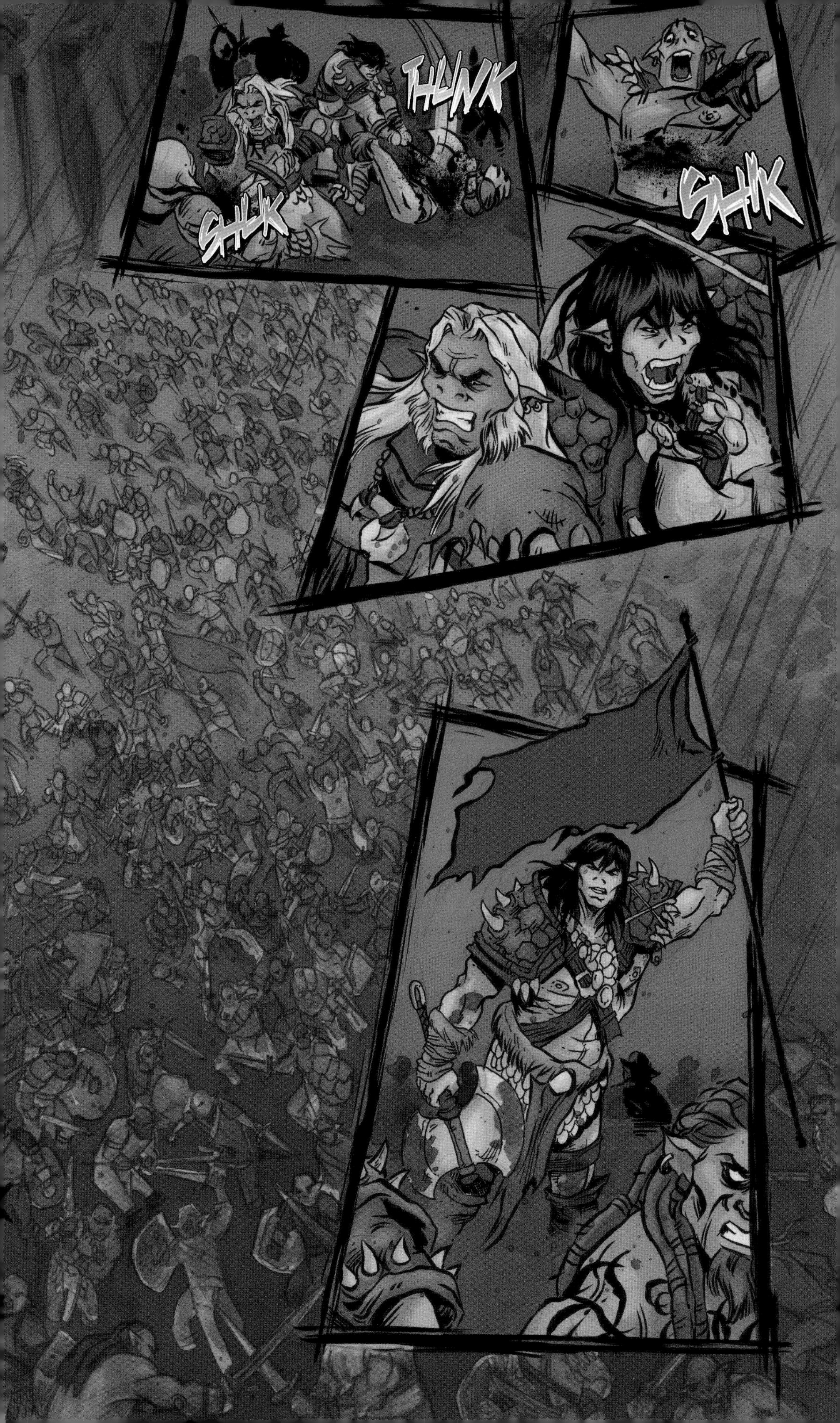
THUNK
SHUK
SHUK

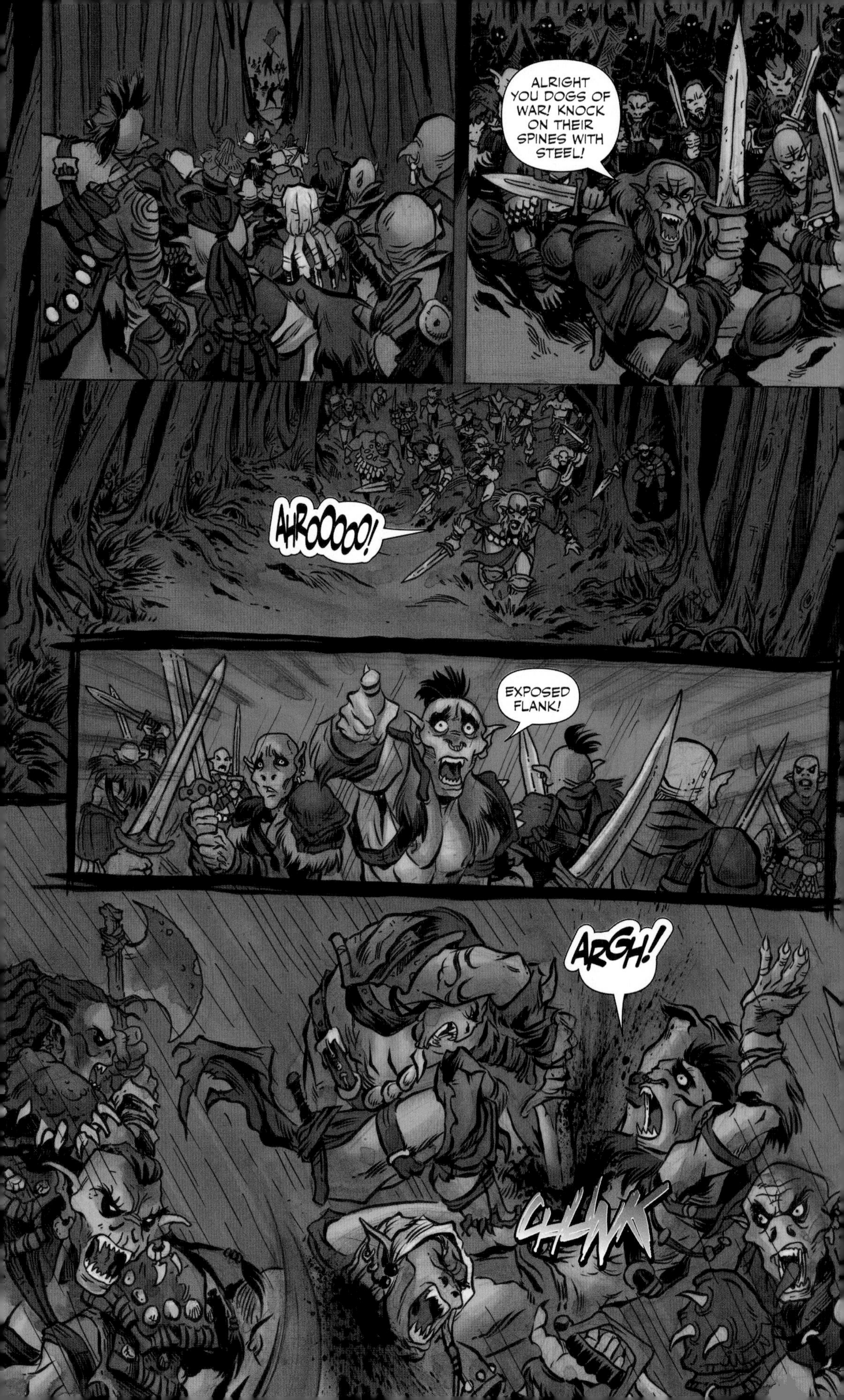
ALRIGHT YOU DOGS OF WAR! KNOCK ON THEIR SPINES WITH STEEL!
AHROOOOO!
EXPOSED FLANK!
ARGH!
CHUNK

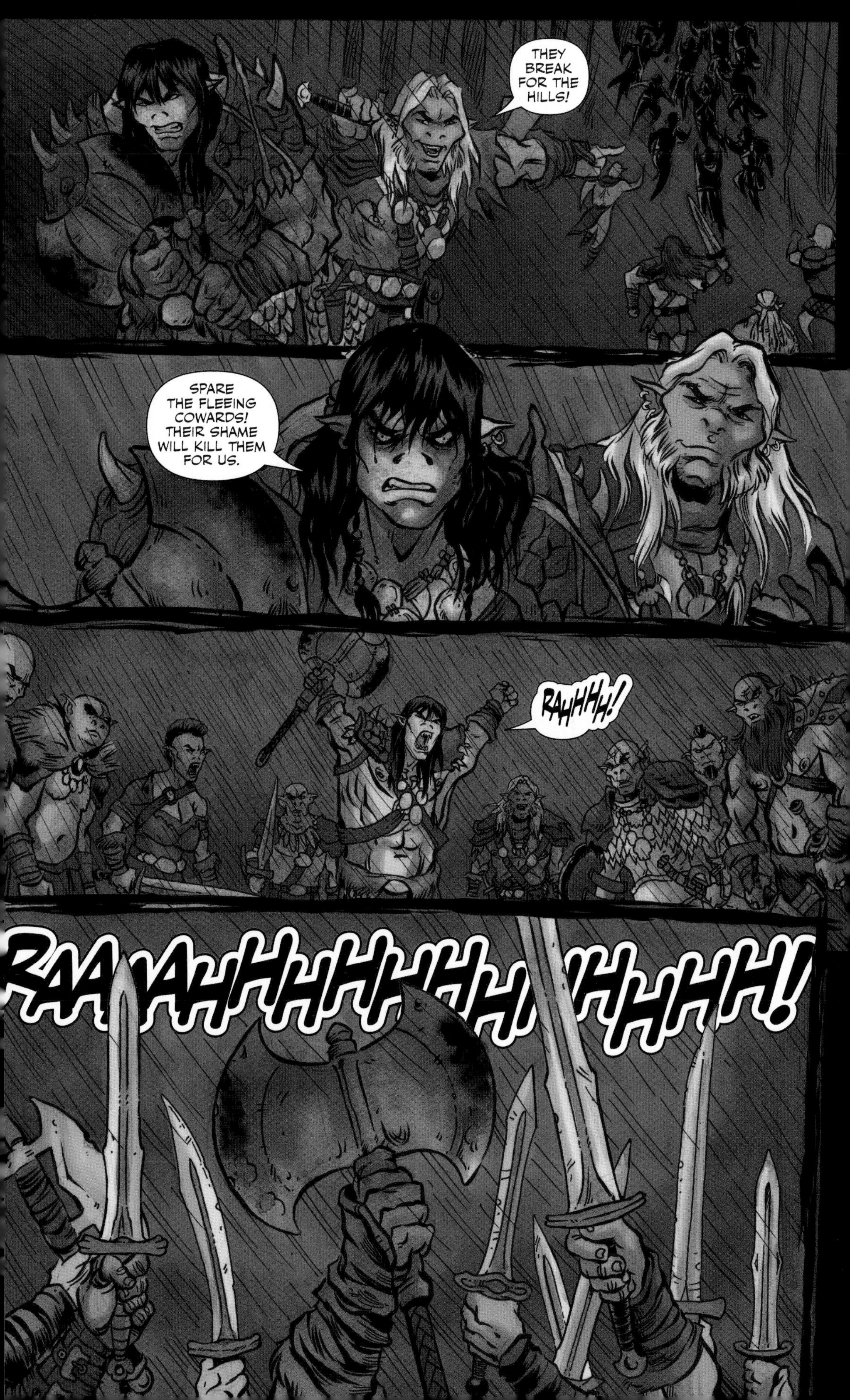
THEY BREAK FOR THE HILLS!
SPARE THE FLEEING COWARDS! THEIR SHAME WILL KILL THEM FOR US.
RAHHHH!
RAAAAHHHHHHHHHHHH!

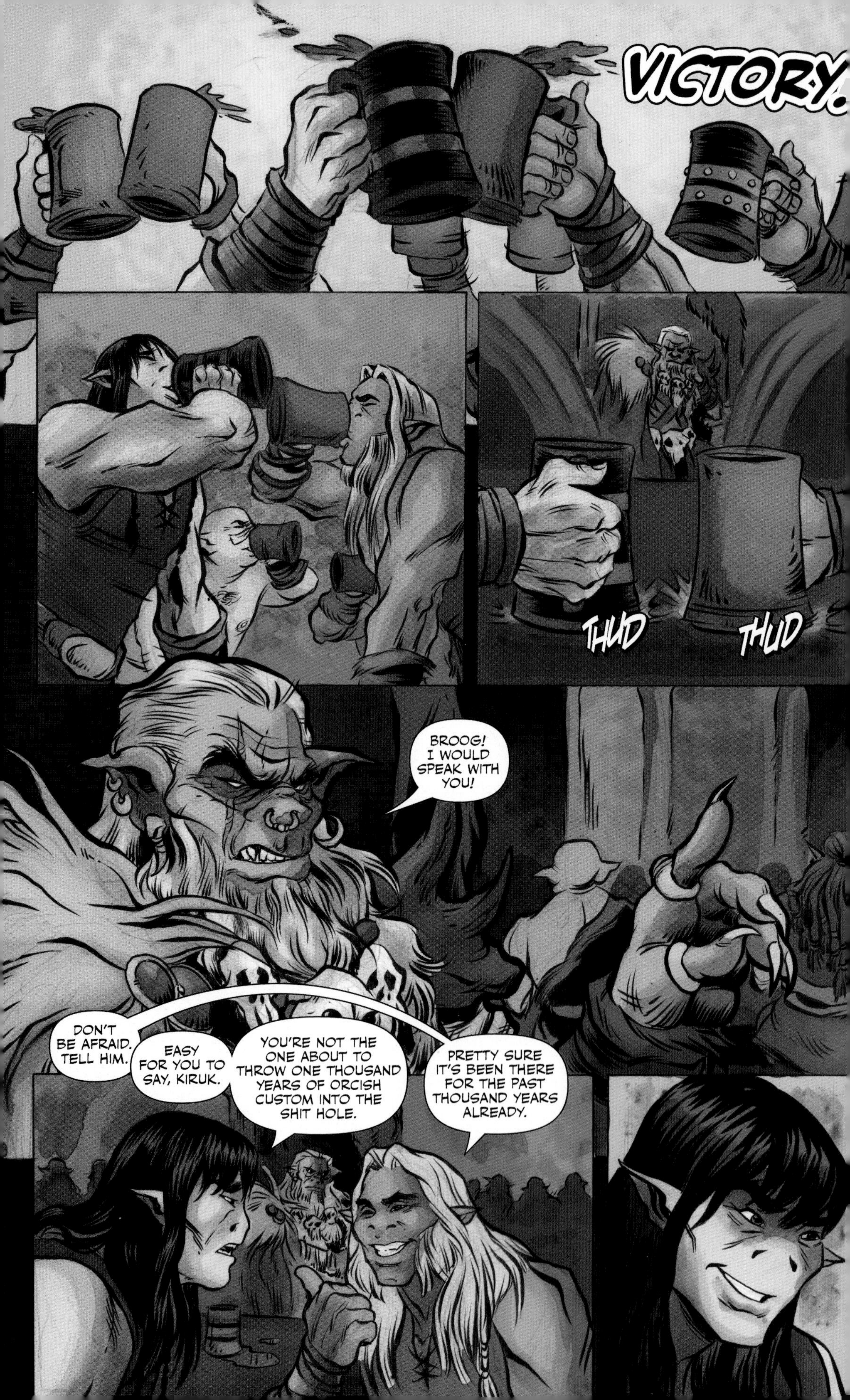
VICTORY.
THUD
THUD
BROOG! I WOULD SPEAK WITH YOU!
DON'T BE AFRAID. TELL HIM.
EASY FOR YOU TO SAY, KIRUK.
YOU'RE NOT THE ONE ABOUT TO THROW ONE THOUSAND YEARS OF ORCISH CUSTOM INTO THE SHIT HOLE.
PRETTY SURE IT'S BEEN THERE FOR THE PAST THOUSAND YEARS ALREADY.

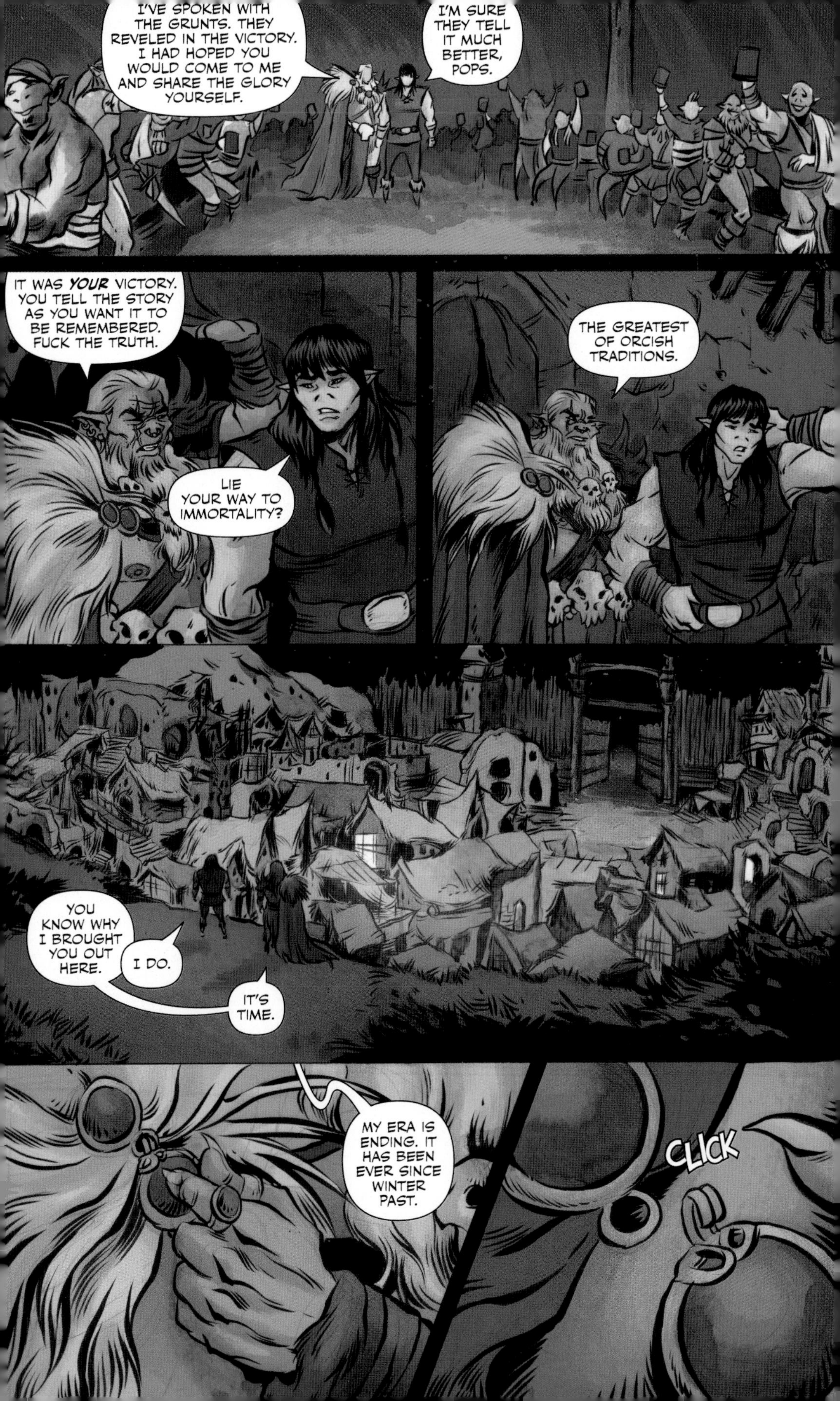
I'VE SPOKEN WITH THE GRUNTS. THEY REVELED IN THE VICTORY. I HAD HOPED YOU WOULD COME TO ME AND SHARE THE GLORY YOURSELF.
I'M SURE THEY TELL IT MUCH BETTER, POPS.
IT WAS YOUR VICTORY. YOU TELL THE STORY AS YOU WANT IT TO BE REMEMBERED. FUCK THE TRUTH.
LIE YOUR WAY TO IMMORTALITY?
THE GREATEST OF ORCISH TRADITIONS.
YOU KNOW WHY I BROUGHT YOU OUT HERE.
I DO.
IT'S TIME.
MY ERA IS ENDING. IT HAS BEEN EVER SINCE WINTER PAST.
CLICK

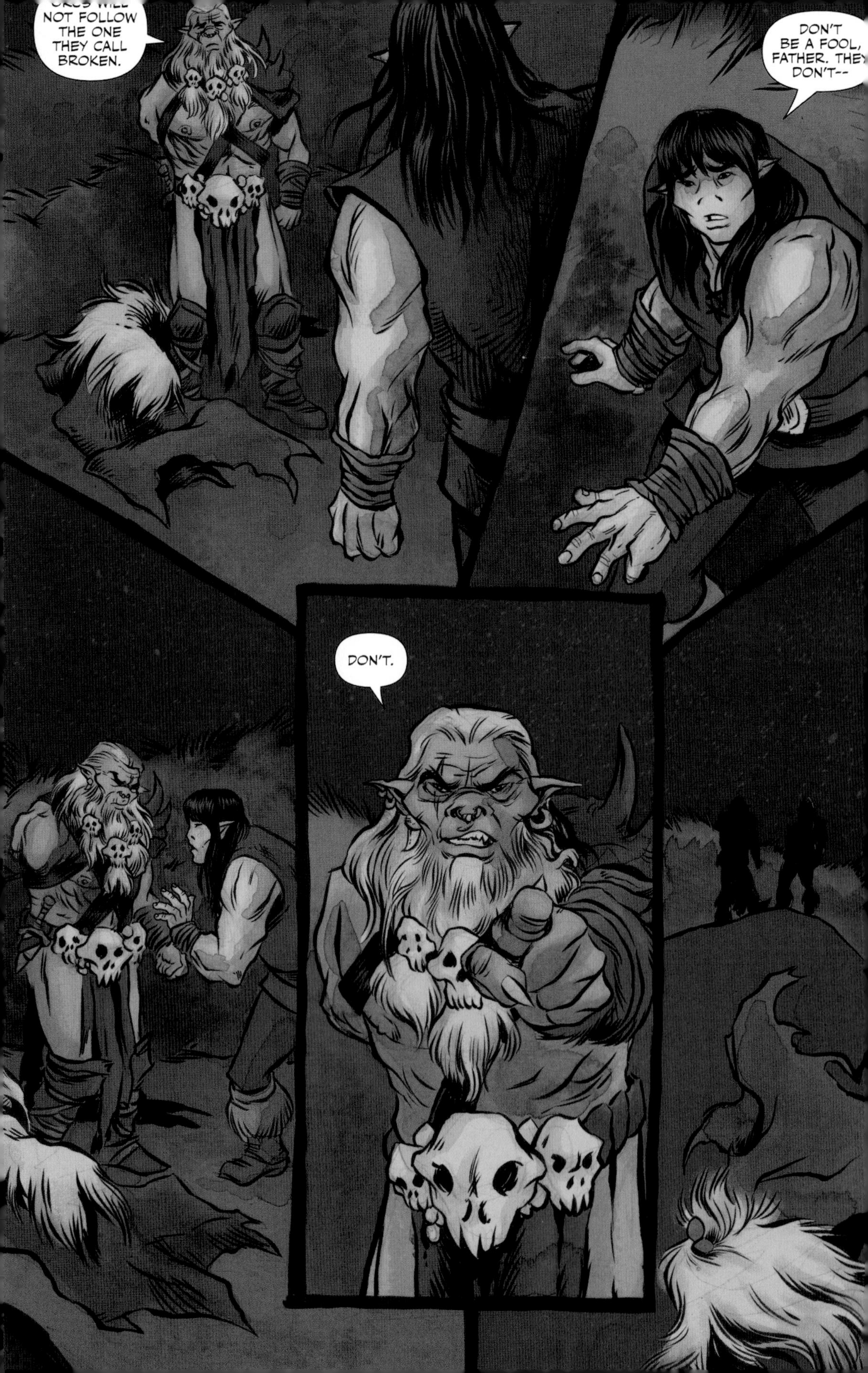
NOT FOLLOW THE ONE THEY CALL BROKEN.
DON'T BE A FOOL, FATHER. THEY DON'T--
DON'T.

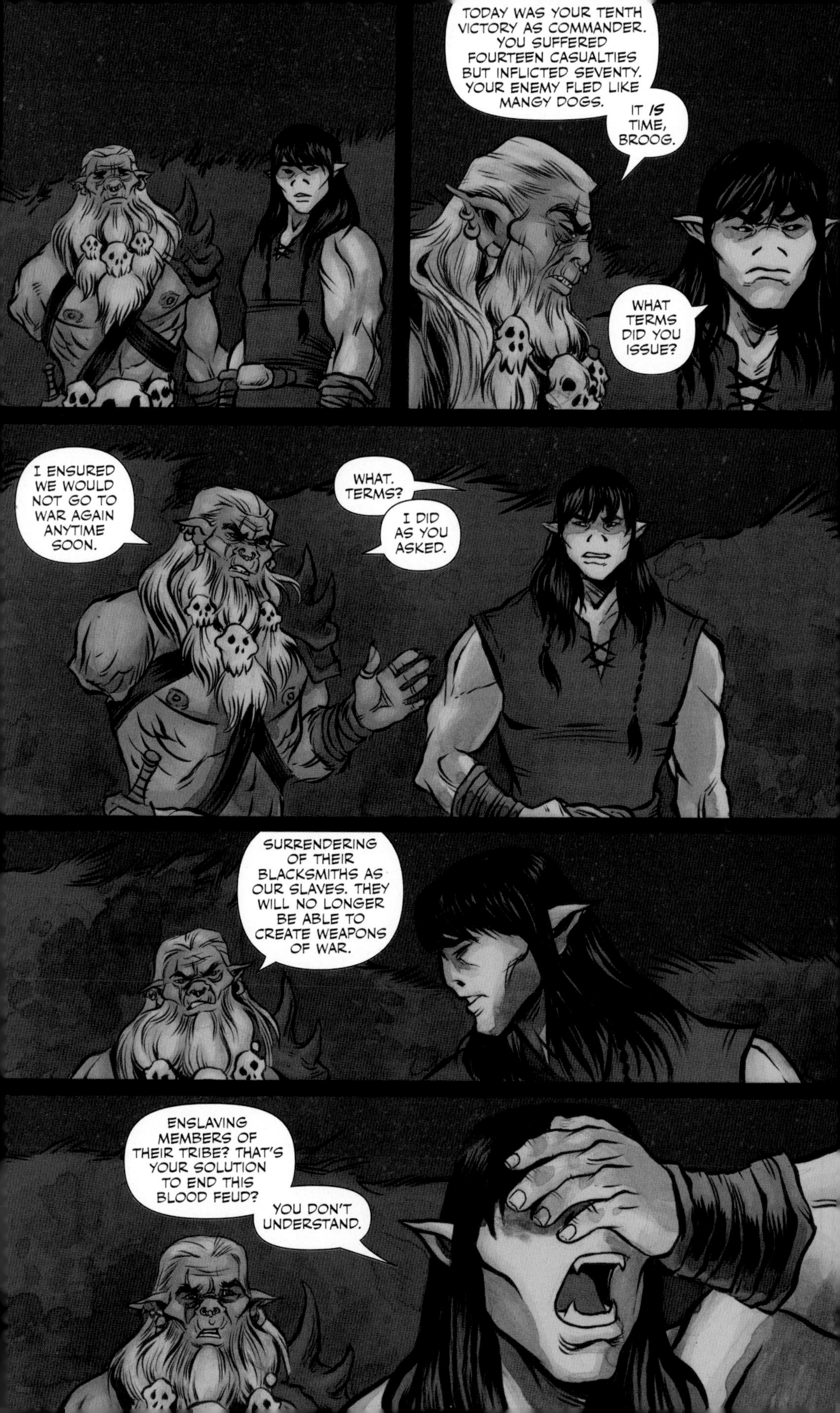
TODAY WAS YOUR TENTH VICTORY AS COMMANDER. YOU SUFFERED FOURTEEN CASUALTIES BUT INFLICTED SEVENTY. YOUR ENEMY FLED LIKE MANGY DOGS.
IT *IS* TIME, BROOG.
WHAT TERMS DID YOU ISSUE?
I ENSURED WE WOULD NOT GO TO WAR AGAIN ANYTIME SOON.
WHAT. TERMS?
I DID AS YOU ASKED.
SURRENDERING OF THEIR BLACKSMITHS AS OUR SLAVES. THEY WILL NO LONGER BE ABLE TO CREATE WEAPONS OF WAR.
ENSLAVING MEMBERS OF THEIR TRIBE? THAT'S YOUR SOLUTION TO END THIS BLOOD FEUD?
YOU DON'T UNDERSTAND.

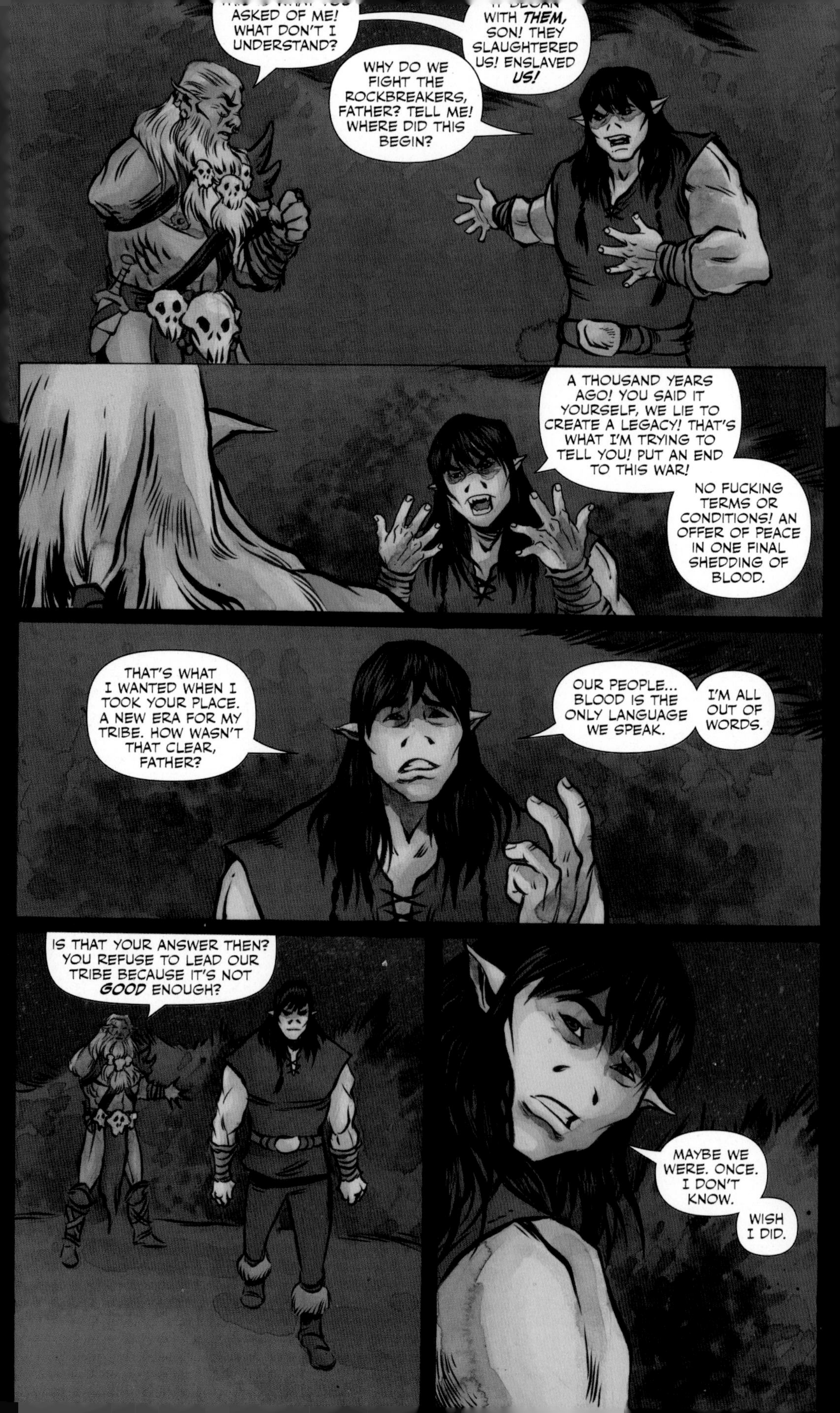
ASKED OF ME! WHAT DON'T I UNDERSTAND?
WITH *THEM,* SON! THEY SLAUGHTERED US! ENSLAVED *US!*
WHY DO WE FIGHT THE ROCKBREAKERS, FATHER? TELL ME! WHERE DID THIS BEGIN?
A THOUSAND YEARS AGO! YOU SAID IT YOURSELF, WE LIE TO CREATE A LEGACY! THAT'S WHAT I'M TRYING TO TELL YOU! PUT AN END TO THIS WAR!
NO FUCKING TERMS OR CONDITIONS! AN OFFER OF PEACE IN ONE FINAL SHEDDING OF BLOOD.
THAT'S WHAT I WANTED WHEN I TOOK YOUR PLACE. A NEW ERA FOR MY TRIBE. HOW WASN'T THAT CLEAR, FATHER?
OUR PEOPLE... BLOOD IS THE ONLY LANGUAGE WE SPEAK.
I'M ALL OUT OF WORDS.
IS THAT YOUR ANSWER THEN? YOU REFUSE TO LEAD OUR TRIBE BECAUSE IT'S NOT *GOOD* ENOUGH?
MAYBE WE WERE. ONCE. I DON'T KNOW.
WISH I DID.

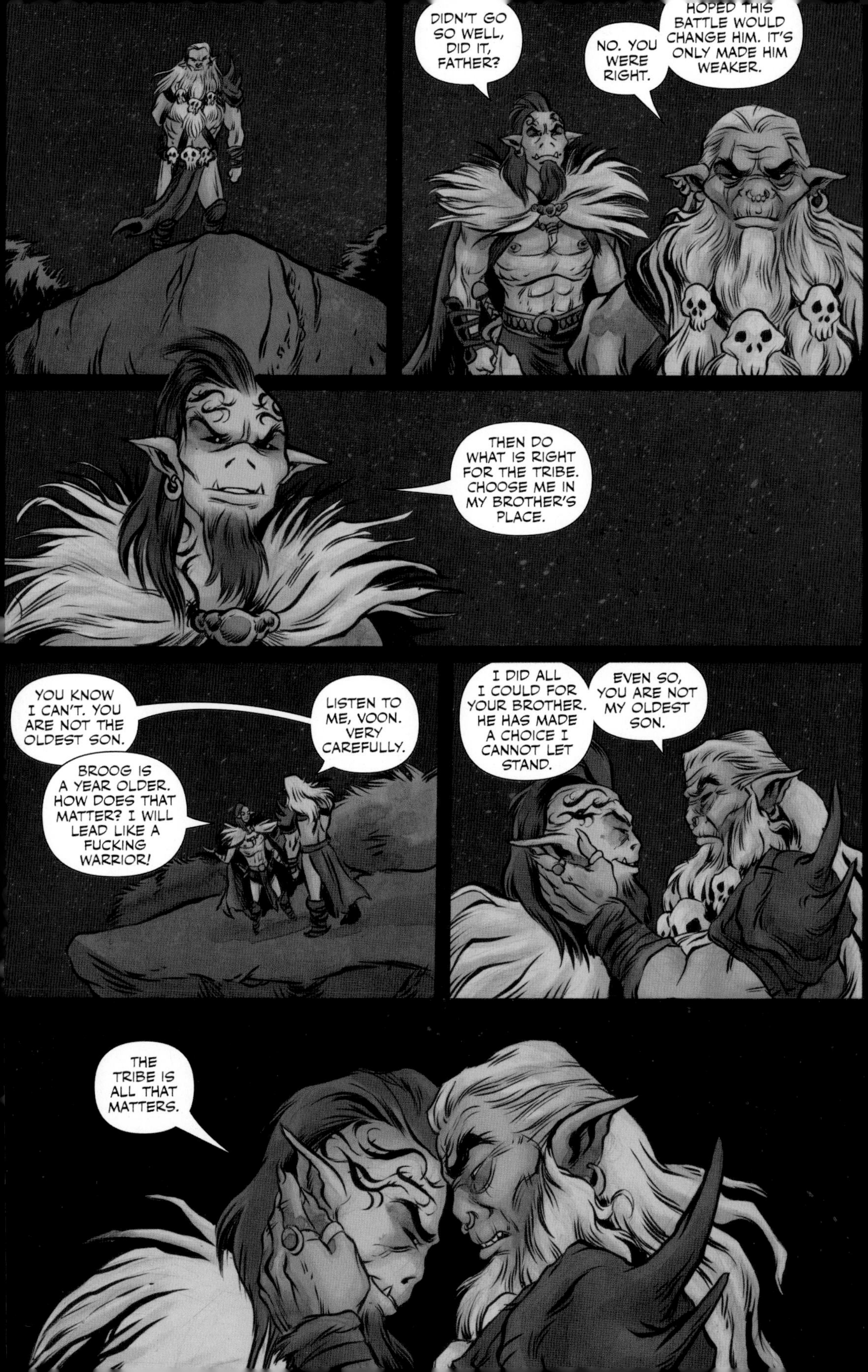
DIDN'T GO SO WELL, DID IT, FATHER?
NO. YOU WERE RIGHT.
HOPED THIS BATTLE WOULD CHANGE HIM. IT'S ONLY MADE HIM WEAKER.
THEN DO WHAT IS RIGHT FOR THE TRIBE. CHOOSE ME IN MY BROTHER'S PLACE.
YOU KNOW I CAN'T. YOU ARE NOT THE OLDEST SON.
BROOG IS A YEAR OLDER. HOW DOES THAT MATTER? I WILL LEAD LIKE A FUCKING WARRIOR!
LISTEN TO ME, VOON. VERY CAREFULLY.
I DID ALL I COULD FOR YOUR BROTHER. HE HAS MADE A CHOICE I CANNOT LET STAND.
EVEN SO, YOU ARE NOT MY OLDEST SON.
THE TRIBE IS ALL THAT MATTERS.

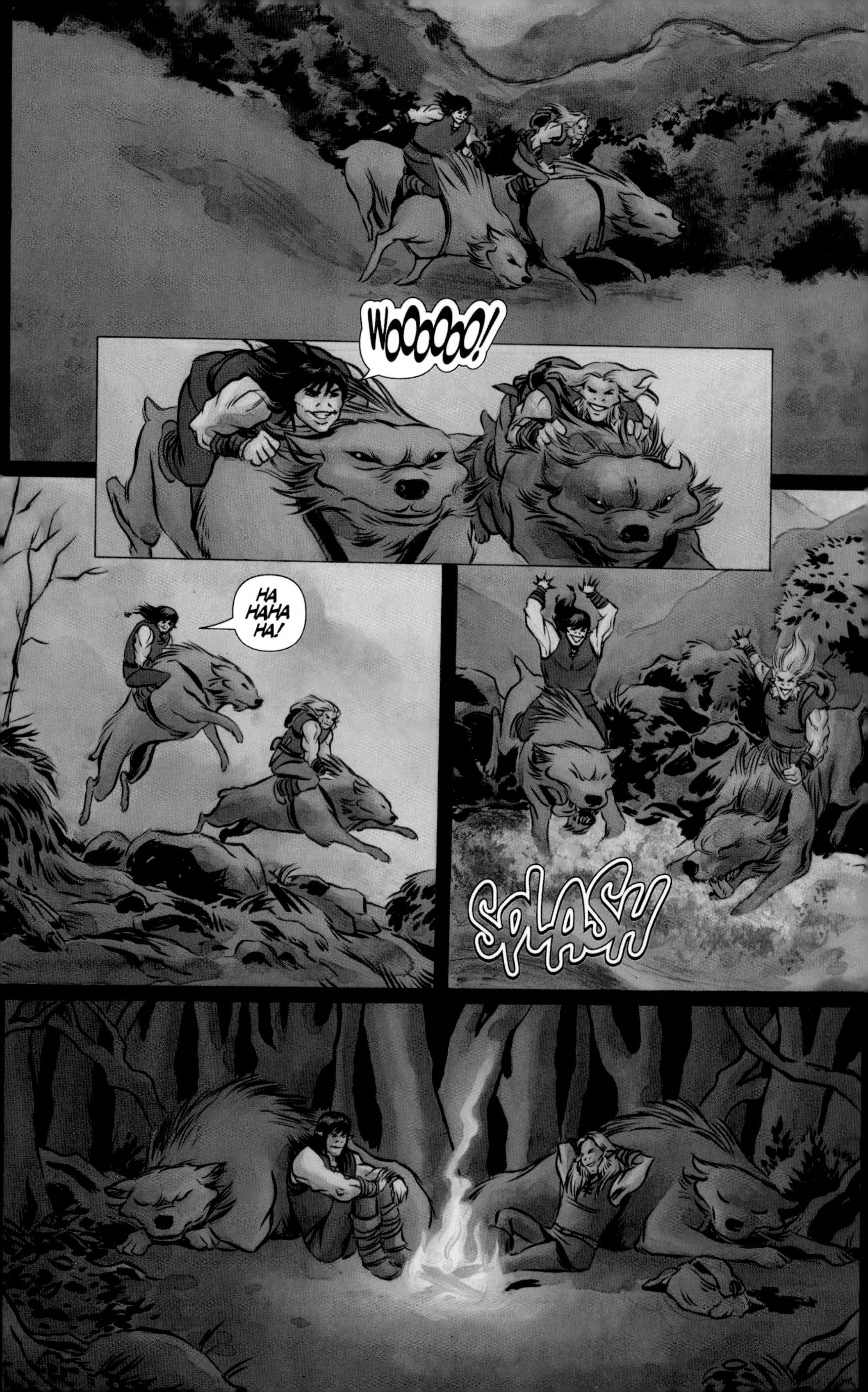
WOOOOOO!
HA HAHA HA!
SPLASH

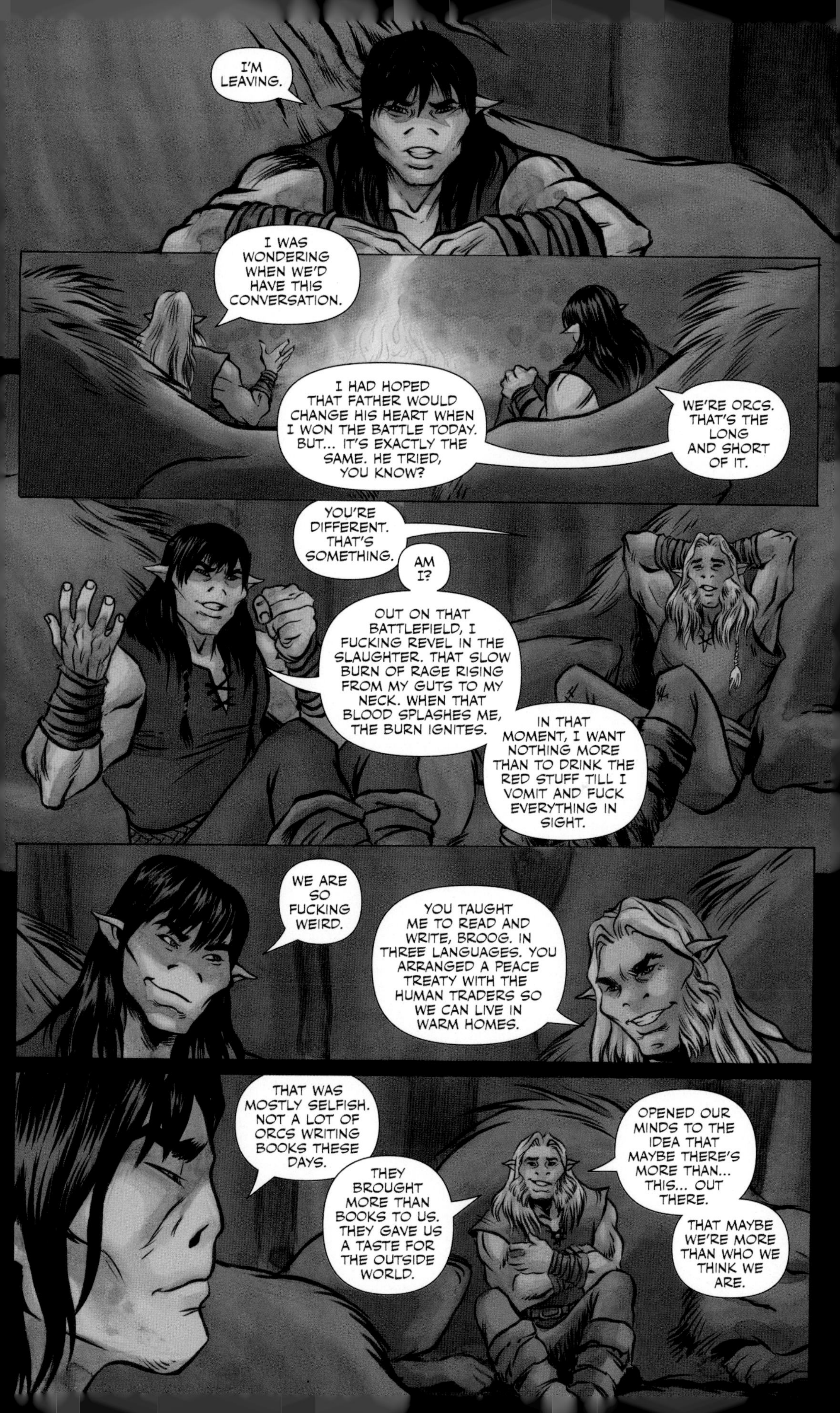
I'M LEAVING.
I WAS WONDERING WHEN WE'D HAVE THIS CONVERSATION.
I HAD HOPED THAT FATHER WOULD CHANGE HIS HEART WHEN I WON THE BATTLE TODAY. BUT... IT'S EXACTLY THE SAME. HE TRIED, YOU KNOW?
WE'RE ORCS. THAT'S THE LONG AND SHORT OF IT.
YOU'RE DIFFERENT. THAT'S SOMETHING.
AM I?
OUT ON THAT BATTLEFIELD, I FUCKING REVEL IN THE SLAUGHTER. THAT SLOW BURN OF RAGE RISING FROM MY GUTS TO MY NECK. WHEN THAT BLOOD SPLASHES ME, THE BURN IGNITES.
IN THAT MOMENT, I WANT NOTHING MORE THAN TO DRINK THE RED STUFF TILL I VOMIT AND FUCK EVERYTHING IN SIGHT.
WE ARE SO FUCKING WEIRD.
YOU TAUGHT ME TO READ AND WRITE, BROOG. IN THREE LANGUAGES. YOU ARRANGED A PEACE TREATY WITH THE HUMAN TRADERS SO WE CAN LIVE IN WARM HOMES.
THAT WAS MOSTLY SELFISH. NOT A LOT OF ORCS WRITING BOOKS THESE DAYS.
THEY BROUGHT MORE THAN BOOKS TO US. THEY GAVE US A TASTE FOR THE OUTSIDE WORLD.
OPENED OUR MINDS TO THE IDEA THAT MAYBE THERE'S MORE THAN... THIS... OUT THERE.
THAT MAYBE WE'RE MORE THAN WHO WE THINK WE ARE.

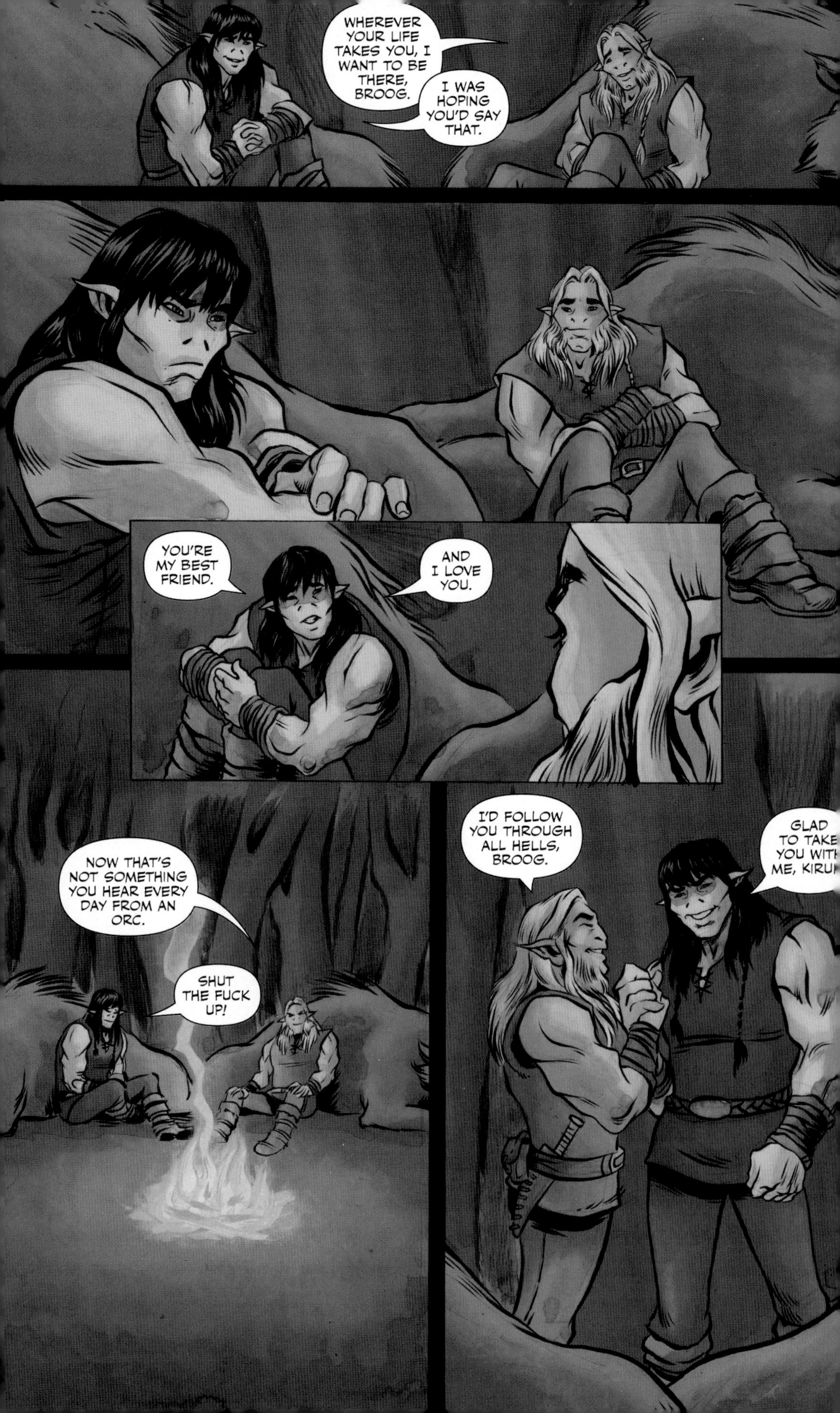
WHEREVER YOUR LIFE TAKES YOU, I WANT TO BE THERE, BROOG.
I WAS HOPING YOU'D SAY THAT.
YOU'RE MY BEST FRIEND.
AND I LOVE YOU.
NOW THAT'S NOT SOMETHING YOU HEAR EVERY DAY FROM AN ORC.
SHUT THE FUCK UP!
I'D FOLLOW YOU THROUGH ALL HELLS, BROOG.

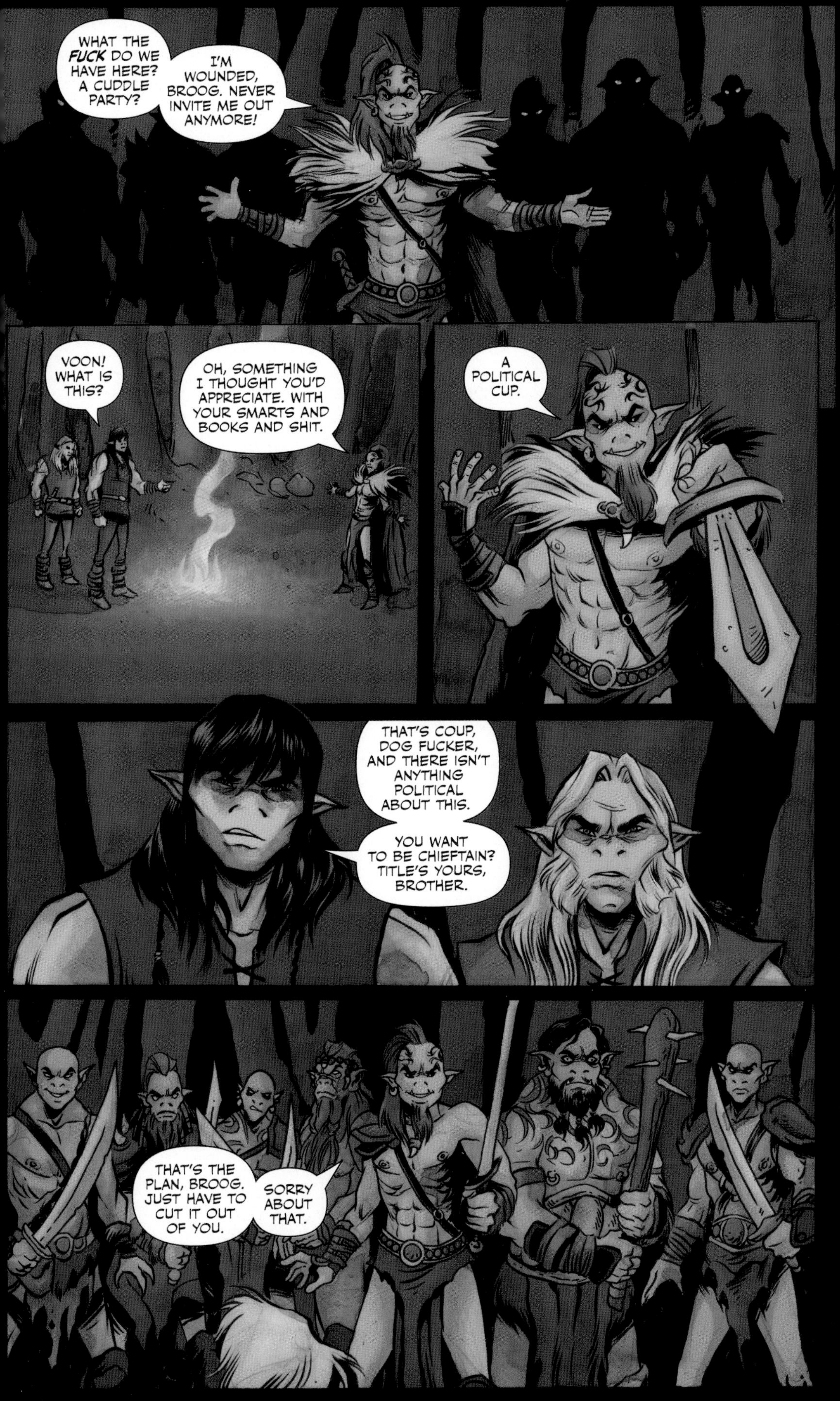
WHAT THE *FUCK* DO WE HAVE HERE? A CUDDLE PARTY?
I'M WOUNDED, BROOG. NEVER INVITE ME OUT ANYMORE!
VOON! WHAT IS THIS?
OH, SOMETHING I THOUGHT YOU'D APPRECIATE. WITH YOUR SMARTS AND BOOKS AND SHIT.
A POLITICAL CUP.
THAT'S COUP, DOG FUCKER, AND THERE ISN'T ANYTHING POLITICAL ABOUT THIS.
YOU WANT TO BE CHIEFTAIN? TITLE'S YOURS, BROTHER.
THAT'S THE PLAN, BROOG. JUST HAVE TO CUT IT OUT OF YOU.
SORRY ABOUT THAT.

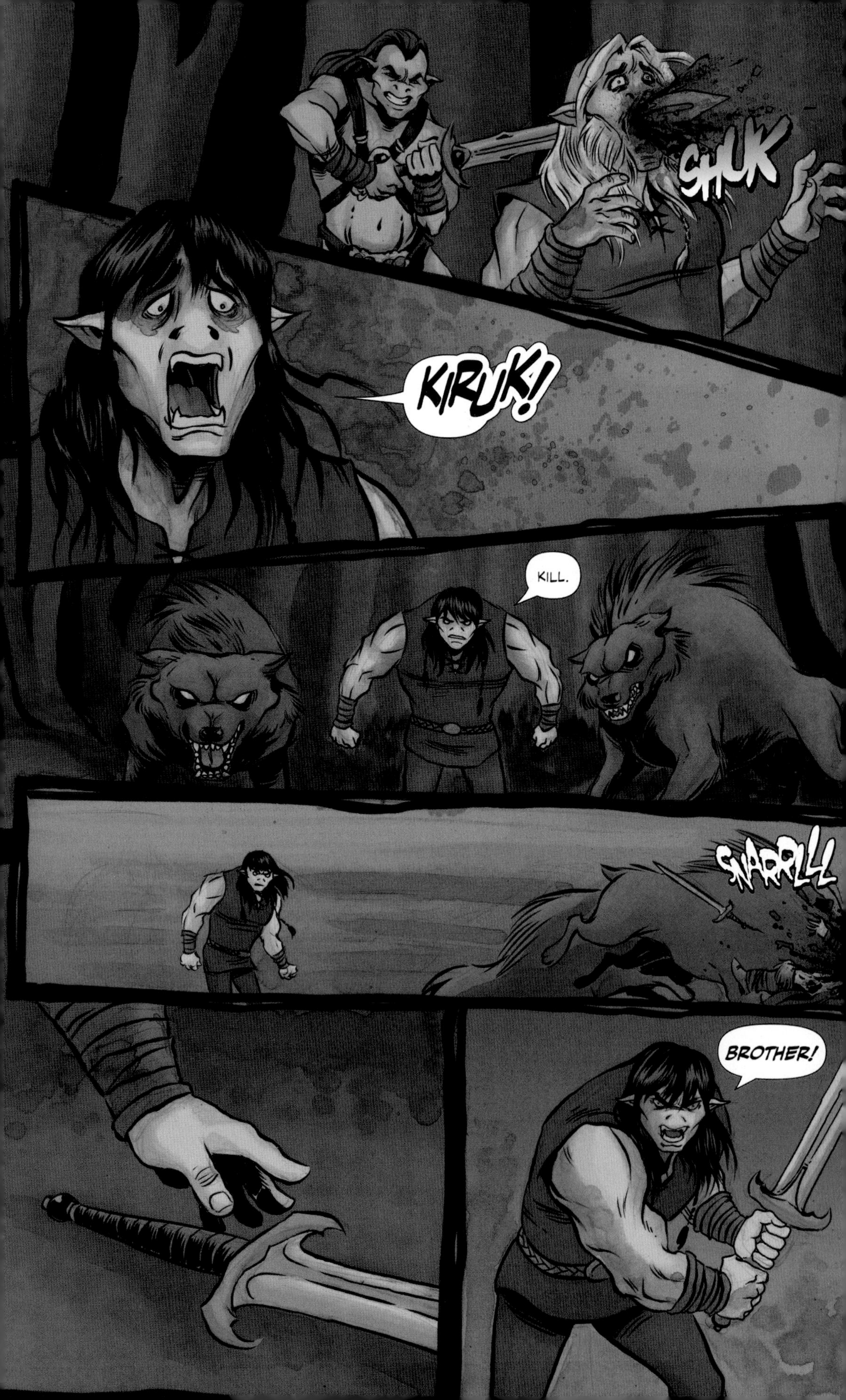
SHUK
KIRUK!
KILL.
SNARRLLL
BROTHER!

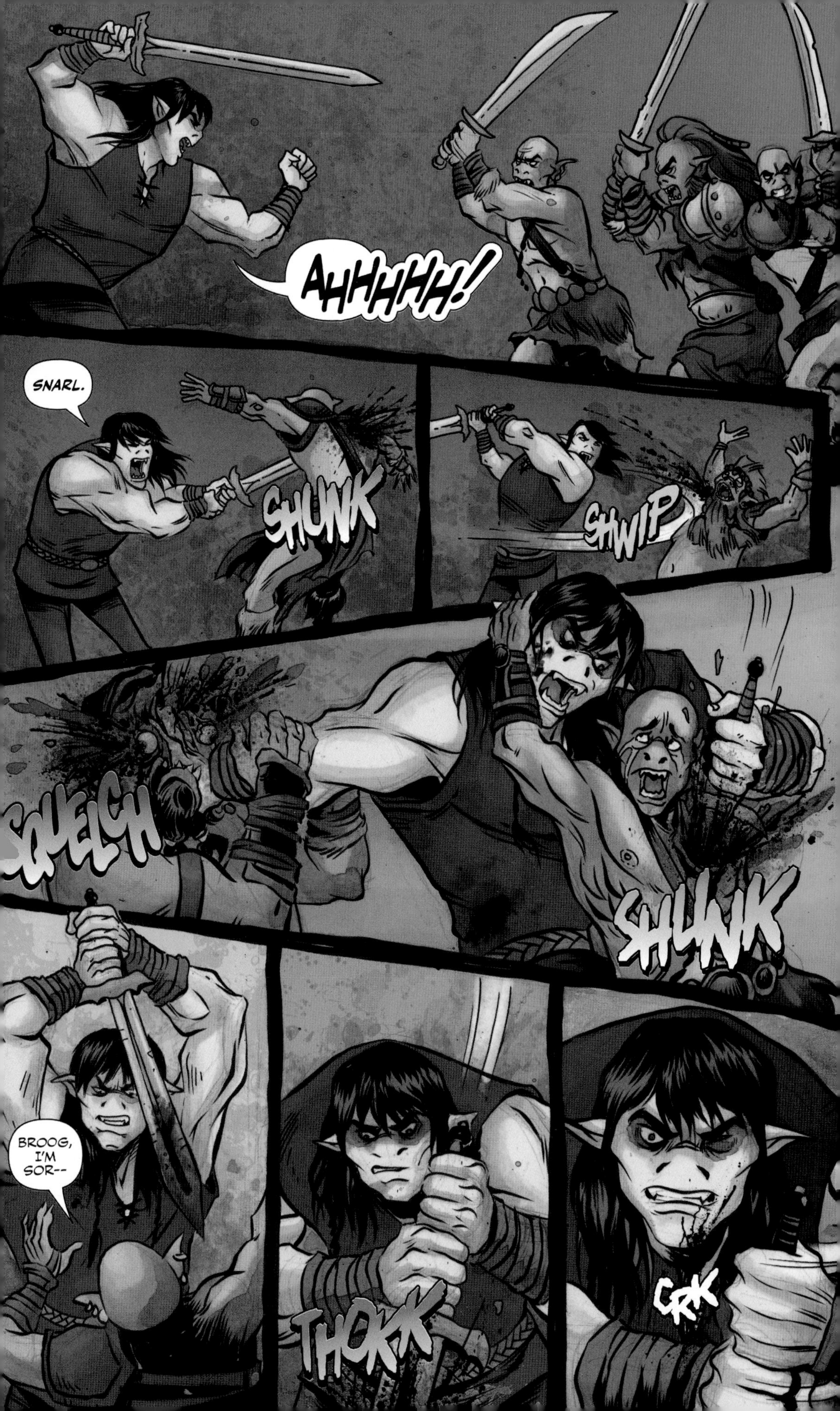
AHHHHH!
SNARL.
SHUNK
SHWIP
SQUELCH
SHUNK
BROOG, I'M SOR--
THOKK
GRK

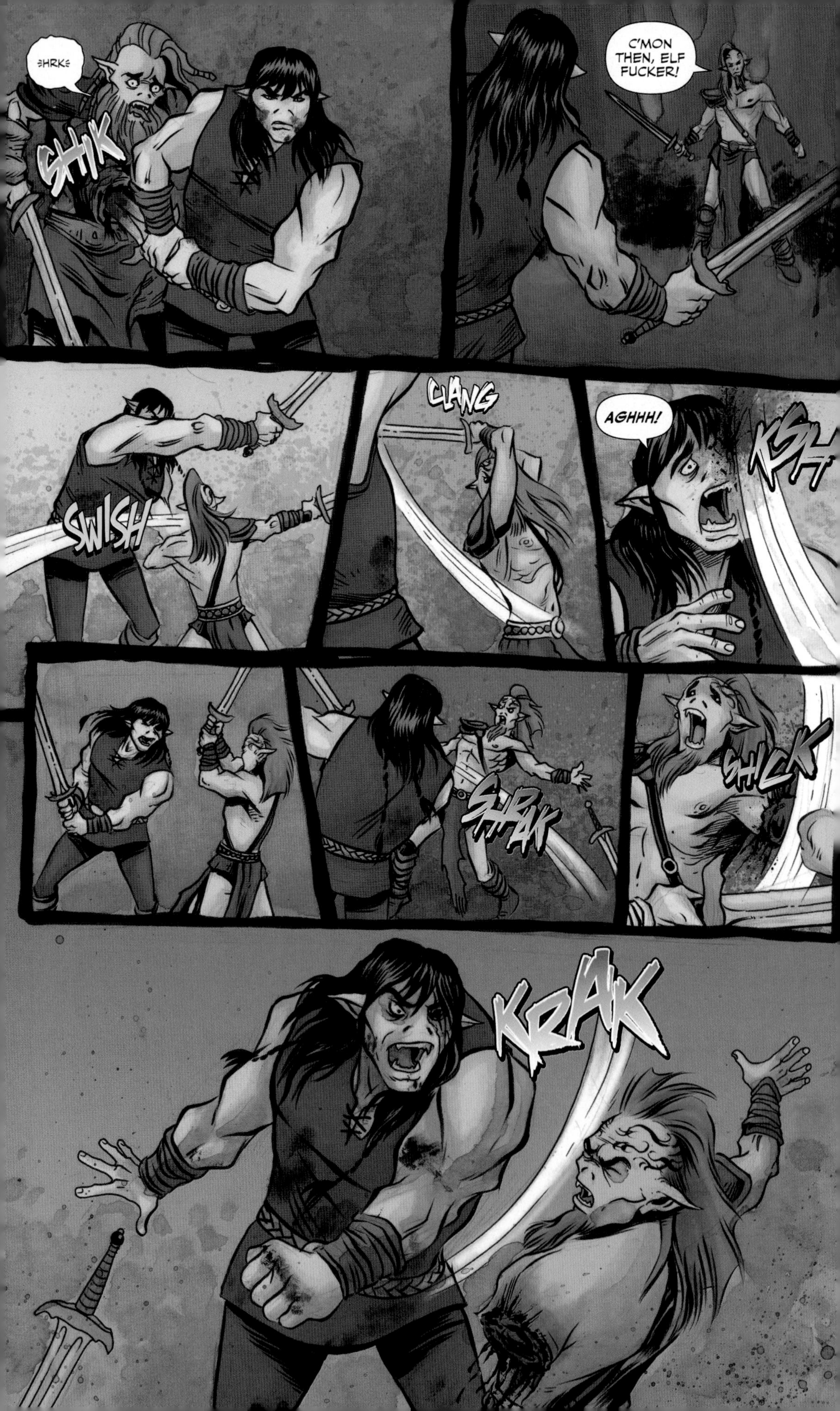

HRK
SHIK
C'MON THEN, ELF FUCKER!
SWISH
CLANG
AGHHH!
KSH
SHRAK
SHICK
KRAK

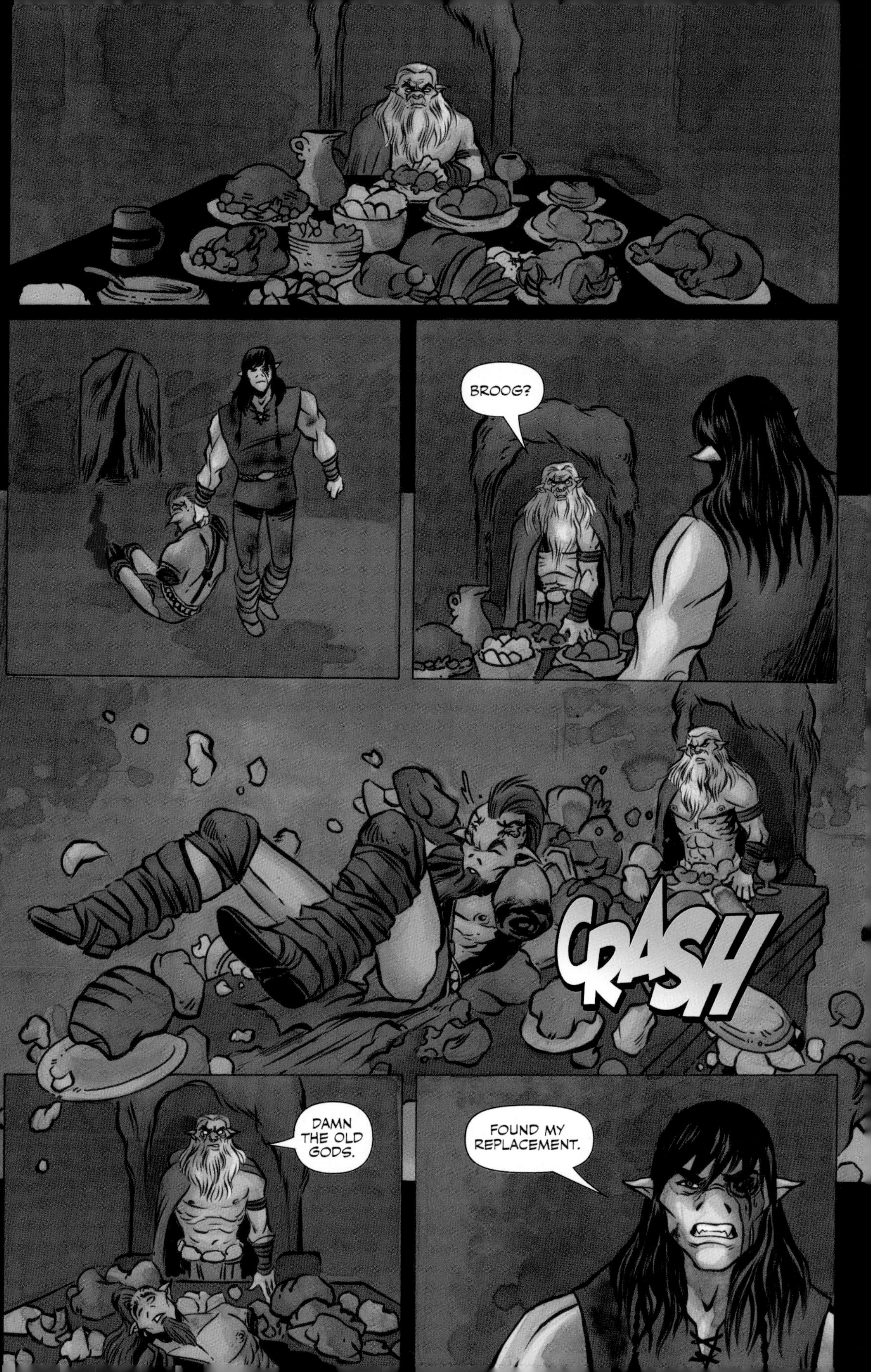
BROOG?
CRASH
DAMN THE OLD GODS.
FOUND MY REPLACEMENT.

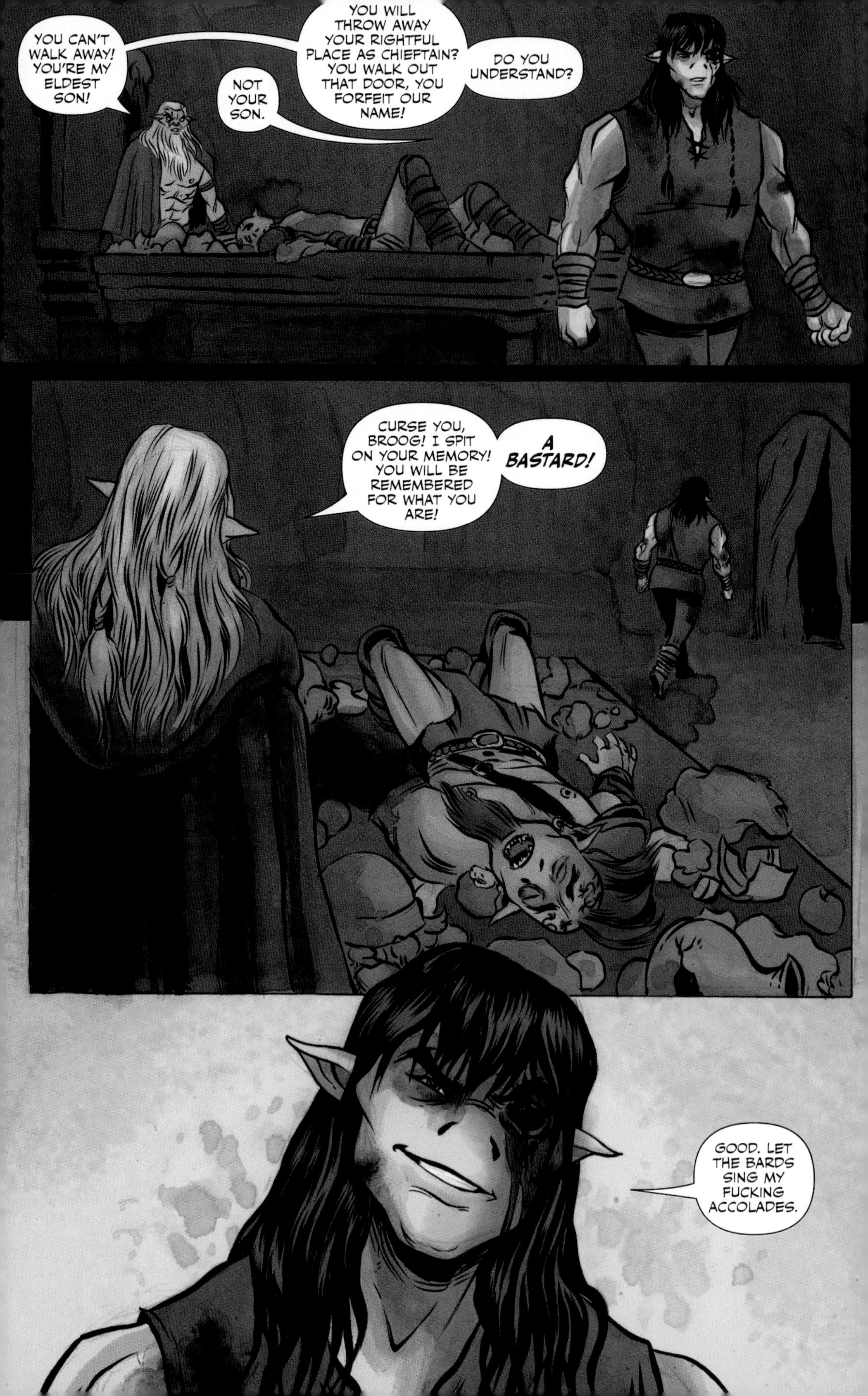

YOU CAN'T WALK AWAY! YOU'RE MY ELDEST SON!
YOU WILL THROW AWAY YOUR RIGHTFUL PLACE AS CHIEFTAIN? YOU WALK OUT THAT DOOR, YOU FORFEIT OUR NAME!
DO YOU UNDERSTAND?
NOT YOUR SON.
CURSE YOU, BROOG! I SPIT ON YOUR MEMORY! YOU WILL BE REMEMBERED FOR WHAT YOU ARE!
A BASTARD!
GOOD. LET THE BARDS SING MY FUCKING ACCOLADES.

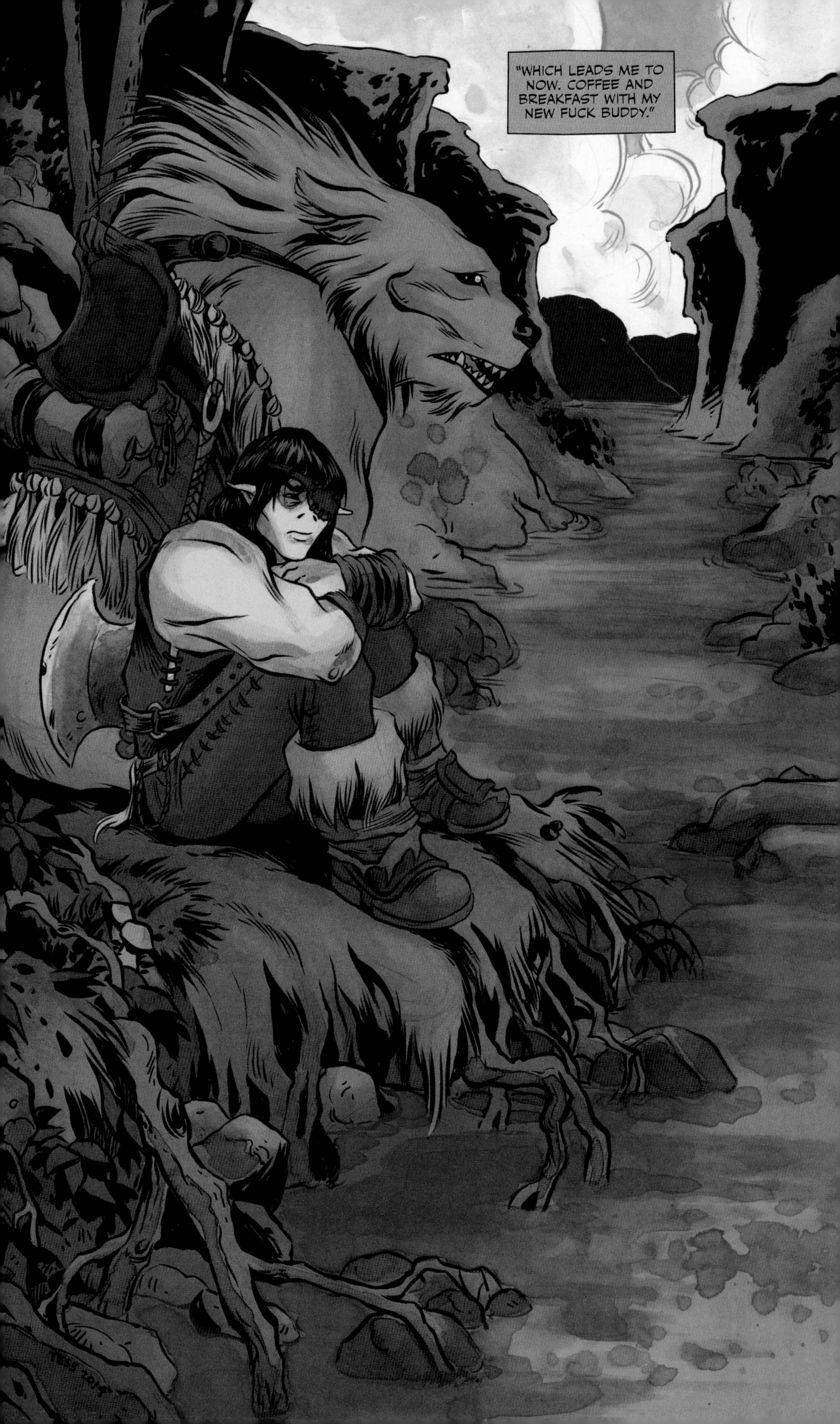
"WHICH LEADS ME TO NOW. COFFEE AND BREAKFAST WITH MY NEW FUCK BUDDY."

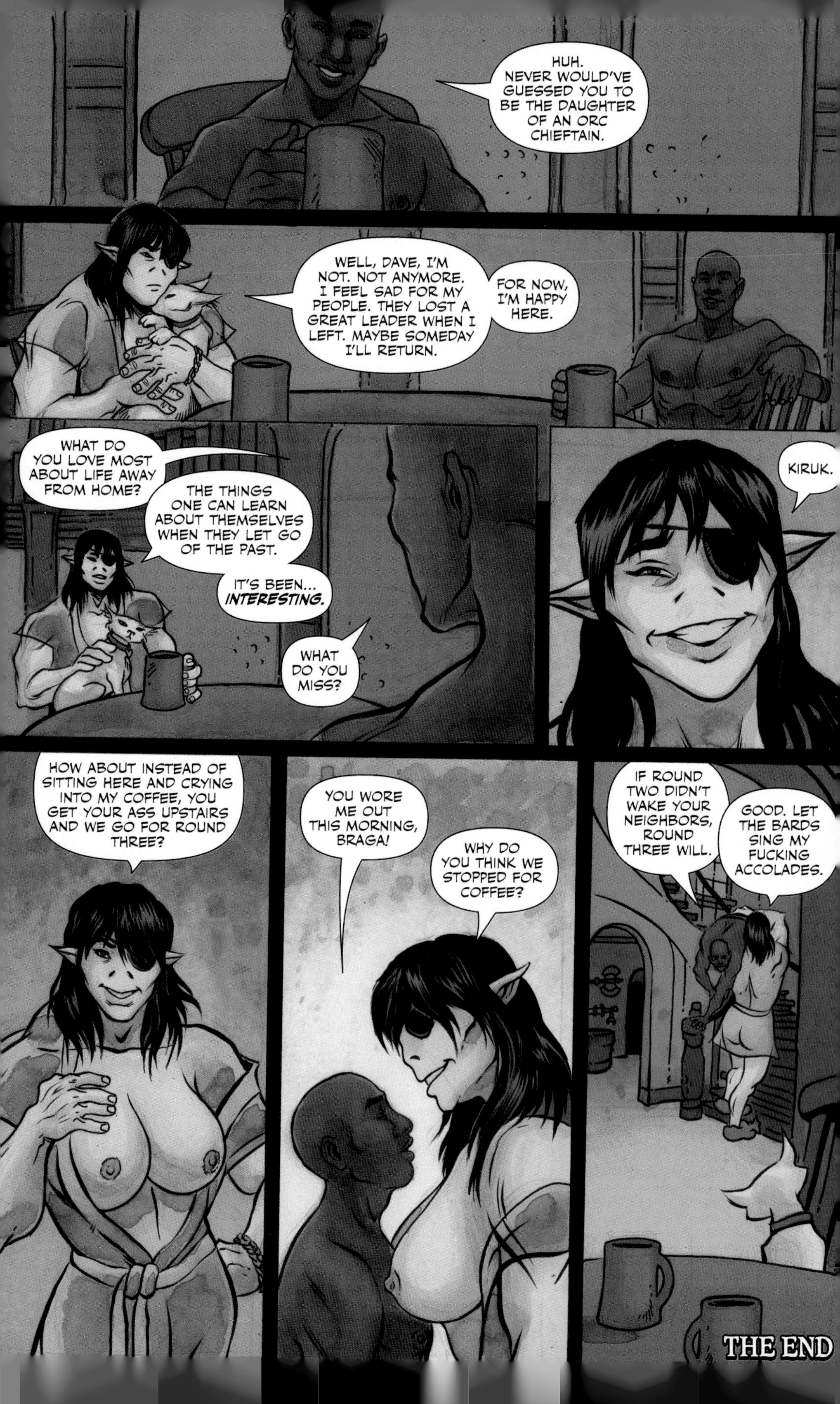
HUH. NEVER WOULD'VE GUESSED YOU TO BE THE DAUGHTER OF AN ORC CHIEFTAIN.
WELL, DAVE, I'M NOT. NOT ANYMORE. I FEEL SAD FOR MY PEOPLE. THEY LOST A GREAT LEADER WHEN I LEFT. MAYBE SOMEDAY I'LL RETURN.
FOR NOW, I'M HAPPY HERE.
WHAT DO YOU LOVE MOST ABOUT LIFE AWAY FROM HOME?
THE THINGS ONE CAN LEARN ABOUT THEMSELVES WHEN THEY LET GO OF THE PAST.
IT'S BEEN... ***INTERESTING.***
WHAT DO YOU MISS?
KIRUK.
HOW ABOUT INSTEAD OF SITTING HERE AND CRYING INTO MY COFFEE, YOU GET YOUR ASS UPSTAIRS AND WE GO FOR ROUND THREE?
YOU WORE ME OUT THIS MORNING, BRAGA!
WHY DO YOU THINK WE STOPPED FOR COFFEE?
IF ROUND TWO DIDN'T WAKE YOUR NEIGHBORS, ROUND THREE WILL.
GOOD. LET THE BARDS SING MY FUCKING ACCOLADES.
THE END

EXTRAS

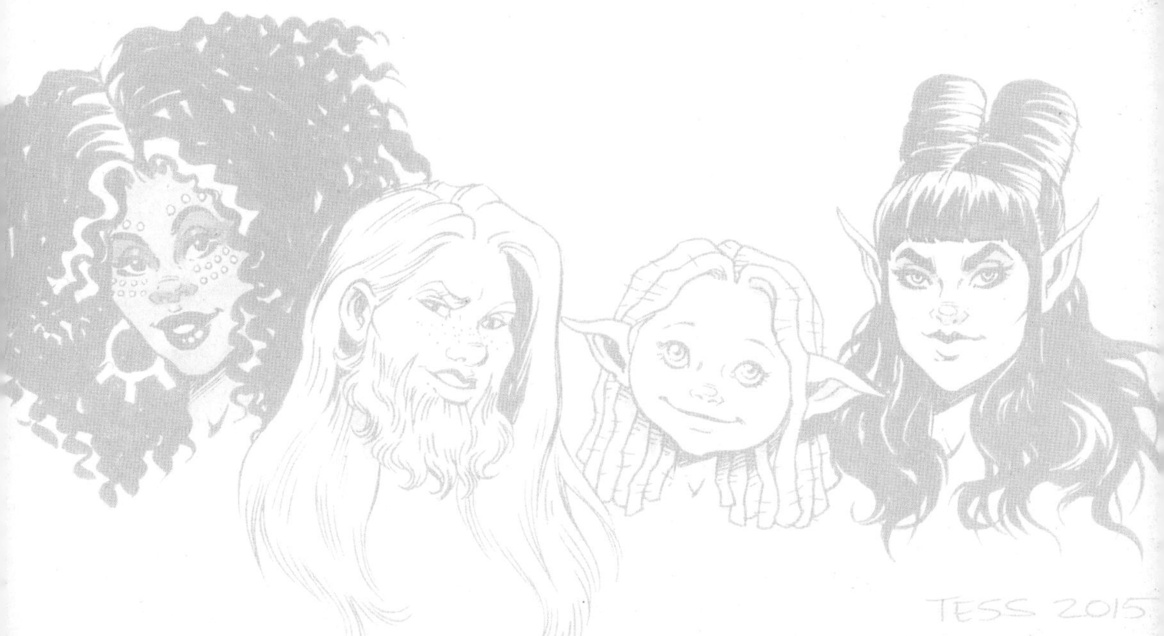
TESS 2015

Over the next few pages, we'll give you a look at Tess' creative process--including sketches, pencils and finished inks. Below are her thumbnails for issue 13. By laying out the pages like this, she's able to pace the story for maximum effect.

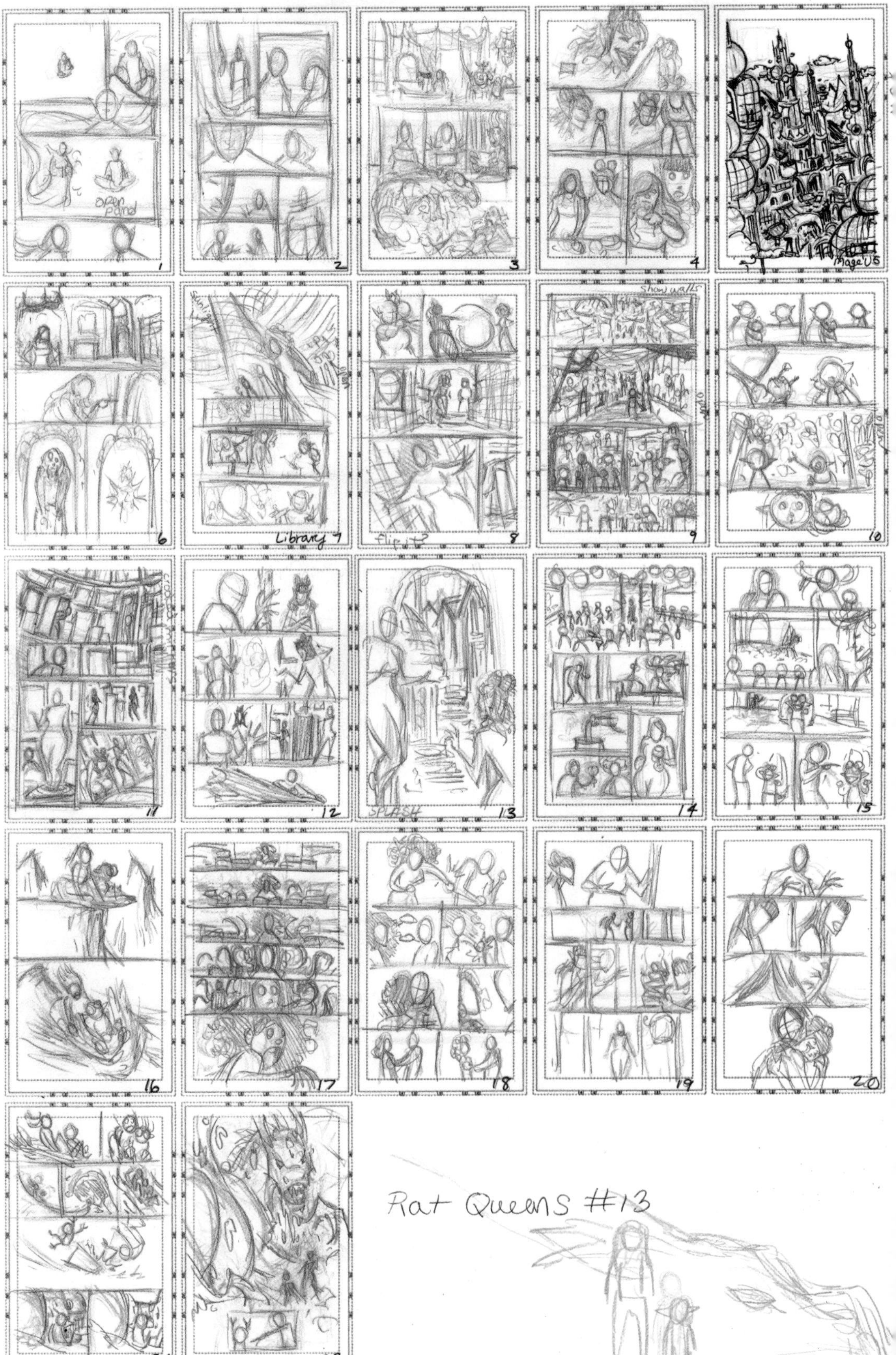

open pond
Library
SPLASH
Rat Queens #13

Three attempts at this volume's cover. Can you pick out the subtle differences between the rejected covers to the left and directly below...

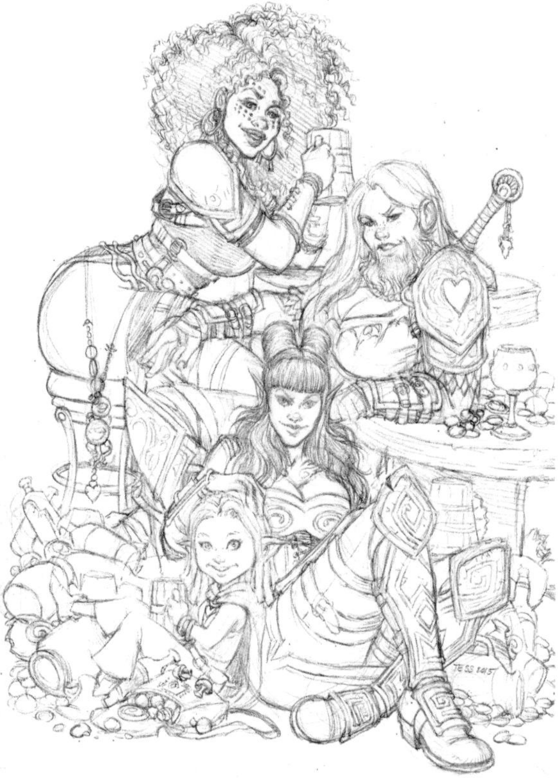
TESS 2015

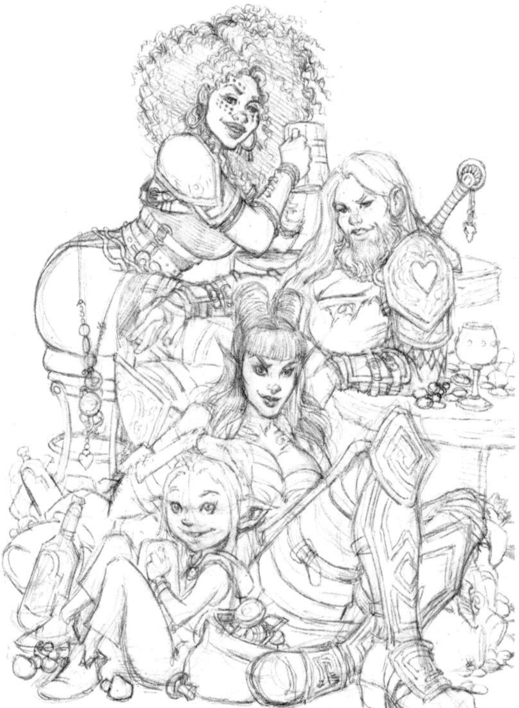

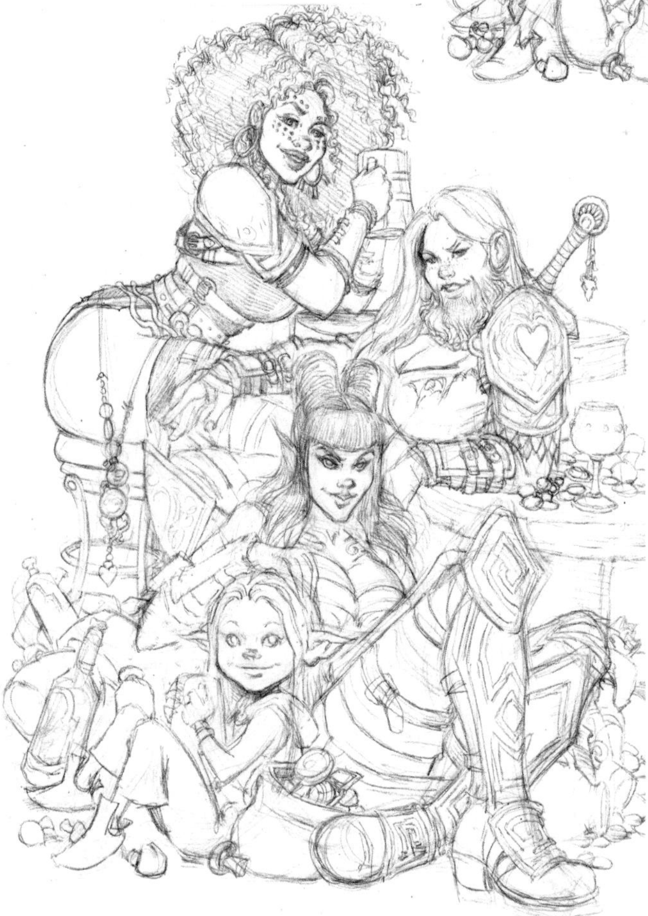

...To this (left), the final pencils for this volume's cover.

By the way, it was Tess who rejected the above two, proving once again that an artist is always her own worst critic!

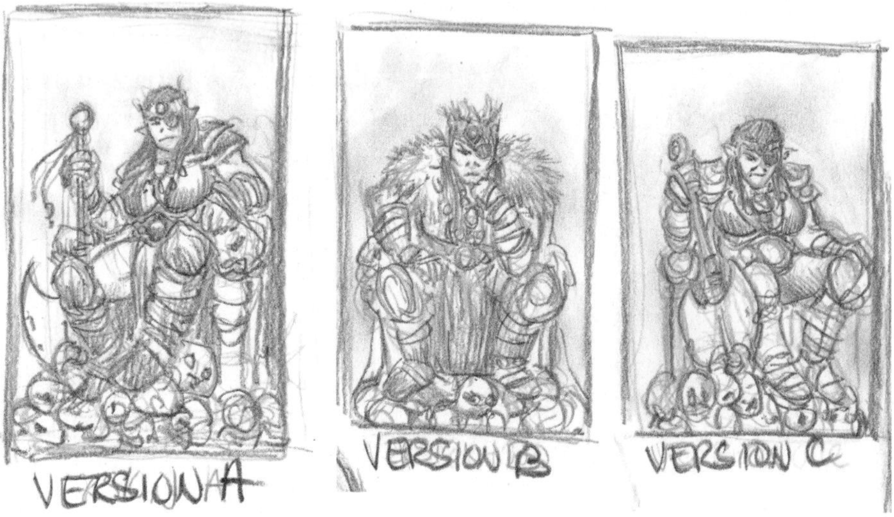
VERSION A
VERSION B
VERSION C

ABOVE:
Tess' sketches for the cover of the Braga Special, her first foray into the world of the Rat Queens.

Version A was chosen as best and the original pencils appear to the right.

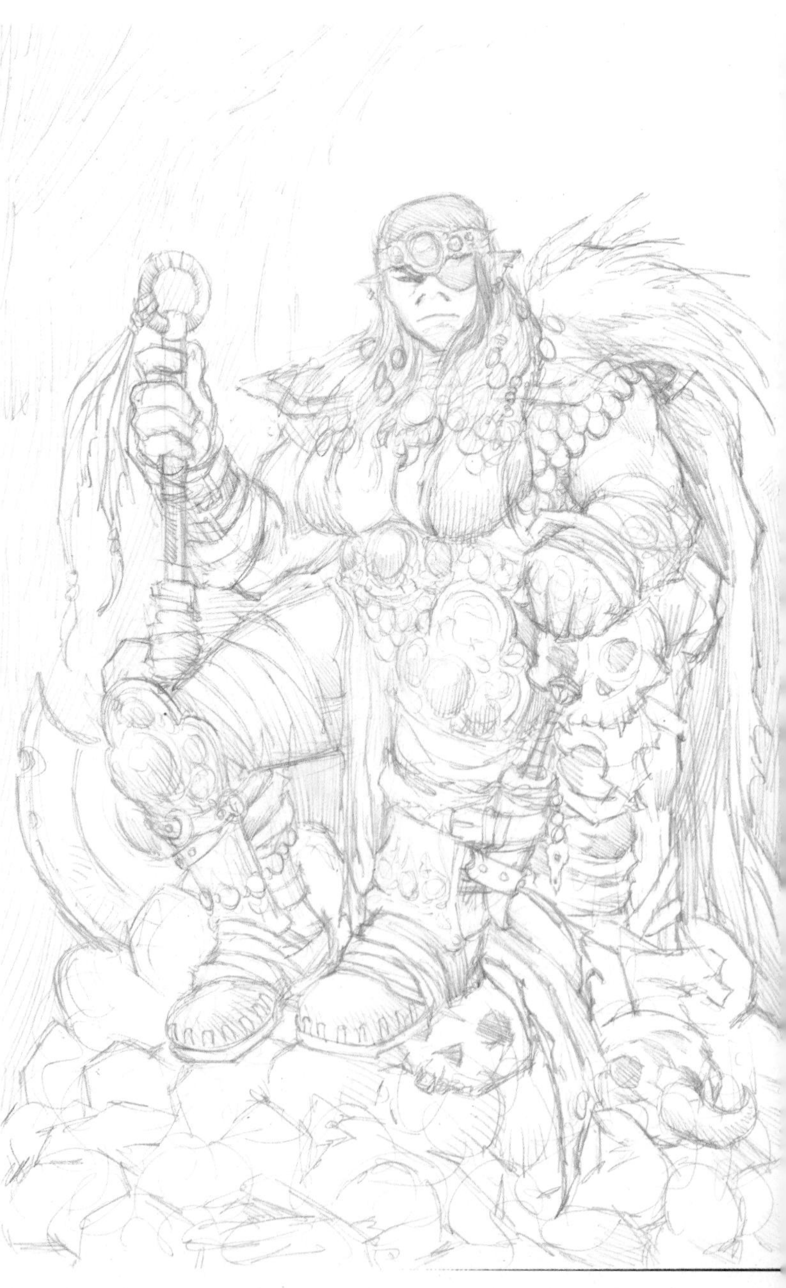

And, the final inks to the Braga Special cover. Art by Tess Fowler.

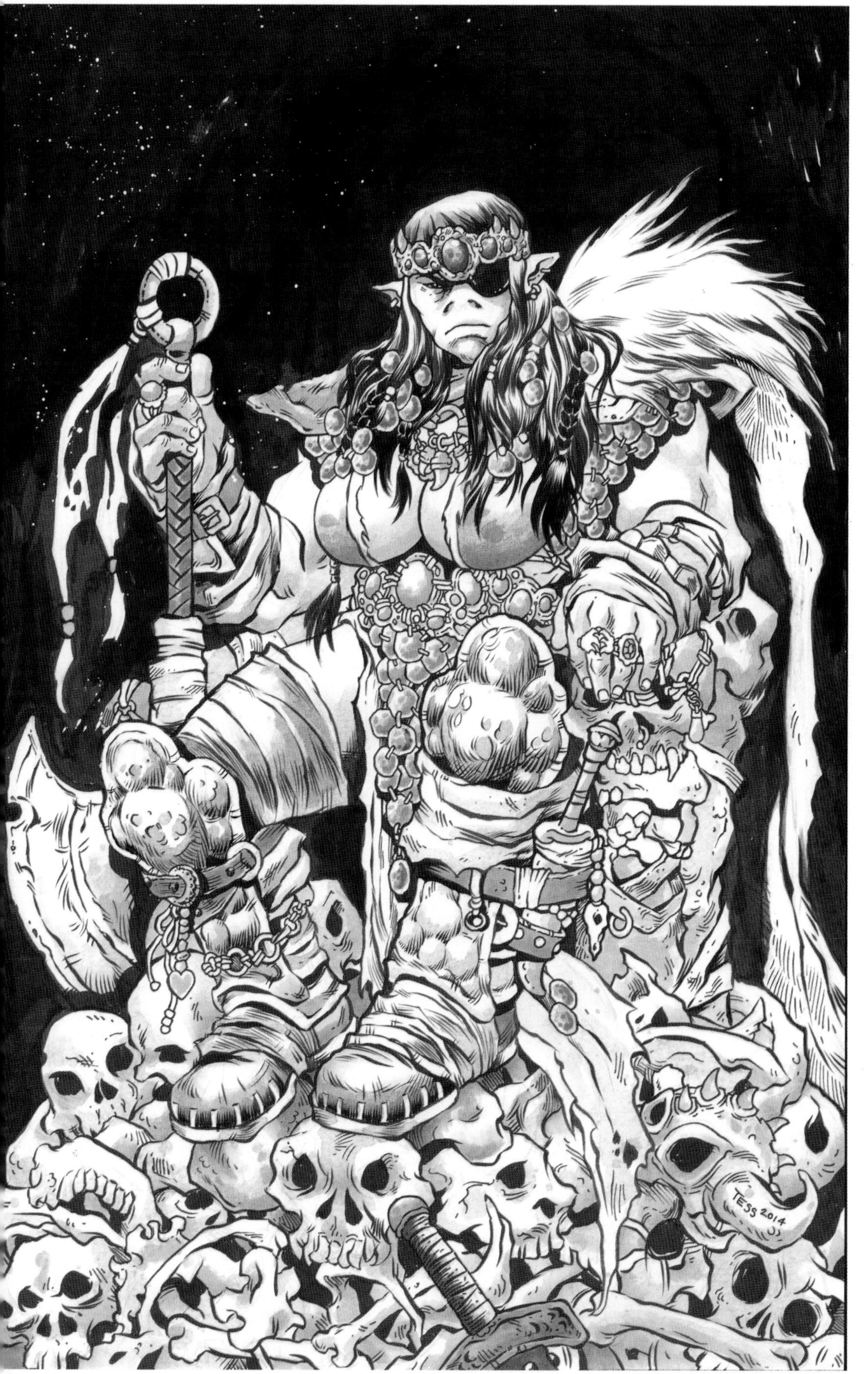
TESS 2014

Tess gives us some costume changes for the Queens. In the top row we see them in their regular outfits. The middle row is casual clothing and on the bottom the Queens are in winter gear.

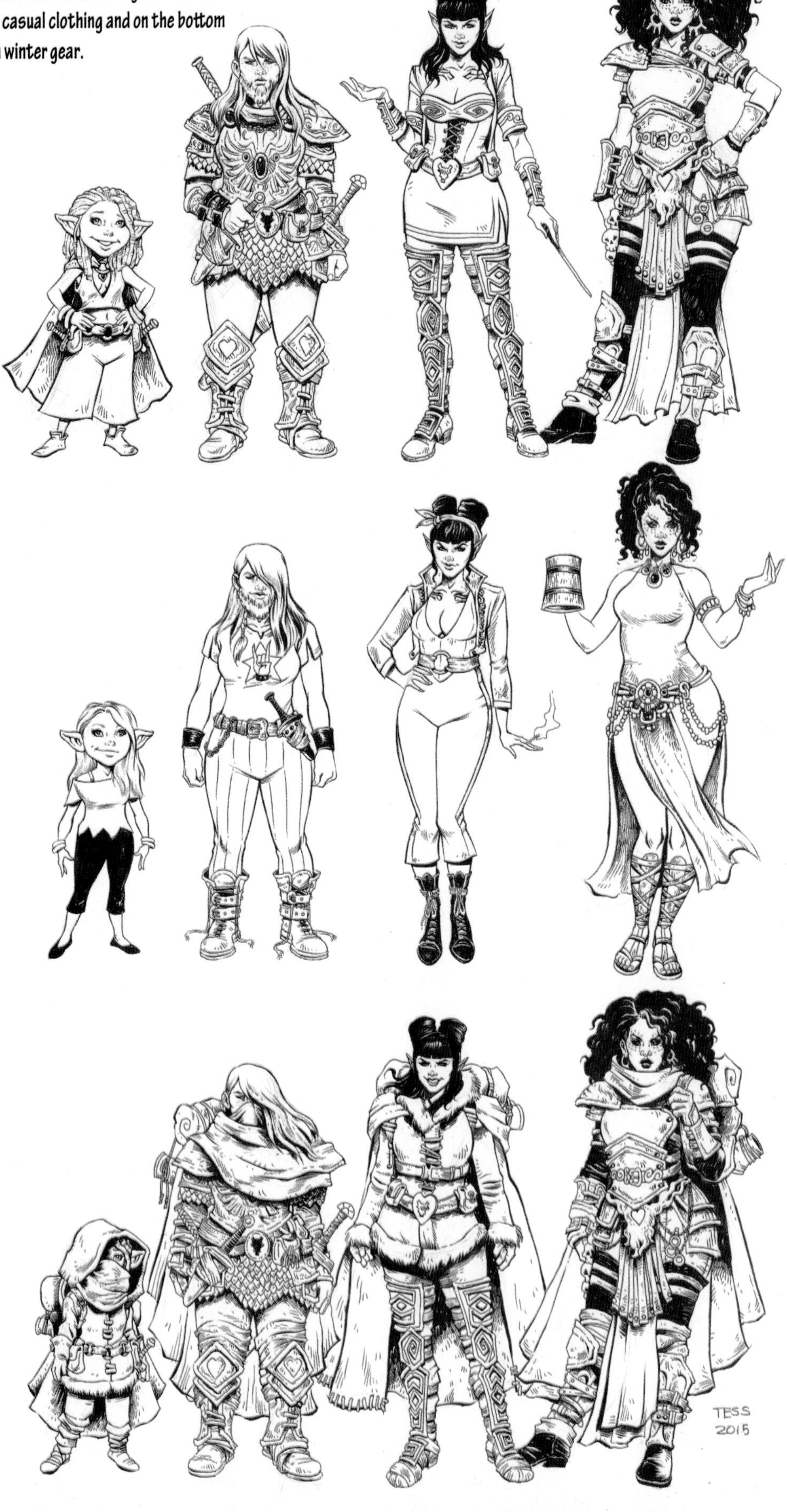
TESS
2015

at better way to close this volume than Tess'
rable self-portrait sketch with the baby Queens!

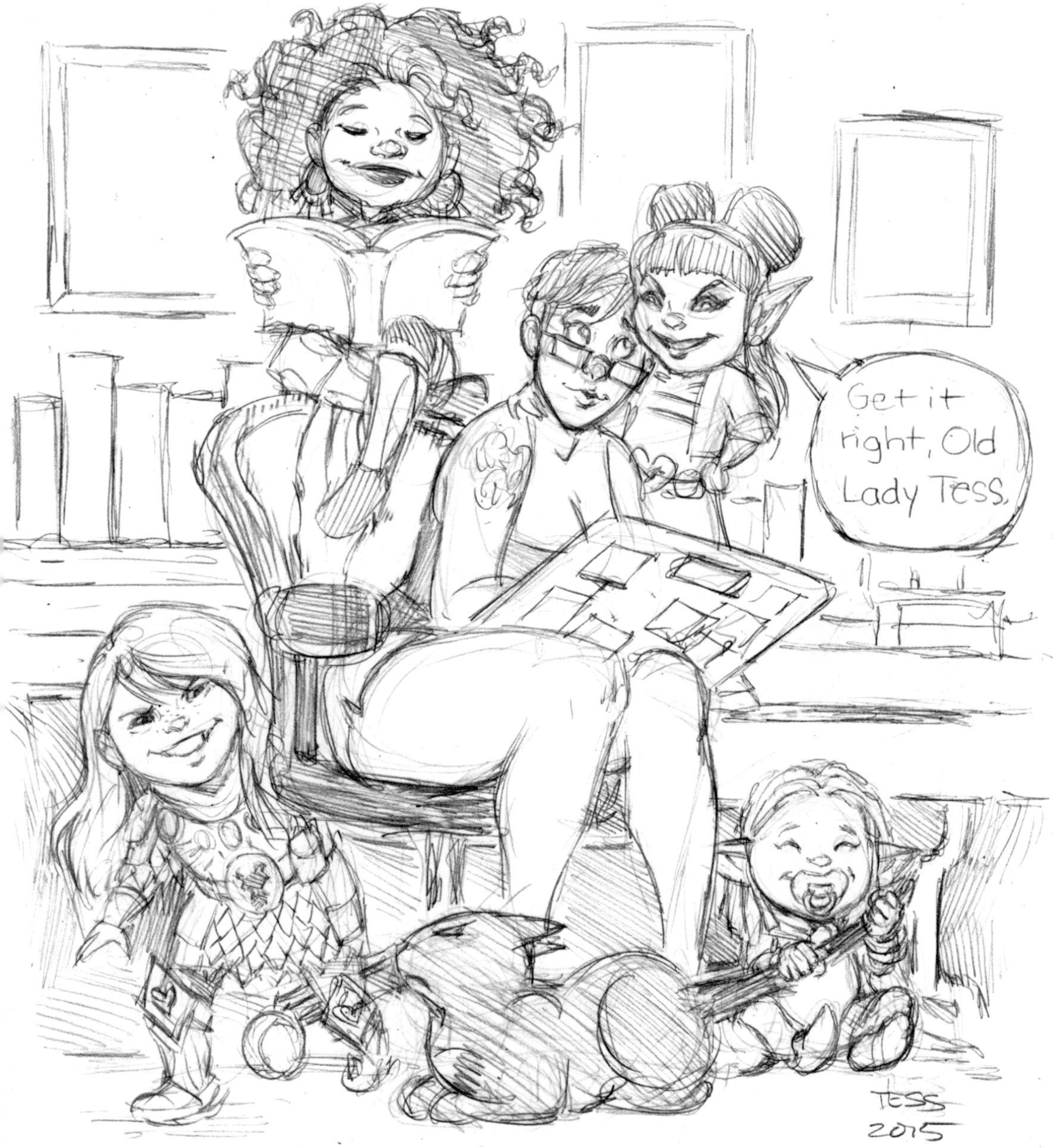
Get it right, Old Lady Tess.
TESS 2015

"ME AND MY SUGAR-MUFFINS"

THIS is diversity! Graphic Novels For the Discriminating Reade

HORROR

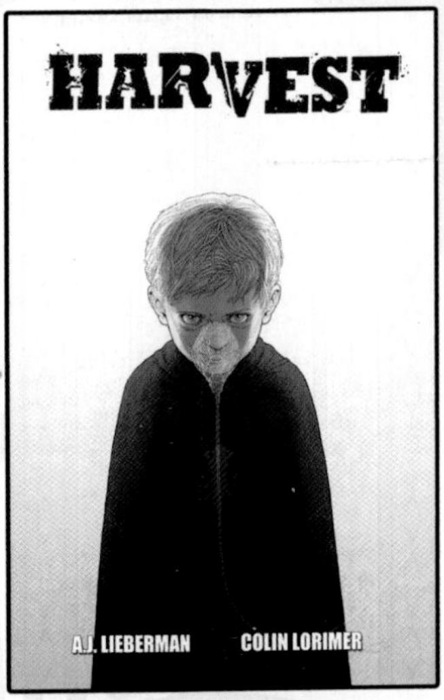
HARVEST
A.J. LIEBERMAN
COLIN LORIMER

HUMOR

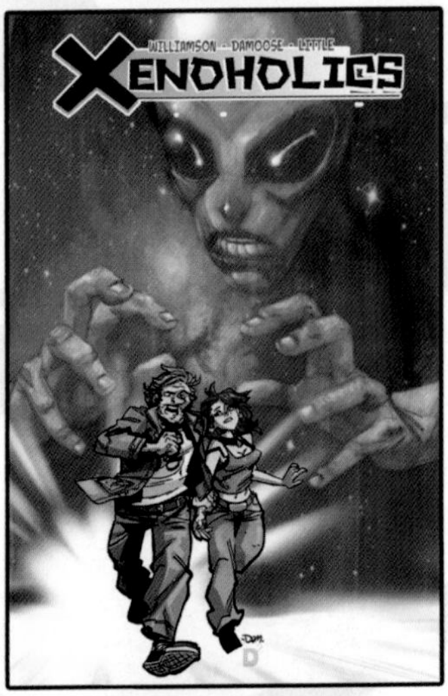
WILLIAMSON DAMOOSE LITTLE
XENOHOLICS

HISTORICAL FICTION

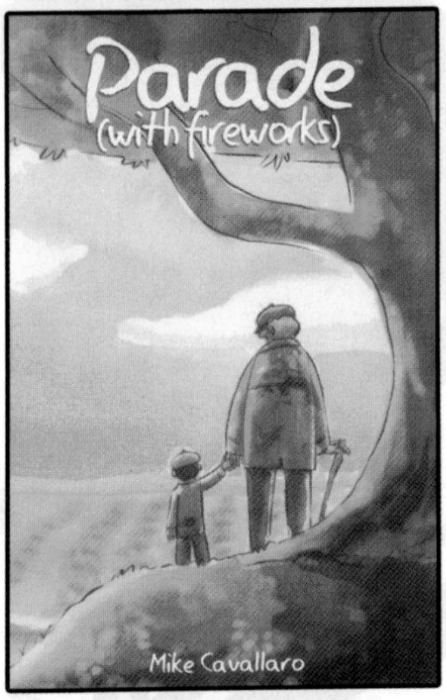
Parade
(with fireworks)
Mike Cavallaro

SUPER-HERO

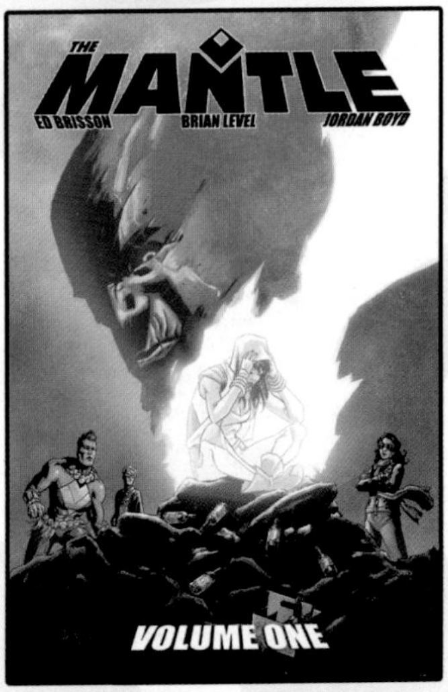
THE MANTLE
ED BRISSON
BRIAN LEVEL
JORDAN BOYD
VOLUME ONE

SCIENCE-FICTION

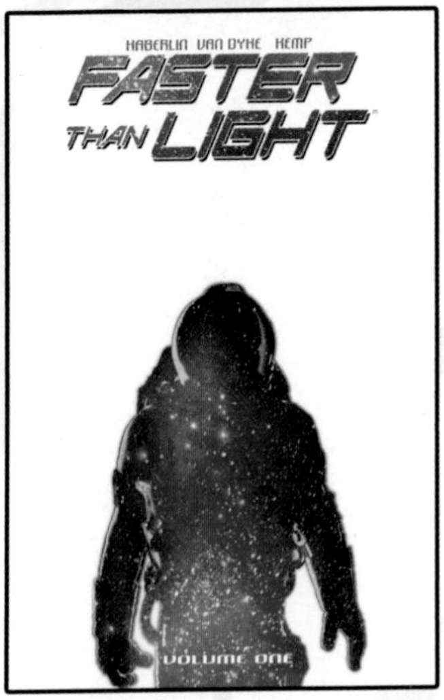
HABERLIN VAN DYKE HEMP
FASTER THAN LIGHT
VOLUME ONE

ADULT CONTENT

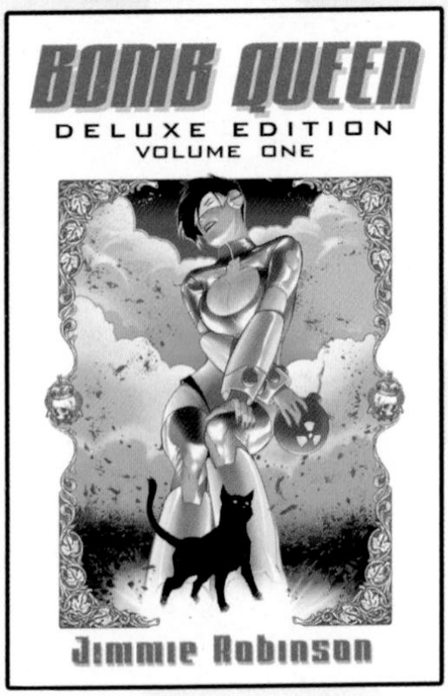
BOMB QUEEN
DELUXE EDITION
VOLUME ONE
Jimmie Robinson

Follow ShadowlineComics on f and t